For Lester,
who made this
possible,
Fondly,
Sharon

Approaches to Poverty in Medieval Europe

INTERNATIONAL MEDIEVAL RESEARCH

Previously published volumes in this series are listed at the back of the book.

VOLUME 22

Approaches to Poverty in Medieval Europe

Complexities, Contradictions, Transformations, *c.* 1100–1500

Edited by

Sharon Farmer

BREPOLS

British Library Cataloguing in Publication Data

A catalogue record for this book is available from the British Library.

D/2016/0095/37
ISBN: 978-2-503-55547-8
e-ISBN: 978-2-503-56206-3
Printed in the EU on acid-free paper

Contents

List of Illustrations

Tables

Maps

Figures

Introduction

Sharon Farmer

The essays in this volume — which draw on a variety of sources from England, France, the Low Countries, Italy, and Iberia — grew out of papers that were presented within the auspices of the special thematic strand, 'Poor... Rich', of the 2011 International Medieval Congress at the University of Leeds. While the thematic strand lent itself to a broad range of topics, from 'conspicuous consumption and magnificence' to 'vagrancy and homelessness', the essays that were selected for this volume focus on the poor end of the spectrum (including both the involuntary and the voluntary poor) and on secular and religious responses to the poor.

Historiographical Background

Anyone who chooses, in the twenty-first century, to write about the history of medieval poverty and the medieval poor builds on foundations that were laid by the French scholar Michel Mollat (1911–96) and by the Polish scholar and politician Bronislaw Geremek (1932–2008). The two scholars drew on each other's work, but they also developed notably different perspectives, especially concerning the role of the Christian religion in shaping attitudes towards the poor; Geremek, moreover, carried his analysis across a much broader period of time, seeking, in his discussion of medieval poverty, to trace the roots of certain early modern and modern European attitudes towards and classifications of the poor.

Sharon Farmer (farmer@history.ucsb.edu) is Professor of History at the University of California, Santa Barbara. Her research focuses on the social history of medieval France.

Approaches to Poverty in Medieval Europe: Complexities, Contradictions, Transformations, c. 1100–1500, ed. by Sharon Farmer, IMR 22 (Turnhout: Brepols, 2016) pp. 1–22
BREPOLS PUBLISHERS 10.1484/M.IMR-EB.5.105457

For over a decade, beginning in 1962, Mollat's seminar on the history of medieval poverty spawned scores of publications by dozens of scholars on the subjects of medieval poverty and charity, governmental responses to the poor, and religious attitudes towards the poor.[1] That work culminated, in 1971, in Mollat's joint publication, with Philippe Wolfe, of a study of popular protest movements of the fourteenth and fifteenth centuries, *Ongles bleus, Jacques et Ciompi: les révolutions populaires en Europe aux XIVe et XVe siècles*, published in English in 1973 as *Popular Revolutions of the Late Middle Ages*; and, in 1978, in Mollat's monumental work *Les pauvres au Moyen Âge*, which appeared in English in 1986 as *The Poor in the Middle Ages: An Essay in Social History*.

As Samuel K. Cohn, Jr, recently pointed out, for over three decades Mollat and Wolfe's *Popular Revolutions* remained the only attempt at a truly comparative study of late medieval protest movements.[2] Similarly, Mollat's monograph on the medieval poor, which drew on evidence from every part of Western Europe, and much of Eastern Europe as well, created an enduring scholarly consensus concerning the basic contours of the history of poverty within medieval European Christian society.

In the early medieval Christian West, Mollat suggested, virtually the only organized charitable responses to the plight of the poor came from the church — first its bishops, and then its monks.[3] That era was followed by a 'revolution in charity' in the twelfth and thirteenth centuries, which saw an outpouring of royal, noble, and bourgeois generosity, resulting in an explosion of new foundations of charitable institutions and in other caritative acts.[4] Then, for the fourteenth and fifteen centuries, Mollat (who drew here on some of Geremek's work) painted a picture of increasing levels of poverty and vagrancy (brought about by war, famine, and plague) followed by greater statutory efforts to 'police the poor' by freezing wage levels and outlawing vagabondage.[5] Such circumstances were made even worse, Mollat argued, because charitable efforts to ameliorate the plight of the poor met with increasing challenges, as endowed

[1] Some of those articles were published in Mollat, *Études sur l'histoire de la pauvreté*. Other articles that grew out of the seminar were listed at the end of volume II of that collection.

[2] Cohn, *Lust for Liberty*, p. 3.

[3] Mollat, *The Poor in the Middle Ages*, trans. by Goldhammer, pp. 38–53.

[4] Mollat, *The Poor in the Middle Ages*, trans. by Goldhammer, pp. 87–157. He uses the expression 'revolution in charity' on p. 135, citing Vauchez, 'Charité et pauvreté'.

[5] Mollat, *The Poor in the Middle Ages*, trans. by Goldhammer, pp. 191–293. The influence of Geremek's work is especially apparent at pp. 290–93, which draw on Geremek, 'La lutte contre le vagabondage à Paris'.

institutions struggled with declining landed revenues, or were simply destroyed by marauding troops.[6] In the meantime, underemployment, low wages, new forms of taxation that accompanied warfare, predatory demands from mercenary troops, and the failure, on the part of the armed nobility, to protect the poor and the weak, helped to mobilize new forms of social protest. For the most part, those movements were not successful — and indeed, Mollat's study suggests that these pressures from below contributed to increasingly negative portrayals and repressive measures on the part of intellectual and ruling elites.[7] Another strand that contributed to ideas about controlling the poor came, Mollat argued, from humanist intellectuals who emphasized that rulers and legislators should help prevent threats to the social order by outlawing public begging. 'With humanism,' Mollat asserted, 'contempt for the poor took a subtle and perfidious turn, becoming disdainful and philosophical.'[8] Mollat thus suggested that the dramatic revolution in systems of social welfare that began to take shape in the 1520s (with the establishment of centralized urban systems of poor relief and the outlawing of outdoor begging) actually had its roots in ideas that had already been articulated in the fifteenth century.

One underlying theme of Mollat's study is that, while economic, social, and environmental factors all played their part in the history of medieval poverty and responses to it, Christian ideas and preaching — most especially those of the new mendicant religious orders that took shape in the early thirteenth century — played a major role in helping to ameliorate the plight of the poor. Mollat emphasized that the ideas and behaviour of Saints Francis and Dominic — the founders of the two most important mendicant orders — marked a major turning point because they validated the sacred humanity of the poor themselves:

> Both Dominic and Francis were irresistibly drawn to the humiliated Christ, on whom they modelled their lives. In a society where money tended to augment the power of those who had it and to diminish the status of those who did not, their role was to preach that the poor have value as human beings, and indeed that they are sacred images of Christ.[9]

[6] Mollat, *The Poor in the Middle Ages*, trans. by Goldhammer, pp. 268–69.

[7] Mollat, *The Poor in the Middle Ages*, trans. by Goldhammer, pp. 205–32.

[8] Mollat, *The Poor in the Middle Ages*, trans. by Goldhammer, p. 255.

[9] Mollat, *The Poor in the Middle Ages*, trans. by Goldhammer, p. 121.

And that was not all. According to Mollat, mendicant preaching helped to foster the spread of the 'revolution in charity' by 'educating consciences'; and indeed, new charitable work was promulgated 'if not by the mendicants themselves, then at least under their influence'.[10]

Bronislaw Geremek shared Mollat's perception that the twelfth and thirteenth centuries saw a revolution in charity and a new recognition of the spiritual value of poverty, and that the later Middle Ages constituted a period of large-scale pauperization and increasingly negative responses to the poor. Nevertheless, his interpretive and analytical emphases were somewhat different. In analysing ideas about the poor, he was especially interested in tracing the origins of modern hierarchies concerning the deserving and the undeserving poor, as well as the roots of widespread tendencies to vilify the poor. He argued that the roots of negative images of the poor and of beggars could be traced back to the period of late antiquity, but that they saw an increase during the twelfth and thirteenth centuries precisely because churchmen, who identified with and praised the spiritual value of 'the voluntary poor' (who gave up what they had and *chose* poverty), emphasized the inherent greed and idleness of the involuntary poor (who had no 'taste' for poverty, and thus did not voluntarily *choose* the poverty that engulfed them).[11] More than was the case with Mollat, moreover, Geremek sought structural explanations for late medieval pauperization, which, he assumed, underlay the increasingly negative attitudes towards the poor and towards beggars.[12] Along lines that implicitly agreed with Geremek's negative portrayal of the relationship between the mendicant orders and the involuntary poor, Lester K. Little emphasized that the religious poverty of the mendicants served the needs of the wealthy merchants who dominated urban culture, rather than those of the involuntary poor.[13]

In the decades since Mollat and Geremek laid the groundwork for the study of medieval poverty and the ways in which it was handled and represented, a number of works have added detail and nuance to their basic theses. Concerning the 'revolution in charity' of the twelfth and thirteenth centuries, the work of François-Olivier Touati, Daniel Le Blévec, James Brodman, John Henderson, Sethina Watson, and others has enabled us to chart in much greater detail the size and impact of this important charitable turn. In England,

[10] Mollat, *The Poor in the Middle Ages*, trans. by Goldhammer, pp. 127–28.

[11] Geremek, *Poverty*, trans. by Kolakowska, pp. 15–30.

[12] Geremek, *Poverty*, trans. by Kolakowska, pp. 73–119.

[13] Little, *Religious Poverty and the Profit Economy*.

as Watson has argued, no separate charitable institutions, such as hospitals, existed before 1085; by the year 1200, however, there were more than four hundred.[14] In the lower Rhône Valley, as Le Blévec's extensive research has shown, the number of independent charitable institutions jumped from two in the year 1100 to twenty-three by the year 1200 and ninety-six by the year 1300.[15] Along similar lines, Touati has demonstrated that in the French ecclesiastical province of Sens, which encompassed the dioceses of Sens, Chartres, Paris, Orléans, Meaux, Troyes, Auxerre, and Nevers, the number of long-term residences for lepers jumped from five or six in the year 1100 to nearly four hundred by the early fourteenth century. Unlike Mollat, moreover, Touati (along with Carole Rawcliffe and others) interprets the huge increase in the number of leprosaria as a part of the new charitable impulse, rather than evidence of attempts to marginalize and contain lepers.[16] James Brodman, John Henderson, and Luise Windemuth have also described increases in numbers of charitable institutions in Italy, Iberia, and Germany.[17]

Concerning the role played by the new mendicant orders of the thirteenth century in constructing either positive or negative attitudes towards the poor, historians continue to align with both sides of the debate. Jussi Hanska and Adam Davis (who has contributed to this volume) number among those who emphasize the role played by mendicant leaders in constructing positive, or more compassionate, attitudes towards the poor; Kenneth Baxter Wolf and Allison Edgren (another contributor to this volume) number among those who tend to emphasize the negative impact of the mendicant religious orders. James Brodman and Daniel Le Blévec have documented a general lack of interest, on the part of the mendicant orders, in supporting hospitals; however, both scholars also emphasize that in addition to the rise of the mendicant orders, the era of the revolution in charity saw a general rise in the popularity of hospital service as a form of religious life.[18]

Recent scholars have also added detail and nuance to our understanding of the negative turn, for the poor, in the fourteenth and fifteenth centuries. New

[14] Watson, 'The Origins of the English Hospital', pp. 75–76.

[15] Le Blévec, *La part du pauvre*, I, 18–38; II, 595, 824–25.

[16] Touati, *Maladie et société*; Rawcliffe, *Leprosy in Medieval England*, pp. 104–54.

[17] Brodman, *Charity and Welfare*, pp. 28–46; Henderson, *The Renaissance Hospital*, p. 6; Windemuth, *Das Hospital als Träger der Armenfürsorge*, pp. 46–53, 75–78.

[18] Hanska, '*And the Rich Man Also Died*'; Wolf, *The Poverty of Riches*; Le Blévec, *La part du pauvre*; Brodman, *Charity and Religion*; and see the essays by Davis and Edgren in this volume.

developments in the study of human remains have enabled medical anthropologists and microbiologists to affirm what written documentation had already suggested to Mollat and others — that poverty and malnutrition enhanced people's vulnerability to the Black Death.[19] Much like Geremek, A. L. Beier and Judith Bennett have argued that the repressive measures of the English ordinance of labourers of 1349 marked the beginning of a trend that lasted well into the early modern period; Robert Braid and James Brodman, moreover, have added more comprehensive comparative discussions of legislation outlawing vagabondage; and Elaine Clark has demonstrated that some anti-vagabond legislation took root in England in the thirteenth century.[20] Like Mollat and Wolfe, Samuel K. Cohn has taken a comparative approach to late medieval popular protests; unlike the two earlier scholars, however, Cohn draws sharp distinctions between urban and rural protests, and he is more attuned to regional differences.[21] Annie Saunier and Marjorie McIntosh have affirmed, for Northern France and England, Mollat's thesis that, as a result of declining incomes and the ravages of war, many charitable institutions suffered decline in the fourteenth and fifteenth centuries.[22] Le Blévec and Henderson have found, however, that despite the crises of the later Middle Ages, the repercussions of the charitable revolution continued to be felt well into the fourteenth century. Indeed, in Florence and the Rhône Valley, more charitable institutions were founded in the fourteenth century than in either the twelfth or thirteenth, and a number of towns in Northern Italy saw the foundation of their largest and most important hospitals in the second half of the fourteenth century.[23] James Brodman and others have also noted that increasingly in the fourteenth century charitable organizations began to favour the 'shame-faced' poor — people of some means who had fallen into hard times — over the truly indigent.[24]

[19] Crubézy, Duchesne, and Arlaud, *La mort, les morts et la ville*, p. 403. For a survey of the emerging consensus among microbiologists that *Y. pestis* was indeed the cause of the Black Death, see Little, 'Review Article: Plague Historians in Lab Coats'; Green, 'Taking Pandemic Seriously'.

[20] Bennett, 'Compulsory Labor Service'; Beier, 'A New Serfdom'; Braid, '"Et non ultra"'; Clark, 'Institutional and Legal Responses', pp. 258–59; Brodman, *Charity and Welfare*, p. 5

[21] Cohn, *Lust for Liberty*.

[22] Saunier, 'Les incidences de la guerre de cent ans', pp. 50, 64; McIntosh, *Poor Relief in England*, p. 303.

[23] Le Blévec, *La part du pauvre*, II, 595; Henderson, *The Renaissance Hospital*, p. 6; Henderson, *Piety and Charity*, pp. 344–53. On an upsurge in charity during the Great Famine, see Jordan, *The Great Famine*, pp. 157–58.

[24] Brodman, *Charity and Welfare*, p. 5.

Recent historians and archaeologists have also transformed our understanding of the underlying structural causes and consequences of endemic poverty — both in the early Middle Ages and in the period around 1300. Concerning the early Middle Ages, the work of historians Chris Wickham and Robin Fleming, who draw on recent scholarship in the fields of archaeology and medical anthropology, has transformed our understanding of the fundamental societal poverty that prevailed in Britain after the withdrawal of the Romans.[25] Concerning the late thirteenth and early fourteenth centuries, Bruce Campbell has countered earlier arguments that harsh seigniorial demands exacerbated the poverty of the peasantry. Campbell argues instead that in Britain, at least, the poverty of the peasantry was caused in large part by the leniency of seigniorial lords, who allowed peasants to divide up their holdings; for that reason, he argues, far too many peasants were unable to support themselves in the decades surrounded the year 1300.[26] Concerning Geremek's assumption that a pattern of widespread pauperization must have continued into the fifteenth century, Christopher Dyer has argued for Britain that, in fact, standards of living were rising in the fifteenth century.[27] Recent scholars have also found inspiration in the work of Amartya Sen, who has called attention to the role that international markets could play in leaching fundamental resources from less wealthy to more wealthy regions, thus contributing to, or even causing, famines.[28]

Although Mollat's and Geremek's work continues to provide the basic road map for the study of medieval poverty and of the ways in which the non-poor responded to it, in recent decades four major historiographical developments have taken the field in altogether new directions. First, Peter Brown has argued that the idea of 'the poor' was invented by bishops of the fourth century, and, building on that argument, Peregrine Horden has argued that that invention had major consequences in the development of the hospital as an institutional response to poverty and suffering. The first hospitals, Horden argues, were

[25] Fleming, *Britain after Rome*; Fleming, 'Bones for Historians'; Wickham, *Framing the Early Middle Ages*, pp. 306–23, 339–54, 428–34. Fleming returned to the issue of societal poverty in post-Roman Britain in her plenary address at the 2011 International Medieval Congress at Leeds: 'Recycling in Britain after the Fall of Rome's Metal Economy'.

[26] Campbell, 'The Agrarian Problem in the Early Fourteenth Century'.

[27] Dyer, 'Poverty and its Relief in Late Medieval England', pp. 42–43; Dyer, *Making a Living in the Middle Ages*.

[28] Bourin, Drendel, and Menant, *Les disettes dans la conjoncture de 1300*. See especially in that volume: Bourin and Menant, 'Les disettes dans la conjoncture de 1300 en Méditerranée', pp. 20–25; Benito i Monclús, 'Famines sans frontières en Occident'; Drendel, 'Conclusion'.

founded in the eastern Roman Empire in the fourth century. From there, they spread across the Mediterranean region, finding roots in Western Europe and in Islamic societies.[29] Second, recent work on women and gender in the Middle Ages has called attention to differences in men's and women's patterns of charitable generosity, in poor men's and poor women's experiences of poverty, and in the ways in which poor men and women were perceived and represented.[30] Third, scholars — including Christopher Dyer, in his plenary address to the 2011 International Medieval Congress at Leeds — have uncovered new sources that reveal the voices, agency, and daily experiences of the poor.[31] And finally, recent historians have taken a more comparative approach to patterns of poverty and charity in Muslim, Jewish, and Christian societies, and several of those historians have emphasized the ways in which minority and majority communities influenced each other in their pious and pragmatic responses to the poor.[32]

Approaches to Poverty I: Reexamining the 'Revolution in Charity'

The essays in this volume re-examine the two major high and late medieval turning points in the relationship between rich and poor that were emphasized by Mollat and Geremek, adding new perspectives on the agency of the poor, the influence of gendered forms of devotion, parallels in Christian and Jewish representations of the deserving and undeserving poor, and the effect of mendicant piety on the status of the involuntary poor. Several of our essays, moreover,

[29] Brown, *Poverty and Leadership*, p. 8; Brown, *Through the Eye of a Needle*; Horden, 'The Earliest Hospitals'.

[30] On gendered patterns of charity and palliative care, see Cullum, '"And hir name was charite"'; McNamara, 'The Need to Give'; Farmer, 'Persuasive Voices'; Farmer, 'The Leper in the Master Bedroom'; Wolf, 'Introduction', in *The Life and Afterlife of St. Elizabeth of Hungary*, trans. by Wolf, pp. 55–79; Rawcliffe, 'Hospital Nurses and their Work'; Baumgarten, *Practicing Piety*, pp. 103–37; Baumgarten, 'Charitable Like Abigail'. On differences in the ways in which men and women experienced poverty, see Farmer, *Surviving Poverty*, pp. 74–104, 136–64; Bennett, 'Compulsory Labor Service'. On differences in stereotypes and representations of poor men and poor women, see Farmer, *Surviving Poverty*, pp. 39–73, 105–135.

[31] Dyer, 'The Experience of Being Poor'; Farmer, *Surviving Poverty*, pp. 74–104, 136–64; Cohen, *Poverty and Charity*.

[32] Sabra, *Poverty and Charity in Medieval Islam*; Cohen, *Poverty and Charity*; Galinsky, 'Jewish Charitable Bequests and the Hekdesh Trust'; Zytnicki and Sibon, 'Introduction au dossier'; Denjean, Sibon, and Soussen, 'Charité bien ordonée'; Frankel and Lev, *Charity and Giving in Monotheistic Religions*; Baumgarten, *Practicing Piety*, pp. 103–37.

suggest that medieval studies of poverty and wealth need to pay more attention to the role of rulers, ruling elites, and public policy.

In the first two essays of this volume Adam Davis, who focuses primarily on French sources, and Janice Musson, who focuses on England, help us to rethink the origins of the 'revolution in charity' of the twelfth and thirteenth centuries and the impact of new royal efforts to dispense justice in those same centuries. The three subsequent essays — by Alyssa Gray, Allison Edgren, and Jill Moore — highlight contradictions and limitations in twelfth- and thirteenth-century attitudes towards the poor. Gray looks at an important effort by a twelfth-century rabbi to redefine the deserving poor, while Edgren and Moore focus on questions concerning mendicant piety and the plight of the involuntary poor.

Drawing on recent work on twelfth- and thirteenth-century female religious devotion to the suffering Christ, Davis suggests that we need to re-examine the reasons for the explosion of charitable generosity and service in the twelfth and thirteenth centuries. The new 'culture of compassion' for the sick and the poor, he argues, was a consequence of the emergence of new forms of intensely personal devotion to and compassion for the sufferings of Christ. Expanding on the arguments of Sarah McNamer, who suggests that the new affective devotion of the High Middle Ages, which was highly gendered, led to the *invention* of compassion, Davis argues that even as they began to cultivate feelings of compassion for Christ, pious individuals of the High Middle Ages, many of whom were women, were awakened to compassion for their suffering neighbours as well.[33] His essay implicitly moves us away from the special agency of Saints Francis and Dominic, suggesting that women's religious devotion may have provided special impetus for the 'revolution in charity' as well.

Most scholarship has emphasized that, in the twelfth and thirteenth centuries, care for the poor was more a matter of personal and religious charity than of public policy. Janice Musson's essay on the impact of King Henry II's assize of novel disseisin reminds us, by contrast, that the degree to which rulers took seriously their responsibility to provide justice for their subjects could have a major impact on the well-being of the more modest members of society, even working to prevent some of them from falling into dependent poverty.

During the tenth and eleventh centuries, such justice was difficult to find in much of Western Europe, as territorial lords grabbed whatever land and power they could take, paying little heed to the responsibilities of public office. The twelfth century, as is well known, saw the beginning of the end of 'personal-

[33] McNamer, *Affective Meditation.*

proprietary' lordships, as royal and princely rulers in various regions began to exercise more effective governance.[34] As Thomas Bisson has recently argued, however, we cannot assume that improvements in the bureaucratic efficiency of government automatically resulted in efforts to serve the people with greater justice. Indeed, Bisson argues, it took much of the twelfth century for the will to dispense justice to catch up with the capacity to wield power. The England that Henry II inherited in 1154, for instance, had developed an efficient system for keeping track of royal accounts, but, Bisson claims, it 'was hardly more "governed", hardly less "dominated"' than other, less sophisticated lordships.[35] Henry II's legal reforms went a long way in bringing about a more 'governed', less 'dominated' society — and his interest in preventing powerful individuals from dispossessing less powerful landholders, an interest that he codified in the assize of novel disseisin around 1166, constituted one of his more important efforts to transform royal power into a form of governance that served the interests of the people.[36]

To what degree, however, did the assize of novel disseisin address the needs of modest landholders — those who either experienced or were threatened by poverty, even to the point of destitution? Henry II's interest in the issue of dispossession seems to have been peaked, at least in part, by cases in which extremely wealthy monasteries claimed to be the victims of dispossession.[37] The question thus begs to be asked: how far down the social and economic ladder did the assize of novel disseisin actually reach?

Janice Musson's discussion of actual court cases from 1194 to 1215 provides a badly needed answer to this question. Her evidence suggests that royal justice really did work in behalf of the lowliest freeholders — and that compassion for the poor had its place in the courts, at least when it came time to decide whether or not a loosing party had to pay the required court fine. Her discussion also reveals the agency of even the most modest of freeholders, who developed sophisticated knowledge of how the legal system worked and how they could make it work to their advantage.

The outpouring of charitable generosity in twelfth- and thirteenth-century Western Christian society might lead us to believe that charity came to

[34] Bisson, *The Crisis of the Twelfth Century*. The phrase 'personal-proprietary' is taken from p. 13.

[35] Bisson, *The Crisis of the Twelfth Century*, p. 379.

[36] Bisson, *The Crisis of the Twelfth Century*, pp. 379–81.

[37] Bisson, *The Crisis of the Twelfth Century*, p. 381.

be dispensed indiscriminately, but this was hardly the case. Indeed, building on ideas that had their roots in late antiquity, Christian canon lawyers of the twelfth century articulated sharp distinctions between the 'deserving' and the 'undeserving' poor. The principal line of thinking distinguished between those whose infirmity of mind, body, or social position rendered them deserving of charitable support because they were incapable of supporting themselves, and those who were able to support themselves, and were thus undeserving of charity. However, a second line of thought built on the writings of Saint Augustine, who had taught that Christians should withhold charity from those 'who follow an evil way of life' — a category that encompassed infamous professions such as prostitution and entertaining.[38]

In her contribution to this volume, Alyssa Gray highlights a parallel line of discussion within Jewish legal thought. In his 'Book of Those Who Fear God', Rabbi Eliezer of Metz (d. 1198) argued that Jews who were 'deliberate transgressors' of Jewish law were, much like the canon lawyers' followers of 'an evil way of life', undeserving of charitable support. Unlike the canon lawyers, however, Rabbi Eliezer articulated a position that built on no previous discussion within his textual tradition. In her explanatory analysis of Rabbi Eliezer's innovative thinking, Gray carefully lays out traditional rabbinic discussions of charity to fellow Jews, on the one hand, and treatment of Jews who disobeyed the law, on the other. Gray points out that earlier legal commentators had kept those two discussions entirely separate, and, in their discussions of Jews who disobeyed the law, they had recommended relative leniency for those who transgressed for reasons of appetite rather than spite. Rabbi Eliezer, by contrast, blurred both distinctions, bringing together discussions of charity and discussions of transgressors, and viewing any intentional transgression of any aspect of Jewish law as equally deserving of rejection and exclusion.

Gray argues that Rabbi Eliezer's new harsh attitude toward all transgressors of Jewish law should be interpreted within the context of increasing persecution of Jews and increasing incidents of Jewish apostasy that resulted from such persecutions. Rabbi Eliezer came to view each and every intentional transgression of Jewish law as the beginning of a slippery slope leading to apostasy. As Christian efforts at boundary maintenance increased in the new 'persecuting society', some Jewish leaders responded in kind, monitoring the behaviour of

[38] Tierney, 'The Decretists and the "Deserving Poor"', pp. 368–69. In the 1180s John of Salisbury brought this perspective to the English royal court: Clark, 'Institutional and Legal Responses', p. 458.

the members of their community and advocating increasingly harsh responses to those who failed to live up to their expectations.

Like Gray, Allison Edgren and Jill Moore address complexities and contradictions within the revolution in charity of the twelfth and thirteenth centuries. Both of their essays focus on the new mendicant religious orders, and both bring to our attention the degree to which the mid- and late thirteenth-century members of those orders moved away from the ideals and aspirations of the early thirteenth-century founders.

In a nuanced discussion of the evolution of Franciscan attitudes towards begging during the first seventy years of the order's existence (1210–80), Allison Edgren highlights the degree to which Saint Francis's spiritual ideal of both expressing humility and practicing religious poverty by begging door to door served as a flashpoint for conflicting aspects of the life of voluntary poverty. If it was 'better to give than to receive', as the Gospels taught, and if able-bodied Christians were supposed to work rather than beg, how could the Franciscans justify their identity as *mendicants*? How, indeed, could they ask for material support without appearing to be greedy? As Edgren points out, the earliest Franciscan texts avoided associating the brothers themselves with the verb *mendicare*, and they justified the Franciscans' public quests for alms by portraying Francis and his earliest followers as mere conduits for the redistribution of wealth: they sought Christian alms in order to give those same alms to the involuntary poor. Increasingly, however, Franciscan texts emphasized that the brothers had a right to beg because they engaged in spiritual, rather than manual, labour; they indicated, moreover, that unlike the involuntary poor, whose begging was tainted by greed, Franciscan brothers begged for spiritual rather than material reasons. By calling into question the motives of weak and disabled beggars, and highlighting the spiritual benefits of giving alms to themselves, the Franciscans of the mid- and later thirteenth century, Edgren suggests, augmented the plight of the involuntary poor.

At the same time that they struggled with the idea and practice of holy mendicancy, the Franciscans struggled with, and eventually gave into, the temptation to modify or abandon Francis's wholehearted commitment to a life of voluntary poverty. As Edgren reminds us, already in 1239 the Master General of the order, Elias of Cortona, was deposed amid complaints of corruption and rich living. By the end of the century, however, the problem was more endemic and more institutionalized — at least in Italy. In 1292 the Franciscan province of Tuscany passed statutes that overtly contradicted those of the Chapter General of the order, thereby allowing brothers within the province to receive personal gifts and legacies and to serve as executors of wills.[39] Within a short time, brothers from prominent local families who had joined the convent of Santa Croce in Florence were receiving legacies from their relations.[40] A number of those friars then invested their wealth in the most portable of valuable objects — books, some of which they had richly decorated by the most prominent artists of the time, such as Taddeo Gaddi.[41]

As Jill Moore's essay in this volume suggests, one factor that contributed to the abandonment of a life of voluntary poverty among Italian Franciscans and Dominicans was the fact that individual friars were given the responsibility of holding the office of Master Inquisitor, in which capacity they managed large budgets that were funded by properties that had been confiscated from convicted heretics. A division of resources and responsibilities between inquisitors and Italian communes should have served as a means of preventing corruption, but that division often broke down, offering Master Inquisitors the opportunity to manage their affairs however they pleased. In some cases, moreover, the Franciscan or Dominican superiors of inquisitors put pressure on them to spend money in lavish ways.

In her essay, Moore draws on the account books of individual inquisitors in order to determine how often and to what degree those who operated in northern Italy in the late thirteenth and early fourteenth centuries ended up breaking their vows of voluntary poverty, as defined in the rules for their orders. She then demonstrates that, while the temptations were the same for all, friars varied in their responses to the temptations — with some remaining true to their vows of voluntary poverty, a large number giving into temptations, and some behaving in overtly criminal ways.

Some of the most astonishing evidence for the outright criminal behaviour of Franciscan inquisitors comes from the *Liber contractuum*, a compilation of notarial documents concerning the activities of the Franciscan convents of Padua and Vicenza that the papal curia put together in 1302 in response to requests from the bishop and commune of Padua.[42] As Moore's discussion makes clear, the *Liber contractuum* indicates that the Franciscan inquisitors and their staffs were falsifying accounts in order to deprive Padua and Vicenza of

[39] Piron, 'Un couvent sous influence', pp. 327–28.

[40] Piron, 'Un couvent sous influence', p. 344.

[41] Piron, 'Un couvent sous influence', pp. 347–48; Moore's essay in this volume, at n. 56.

[42] On the background to this text, see Piron, 'Un couvent sous influence', p. 324; Grieco, 'Pastoral Care, Inquisition and Mendicancy', pp. 144–45.

their due share in the revenues of the inquisition, selling confiscated properties at discount prices to their own relatives, and diverting properties left for charity to personal uses. In one case, the inquisitor threatened a secular cleric with prosecution for heresy in order to force him to designate a group of notaries as *pauperes Christi* so that they could draw on the income of a testamentary bequest intended for orphans, poor widows, and indigents. It seems that by the early fourteenth century many Franciscans in Italy had abandoned not only Francis's life of voluntary poverty but also his compassion for the poor.

Approaches to Poverty II: Crises of the Later Middle Ages

In this section, Samuel K. Cohn takes another look at rising standards of living in the late fourteenth and fifteenth centuries, arguing that politics and the power of urban elites played a strong role in determining just who benefited from improving standards of living and who got left out. Pol Serrahima offers an example of a fifteenth-century Iberian war, which, much like the Hundred Years' War in France, precipitated a major downturn in the numbers of charitable resources that were available for the involuntary poor. Sarah Lynch picks up on some of the themes of Christopher Dyer's recent work, demonstrating that the men who identified with a particular category of work could experience a wide spectrum of standards of living.[43] Like the essays of Cohn and Serrahima, moreover, her essay supports Brodman's point that in the later Middle Ages elites found various ways to shift public and charitable resources away from the indigent poor, favouring, instead, people who had more resources to begin with. In the final essay, Anne Scott's discussion of gendered representations of the poor in three high and late medieval literary texts supports the contention that, despite rising standards of living for the poor, elite representations of the poor became increasingly harsh and negative in the later Middle Ages. Her essay suggests that this negative turn was a consequence of elite fears of losing status and wealth.

Samuel K. Cohn's examination of the 'political paradox of post-plague economics' emphasizes that in the late fourteenth and fifteenth centuries the actions and decisions of ruling urban elites negatively affected the lives of some people who lacked wealth and power. Drawing on a sweeping array of examples from northern and central Italy, England, the Low Countries, and Iberia, Cohn argues convincingly that the new economic conditions of the post-Black

[43] Dyer, *Making a Living in the Middle Ages*.

Death period had differing political effects for peasants and urban artisans: while standards of living improved for nearly everyone after 1375, and peasants throughout Western Europe gained greater economic and political rights, urban artisans lost both political power and economic position, thus becoming victims of a new 'political poverty'. While acknowledging that we may not yet be in a position to fully explain this widespread pattern, Cohn analyses one particular example that may help us understand some of the broader causal factors: in late fourteenth-century Florence, prominent artisans gained favours from powerful elites through a new patronage network. That network, Cohn argues, 'atomized power', breaking up corporatist identities and undermining the possibility of collective action. It also drove a wedge between middling artisans — the ones who profited from the patronage system — and those who constituted a more marginalized lower class.

Cohn argues that changing patterns of charity reflected new social divisions among artisans and the working poor of Florence: after the Black Death Florentine charitable priorities shifted away from the indigent poor towards marriageable girls whose good characters, along with those of their families, were made manifest by their 'buon costume'. John Henderson has argued that this shift in charitable priorities reflected the desire on the part of Florence's civic and confraternal leaders to rebuild the population in the wake of the plague.[44] Cohn argues that it was also symptomatic of a growing social gap between middling artisans who were considered respectable, and the lowliest artisans, who became increasingly marginalized in the fourteenth and fifteenth centuries.

Pol Serrahima's essay examines yet another shift in charitable priorities that siphoned resources away from the indigent poor. Drawing on the extensive financial records of the *Almoina*, a charitable institution administered by the canons of Barcelona's cathedral, Serrahima both reinforces our understanding of the practical consequences of the charitable revolution of the twelfth century and demonstrates its reshaping in the fifteenth. The *Almoina* had its origins in a single testamentary bequest of 1161, in which a cleric of Barcelona provided an endowment for daily year-round meals for three people. Over the course of the next hundred years or so, additional bequests, primarily from lay benefactors, enhanced that original endowment to the point that the cathedral chapter was able to provide 288 poor people with daily year-round meals. During the Catalan civil war of 1462–72, however, the endowed incomes of the charity

[44] Henderson, *Piety and Charity*, p. 11.

declined sharply, and in their efforts to manage their dwindling resources the canons instituted drastic budget cuts, reducing their allocations for poor relief by 93 per cent. At the same time, the canons cut back on their expenditures for liturgical needs and pensions for priests, but only by 41 per cent. Serrahima reminds us that in shifting their priorities from poor relief to sacramental needs, the canons of the cathedral remained true to Christian definitions of charity — which encompassed both love of God and love of ones neighbour. Nevertheless, it seems that the canons' choices were out of alignment with the charitable priorities of Barcelona's lay people, who, for the most part, ceased to establish new endowments with the *Almoina* after 1472. While that institution stagnated, however, the resources of the city's main municipal hospital, which was under the administrative control of the urban government, grew dramatically.

Like Cohn's essay, Sarah Lynch's richly researched examination of the economic standing of elementary and grammar school teachers in late medieval Lyon provides another discussion of the ways in which funds that were intended for the public welfare came to be used in ways that enhanced class division. Lynch's essay, which makes a major contribution to the social history of late medieval education, describes three different groups of schoolteachers in Lyon: those at the cathedral, which constituted the city's oldest educational institution; those who were outside of the cathedral and often somewhat marginal both socially and economically; and those, beginning in the early fifteenth century, who had close ties with the municipal authorities and tended to receive high levels of civic remuneration as well as special privileges such as tax exemptions. Lynch's discussion of this third group further supports Cohn's claim that late medieval urban elites often consolidated their social and political position, widening the distance between themselves and more modest members of society. The municipal leaders' use of public funds to enhance the status of teachers who educated their own children suggests that, here again, we see a channelling of resources away from the neediest members of society.

In the final essay of this volume, Anne Scott draws together evidence and themes from both periods under discussion here, while reinforcing Cohn's and Lynch's evidence that the gap between elites and the poor grew considerably in the later Middle Ages. Scott's discussion highlights the roles of powerful poor women, or hags, in three literary texts of the thirteenth, fourteenth, and fifteenth centuries: Lady Poverty in the Franciscan 'Sacred Exchange of Saint Francis with Lady Poverty', which was written in Italy around 1227; the hag in Chaucer's 'Wife of Bath's Tale', written in England in the 1380s; and Glad Poverty in Book III of Lydgate's *Fall of Princes*, written in England in the 1430s. The representations of these three hags reveal both a persistent negative attitude towards the poor on the part of elites, and a fear of falling into poverty that grew more acute as the later Middle Ages progressed. Singling out the graphic descriptions of a despicable Glad Poverty in Lydgate's text, Scott reminds us that for many of those for whom material prosperity, or even stability, was a priority, poverty was an extremely frightening and hateful prospect. Her essay helps us to understand why assistance for the shame-faced poor — people of means who had suffered a loss of status through loss of wealth — became an increasingly important aspect of charity in the later Middle Ages.

Gaps in Coverage: New Directions in the Field

The 2011 International Medieval Congress at Leeds included papers that were illustrative of two recent developments in the arena of medieval poverty studies that are not included in this volume — studies of poverty, charity, and attitudes towards the poor in medieval Islamic societies, and studies that draw on archaeological and human remains in order to provide new insights concerning the daily lives and physical sufferings of the poor.[45] Because scholars in these fields often publish in venues that differ from those of mainstream European medievalists, we were unable to include any of those papers in this volume. There is no question, however, that in the future more and more historians of medieval poverty will want to incorporate evidence from the fields of archaeology and medical anthropology into their work, and that historians of medieval European charity will want to take a more comparative approach, one that considers patterns of charity in Christian, Jewish, and Islamic societies. Alyssa Gray's essay in this volume is indicative of the fruitful potential in the approach to ideas about charity that takes into consideration both Christian and Jewish perspectives.

There were surprisingly few papers at the 2011 congress that looked explicitly at questions concerning women's and men's differing experiences of involuntary poverty and men's and women's differing approaches to charitable generosity. Nevertheless, as the essays of Davis and Scott suggest, the gendered approach to medieval poverty studies is a fruitful area of research, and, indeed, we need to know much more about the differing experiences and differing

[45] See, in the online programme for the 2011 International Medieval Congress, descriptions of papers by Julia Bray and Yaacov Lev on poverty and charity in Islamic societies, and descriptions of papers by Simone Kahlow, Nat Alcock, and Fabian Kanz, which drew on archaeological and human remains in order to elucidate aspects of the lives of the medieval poor: <www.leeds.ac.uk/ims/imc/imc2011.html> [accessed 25 June 2015].

forms of agency of poor men and women and of the men and women who responded to their needs.

Concerning the impact of the mendicant religious orders on the status and well-being of the involuntary poor, the differing interpretations of Davis, Edgren, and Moore in this volume suggest that we need more work in this area as well. Davis's and Moore's use of unpublished archival sources and Edgren's meticulous examination of changing uses of words and concepts suggest that there are sources out there that have yet to be examined, and that well-known sources can yield new insights when read with a fresh approach.

Finally, when read in light of each other, the essays in this volume by Musson, Cohn, Serrahima, and Lynch suggest that studies of medieval poverty need to explore in more depth the role of governments, bureaucrats, and public policy in shaping the lives of the medieval poor. Medieval governments sometimes helped to ameliorate the plight of the poor, but they sometimes caused people to fall into the ranks of the poor. We need to gain a deeper understanding of medieval poverty as a public and regulated issue, and to analyse more fully the medieval roots of early modern systems of public welfare.

Works Cited

Primary Sources

The Life and Afterlife of St. Elizabeth of Hungary: Testimony from her Canonization Hearings, trans. by Kenneth Baxter Wolf (Oxford: Oxford University Press, 2011)

Secondary Studies

Baumgarten, Elisheva, 'Charitable Like Abigail: The History of an Epitaph', *Jewish Quarterly Review*, 105.3 (2015), 312–39

——, *Practicing Piety in Medieval Ashkenaz* (Philadelphia: University of Pennsylvania Press, 2014)

Beier, Augustus Leon, 'A New Serfdom', in *Cast Out: Vagrancy and Homelessness in Global and Historical Perspective*, ed. by Augustus Leon Beier and Paul Ocobock (Athens, Ohio: Ohio University Press, 2008), pp. 35–63

Benito i Monclús, Pere, 'Famines sans frontières en Occident avant la "conjoncture de 1300": à propos d'une enquête en cours', in *Les disettes dans la conjoncture de 1300 en Méditerranée occidentale*, ed. by Monique Bourin, John Drendel, and François Menant, Collection de l'École française de Rome, 450 (Rome: École française de Rome, 2011), pp. 37–86

Bennett, Judith, 'Compulsory Labor Service in Late Medieval England', *Past & Present*, 209 (2010), 7–51

Bisson, Thomas, *The Crisis of the Twelfth Century: Power, Lordship, and the Origins of European Government* (Princeton: Princeton University Press, 2009)

Bourin, Monique, John Drendel, and François Menant, eds, *Les disettes dans la conjoncture de 1300 en Méditerranée occidentale*, Collection de l'École française de Rome, 450 (Rome: École française de Rome, 2011)

Bourin, Monique, and François Menant, 'Les disettes dans la conjoncture de 1300 en Méditerranée', in *Les disettes dans la conjoncture de 1300 en Méditerranée occidentale*, ed. by Monique Bourin, John Drendel, and François Menant, Collection de l'École française de Rome, 450 (Rome: École française de Rome, 2011), pp. 9–33

Braid, Robert, '"Et non ultra": Politiques royales du travail en Europe occidentale au XIVe siècle', *Bibliothèque de l'École des Chartes*, 161 (2003), 437–91

Brodman, James William, *Charity and Religion in Medieval Europe* (Washington, DC: Catholic University of America Press, 2009)

——, *Charity and Welfare: Hospitals and the Poor in Medieval Catalonia* (Philadelphia: University of Pennsylvania Press, 1998)

Brown, Peter, *Poverty and Leadership in the Later Roman Empire* (Hanover: University Press of New England, 2002)

——, *Through the Eye of a Needle: Wealth, the Fall of Rome, and the Making of Christianity in the West, 350–550 AD* (Princeton: Princeton University Press, 2012)

Campbell, Bruce, 'The Agrarian Problem in the Early Fourteenth Century', *Past & Present* 188 (2005), 3–70

Clark, Elaine, 'Institutional and Legal Responses to Begging in Medieval England', *Social Science History*, 26 (2002), 447–73

Cohen, Mark, *Poverty and Charity in the Jewish Community of Medieval Egypt* (Princeton: Princeton University Press, 2005)

Cohn, Samuel K., Jr, *Lust for Liberty: The Politics of Social Revolt in Medieval Europe* (Cambridge, MA: Harvard University Press, 2006)

Crubézy, Éric, Sylvie Duchesne, and Catherine Arlaud, *La mort, les morts et la ville: Saint Côme et Saint-Damien, Montpellier, x^e^–xvie siècles* (Paris: Errance, 2006)

Cullum, Patricia, '"And hir name was charite": Women and Charity in Medieval Yorkshire', in *Woman is a Worthy Wight: Women in Medieval English Society, 1200–1500*, ed. by P. J. P. Goldberg (Stroud: Sutton, 1992), pp. 182–211

Denjean, Claude, Juliette Sibon, and Claire Soussen, 'Charité bien ordonée: acteurs et institutions de la *tsédaqah* en Europe méditerranéenne au bas Moyen Age', *Les Cahiers de Framespa*, 15 (2014) <http://framespa.revues.org/2708> [accessed 25 June 2015]

Drendel, John, 'Conclusion', in *Les disettes dans la conjoncture de 1300 en Méditerranée occidentale*, ed. by Monique Bourin, John Drendel, and François Menant, Collection de l'École française de Rome, 450 (Rome: École française de Rome, 2011), pp. 417–22

Dyer, Christopher, 'The Experience of Being Poor in Late Medieval England,' in *Experiences of Poverty in Late Medieval and Early Modern England and France*, ed. by Anne M. Scott (Farnham, Surrey: Ashgate, 2012), pp. 19–39

——, *Making a Living in the Middle Ages* (New Haven: Yale University Press, 2002)

——, 'Poverty and its Relief in Late Medieval England', *Past & Present*, 216 (2015), 41–78

Farmer, Sharon, 'The Leper in the Master Bedroom: Thinking Through a Thirteenth-Century Exemplum', in *Framing the Family: Narrative and Representation in the Medieval and Early Modern Periods*, ed. by Rosalynn Voaden and Diane Wolfthal (Tempe: Arizona Center for Medieval and Renaissance Studies, 2005), pp. 79–100

——, 'Persuasive Voices: Clerical Images of Medieval Wives', *Speculum* 61 (1986), 517-43

——, *Surviving Poverty in Medieval Paris: Gender, Ideology and the Daily Lives of the Poor* (Ithaca: Cornell University Press, 2001)

Fleming, Robin, 'Bones for Historians: Putting the Body Back in Biography', in *Writing Medieval Biography, 750–1250: Essays in Honour of Frank Barlow*, ed. by David Bates (Woodbridge: Boydell, 2006), pp. 29–48

——, *Britain after Rome: The Fall and Rise, 400–1070* (London: Penguin, 2010)

——, 'Recycling in Britain after the Fall of Rome's Metal Economy', *Past & Present*, 217 (2012), 3–45

Frankel, Miriam, and Yaacov Lev, eds, *Charity and Giving in Monotheistic Religions* (Berlin: Gruyter, 2009)

Galinsky, Judah D., 'Jewish Charitable Bequests and the Hekdesh Trust in Thirteenth-Century Spain,' *Journal of Interdisciplinary History* 35 (2005), 423–40

Geremek, Bronislaw, 'La lutte contre le vagabondage à Paris aux XIVe et XVe siècles', in *Ricerche storiche ed economiche in memoria di Corrado Barbagallo*, ed. by Luigi di Rosa (Naples: Edizioni scientifiche italiane, 1970), pp. 213–36

——, *Poverty: A History*, trans. by Agnieszka Kolakowska (Oxford: Oxford University Press, 1994)

Green, Monica, 'Taking "Pandemic" Seriously: Making the Black Death Global', *The Medieval Globe*, 1 (2014), 27–61

Grieco, Holly, 'Pastoral Care, Inquisition and Mendicancy in the Medieval Franciscan Order', in *The Origin, Development, and Refinement of Medieval Religious Mendicancies*, ed. by Donald Prudlo (Leiden: Brill, 2011), pp. 117–56

Hanska, Jussi, *'And the Rich Man Also Died; and He Was Buried in Hell': The Social Ethos of Mendicant Sermons* (Hensinki: Suomen Historiallinen Seura, 1997)

Henderson, John, *Piety and Charity in Late Medieval Florence* (Chicago: University of Chicago Press, 1994)

——, *The Renaissance Hospital: Healing the Body and Healing the Soul* (New Haven: Yale University Press, 2006)

Horden, Peregrine, 'The Earliest Hospitals in Byzantium, Western Europe, and Islam', *Journal of Interdisciplinary History*, 35 (2005), 361–89

Jordan, William Chester, *The Great Famine: Northern Europe in the Early Fourteenth Century* (Princeton: Princeton University Press, 1996)

Le Blévec, Daniel, *La part du pauvre: l'assistance dans les pays du bas-Rhône du XIIe siècle au milieu du XVe siècle*, 2 vols (Rome: École française de Rome, 2000)

Little, Lester K., *Religious Poverty and the Profit Economy in Medieval Europe* (Ithaca: Cornell University Press, 1978)

——, 'Review Article: Plague Historians in Lab Coats', *Past & Present*, 213 (2011), 267–90

McIntosh, Marjorie, *Poor Relief in England, 1350–1600* (Cambridge: Cambridge University Press, 2012)

McNamara, Jo Anne, 'The Need to Give: Suffering and Female Sanctity in the Middle Ages', in *Images of Sainthood in Medieval Europe*, ed. by Renate Blumenfeld-Kosinski and Timea Szell (Ithaca, NY: Cornell University Press, 1991), pp. 199-221

McNamer, Sarah, *Affective Meditation and the Invention of Medieval Compassion* (Philadelphia: University of Pennsylvania Press, 2010)

Mollat, Michel, *The Poor in the Middle Ages: An Essay in Social History*, trans. by Arthur Goldhammer (New Haven: Yale University Press, 1986)

——, ed., *Études sur l'histoire de la pauvreté: Moyen Âge-XVIe siècle*, 2 vols (Paris: Publications de la Sorbonne, 1974)

Mollat, Michel and Philippe Wolfe, *Popular Revolutions of the Late Middle Ages*, trans. by A. L. Lytton-Sells (London: Allen and Unwin, 1973)

Piron, Sylvain, 'Un couvent sous influence: Santa Croce autour de 1300', in *Économie et religion: l'expérience des orders mendiants (XIIIe–XVe siècle)*, ed. by Nicole Bériou and Jacques Chiffoleau (Lyon: Presses Universitaires de Lyon, 2009), pp. 321–55

Rawcliffe, Carole, 'Hospital Nurses and their Work', in *Daily Life in the Middle Ages*, ed. by Richard Britnell (Stroud, UK: Sutton, 1998), pp. 43-64

Sabra, Adam, *Poverty and Charity in Medieval Islam: Mamluk Egypt, 1250–1517* (Cambridge: Cambridge University Press, 2000)

Saunier, Annie, 'Les incidences de la guerre de cent ans sur les établissements hospitaliers du nord de la France', *Les hôpitaux enjeux de pouvoir: France du Nord et Belgique (IVe–XXe siècle)*, ed. by Marie-Claude Dinet-Lecomte, Revue du nord, Hors série, Collection Histoire, 22 (Villeneuve-d'Ascq: Université Charles-de-Gaulle-Lille 3, 2008), pp. 46–66

Tierney, Brian, 'The Decretists and the "Deserving Poor"', *Comparative Studies in Society and History*, 1(1958–59), 360–73

Touati, François-Olivier, *Maladie et société au Moyen Âge: la lèpre, les lépreux et les léproseries dans la province ecclésiastique de Sens jusqu'au milieu du XIVe siècle*, Bibliothèque du Moyen Âge, 11 (Paris: De Boeck, 1998)

Vauchez, André, 'Charité et pauvreté chez Elisabeth de Thuringe d'après les actes du procès de canonisation', in *Études sur l'histoire de la pauvreté: Moyen Âge-XVIe siècle*, ed. by Michel Mollat, 2 vols (Paris: Publications de la Sorbonne, 1974), I, 163–73

Watson, Sethina, 'The Origins of the English Hospital', *Transactions of the Royal Historical Society*, 16 (2006), 75–94

Wickham, Chris, *Framing the Early Middle Ages: Europe and the Mediterranean, 400–800* (Oxford: Oxford University Press, 2005)

Windemuth, Marie-Luise, *Das Hospital als Träger der Armenfürsorge im Mittelalter* (Stuttgart: Steiner, 1995)

Wolf, Kenneth Baxter, *The Poverty of Riches: Saint Francis of Assisi Reconsidered* (Oxford: Oxford University Press, 2003)

Zytnicki, Colette, and Juliette Sibon, 'Introduction au dossier: charité et bienfaisance dans le monde juif en diaspora,' *Cahiers de Framespa* 15 (2014) <http://framespa.revues.org/2708> [accessed 25 June 2015]

IN THE SPIRIT OF THE STUDIO **Open with**

"IN THE SP

July , 202
A two-day
Focusing
In Reggic

Day 1

9:00 – 9:30 Student -faculty Introdu
Students work in pairs;
Faculty participate
Kristina has 5 interviev
Students introduce ea

9:30 – 10:30 Lella identifies and shar

. These principles are prepared a
resource to which parti
Students encouraged t

10:30 - 10:40 Break

10:40 - 12:00 Students view slides of
Try to identify principle

Key descriptive words l

- The power and pleas
- collaboration
- organization of spac
- Image of the child
- awareness
- interconnected even
- Techniques (experim
- Transforming a mate
- Properties of each m

1:00 Lunch

.00 Materials, Collections in the

Hospitals, Charity, and the Culture of Compassion in the Twelfth and Thirteenth Centuries

Adam J. Davis

During the twelfth and thirteenth centuries hundreds of hospitals and leper houses were founded all over Europe to care for the sick and poor. Hospitaller and military orders, lay confraternities, monasteries, and penitential groups were also actively engaged in charitable work. This period clearly represented a turning point in the way that women and men thought about and acted toward their poor and needy neighbours. Various theories have been put forward for why new charitable institutions were founded and became the objects of such broad popular support, ranging from lay and ecclesiastical lords, to knights and townspeople. One possible explanation is that the political emergence of towns fostered new institutional forms of charity.[1] Charitable giving also seems to have been tied to the outpouring of lay religious devotion and growing concern with salvation, since medieval donors linked their giving to the welfare of their souls and believed in the intercessory powers of the sick and poor recipients of their gifts. Moreover, the traditional theological notion of an almost quantifiable link between salvation and almsgiving became all the more vital with the development of the doctrine of purgatory.[2] The growing sanctification of charity was also evident in the large number of saints from this period

[1] Watson, 'City as Charter'.

[2] Le Goff, *The Birth of Purgatory*, trans. by Goldhammer.

Adam J. Davis (davisaj@denison.edu) is Associate Professor and William T. Utter/Clyde E. Williams, Jr, Professor of History at Denison University.

Approaches to Poverty in Medieval Europe: Complexities, Contradictions, Transformations, c. 1100–1500, ed. by Sharon Farmer, IMR 22 (Turnhout: Brepols, 2016) pp. 23–45
BREPOLS PUBLISHERS 10.1484/M.IMR-EB.5.105458

who were venerated for their acts of compassion, which often included founding and working in a hospital.[3] Support for charitable institutions may also have been fuelled by guilt about growing prosperity, with charity serving to justify profit making when some of those profits were channelled toward alms.[4] In this regard, a thirteenth-century treatise on the vices and virtues suggested that the works of mercy — which its author called expressions of 'dolore e compassione avere d'altrui male, e d'altrui necessitade' (sorrow and compassion for the misfortunes and needs of others) — were the ideal antidote for the sin of avarice.[5]

This essay contends both that a new culture of compassion emerged during the twelfth and thirteenth centuries, evident in hagiographical texts, devotional literature, visual images, and theology, and that this culture of compassion, heretofore largely neglected by scholars, helped fuel the medieval charitable revolution. The emergence of this new culture of compassion, I argue, was closely related to the rise of new forms of devotion to the suffering and humanity of Jesus.

How were ideas about almsgiving, the works of mercy, and compassion reflected in medieval charitable practices? In particular, this essay examines how compassion figured both in the financial support given to hospitals for the sick and poor and in the decision of some women and men to dedicate their lives to caring for the *miserabiles* in these institutions.

Some modern scholars have challenged the notion that medieval charity as practiced in hospitals was a reflection of genuine piety, let alone compassion. They point to the 'non-caring activities in which hospitals engaged [...] under the guise of charity', thereby casting medieval charity as merely ceremonial, or a self-serving, calculated display of the giver's power and prestige.[6] By highlighting the instrumental aspects of medieval charity, these scholars echo the suspicion with which Enlightenment *philosophes* viewed religious charity: namely, as

[3] Vauchez, *Sainthood*, trans. by Birrell.

[4] Little, *Religious Poverty and the Profit Economy*.

[5] This treatise was the *Esposizione del paternostro*, a Tuscan translation of *La somme le roi*. See Botana, *The Works of Mercy*, p. 68.

[6] Rubin, 'Imagining Medieval Hospitals'. See also Ruiz, *From Heaven to Earth*; Rawcliffe, '"A Word from Our Sponsor"'. For a counter-argument, see Brodman, *Charity and Religion*. Even Michel Mollat, who did pioneering work on medieval attitudes toward the poor, suggests that the motivation behind traditional alms was not *bienfaisance* or the relief of the afflicted. Rather, he suggests that medieval almsgiving was inherently 'egocentric in a sense [since] it is aimed at the salvation of the donor through the intervening of the beneficiary': see Mollat, 'L'hôpital dans la ville au moyen âge en France', p. 11.

a form of *égoïsme*, stemming solely from the giver's concern with his or her own salvation (as opposed to the recipient's material or spiritual state).[7] What this explanatory model ignores, however, is that a donor's concern with his or her own salvation (or social status) could easily coexist with genuine concern for the recipient's material or spiritual state.[8]

Recent work by social psychologists, neuroscientists, and evolutionary theorists has deepened our understanding of human emotions like compassion. And while historians have also begun to examine the important role of emotions, altruistic motives, and 'moral sentiments' in history, there remains a need, particularly in studying the history of charity and altruism, to move away from a *homo economicus* model of human nature in which humans are thought to always act purely out of 'rational' self-interest.[9] Many scientists now believe that compassion is biologically innate and a product of evolutionary processes, a point that even Darwin made in *The Descent of Man*.[10] Neuroscientists have sought to identify the neural underpinnings of empathy in the brain to demonstrate that altruistic behaviour actually stimulates pleasure sensors in the brain. But it is not at all clear that altruism is merely the result of the way humans are biologically wired. In fact, there is compelling evidence that compassion and altruism are learned emotions and behaviours fulfilling specific social roles and the products of a particular culture, discourse, and 'emotional community'.[11] Even if to provide care to a needy stranger or voluntarily give up one's property does not run counter to human nature, the nature and scale of charitable practices has varied across space and time, and there is a need to explain why. What is the relationship between emotions (such as compassion and empathy) and charitable behaviour in the particular cultural context of high medieval Europe?

[7] Whereas the *philosophes* associated religious charity with *égoïsme*, they argued that *bienfaisance* represented a more pure, selfless form of altruism, in large part because it was stripped of religious values. See Jones, *Charity and Bienfaisance*, pp. 2–3.

[8] For a fuller discussion of these issues, see Davis and Taithe, 'From the Purse and the Heart'.

[9] On emotions in history, see Rosenwein, *Emotional Communities*; Rosenwein, 'Worrying about Emotions in History'.

[10] For a review of the vast literature on this subject, see Goetz, Keltner, and Simon-Thomas, 'Compassion: An Evolutionary Analysis and Empirical Review'. E. O. Wilson and some others have advanced a controversial theory called 'group selection' to explain how altruism and self-sacrifice benefit a group at the expense of an individual. See Lehrer, 'Kin and Kind'. For a critique of this theory, see Pinker, 'The False Allure of Group Selection'.

[11] Rosenwein, 'Problems and Methods in the History of Emotions'.

In trying to understand medieval Christians' expressions of support for new charitable institutions like hospitals, we need to consider how specific cultural and devotional experiences might have conditioned people to feel compassion and behave charitably toward those in need of assistance. The historian Lynn Hunt has proposed a causal relationship between the rise of humanitarian concerns during the eighteenth century and cultural experiences, such as the reading of epistolary novels.[12] Just as these novels provoked 'imagined empathy' in their readers for the plight of the novels' characters, the medieval faithful projected their own 'imagined relationship' with a suffering Jesus and compassionate Mary, evoked in preachers' sermons and in visual representations in churches, onto the *miserabiles* of their own community.[13] This essay examines how developments in medieval spirituality, including a greater emphasis on the humanity of Jesus and Mary, made it easier for medieval Christians to empathize with a suffering stranger, to see themselves, a family member, or Jesus in the sufferer (or, for that matter, in the one who sought to alleviate the suffering). The notion of serving others and seeing Christ in those who were suffering was of course a central part of New Testament teaching. Yet, as Peter Brown has recently shown, it was only during the late fourth century that 'the poor', a category essentially created by late Roman bishops, became objects of material and religious concern in the Roman West, as giving gradually shifted from the traditional, pagan civic generosity, in which the wealthy gave large gifts to their city, to a new Christian model in which the 'middling' classes gave what modest gifts they could to the poor and their local church.[14] Thus, the distant roots of a culture of compassion that emerged in the twelfth and thirteenth centuries can be found in late antiquity, when the relationship between the spiritual and material was being redefined. The emphasis on the value of charity and the works of mercy, however, became a focus of Christian practice in novel ways during the High Middle Ages.

Michel Mollat, André Vauchez, and others have observed a cultural shift in attitudes toward the poor during the twelfth and thirteenth centuries that had important implications for the proliferation of hospitals.[15] As these scholars readily acknowledge, the poor continued to be stigmatized and harassed, and

[12] Hunt, *Inventing Human Rights*.

[13] McNamer, *Affective Meditation*. On imitative devotion to Christ and Mary during the Middle Ages, see also Fulton, *From Judgment to Passion*.

[14] Brown, *Through the Eye of a Needle*.

[15] Longère, 'Pauvreté et richesse chez quelques prédicateurs'; Mollat, *The Poor in the Middle Ages*, trans. by Goldhammer; Vauchez, *La spiritualité du moyen âge occidental*, pp. 118–23.

there was suspicion that some beggars were able-bodied and therefore 'undeserving' of assistance. The hagiographic topos of a saint's humble, personal ministry to the sick poor continued to have force in the High Middle Ages precisely because the *miserabiles* were still met with disdain, and it was thus considered unnatural for someone to wish to care for them. Yet in terms of collective attitudes, poverty was also increasingly regarded as a sign of divine election, with the poor seen as Christ's vicars on earth.[16] The status of the *pauperes Christi*, traditionally those who took religious vows of voluntary poverty, was gradually extended to include the *miserabiles*, a category that according to the churchman Jacques de Vitry (d. 1240) included the involuntary poor, invalid, timid, feeble-minded, miserable, hungry, leprous, and those who cry.[17]

The exaltation of voluntary religious poverty may even have played a role in the parallel rise in the status of the involuntary poor. In the words of Bronislaw Geremek, 'the heroism of renunciation, doctrinally presented both as an end in itself [...] and as a means to salvation, played another role: it stimulated compassion. Thus it was beneficial both to professional beggars and to the poor in general'.[18] In his first *Rule*, Saint Francis told his fellow Minors 'gaudere, quando conversantur inter viles et despectas personas, inter pauperes et debiles et infirmos et leprosos et iuxta viam mendicantes' (to rejoice when they live among vile and despised people, the poor and powerless, the sick, the lepers, and the beggars in the street).[19] The involuntary poor were thought to serve a salvific function for those who were not poor and who gave charity. Thus, the involuntary poor served a crucial function in providing the opportunity for penitential acts of almsgiving. A parallel phenomenon was also taking place with regard to medieval attitudes toward lepers. Indeed, the French historian François-Olivier Touati has called the twelfth-century laity's expressions of mercy toward the sick and leprous nothing short of a 'mutation de conscience'.[20]

[16] In his study of the problem of wealth in late antiquity, Peter Brown likewise cites many examples of the poor being both the objects of scorn and admiration. The fantastically wealthy Pinianus and Melania the Younger so wished to identify with the poor that they enlisted on the poor roll of the church of Jerusalem in 417. See Brown, *Through the Eye of a Needle*, p. 300.

[17] Mollat, *The Poor in the Middle Ages*, trans. by Goldhammer, p. 102.

[18] Geremek, *Poverty*, trans. by Kolakowska, p. 36. This runs counter to Kenneth Baxter Wolf's somewhat controversial argument that the Franciscans' pursuit of voluntary poverty actually hurt the status of the involuntary poor, a position echoed in the essay by Allison Edgren in this volume. See Wolf, *The Poverty of Riches*.

[19] Francis of Assisi, *Regula non bullata*, ed. by Esser, p. 141.

[20] Touati, *Maladie et société*, p. 214.

This transformation of conscience is evident in the frequency of twelfth- and thirteenth-century charitable giving and the mushrooming of hospital foundations. These developments suggest a medieval 'charitable imperative', to borrow from the title of Colin Jones's book about hospitals in *ancien régime* and revolutionary France.[21] For example, a study of thirteenth-century testaments in Flanders found that 85 per cent of testaments included charitable bequests (to aid lepers, hospitals, beguinages, widows, the ransoming of captives, etc.), and 44 per cent included a bequest to at least one hospital.[22] Two-thirds of all wills from *c.* 1300 in east-central France included distributions of coin and/or food to the poor.[23] Forty per cent of all testaments in thirteenth-century Barcelona included bequests to a hospital, as did 90 per cent of testaments in Rodez in the south of France *c.* 1300.[24]

It was common for twelfth- and thirteenth-century testaments to indiscriminately include bequests to all of the religious and charitable institutions of a city or region. In his famous will of 1248, the French royal cook, Adam, made bequests to some one hundred different religious houses and seventeen leprosaries in the Paris region.[25] The wealthy Parisian bourgeois couple, Étienne Haudri and his wife Jeanne Barbou, who were draper merchants, not only founded a hospital for poor widows but left testamentary bequests to lepers, the blind, orphans, prisoners, students who were without support, those suffering from ergotism, the poor who had fallen on hard times, hospices for the sick, and poor girls who wished to marry. The size of Étienne's charitable bequests was approximately ten times his bequests to churches and religious houses, and about the same size as his bequests to family members and household servants and clerics. But 80 per cent of his wife, Jeanne's, testamentary bequests were directed at hospitals and other charitable causes.[26]

Testators could be quite discriminating in their giving by leaving the largest gifts to a particular hospital, requesting burial in the hospital's cemetery, and asking that the hospital's *magister* be the executor for the will. It is of course difficult to know what might have moved a donor to make a bequest to a hospital,

[21] Jones, *The Charitable Imperative*.

[22] Godding, 'La pratique testamentaire en Flandre au XIIIe siècle', pp. 289–90.

[23] Vauchez, 'Assistance et charité en occident'.

[24] Brodman, *Charity and Religion*, p. 40. Mollat, 'L'hôpital dans la ville au moyen âge en France', p. 10.

[25] Touati, 'Les groupes des laïcs', p. 146 and n. 27.

[26] Bove, 'vie et mort d'un couple de marchands-drapiers Parisiens', p. 50.

and we should be wary of reductionist explanations for charitable practices, since a multiplicity of factors and motivations probably underlay any given gift.[27] Hospitals provided a wide range of services which extended beyond what we traditionally associate with 'care', from saying masses for donors' souls, to acting as creditors for those in need of short term capital. Some donation charters indicate that a donation was made to a hospital in gratitude for specific services it provided the donor or his/her relatives. In 1271 the knight Jean de Lunay gave the *hôtel-Dieu* of Provins in Champagne a rent as gratitude 'pro servicio dicti militis et uxoris sue defuncte in dicta Domo Dei annuatim faciendo' (for the service that had been done annually for him and his late wife in the *domus Dei*).[28] Some donations were directed at a relative working in the hospital. In 1269 the squire Jacques de Saint Martin de Hupeelo gave a lifetime rent of oats and wheat to his sister Alice, who was a sister at the *hôtel-Dieu* of Provins.[29] A charter from that same year confirmed an earlier donation made to Marguerite, a *conversa* in the hospital, by her mother, the late noblewoman Agnes de Courbouzon, of an annual rent of half a *muid* of grain.[30]

Donation charters and testamentary bequests to hospitals were at times explicit in saying that a benefactor acted out of a sense of piety or compassion. When Jacques Bernier, a cleric in the diocese of Sens who had grown up in Provins, donated a rent to the hospital there, he acknowledged 'devocionem quam habuerat et habebat circa pauperes Domus Dei de Pruvino ante fontem dicte ville et erga Domum predictam et eorum miserabilem paupertatem' (the devotion that he had had and continued to have for the poor of the *domus Dei* of Provins in front of the fountain of the said city and toward the said house and their miserable poverty).[31] The bourgeoise Jacqueline la Coypelle donated

[27] A potentially valuable source in this regard would be the recruiting messages of the *quaestors* who collected alms on behalf of hospitals. This would at least permit a sense of what hospitals believed would resonate with potential donors. For words of caution on the impossibility of reconstructing the motives behind charitable giving, see Rawcliffe, '"A Word from Our Sponsor"', p. 118.

[28] Seine-et-Marne, Archives départementales [henceforth AD] Seine-et-Marne 11HdtA12, fol. 57v; 'Les cartulaires', ed. by Dupraz, act no. 191.

[29] AD Seine-et-Marne 11HdtA12, fol. 66r–v; 'Les cartulaires', ed. by Dupraz, act no. 220.

[30] AD Seine-et-Marne 11HdtA12, fol. 32r–v; 'Les cartulaires', ed. by Dupraz, act no. 104. In 1247 the squire Guyard de Fonteneto amortized the donation that his late mother, Agnes, had made to his sister, Marguerite, a sister of the hôtel-Dieu. See AD Seine-et-Marne 11HdtA12, fol. 32r; 'Les cartulaires', ed. by Dupraz, act no. 102.

[31] AD Seine-et-Marne 11HdtA12, fol. 107r–v; 'Les cartulaires', ed. by Dupraz, act no. 358.

land out of a sense of 'affectionem et devocionem' (affection and devotion) which she had for the *domus Dei* and the poor there.[32] The knight Pierre des Barres confirmed a donation of a rent that his mother, Heloise des Barres, 'Dei amore et pietatis intuit, donavit ad sustentationem pauperum Domus Dei de Provins' (made with love of God and in a spirit of piety for the sustenance of the poor of the *domus Dei* of Provins).[33] In her 1238 entrance charter to serve as a sister in a leprosary, Jacqueline de Louasville stated her intention 'Deo servire et compassione salubri succurrere posset debilibus et infirmis' (to serve God and to be a measure of help by her aid and compassion to the most weak and sick).[34] These of course might merely represent stock phrases or formulas, but there is quite a bit of variation in the wording of charters, with some clauses being quite personalized. Even if some phrases are formulaic, they indicate that hospitals were considered important sites for the performance of the spiritual and corporal works of mercy.

While most medieval Christians expressed their compassion through charitable bequests, some laywomen and men displayed a personal commitment to the works of mercy by dedicating their lives to caring for the sick poor in a hospital. This charitable service emerged as part of the larger apostolic movement of the twelfth and thirteenth centuries. As André Vauchez has put it, 'a new category of saint' developed as part of the apostolic movement, with sanctity increasingly tied to the practice of charity.[35] Saint Francis of Assisi did much to popularize this charity-driven spirituality:

> To the Poverello, the love of God was indissociable from the love of men. It was not enough to imitate Jesus in gestures and conduct; it was also necessary to seek out and love him in the most wretched of his creatures.[36]

[32] AD Seine-et-Marne 11HdtA12, fol. 133v–134r; 'Les cartulaires', ed. by Dupraz, act no. 460.

[33] AD Seine-et-Marne 11HdtA13 ('petit cartulaire'), fol. 71r; 'Les cartulaires', ed. by Dupraz, act no. B11.

[34] Touati, *Maladie et société*, p. 407.

[35] Vauchez, *Sainthood*, trans. by Birrell, p. 199. For the relationship between charity and female sanctity, see Le Blévec, 'Le rôle des femmes dans l'assistance et la charité'.

[36] Vauchez, *Sainthood*, trans. by Birrell, p. 390. Admittedly, while Francis and some of the earliest brothers did work among the poor (and some brothers lived in hospitals with the poor), the primary occupation of the earliest brothers was not to improve the social and economic conditions of the poor. Still, Francis and the earliest friars displayed a radical commitment to living as the poor and among the poor, and inspired later social agents of change, particularly among the tertiaries who worked in hospitals.

Admittedly, the image of the charitable saint helping the beggar or leper had been a hagiographical topos stretching back to Saint Martin of Tours in the fourth century, to say nothing of earlier, foundational examples in the New Testament. Yet unlike most of the saints during the periods immediately before and after the twelfth and thirteenth centuries, whom Vauchez calls 'contemplative', many of the saints from the late twelfth and thirteenth centuries (or those regarded as having lived exemplary lives even if they were not formally canonized) were distinctly charitable — venerated for founding and/or working in hospitals — and a striking number were Franciscan tertiaries, reflecting the influence of Franciscan spirituality.[37] Moreover, even as the First Order shifted its attention away from the kind of caritative work that friars like Anthony of Padua, Gerard of Modena, and Henry of Milan had been engaged in during the late 1220s and 1230s, to the clerical and pastoral work of preaching and hearing confession, the penitential spirituality of the Third Order, inspired as it was by Franciscan charism, became increasingly defined by caritative work.[38]

The close association between care-giving and spirituality is vividly illustrated by the life of the beguine Marie of Oignies, who spent years with her

[37] These included Margherita of Cortona (d. 1297), a Franciscan tertiary, who after her husband's death founded a hospital and charitable confraternity; Angela of Foligno (d. 1309), a wealthy widow and tertiary who cared for lepers in a hospital in Foligno; Agnes of Bohemia (d. *c.* 1281), a tertiary who founded a hospital in Prague and also founded the Crosiers of the Red Star, a lay confraternity which served the sick and ran dozens of hospitals in Eastern Europe; Douceline of Digne (d. 1274), a Franciscan tertiary and beguine who first cared for the poor her father took into his own home and, following his death, who worked in the hospital of Hyères; Jutta of Huy, a wealthy married woman who had close ties to the Cistercians and worked for eleven years caring for lepers; Aldobrandesca (d. *c.* 1309), a Humiliati and widow who worked in a hospital in Siena; Saint Ubaldesca (d. 1206), a lay sister who served the sick in the hospital of Saint John of Jerusalem in Pisa; Raimondo Palmerio of Piacenza (d. 1200), a shoemaker and married father who founded a hospice for abandoned children and a hospital for poor women; Saint Omobon of Cremona (d. 1197), a tailor who founded a hospital; Saint Gerard Tintori of Monzo (d. 1207), who founded and worked in a hospital; Saint Walter of Lodi (d. 1224), who founded a hospital; Saint Andrew Gallerani, who founded the hospital of the Confraternity of Mercy in Siena; and Saint Gerardo Tintore, who established a hospital in Milan. See Vauchez, *Sainthood*, trans. by Birrell, pp. 200–01; Thompson, *Cities of God*, pp. 180–81, 196; Pieper, 'Saint Elizabeth of Hungary', pp. 205, 210, 218–19; Brodman, *Charity and Religion*, pp. 182–83.

[38] Some later Spiritual Franciscans, like Ubertino of Casale and Angelo Clareno, living outside the cities in hermitages, also displayed a genuine concern about the problem of material poverty for the involuntary poor. See Cusato, 'Where Are the Poor?'; Cusato, 'Two Uses of the *Vita Christi* Genre in Tuscany, *c.* 1300'. I am grateful to Michael Cusato for his help in clarifying the Franciscan Order's interest in material poverty during the thirteenth century.

husband serving lepers in the hospital of Willambrouk before retiring to a hermit's cell to lead a life of mystical contemplation. In writing about Marie's works of mercy, Jacques de Vitry not only underscores her spiritual powers, like the curative power of her prayers, but also calls attention to the fact that Marie was more troubled by the suffering of others than her own travails.[39] In fact, while expressing compassion for the sufferings of others, she rejoiced in her own tribulations and wished that she could take on the afflictions of others. Marie regarded physical suffering as spiritually valuable in teaching patience and discipline. For Jacques, who believes that women were in some ways better suited than men for the holy work of caring for the *miserabiles*, Marie's willingness to do revolting work, such as washing lepers' sores, rendered her a kind of holy martyr and an example of selfless service to others.

Another lay woman known for her compassion for the *miserabiles* was Elizabeth of Hungary, the daughter of King Andrew II of Hungary, about whom a great deal is known due to a number of hagiographical texts as well as the testimony that was part of several canonization inquests that occurred just after her death in 1231.[40] After the death of her husband, Louis IV of Thuringia, Elizabeth developed close ties to the Franciscans and may have become a Franciscan tertiary and beguine.[41] She distributed food to the poor and sick, washed their feet each year on Holy Thursday, made them clothes and habits for burying their dead, and used 2000 marks from her dower to found a hospital for the poor dedicated to Saint Francis at Marburg in Thuringia.

Despite her elite upbringing, Elizabeth joined the hospital brothers and sisters in preparing and serving meals, dressing and undressing patients, bathing them, washing their linens, and personally performing the most miserable tasks so that she might experience the misery of the poor herself. She kissed the sores of the leprous and washed the wounds of a beggar with an ulcerous head and would cut his hair while holding his head in her lap. Elizabeth was drawn to the sickest, most abject patients in her hospital. Her disciple, Isentrude, described how Elizabeth wiped filth from the mouths, ears, and noses of the sick in the hospital. She not only endured sights and smells that her handmaids in the hospital could not begin to tolerate, but took delight in doing so, often smiling and

[39] Jacques de Vitry, *The Life of Marie d'Oignies*, trans. by King, pp. 85, 100–01.

[40] Ancelet-Hustache, *Gold Tried by Fire*; *The Life and Afterlife of St. Elizabeth of Hungary*, trans. by Wolf.

[41] There is debate about whether Elizabeth became a Tertiary. See Vauchez, 'Charité et pauvreté', pp. 171–72; Pieper, 'Saint Elizabeth of Hungary', pp. 44–45, 51–55.

laughing. For a while Elizabeth cared for a paralysed orphan boy who hemorrhaged blood, often cleaning his bloody (and soiled) clothes. When this child died, she adopted a malodorous leprous girl, who until that point had always been shunned. Elizabeth hid the sickly girl in her own house and cared for her until Elizabeth's harsh confessor, Conrad of Marburg, discovered the hidden child. He expelled the girl from Elizabeth's house, only to have Elizabeth adopt a new child, this one afflicted with ringworm. What Elizabeth's hagiographers emphasized was the fervour and love with which she devoted herself to assisting the most helpless. Elizabeth's charity, which involved unpleasant, self-humiliating labour, carried as much meaning for her as it did for the recipient, and required that she personally experience the sufferings of the afflicted, in short, that she experience *compassio*, which was the defining feature of her spirituality.[42]

Although hagiographers and witnesses who gave testimony about Elizabeth's sanctity as part of the canonization inquest were intent on promoting her sanctity as exceptional, their own accounts make clear that Elizabeth was not working alone but collaborating with a team of hospital workers at Marburg that was engaged in difficult and often unpleasant work. This group of hospital workers included the servants Irmingard, (a different) Elizabeth, and Hildegunde, as well as the *custos* of the hospital, Hermann and his wife Irmentrude. Yet most of the people around Elizabeth, including her confessor, are depicted by witnesses as having been incapable of understanding the depth of her charity, such as her willingness to risk contracting contagious diseases or the pleasure she derived from giving away all of her wealth in the form of alms. In the face of the wretched, Elizabeth seemed to have none of the natural human feelings of revulsion. And whereas Elizabeth's confessor cast her charity in terms of her spiritual development — as an antidote to her pride and a way to obtain merit in the eyes of God — witnesses described Elizabeth as focused squarely on the recipients of her charity, not on the way her charity might benefit her.[43]

The Franciscans were quick to highlight their association with Elizabeth, whom they depicted as embodying the Franciscan virtues of poverty and love of the poor. In loving the poor as brothers and sisters in Christ rather than as mere instruments of her own salvation, Elizabeth was inspired by the example of

[42] Vauchez, 'Charité et pauvreté'.

[43] The *vita* of Yvette of Huy by Hugh of Floreffe, in contrast, largely ignores the lepers who were cared for by Yvette, focusing instead on how she embodied pious humility, dramatized by her efforts to contract leprosy (bathing with the lepers and even mixing her blood with theirs). See *Living Saints of the Thirteenth Century*, ed. by Mulder-Bakker, pp. 93–95.

Saint Francis.[44] In the left lancet window in the cathedral of Strasbourg, erected in the mid-thirteenth century, Elizabeth is depicted engaged in each of the six corporal works of mercy. In the rose window at the apex, she is rewarded by being crowned by the Virgin Mary, taking her place among the Elect on Christ's right-hand side.[45] And when Margaret of Burgundy, the queen of Sicily and widow of Charles of Anjou, founded a hospital in 1293 at her castle in Tonnerre (where she was countess), she dedicated altars in the hospital chapel to the Virgin Mary, John the Baptist, Mary Magdalene, and Elizabeth of Hungary.[46]

What also distinguished a number of the charitable saints from this period was their own experiences of suffering, which made them identify with the afflictions of others and led them to act compassionately. For example, representations of the adversities faced by the saintly French king Louis IX — his frequent illnesses, his ascetic lifestyle, his crusading failures, and the loss of family members — embodied what Jacques Le Goff has termed the thirteenth-century 'valorisation de la souffrance' (valorization of suffering), a suffering that hagiographers linked to Louis's compassion for the downtrodden.[47] Guillaume de Saint-Pathus, who detailed the king's many acts of charity, including founding and patronizing hospitals, underscored that the king 'eut une tendresse merveilleuse de compassion pour ceux dans le mésaise' (had a marvelous tender compassion for people who were in a bad way).[48] A litany of anecdotes was invoked by Louis's hagiographers to illustrate his compassion: picking up the bodies and limbs of the Christians who were killed at Sidon, or using his own fingers to wash away the grime between the toes of a poor man. Iconographic images of the humble and compassionate king performing each of the seven works of mercy, in some cases in a hospital setting, appeared in the Books of Hours of Jeanne d'Evreux and Marie of Navarre, as well as in public spaces, such as the now lost altar retable in the lower chapel of the Sainte Chapelle in Paris.[49] In representations of charitable saints, compassion was depicted as a central motivator for religiously exemplary behaviour. This sanctification of compassionate

[44] Pieper, 'Saint Elizabeth of Hungary', pp. 171–79.

[45] Holladay, 'The Education of Jeanne d'Evreux', p. 593.

[46] Courtenay, 'The Hospital of Notre Dame des Fontenilles at Tonnerre', pp. 84–85.

[47] Le Goff, *Saint Louis*, pp. 858–86.

[48] Le Goff, *Saint Louis*, pp. 878–79.

[49] For the *vitae* by Geoffrey of Beaulieu and William of Chartres, see *The Sanctity of Louis IX*, ed. by Gaposchkin and Field. See also Holladay, 'The Education of Jeanne d'Evreux'; Guest, 'A Discourse on the Poor'; Gaposchkin, *The Making of Saint Louis*, p. 201.

behaviour may have been what inspired lay women and men (and clergy) to provide support to hospitals, where the works of mercy were performed daily.

In addition to saints' lives, however, models for teaching charity and compassion abounded in the Middle Ages, including the Bible, books of hours, *exempla* in sermons, and visual representations.[50] Although relatively few images of the works of mercy survive, Federico Botana has established that beginning in the twelfth century there was a burgeoning imagery of the works of mercy, including mural panel paintings, manuscripts, sculptures, and stained glass.[51] On the baptistery in Parma, constructed in 1196, six reliefs on the west portal, one for each of the works of mercy in Matt. 25. 35–36, contain verses on their base to help the viewer recognize and learn how to properly perform the work of mercy depicted: 'juxta hoc exemplum peregrinis hostia pandas' (this is an example of how you should open the door to pilgrims), 'cum multa cura lavat hic egro sua crura' (this one washes the legs of the sick with much care), and so forth.[52] Likewise, texts such as *La voie de paradis* and the *Breviari d'amor* included both textual and visual demonstrations on how to practise the works of mercy, making theological concepts accessible to the laity.[53] The late thirteenth-century *Miroir des bonnes femmes* is comprised of thirty *exempla* illustrating 'good women', including women from the Bible and female saints, many of whom were notable because of their compassion and charitable activities.[54] Even in the *Enseignements* that King Louis IX composed for his children, he urged them to feel compassion for the poor and all those who were suffering.[55]

In trying to understand what might have made a hospital donor identify with the anonymous sick and poor residents of a hospital, it is worth recalling that it was common for visual representations of the works of mercy to depict the works being performed in hospitals, thereby strengthening the association of hospitals as sites of such works of compassion.[56] Furthermore, Christ frequently appears in visual representations as one of the beneficiaries of the works of mercy, thereby linking Christ with the contemporary suffering stranger.[57]

[50] Holladay, 'The Education of Jeanne d'Evreux'.

[51] Botana, *The Works of Mercy*, p. 7.

[52] Botana, *The Works of Mercy*, pp. 30–31 n. 63.

[53] Botana, *The Works of Mercy*, p. 58.

[54] Holladay, 'The Education of Jeanne d'Evreux', p. 602.

[55] Le Goff, *Saint Louis*, p. 878.

[56] Botana, *The Works of Mercy*, pp. 44–46.

[57] Botana, *The Works of Mercy*, p. 158 n. 31.

In a fourteenth-century fresco cycle in the baptistery of Parma depicting the seven works of mercy, Christ appears from a cloud in each scene, holding the Scriptures with one hand and pointing to the beneficiaries of the works of mercy with his other hand, thereby recalling the Prophecy of the Last Judgement in Matt. 25. 40: 'quamdiu fecistis uni ex his fratribus meis minimis, mihi fecistis' (as long as you did it to one of these my least brethren, you did it to me).[58]

Medieval *exempla* also frequently drew a linkage between the tribulations of the contemporary sick poor and Christ's own suffering. For instance, Jacques de Vitry cited an *exemplum* in which a noble matron allowed a male leper to seek repose in her house and bed, thereby risking the anger of her husband who hated lepers. When her husband returned from hunting, the leper had miraculously disappeared, leaving behind a wonderful aroma, signifying paradise and the fact that the leper had in fact been Christ in disguise. In the words of Jacques de Vitry, 'Qui igitur predictis modis miseretur proximo accommodat Deo [....] dicente Domino, "Esurivi et dedisti michi manducare"' (Whoever therefore through these works shows charity to his neighbour applies that charity to God [...] as the Lord said, 'I was hungry and you gave me food [Matt. 25. 35]').[59]

While personal salvation was not the sole motivation for charitable acts, the salvific power of mercy was nonetheless frequently emphasized by visually juxtaposing the works of mercy with the Last Judgement or the Heavenly City, thus suggesting that salvation could be attained by performing such good works; by implication, failure to do so would have a far less auspicious result.[60] Artistic renderings of the works of mercy also linked them to the Eucharistic sacrifice, this at a time of increasing Eucharistic fervor. Federico Botana has shown that besides the Crucifixion itself being described in medieval texts as a work of mercy in redeeming humanity, images depicting the performance of works of mercy were at times positioned in a way to create a 'strong association between the works of mercy and the Eucharistic sacrifice'.[61] This was true of the fresco, *I Canevari* (*c.* 1280), which was associated with the *Misericordia* confraternity in Bergamo and depicted four officials distributing food and wine. The fresco was on the lower part of a choir screen in the Bergamo cathedral and was part of a pictorial program that included devotional images and opened up to the high altar.[62]

[58] Botana, *The Works of Mercy*, pp. 86–88.

[59] Farmer, 'The Leper in the Master Bedroom', p. 83.

[60] Botana, *The Works of Mercy*, pp. 47, 197.

[61] Botana, *The Works of Mercy*, p. 188.

[62] Botana, *The Works of Mercy*, pp. 83–85, 184–88.

Just as the Eucharist was thought to make Christ's presence real, so too was Christ believed to be present in the performance of works of mercy (at times disguised as the afflicted), which, like the Eucharist, was cast as an expression of love.

There remains a need to explore the relationship between charitable practices and developments in medieval devotion that involved a new capacity for imagination and empathy. Beginning in the late eleventh century, compassion became a pervasive theme in medieval devotional literature, so much so that J. A. W. Bennett has argued that the popularity of the literary genre of affective meditation on Christ's Passion represented a 'revolution in feeling'.[63] More recently, Sarah McNamer credits affective meditations on the Passion with 'the invention of compassion'.[64] The objective of meditations such as the pseudo-Bonaventurean *Meditationes vitae Christi*, the *Golden Legend*, Nicholas Love's *Mirror of the Blessed Life of Jesus Christ*, or Richard Rolle's *Incendium amoris* was 'to teach their readers, through iterative affective performance, how to feel'.[65] The *Meditationes vitae Christi* implored the meditant 'ut intime compaciaris ac simul pascaris, averte autem parumper oculos a divinitate et eum purum hominem considera' (to make yourself more deeply compassionate and nourish yourself at the same time, turn your eyes away from his divinity for a little while and consider him purely as a man).[66] Through these meditations, the 'distance of space and time is [...] annihilated' as the medieval reader or listener imagines himself or herself present at the crucifixion, experiencing Christ's bodily pain or feeling the grief experienced by the Virgin Mary.[67] This imitative devotion and affective identification with Jesus and Mary could also be stimulated with help from painted rood-screens and crucifixes that were ubiquitous in medieval churches (and hospitals), or the scenes of the Crucifixion and the Man of Sorrows in psalters, missals, and books of hours. Scenes from the evangelical past, whether visual or textual, sought to elicit a sense of compassion and above all, empathy from the meditant.[68]

[63] Bennett, *Poetry of the Passion*, p. 32.

[64] McNamer, *Affective Meditation*.

[65] McNamer, *Affective Meditation*, p. 2.

[66] Iohannis de Caulibus, *Meditaciones vite Christi*, ed. by Stallings-Taney, pp. 267–68; *Meditations on the Life of Christ*, ed. by Ragusa and Green, p. 330.

[67] Bennett, *Poetry of the Passion*, p. 35.

[68] Fulton, *From Judgment to Passion*.

While it is impossible to establish a direct causal link, it is possible that affective devotional experiences made it easier for some people to empathize with their needy neighbours. In short, material support for charitable causes such as hospitals may be related to developments in meditative and devotional practices. Is there any connection, for example, between women's (especially widows') high rate of charitable giving and service in hospitals and the fact that, as McNamer and others have shown, affective devotion was so gendered, with compassion for the suffering Christ associated with 'feeling like a woman'?[69] According to the *Legenda maior* (*c.* 1300), the charity of Saint Hedwig (d. 1243), duchess of Silesia, particularly her love of the poor, was directly tied to her devotion to the suffering of Jesus.[70] Both Julian of Norwich and Margery Kempe also claimed that their visions of a suffering Christ resulted in their feeling greater compassion for their fellow Christians in need, whom they treated as if they were Christ.[71] Admittedly, it was one thing for a Passion narrative to elicit devotion to Christ and another for that compassion to be translated into concrete works of mercy directed at strangers in one's own midst. As Miri Rubin and others have shown, meditations on the Passion could just as easily lead to horrific violence against Jews as inspire acts of compassion for a fellow Christian. Yet for the fourteenth-century English Augustinian Walter Hilton, meditation on the Passion was valuable only insofar as it inspired altruistic behaviour. To worship Christ, according to Hilton, necessarily involved washing Christ's feet, and that meant attending to one's fellow Christians:

> Thanne yif that thou be bisi with al thi wirching and thi myghte for to arraie his heed — that is for to worschipe hymsilf by mynde of his passion and of his othere werkes in his manheed bi devocioun and meditacioun of him — and foryetest his feet — that aren thyn children and thi servauntes, thi tenauntes — and alle thyn evene-Cristen spille for defaute of kepynge, unaraied, unkeped, and not tended to as thei aught for to be: thou plesest him not. Thou doost noo worschipe to him.[72]

> (If you devote all your efforts and energy to adorning his head — in other words, to honouring him by thinking about his passion and the other acts of his incarnation as a way of worshipping him and meditating about him — and neglect his feet — in other words, your children, your servants and your tenants — so that all your

[69] McNamer, *Affective Meditation*, pp. 119–49.

[70] Vauchez, *Sainthood*, trans. by Birrell, pp. 373–74.

[71] McNamer, *Affective Meditation*, p. 150.

[72] Hilton, *Epistle on the Mixed Life*, ed. by Windeatt, p. 117.

> fellow-Christians perish for lack of care — not clothed, provided for, and looked after as they should be — you do not please him. You do him no honour.)

For Langland, it was Christ who 'in a pore mannes apparaille pursueth us evere' (in a poor man's apparel pursues us always).[73]

Late twelfth- and thirteenth-century theologians and canonists, meanwhile, drew on scriptural and patristic texts in developing a theology of almsgiving, one that reflected a new cultural ethos of giving and recognized the involuntary poor as a class of people with important status.[74] It was only in the twelfth century that the six good deeds in Matt. 25. 35–36 were established as the canonical corporal works of mercy, along with a seventh work, burying the dead (from Tobit 12. 12), which was added in the late twelfth century.[75] The influential Parisian theologian Peter the Chanter argued that mercy is exalted above every other virtue and that the way to imitate Christ is through the performance of works of mercy.[76] Addressing the regular clergy in his *Verbum adbreviatum*, the Chanter warns of the danger that the offices and prayers — the *horae vocales* — recited in the cloister, would be done at the expense of the seven *horae reales*, the active hours outside of prayer time, which corresponded, he argues, to the seven works of mercy. In addressing a point that had long been debated by Christians — the relative merits of the active and contemplative life — the Chanter here emphasizes the value of the active life and the supreme importance of the works of mercy.[77] In his discussion of almsgiving, he argues that 'pietas enim dantis condit elemosinam, non quantitas dati' (the piety of giving makes the alms, not the quantity of the gift), and he frowns on forced almsgiving, which he believes was not pleasing to God, since it is 'elemosinam enim condiat caritas, non autem dandi necessitas' (charity that makes alms, moreover, not the necessity of giving).[78]

Jacques de Vitry, who was part of the Chanter's circle and composed several model sermons directed at hospital audiences, echoed his teacher on the

[73] Langland, *Piers Plowman*, ed. by Robertson and Shepherd, B.xi.186, pp. 172–73; Bennett, *Poetry of the Passion*, p. 61.

[74] Imbert, *Histoire des hôpitaux en France*, pp. 47–48; Tierney, *Medieval Poor Law*; Tierney, 'The Decretists and the "Deserving Poor"'.

[75] Botana, *The Works of Mercy*, pp. 1–2.

[76] Petrus Cantor Parisiensis, *Verbum adbreviatum*, ed. by Boutry, pp. 638–39.

[77] Botana, *The Works of Mercy*, pp. 30, 37–39; Petrus Cantor Parisiensis, *Verbum adbreviatum*, ed. by Boutry, pp. 525–26.

[78] Petrus Cantor Parisiensis, *Verbum adbreviatum*, ed. by Boutry, p. 660.

importance of intention and motivation in almsgiving. According to Jacques, the giving of alms should not be done to win praise, or under the presumption that it would secure one a place in heaven. And the amount of alms mattered far less than where they came from and how they were to be used.[79] Other theologians debated when alms should be given, in what form, and by and to whom. Theologians, preachers, and various kinds of writers also invoked the image of the *corpus mysticum* to suggest that just as the various organs and members of the human body are interdependent, so too does a Christian society require that all of its members assist one another in a spirit of charity.[80] For example, in his thirteenth-century *Summa de poenitentia*, the Franciscan Servisanto of Faenza urges the members of the spiritual body to look after their neighbours just as the various parts of a physical body work in tandem.[81]

In considering compassion's place in charitable practices, I have not sought to argue that all support of hospitals was principally motivated by compassion, whether in the form of caring for inmates or the giving of alms. A system of incentives and rewards was built into the Christian theology of almsgiving. Medieval visual representations of almsgiving almost always focussed on the almsgiver, not the nameless recipient.[82] As Marcel Mauss's classic work on the gift illustrates,[83] the dynamics of giving are inherently complex as is defining what actually constitutes a gift. Some medieval charters that purported to be charitable donations were in fact exchanges or disguised sales. Hospital donors not only hoped that the prayers of the poor would help shorten their time in purgatory, but some also made gifts to ensure that they or a family member would be received in the hospital as a resident, nurse, or *donatus*. Others wished to establish a good relationship with a hospital, which in some cases served as a significant landholder and creditor in the town. Likewise, some of the women and men who became hospital *conversi*, dedicating their lives to car-

[79] Davis, 'Preaching in Thirteenth-Century Hospitals'; Bird, 'Medicine for Body and Soul', p. 101.

[80] Botana, *The Works of Mercy*, pp. 182–84.

[81] Botana, *The Works of Mercy*, p. 183. As Federico Botana has shown, this application of the *corpus mysticum* to the works of mercy was also used both by the Occitan poet and jurist Matfre Eremegaud in his *Breviari d'amor*, an encyclopaedic poem (*c.* 1290), and in a Tuscan translation of the enormously popular *La somme le roi*, a treatise on the vices and virtues originally composed for the future French king Philip IV. See Botana, *The Works of Mercy*, pp. 183–84.

[82] Guest, 'A Discourse on the Poor', p. 162.

[83] Mauss, *The Gift*, trans by Halls.

ing for hospital inmates, were as much looking for material and spiritual security for themselves as thinking about the needs of others.

But the mere fact that self-interest often (or even always) underlay gifts and service does not preclude the possibility that a giver simultaneously felt a desire to help the poor and sick. A donor might have felt compassion as a result of giving even if compassion was not the original impetus for the gift. This was a culture steeped in images of compassion and altruism, whether in art, affective meditations, *exempla*, or hagiography. These religious and cultural forms were meant to elicit compassion and in some cases, teach people how to perform the works of mercy, ultimately propelling them to action. In the medieval imagination, hospitals were the sites par excellence for works of mercy and thereby the ideal place to channel one's compassion for Christ onto those who fell under the abstract category of the poor. Hospitals not only cared for a limited number of poor and sick residents, but often also oversaw the distribution of food and clothes to the urban poor outside the hospitals' walls, so many townspeople were familiar with their local hospitals. Hospitals were part of the consciousness of testators thinking about the needs of the sick poor. Supporting a hospital was viewed as a way to imitate the charitable examples of Christ and the saints, and it was believed that in doing works of mercy one was simultaneously imitating and caring for Christ. The humanization of Jesus and Mary and increased identification with their suffering contributed to the growing sensitivity to the immediate needs for poor relief. Hospital donors also recognized, as the language of their charters made clear, that one day they might well be suffering and in need of another's mercy and compassion. Compassion thus not only represents a chapter in the history of emotions, but was part of a cultural shift in sensibility in the High Middle Ages, evident in the strong support of charitable institutions. Indeed, compassion was central to the mission of medieval hospitals and the support they received.

Works Cited

Archival Sources

Seine-et-Marne, Archives départementales Seine-et-Marne 11HdtA12
——, Archives départementales Seine-et-Marne 11HdtA13

Primary Sources

'Les cartulaires de l'Hôtel-Dieu de Provins: éditions critique', ed. by Dominique Dupraz (unpublished thesis, École des Chartes, Paris, 1973)

Francis of Assisi, *Regula non bullata*, in *Écrits*, ed. by Kajetan Esser, trans. by Théophile Desbonnets and others, Sources Chrétiennes, 285 (Paris: Cerf, 1981), pp. 122–79

Hilton, Walter, *Epistle on the Mixed Life*, in *English Mystics of the Middle Ages*, ed. by Barry Windeatt (Cambridge: Cambridge University Press, 1994), pp. 108–30

Iohannis de Caulibus, *Meditaciones vite Christi*, ed. by Mary Stallings-Taney, Corpus Christianorum Continuatio Mediaevalis, 153 (Turnhout: Brepols, 1997)

Jacques de Vitry, *The Life of Marie d'Oignies*, trans. by Margot H. King (Toronto: Peregrina, 1993)

Langland, William, *Piers Plowman*, ed. by Elizabeth Robertson and Stephen H. A. Shepherd (New York: Norton, 2006)

The Life and Afterlife of St. Elizabeth of Hungary: Testimony From Her Canonization Hearings, trans. by Kenneth Baxter Wolf (Oxford: Oxford University Press, 2011)

Living Saints of the Thirteenth Century: The Lives of Yvette, Anchoress of Huy; Juliana of Cornillon, Author of the Corpus Christi Feast; and Margaret the Lame, Anchoress of Magdeburg, ed. by Anneke B. Mulder-Bakker, trans. by Jo Ann McNamara (Turnhout: Brepols, 2011)

Meditations on the Life of Christ: An Illustrated Manuscript of the Fourteenth Century, ed. by Isa Ragusa and Rosalie B. Green and trans. by Isa Ragusa (Princeton: Princeton University Press, 1961)

Petrus Cantor Parisiensis, *Verbum adbreviatum: Textus conflatus*, ed. by Monique Boutry, Corpus Christianorum Continuatio Mediaevalis, 196 (Turnhout: Brepols, 2004)

The Sanctity of Louis IX: Early Lives of Saint Louis by Geoffrey of Beaulieu and William of Chartres, ed. by M. Cecilia Gaposchkin and Sean L. Field, trans. by Larry F. Field (Ithaca: Cornell University Press, 2013)

Secondary Studies

Ancelet-Hustache, Jeanne, *Gold Tried by Fire: St. Elizabeth of Hungary* (Chicago: Franciscan Herald Press, 1963)

Bennett, Jack Arthur Walter, *Poetry of the Passion: Studies in Twelve Centuries of English Verse* (Oxford: Clarendon Press, 1982)

Bird, Jessalyn, 'Medicine for Body and Soul: Jacques de Vitry's Sermons to Hospitallers and their Charges', in *Religion and Medicine in the Middle Ages*, ed. by Joseph Ziegler and Peter Biller (York: York Medieval Press, 2001), pp. 91–108

Botana, Federico, *The Works of Mercy in Italian Medieval Art (c. 1050–c. 1400)* (Turnhout: Brepols, 2012)

Bove, Boris, 'Vie et mort d'un couple de marchands-drapiers Parisiens d'après les testaments de Jeanne et Étienne Haudri (1309, 1313)', *Paris et Ile-de-France, Mémoires* 52 (2001), 19–81

Brodman, James William, *Charity and Religion in Medieval Europe* (Washington, DC: Catholic University of America Press, 2009)

Brown, Peter, *Through the Eye of a Needle: Wealth, the Fall of Rome, and the Making of Christianity in the West, 350–550 AD* (Princeton: Princeton University Press, 2012)

Courtenay, Lynn T., 'The Hospital of Notre Dame des Fontenilles at Tonnerre: Medicine as Misericordia', in *The Medieval Hospital and Medical Practice*, ed. by Barbara S. Bowers (Aldershot: Ashgate, 2007), pp. 77–106

Cusato, Michael, 'Two Uses of the *Vita Christi* Genre in Tuscany, *c.* 1300: John de Caulibus and Ubertino da Casale Compared. A Response to Daniel Lesnick, Ten Years Hence', *Franciscan Studies* 57 (1999), 131–48

——, 'Where are the Poor in the Writings of Angelo Clareno and the Spiritual Franciscans?', in *Angelo Clareno Francescano: Atti del XXXIV Convegno internazionale, Assisi, 5–7 ottobre 2006* (Spoleto: Centro Italiano Di Studi Sull'alto Medioevo, 2007), pp. 123–65

Davis, Adam J., 'Preaching in Thirteenth-Century Hospitals', *Journal of Medieval History*, 36 (2010), 72–89

Davis, Adam J., and Bertrand Taithe, 'From the Purse and the Heart: Exploring Charity, Humanitarianism, and Human Rights in France', *French Historical Studies* 34 (2011), 413–32

Farmer, Sharon, 'The Leper in the Master Bedroom: Thinking Through a Thirteenth-Century Exemplum', in *Framing the Family: Narrative and Representation in the Medieval and Early Modern Periods*, ed. by Diane Wolfthal and Rosalynn Voaden (Tempe: Arizona Center for Medieval and Renaissance Studies, 2005), pp. 79–100

Fulton, Rachel, *From Judgment to Passion: Devotion to Christ and the Virgin Mary, 800–1200* (New York: Columbia University Press, 2002)

Gaposchkin, M. Cecilia, *The Making of Saint Louis: Kingship, Sanctity, and Crusade in the Later Middle Ages* (Ithaca: Cornell University Press, 2008)

Geremek, Bronislaw, *Poverty: A History*, trans. by Agnieszka Kolakowska (Oxford: Blackwell, 1994)

Godding, P., 'La pratique testamentaire en Flandre au XIIIe siècle', *Revue d'histoire du droit*, 58 (1990), 281–300

Goetz, Jennifer L., Dacher Keltner, and Emiliana Simon-Thomas, 'Compassion: An Evolutionary Analysis and Empirical Review', *Pyschological Bulletin*, 136 (2010), 351–74

Guest, Gerald B., 'A Discourse on the Poor: The Hours of Jeanne d'Evreux', *Viator*, 26 (1995), 153–80

Holladay, Joan A., 'The Education of Jeanne d'Evreux: Personal Piety and Dynastic Salvation in her Book of Hours at the Cloisters', *Art History*, 17 (1994), 585–611

Hunt, Lynn Avery, *Inventing Human Rights: A History* (New York: Norton, 2007)

Imbert, Jean, ed., *Histoire des hôpitaux en France* (Toulouse: Privat, 1982)

Jones, Colin, *The Charitable Imperative: Hospitals and Nursing in Ancien Régime and Revolutionary France* (London: Routledge, 1989)

——, *Charity and Bienfaisance: The Treatment of the Poor in the Montpellier Region, 1740–1815* (Cambridge: Cambridge University Press, 1982)

Le Blévec, Daniel, 'Le rôle des femmes dans l'assistance et la charité', in *La femme dans la vie religieuse du Languedoc (XIII–XIVe s.)*, Cahiers de Fanjeaux, 23 (Toulouse: Privat, 1988), pp. 171–90

Le Goff, Jacques, *The Birth of Purgatory*, trans. Arthur Goldhammer (Chicago: University of Chicago Press, 1984)

——, *Saint Louis* (Paris: Gallimard, 1996)

Lehrer, Jonah, 'Kin and Kind: A Fight about the Genetics of Altruism', *The New Yorker*, 5 March 2012, pp. 36–42

Little, Lester K., *Religious Poverty and the Profit Economy in Medieval Europe* (Ithaca: Cornell University Press, 1978)

Longère, Jean, 'Pauvreté et richesse chez quelques prédicateurs durant la seconde moitié du XIIe siècle', in *Études sur l'histoire de la pauvreté: Moyen Âge–XVIe siècle*, ed. by Michel Mollat, 2 vols (Paris: Publications de la Sorbonne, 1974), I, 255–73

Mauss, Marcel, *The Gift: The Form and Reason for Exchange in Archaic Societies*, trans. by W. D. Halls, intro. by Mary Douglas (New York: Norton, 1990)

McNamer, Sarah, *Affective Meditation and the Invention of Medieval Compassion* (Philadelphia: University of Pennsylvania Press, 2010)

Mollat, Michel, 'L'hôpital dans la ville au moyen âge en France', *Société française d'histoire des hôpitaux*, 47 (1983), 6–17

——, *The Poor in the Middle Ages: An Essay in Social History*, trans. by Arthur Goldhammer (New Haven: Yale University Press, 1986)

Pieper, Lori, 'Saint Elizabeth of Hungary: The Voice of a Medieval Woman and Franciscan Penitent in the Sources for Her Life' (unpublished doctoral dissertation, Fordham University, 2002)

Pinker, Steven, 'The False Allure of Group Selection', *Edge: Conversations on the Edge of Human Knowledge*, 18 June 2012 <http://edge.org/conversation/the-false-allure-of-group-selection> [accessed 12 October 2015]

Rawcliffe, Carole, '"A Word from Our Sponsor": Advertising the Patron in the Medieval Hospital', in *The Impact of Hospitals, 300–2000*, ed. by John Henderson, Peregrine Horden, and Alessandro Pastore (Bern: Peter Lang, 2007), pp. 167–93

Rosenwein, Barbara H., *Emotional Communities in the Early Middle Ages* (Ithaca: Cornell University Press, 2006)

——, 'Problems and Methods in the History of Emotions', *Passions in Context: International Journal for the History and Theory of Emotions*, 1 (2010), 1–32

——, 'Worrying About Emotions in History', *American Historical Review*, 107 (2002), 821–45

Rubin, Miri, 'Imagining Medieval Hospitals: Considerations on the Cultural Meaning of Institutional Change', in *Medicine and Charity before the Welfare State*, ed. by Colin Jones and Jonathan Barry (London: Routledge, 1991), pp. 14–25

Ruiz, Teofilo F., *From Heaven to Earth: The Reordering of Castilian Society, 1150–1350* (Princeton: Princeton University Press, 2004)

Thompson, Augustine, *Cities of God: The Religion of the Italian Communes, 1125–1325* (University Park: Pennsylvania State University Press, 2005)

Tierney, Brian, 'The Decretists and the "Deserving Poor"', *Comparative Studies in Society and History*, 1 (1959), 360–73

——, *Medieval Poor Law: A Sketch of Canonical Theory and its Application in England* (Berkeley: University of California Press, 1959)

Touati, François-Olivier, 'Les groupes des laïcs dans les hôpitaux et les léproseries au moyen âge', in *Les mouvances laïques des ordres religieux*, ed. Nicole Bouter, Actes du troisième colloque international du C.E.R.C.O.R., Tournus, 17–20 juin 1992 (Saint-Étienne: Publications de l'Université de Saint-Étienne, 1996)

——, *Maladie et société au moyen âge: la lèpre, lépreux et les léproseries dans la province ecclésiastique de Sens jusqu'au milieu du XIVe siècle* (Paris: De Boeck Université, 1998)

Vauchez, André, 'Assistance et charité en occident, XIII-XVe siècles', in *Domanda e consumi: livelli e strutture nei secoli (XIII–XVIe)*, ed. by V. Barbagli Bagnoli (Florence: Olschki, 1978), pp. 151–62

——, 'Charité et pauvreté chez Sainte Elisabeth de Thuringe d'après les actes du procès de canonisation', in *Études sur l'histoire de la pauvreté: Moyen Âge-XVIe siècle*, ed. by Michel Mollat, 2 vols (Paris: Publications de la Sorbonne, 1974), I, 163–73

——, *Sainthood in the Later Middle Ages*, trans. Jean Birrell (Cambridge: Cambridge University Press, 1997)

——, *La spiritualité du moyen âge occidental: VIII–XIIIe siècle*, 2nd edn (Paris: Éditions du Seuil, 1994)

Watson, Sethina, 'City as Charter: Charity and the Lordship of English Towns, 1170–1250', in *Cities, Texts and Social Networks, 400–1500: Experiences and Perceptions of Medieval Urban Space*, ed. by Caroline Goodson, Anne E. Lester, and Carol Symes (Farnham: Ashgate, 2010), pp. 235–62

Impoverished Free Litigants in Thirteenth-Century Property Disputes

Janice Musson

Dispossession of property, frequently by violence, was a common experience in the twelfth and thirteenth centuries, leading to social unrest. It was a major problem for English authorities who, in an effort to deal with it, issued the assize of novel disseisin, or recent dispossession, under Henry II, probably in 1166. This law, which asserted the principle that no free person might be disseised lawfully without a court judgement, enabled the dispossessed of every rank and situation, with the notable exception of the unfree, to sue for the return of their holdings, usually land. The action was immediately popular, and the earliest records of its enforcement are filled with cases brought by impoverished men and women of free status. Some defendants were also impoverished, and fall within the scope of the present analysis for that reason. Those who were not are also important to this study for their attitude to the poor whom they opposed.

The records analysed for this discussion are taken mainly from the earliest extant rolls, from 1194 until 1215, when they ceased. They were resumed in 1218. My analysis focuses on two questions: what information can these records add to current knowledge concerning poverty at that time; and how did the poor perceive themselves and authority as personified in their lords, the court, and the crown? The records distinguish between degrees of poverty and show the reaction of the court and others towards it. My discussion begins with a brief outline of the terms of the action and its sphere of influence, followed by an explanation of the criteria that I have used to identify impoverished litigants.

Janice Musson (jmusson.mrs@gmail.com) is a PhD research student at the University of Nottingham, where she also tutors.

Approaches to Poverty in Medieval Europe: Complexities, Contradictions, Transformations, c. 1100–1500, ed. by Sharon Farmer, IMR 22 (Turnhout: Brepols, 2016) pp. 47–66
BREPOLS PUBLISHERS 10.1484/M.IMR-EB.5.105459

These fall into five main categories, as observed in the enrolled cases: firstly, plaintiffs whose poverty can be readily identified; secondly, plaintiffs whose poverty may be inferred from the terminology of the records; thirdly, plaintiffs whose circumstances indicate poverty; fourthly, poor defendants; fifthly, impoverished litigants of both parties who deliberately used the assize for the conveyance of property. Finally, I will analyse some possible reasons for the approaches taken by humble freeholders towards their adversaries and the courts.

The suit of novel disseisin to resolve a disputed tenement could be brought only by a freeholder who held the property in his or her own name. In the hierarchical, land-based society of late twelfth- and early thirteenth-century England, it was free status which held the key to possession and its benefits, which were not precluded by poverty per se. The assize was restricted to the royal courts, either at Westminster or where the king happened to be as he perambulated the country, or in the town or city appointed for a sitting of his circuit justices, whom the king at this early time sometimes joined. Those who were not free, with rare exceptions detailed in *De legibus*, were obliged to take their property disputes to a lower court where the assize did not operate.[1] There seems to have been no difference, other than size, in the types of property held by impoverished and prosperous free persons.

There were three main forms of disseisin: simple, of common, and by nuisance.[2] Simple disseisin concerned the dispossession of a man or woman of his or her main holding. Disseisin of common was the prevention of a tenant of a main holding from exercising his or her right to the use, with others, of further amenities held by another person. Rights of common included common of woodland, fisheries, water, and access, among others, but the most frequent was of pasture. Disseisin by nuisance was the prevention, or diminution, of a freeholder's use of his main holding, or of a right of common, very often through blocking access to it by means of a wall or hedge or ditch.

Any dispossessed freeholder wishing to sue under the assize had first to purchase a writ from the chancery office in Westminster, or from a circuit court. Writs were issued in the king's name to the sheriff of the county wherein the disputed property lay, and specified where and when the case would be heard. The sheriff was directed to assemble twelve men local to the area, known as recognitors, to view the property and assemble the facts. He was also required to obtain sureties from the litigants against their appearance in court and the

[1] Bracton, *De legibus*, ed. by Woodbine, III, 98–106.

[2] Bracton, *De legibus*, ed. by Woodbine, III, 18–25; 166–67, 187–89, 194; 189–93.

payment of any fines and damages. The names of all involved were added to the writ, and on the appointed day every actor was obliged to be present in court. Litigants were able to plead their cause and many did, not least the poor. In court the recognitors constituted a jury and gave a verdict, followed by a judgement from the bench.

In addition to the criteria that a plaintiff must hold freely and in his or her own name, there was a third — that the alleged offence should have occurred no earlier than a previously specified occasion. This was usually an activity of the king, such as his coronation, the date of which limited the time span of a court's authority and prevented it from adjudicating on a disseisin which had occurred before that date. This temporal limitation was part of the opening formula of every record, the clerk sometimes naming the occasion but more frequently writing *infra assisam* (within the assize): that is, within the term of the court's authority. The date was brought forward from time to time with the intention of keeping the disseisin recent or 'novel'. If any one of the three required criteria was transgressed, the case was automatically lost. Although many suits were adjourned for default of recognitors, many more were concluded with untypical speed, which accounted for much of the action's popularity. Damages were often awarded, and the losing party was always subject to a fine, termed an 'amercement' since he or she thereby fell into the mercy of the king.

The assize spread so wide a net across different social groupings and geographical areas and over so long a time that it caught many nuances of circumstance. Scholars agree that its original intention was to prevent forcible ejection and to remove the recovery of property from the sphere of private activity by channelling it through the courts, but they disagree on the severity of the dispossessions that were in question in the late twelfth and early thirteenth centuries.[3] Cecil Anthony Francis Meekings believed that well before 1235, the date of the Surrey eyre which he edited, dispossession was less likely to be violent and more often a matter of 'various infringements'.[4] Donald Sutherland, by contrast, was of the opinion that the assize involved 'putting someone out against his will' until the fourteenth century.[5] These and other views are likely to be

[3] *The 1235 Surrey Eyre*, ed. by Meekings, I, 69; van Caenegem, *The Birth of the English Common Law*, p. ix; Sutherland, *The Assize of Novel Disseisin*, pp. 27–28.

[4] *The 1235 Surrey Eyre*, ed. by Meekings, I, 69. Baker explains that the French word *eyre* came from the Latin term for the justices who travelled the country with the circuit courts, *justicarii in itinere*. Over time the word became identified with the courts themselves: Baker, *An Introduction to English Legal History*, p. 16.

[5] Sutherland, *The Assize of Novel Disseisin*, pp. 22, 145.

complementary rather than contradictory. Nevertheless, the evidence from the beginning of the thirteenth century seems to support Sutherland's interpretation: there were still very many unsuccessful plaintiffs, as noted below, who cannot have been merely infringed upon in minor ways, and they give the impression of severe want. Their poverty was so great that they were pardoned their amercements, and it is difficult to envisage them suffering anything less than physical dispossession. Possibly, the poor were perceived as soft targets, easier to dispossess in a literal fashion than more substantial freeholders. Be that as it may, the rolls show that this was not a view shared by poor freeholders themselves, who demonstrated courage and resolve in defence of their interests.

The impoverished freeholders under discussion include those who held areas too small to sustain them, sometimes fractions of an acre, and who would have needed additional income from labouring or craft work to survive. It excludes the artisans and traders who may have worked alongside them at the selfsame tasks but whose livelihood came solely from their business. Cases of skilled workers who also held land of which they were disseised rarely involve poverty. Peasants who employed labourers and amassed wealth were clearly not impoverished and thus fall outside this discussion, as do those of unfree status.

Poor freeholders were certainly tillers of the soil, but as a whole they were not clods; rather, as revealed in the rolls, very many were knowledgeable and articulate, intelligent and proactive. Their poverty is most clearly demonstrated where the costs were excused, illustrated by Adam and his mother Alice who were pardoned their amercement by the 1208 York eyre when they lost against William, son of Ivo, in Karleton (Carlton), Yorkshire.[6] On the whole, courts accepted the fact that unsuccessful litigants who were very poor could not pay the amercements they attracted, and did not usually try to collect them.[7] Since it is improbable that these plaintiffs could have afforded the originating writ either, it follows that it must have been given to them; indeed, Anthony Musson has argued that the charges were waived if they swore to their poverty.[8]

Musson indicates that the franchise extended to those who had no one to stand surety for them against possible fines and could offer only their word that they would pay the amercement if they lost their case.[9] In 1195 one such

[6] *Curia Regis Rolls*, ed. by Flower, v, 258–59: 'Misericordia perdonatur pro paupertate eorum' (The amercement is pardoned for their poverty).

[7] Musson, *Medieval Law in Context*, pp. 167–68.

[8] Musson, *Medieval Law in Context*, pp. 167–68.

[9] Musson, *Medieval Law in Context*, p. 167.

plaintiff known only as Muriel defaulted on her action against Richard, son of Osain, in Stifield (unidentified), Bedfordshire; the clerk recorded that her faith was her pledge.[10] In other words, there was no one else to pay the fine, which is not given. This was regularly accepted by the court, even when as here the absence of any supporting identification indicates a strong possibility of impoverishment, but it must have been a largely academic exercise given the lack of any pecuniary support. In other cases poverty can be safely deduced from the stated condition of a litigant, such as illegitimacy or dependency.[11] For example, with regard to the amercement of John, son of Walter, by the Lincoln eyre of 1202, the clerk simply noted that he was a servant, implying that he was too poor to pay it.[12] John had failed in his claim against William, son of Uctred, concerning common of pasture in Rike hundred, Lincolnshire. Poor litigants who were successful are much more difficult to identify. The courts had no interest in recording their financial state since, as the winning party, they were not amerced. Yet it is sometimes possible to argue the presence of poverty from the information given, such as the unconscious comparison of one group of litigants with another that appears to be more powerful and prosperous.[13] Litigants in possession of property may have been poor, but they were not destitute.

The poverty revealed in the rolls, then, is not an absolute condition but contains gradations from those still in possession of property, however modest in size, to the destitute. Strictly speaking, poverty is not synonymous with impoverishment, which implies active depression into a less favourable state, although the two terms are here used interchangeably. The rolls identify some who clearly were destitute, in that they had nothing, yet remained free men and women though fallen on hard times. Occasionally, tantalizing glimpses are offered of possible causes for their social and economic decline, including legal technicalities, social unrest, family quarrels, and, doubtless, improvidence.[14] An account of literal impoverishment through extravagance is contained in the case of two sisters who in 1204 at York sued for dispossession of land inher-

[10] *Three Rolls of the King's Court*, ed. by Maitland, p. 131: 'Fides erat plegium' (Her faith was her pledge). At the Bedfordshire and Buckinghamshire eyre.

[11] See below, p. 56.

[12] *The Earliest Lincolnshire Assize Rolls*, ed. by Stenton, *c.* 415: 'Misericordia. Garcio est' (Amercement. He is a servant).

[13] See below, pp. 58–59.

[14] *Rolls of the Justices in Eyre*, ed. by Stenton, pp. lxiii–lxvi, *cc.* 193–94, 119, 52, 918–19.

ited from their father in Pickering, Yorkshire.[15] They had lost it because their mother, who remained with them, became so profligate in her widowhood that they were left with neither money nor chattels to render the service they owed to their lord, who happened to be the king and was present in court on that occasion. The wapentake had taken the land into the king's hand 'sicut consuetude ville est' (as is the custom of the vill) in those circumstances, and the court decided that custom should also settle the sisters' fate.[16] Again, amercement is not mentioned perhaps because the losing party's inability to pay was self evident. In addition to the light it sheds on local practice this depressing case is interesting for its novelty, which may have motivated the clerk to record it, and for its precious glimpse of intimate family life.

Some cases offer indications of how former freeholders might have been depressed into the landless category, perhaps through a misunderstanding of the terms of the assize, such as the time limitation.[17] Other cases illustrate the effort made by plaintiffs to retain their social standing as landholders, however lowly. At the Lincoln eyre of 1202, for example, Margaret, widow of Walter, sued Master Simon de Siwell for the return of her holding.[18] Why she lost it originally is not recorded, but her problems were compounded by the omission of its location from the writ, which should have rendered her case null and void.[19] However, Simon's bailiff undertook to return possession of her tenement to her, and the justices allowed the offer to proceed. The brevity of the record conceals neither Margaret's determination nor her precarious situation, which seems to have been secured only by the good will of her superiors. The greatest difficulty arises at the upper end of this category which shades into

[15] *Pleas before the King*, ed. by Stenton, III, *c.* 897: 'Omnia catalla earum vastavit ita quod dominus Rex non potuit habere servicium suum quod habere debuit de tenemento illo nec aliquid invenire potuit in feudo illo unde districtio fieri posset pro habendo servicio illo' (She wasted all their chattels so that the lord King could not have his service that he should have of that tenement, nor could he find anything in that fee in respect whereof distraint could be made to have that service).

[16] A wapentake was originally a place of administration under the Danes, who settled the eastern part of England in the ninth century. The term came to include the surrounding district, equivalent to the Anglo-Saxon hundred, and became synonymous with the court for that area.

[17] See below, p. 55.

[18] *The Earliest Lincolnshire Assize Rolls*, ed. by Stenton, *c.* 51: 'Venit baliuus ipsius Simonis et cepit in manu quod reddet ei seisinam suam et justicii ei concesserunt' (Simon's bailiff came and undertook to return her seisin to her and the justices permitted him).

[19] Bracton, *De legibus*, ed. by Woodbine, III, 57, 78, 140–41.

peasants who may be considered prosperous enough to withstand a degree of misfortune. Those about whom the rolls give no clue are excluded from consideration in the following analysis.

The number of poor litigants in the early records is small, probably because few of the eyre rolls are extant. More than one hundred eyres were held in four blocks between 1194 and 1209, when they were suspended, but the rolls of only seventeen still exist. From 1209 cases were heard before the king on progress or at Westminster, or his justices at Westminster, until the Hilary term of 1215. The records for this period survive in number, but there are none thereafter until 1218. Altogether, from 1194 until 1215, there are approximately twenty thousand accounts of civil cases of which, by the author's reckoning, rather more than seventeen hundred, about 8.5 per cent, refer to novel disseisin. Of these, approximately forty refer directly to poverty, which may also be discerned, with varying degrees of confidence, in a further ninety-three cases. On the evidence of the comparative numbers before the eyres and the Westminster court, in the years for which the records of both remain, it is clear that many more novel disseisin suits were brought in the country. During 1202, for instance, towards 10.5 per cent of the civil pleas heard before the Lincoln, Northampton, and Bedford eyres were novel disseisin cases, but only a little more than 5 per cent at Westminster.[20] Stenton makes the point that the general eyre that year reduced business at the central court, even though the residue of the eastern circuit was transferred to it.[21] However, in the following year the percentage at Westminster fell to rather less than four, whereas at the Northampton eyre alone it was almost sixty.[22] It seems likely then, taking into account the lost rolls, that novel disseisin formed a significantly greater proportion of the civil pleas than 8.5 per cent.

Turning now to my first category of plaintiffs — approximately forty — whose poverty can be most readily identified, they are those who were unsuccessful in their action and too poor to pay the consequent amercement, duly recorded by the clerk in explanation of the non-payment. This unequivocal

[20] *The Earliest Lincolnshire Assize Rolls*, ed. by Stenton, pp. 1–92, 195–215; *The Earliest Northamptonshire Assize Rolls*, ed. by Stenton, pp. 36–97; *Curia Regis Rolls*, ed. by Flower, II, 90–1059. Approximate figures are 120 out of slightly more than twelve hundred before the eyres, and twenty of fewer than four hundred at Westminster.

[21] *Pleas before the King*, ed. by Stenton, I, 146–48.

[22] *Curia Regis Rolls*, ed. by Flower, II, 1060–1918; *The Earliest Northamptonshire Assize Rolls*, ed. by Stenton, pp. 99–163. Approximate figures are fifty out of some thirteen hundred at Westminster, and 180 out of a little over three hundred at Northampton.

reference to impoverishment appears in, for the most part, straightforward and routine records of which Matilda's case is a good example. Matilda, her only identification, in 1195 failed in her claim against Henry Bat at Longeleia (Langley), Buckinghamshire, but was excused her amercement because of her poverty.[23] Also clearly poor are those plaintiffs who could find no pledges to underwrite the financial consequences of an unsuccessful case and asked the court to rely on their word, their 'faith', alone. Musson writes that those who were not so impoverished but still unable to find pledges were allowed to substitute items of property in their place.[24] However Walter of Quedhavering (Quadring), Lincolnshire, found no pledge other than his word.[25] He lost his case because he failed to appear before the Lincoln eyre of 1202, yet was amerced for one mark (13s. 4d.), twice the usual amount. This relatively steep fine seems to have been imposed, not because the court had reversed its assessment of Walter's financial state but on a point of principal for wasting its time by neither appearing nor excusing himself.[26] Walter was instructed in his absence to pay at Lincoln at a later date, but it cannot be thought likely that he did so. Non-appearance could of course indicate the death of a litigant, but that was often known and recorded, and it seems reasonable to assume that defaulting plaintiffs who had to rely on their word were probably destitute.

My second category of cases is small — eighteen in all — and involves plaintiffs whose poverty may tentatively be inferred from the terminology of the records, specifically the repetition of the term *infra assisam* (within the assize). The phrase referred to a named occasion which, as explained above, limited the time span of a court's authority.[27] It appears in the opening format of every record, unless the occasion itself is given, and was used in the case of Mabel, daughter of Roger, before the Northampton eyre in 1203.[28] Mabel sued

[23] *Three Rolls of the King's Court*, ed. by Maitland, p. 130: 'Matilda quieta de misericordia pro paupertatem' (Matilda is free of amercement for poverty). At the Bedfordshire and Buckinghamshire eyre.

[24] Musson, *Medieval Law in Context*, p. 167.

[25] *The Earliest Lincolnshire Assize Rolls*, ed. by Stenton, c. 1168: 'Non invenit plegios nisi fidem' (He found no pledges except his faith). Walter's suit was against Bartholomew of Muleton (Moulton), concerning a property in Quadring, Lincolnshire.

[26] *The Earliest Lincolnshire Assize Rolls*, ed. by Stenton, c. 1168: 'Walter non venit vel se essoniavit et ideo Walterus in m'ia' (Walter has not come or essoined himself and therefore Walter is in mercy).

[27] Above, p. 49.

[28] *The Earliest Northamptonshire Assize Rolls*, ed. by Stenton, c. 917: 'Willelmus non

William, son of Roger, for dispossession of property in Sirinton (Sherrington), Buckinghamshire, and lost. To their verdict, that William had not disseised her, the jurors added the phrase *infra assisam*. They appear to be giving a reason for their decision. The implication is that Mabel had indeed once possessed, and been wrongfully disseised of, that property, but that her dispossession had occurred earlier than the time limitation of the court before which she brought her case. Mabel had waited too long and lost on a technicality.

The record continues that she was amerced and very poor, indicating that the fine was waived. The time limit referred to was John's third coronation, at Canterbury on Easter Sunday in 1201, so she may have been dispossessed for as long as two-and-a-half years.[29] If it is assumed that she had been too poor to buy the originating writ, it strongly suggests that her poverty was a direct result of her dispossession, possibly by her brother. Mabel was one of six losing plaintiffs before that eyre, about whom the jury used the phrase *infra assisam* in their verdict.[30] One was pardoned his amercement, suggesting poverty, but another was amerced twice, once as the losing party and once for foolish talk (Latin). However this does not necessarily indicate an ability to pay the fines. The nature of the 'foolish talk' is not given, but it is possible that the court was again making a point about wasting its time.[31] It cannot be assumed, then, that all these plaintiffs were impecunious, but their cases do suggest the proximity of poverty and an imperfect understanding of the terms of the assize. This view is supported by a double claim, heard at Lincoln in 1218, brought by a poor woman who won one part of it but lost the other because it was *infra assisam*, out of time.[32]

On the other hand, the same jury at Northampton in 1203 used the identical phrase in twelve cases which were won by the plaintiffs.[33] The eighteen are within a block of forty short accounts, perhaps deliberately grouped together because they were all out of time. It is unlikely that they simply represent the

disseisivit eam [...] infra assisam. Ideo Mabillia in misericordia pro falso clamore et pauperima est' (William has not disseised her [...] within the assize. Therefore Mabel is in mercy for a false claim and she is very poor).

[29] The case was heard on 9 September 1203.

[30] *The Earliest Northamptonshire Assize Rolls*, ed. by Stenton, *cc*. 893, 917, 923, 927, 929, 930.

[31] See the 1202 Lincoln eyre's fine of Walter above.

[32] *Rolls of the Justices in Eyre*, ed. by Stenton, *c*. 52.

[33] *The Earliest Northamptonshire Assize Rolls*, ed. by Stenton, *cc*. 891, 896, 898, 902, 911–12, 914, 916, 918–19, 921, 926.

preferred terminology of a fresh clerk. Clerks were legally precise in their phrasing of verdicts, and this term is not frequently employed. It does seem that it was repeated for a purpose, very possibly because of the nature of the cases. Do they represent nefarious attempts by lords to force possibly poor tenants from their properties? Nine plaintiffs were awarded damages of one mark or less, including one each of 5s., 3s., 12d., and 3d., the remaining being 20s., 30s. and 100s. The amounts were largely balanced by the amercements, except for the smaller sums which attracted the standard fine of half-a-mark. Assuming that the courts were methodical in ordering their business, it is reasonable to conclude that the low damages indicate small holdings. Taken together, the eighteen cases may indicate the resistance, not always successful, of mainly humble peasants to the bullying tactics of their lords. A similar possibility in a different context is discussed below.[34] They cast an oblique light onto one way, perhaps commonly experienced, by which freeholders could be depressed into the landless category. It is not certain how the disseised survived before their cases came to court, which could be several years after the event, but the loss of a tenement, particularly a sole holding, must have pushed many into poverty, if not destitution.

Turning thirdly to plaintiffs whose circumstances indicate poverty, these fall into two distinct groups of people: firstly and most easily discernible, those who were evidently isolated in a weak, dependent situation; secondly, those who may have been humble smallholders opposing much stronger disseisors. The first group, seven in number, is woefully illustrated by the misfortune of a child.[35] Robert, the illegitimate underage son of a priest, became destitute when his father died.[36] He seems to have been too young to be formally seised of his father's holding, in Lafford (Sleaford), Lincolnshire, a method frequently employed by the clergy to circumvent their inability to bequeath property, since, as celibates, they could legally have no heirs. Robert was therefore justly dispossessed by his father's lord, the prior of Hauerholm (Haverholme, Lincolnshire). At Lincoln in 1206, William, son of Alan, pleaded *pro parvo* (for the child) but without avail. Consequently, Robert was left destitute, but

[34] Below, pp. 56–57.

[35] *The Earliest Lincolnshire Assize Rolls*, ed. by Stenton, *cc.* 51, 415, 1335, 1358, 1419; *Pleas before the King*, ed. by Stenton, III, *c.* 899; *Rolls of the Justices in Eyre*, ed. by Stenton, *c.* 923.

[36] *The Earliest Lincolnshire Assize Rolls*, ed. by Stenton, *c.* 1335: 'Ipse sacerdos tenuit terram illam de ipso priore tota vita sua ut prior dixit et in ea obit [...]. Constat quod pater suus obiit seisitus de terra illa et ipse nichil hereditarie potest clamare' (The priest held that land of the prior throughout his life as they prior said and he died holding it [...]. It was certain that his father died seised of that land and he could claim nothing by inheritance).

the justices requested the prior to provide for him 'quousque scierit discernere bonum et malum' (until he knows the difference between right and wrong). Since minors were not amerced, there is no mention of a fine. Similarly, at the 1206 Lincoln eyre, the clerk laconically wrote 'puer est' (he is a boy) to indicate that a second Robert, son of Anketil, was under-age and therefore pardoned his amercement.[37] Minors were evidently able to take out the required writ and bring an action before the court, despite their immunity from amercement, or their cases would have been quashed.

Circumstantial evidence of poverty may be cautiously inferred from two incomplete cases, in the course of which the plaintiffs were restored to their holdings by their lords and so maintained their social standing. In 1206 before the Lincoln eyre, a woman named only as Demilda was found to have been justly disseised by her lord, Robert de Camera, because the disputed holding was not a free tenement, and Demilda had not rendered the service required for it.[38] It is evident that the holding was in villeinage and therefore outside the terms of the assize, but Demilda herself cannot have been unfree or the case could not have proceeded to that conclusion.[39] Robert, her lord, would have challenged her status at the outset. If she had been his villein, she would have held the property in his name and there would have been no case to answer. But, as Bracton explains, a free individual could hold a property for villein services without compromising personal status, and this appears to have been the case here.[40] Robert reinstated her for life on the condition that she paid him three shillings and the customary dues. This was likely to be Demilda's only holding since she had no identification other than her first name, and her situation looks uncertain. Propertied women were usually known by the location of their tenement or the relative through whom they held it. No amercement is mentioned in this case, nor in the widow Margaret's suit given above.[41] It cannot therefore be known if the women had been able to purchase their writs, but

[37] *The Earliest Lincolnshire Assize Rolls*, ed. by Stenton, *c.* 1358. Robert lost his case against Alan and Robert, sons of Acer, over property in Sumercotes (Somercotes), Lincolnshire.

[38] *The Earliest Lincolnshire Assize Rolls*, ed. by Stenton, *c.* 1419: 'Quia ipsa non tenuit libere terram illam […] non potuit facere servicium et consuetudines quod ad terram pertinent' (Because she did not hold that land freely […] (and) could not render the service and customary dues that belong to the land). The location is illegible.

[39] Bracton, *De legibus*, ed. by Woodbine, III, 84–86, 101–02, 107–10.

[40] Bracton, *De legibus*, ed. by Woodbine, III, 84–86, 101–02, 107–10; for examples, see *Rolls of the Justices in Eyre*, ed. by Stenton, *cc.* 174, 176.

[41] Above, p. 52.

both have an air of fragility about them. Neither is there a mention of the fee customarily required for reaching an agreement between the parties in court. Both examples are interesting for the attitude of the lords to these tenants, with whom they seem to have dealt kindly. They also illustrate the court's ability and willingness to be flexible, almost to the point of informality.

The financial circumstances of the second group — thirty-two cases in all — are much more difficult to determine. It is an intriguing category of winning plaintiffs who were awarded often tiny damages in contrast to the much higher amercements levied against their defendants. Of the thirty-two, none received damages of more than half-a-mark (6s. 8d.). Twelve were awarded between 2s. and 4s. inclusive, seven received 12d, and one 3d. No amercement was less than the standard half-mark (6s. 8d.), and several were much more. For example, Eudo the clerk of Hagwrdingham (Hagworthingham), Lincolnshire, received damages of 12d., but his disseisor, William son of Robert, was amerced for half-a-mark, and John of Sauztorp (Sausthorpe), Lincolnshire, received 2s. against Robert Canis's amercement also of half-a-mark.[42] On the other hand, Geoffrey of Normannebi (Normanby le Wold) was amerced 10s. but paid damages of only 12d. to Margery of Beningeworth (Benniworth), whom he had dispossessed of her free tenement in Claxebi (Claxy by Normanby), all in Lincolnshire; similarly Gilbert Scrop paid 3s. to William, son of Robert, in Baston in the same county, against his amercement of one mark (13s. 4d.).[43] It cannot be proved that these plaintiffs were poor. However they are sufficiently alike and are recorded close enough together, although not continuously, on the Lincoln eyre roll of 1206 to hold the reader's attention.[44] Some are also close geographically. The first two examples given above are four miles apart and, with another eight disputed properties, lie in an area to the north and east of Lincoln and bounded by the coast. There is a cluster of five around Boston and a further four centred on Grantham.

Low damages to great lords are not unknown, and the dangers of conflating them with smallholdings and these with smallholders are pointed out by G. Herbert Fowler.[45] He warns that dower and inheritance often fractured estates across a wide area, and that a suit brought for a few acres does not necessarily mean that they were the whole livelihood of the plaintiff. Nevertheless, where

[42] *The Earliest Lincolnshire Assize Rolls*, ed. by Stenton, *cc.* 1457, 1417

[43] *The Earliest Lincolnshire Assize Rolls*, ed. by Stenton, *cc.* 1346, 1378.

[44] *The Earliest Lincolnshire Assize Rolls*, ed. by Stenton, between *cc.* 1310 and 1463.

[45] 'Roll of the Justices in Eyre at Bedford, 1202', ed. by Fowler, p. 140.

there is a cluster of low damages, as here, it is reasonable to consider that they may represent smallholdings which were sole properties. There is also the possibility that like was deliberately placed with like in the order of hearings before the court, strengthened by the inclusion of four adjacent cases in this category from Soham Toney in Norfolk.[46] All but one of these involved damages of 12d. or less. Three concerned common of pasture and the fourth a bank erected to the harm of the plaintiff's holding, fostering the idea that lords were attempting to increase their land. The Lincolnshire examples involved main tenements, and there seems to be no underlying pattern to any of the defendants involved. When taken singly the shortest cases can contain a surprising amount of information. Together they provide a cumulative body of evidence on which to base further research.

Turning fourthly to defendants, those found not guilty remained in seisin, and there is nothing in the records to indicate their financial position, other than that they were obviously not destitute. However, three out of four were found guilty and therefore amerced, but very few were excused the fine because they were poor. This may have been simply because they were prosperous, not least for the wholly practical reason that they had been in possession of property at the expense of the plaintiff for a period of time. Those whose poverty is known — thirty-six individuals in thirteen suits — fall into two categories, principal and secondary defendants.[47] Taking principal defendants first — seven in all — their poverty is plain when, as with plaintiffs, it was recorded directly by the clerk. For instance, in 1202 at Lincoln, the clerk made a marginal note that Benedict, son of John, was a pauper when he was amerced for disseising Gilbert, son of Andrew, of his tenement at Wrenhill (Wrangle), Lincolnshire.[48] Similarly in 1205 at the Northampton eyre, Stephen, son of Roger, was recorded as a poor clerk.[49] In 1214, William Piscator (Fisher) from Northamptonshire was identified as 'pauperimus' (very

[46] *The Earliest Lincolnshire Assize Rolls*, ed. by Stenton, *cc.* 1389–92.

[47] *The Earliest Lincolnshire Assize Rolls*, ed. by Stenton, *c.* 409; *The Earliest Northamptonshire Assize Rolls*, ed. by Stenton, *cc.* 785, 831, 859; *Pleas before the King*, ed. by Stenton, II, *c.* 780; III, *c.* 945; *Curia Regis Rolls*, ed. by Flower, I, 29; III, 345–46; V, 262; VII, 62, 78, 287.

[48] *The Earliest Lincolnshire Assize Rolls*, ed. by Stenton, *c.* 409: 'Pauper nil misericordia' (He is a pauper; no amercement).

[49] *Curia Regis Rolls*, ed. by Flower, III, 346: 'Disseisitor pauper clericus est' (The disseisor is a poor clerk). He was convicted of disseising Stephen, son of Alfred, of property in Colintre (Collingtree), Northamptonshire.

poor).[50] Surprisingly, although the court thus signified that it did not expect any of the amercements to be paid, it awarded damages to the plaintiffs. In the first and last cases they were put at 4d. and 2s. respectively, but set at nothing in the second. It is not clear if the phrasing used, 'reddat dampnum nichil' (let him pay no damages), indicates the court's minimal assessment of the injury caused to the plaintiff or its pragmatic approach to the defendant's inability to pay any sum it might award. The courts cannot have expected the damages they awarded to have been met, given that they had accepted the defendants' poverty regarding their amercements. It is possible that the 1205 eyre was simply being realistic. On the other hand, the fact that reference to damage was made by all three courts might be an indication that it was an important part of the legal process to acknowledge the principle.

Concerning secondary defendants known to be poor — some twenty-nine individuals — Richard Cocus (Cook) is a good example. He was the second-named of six at the 1208 York eyre, and was pardoned his amercement of half-a-mark when all six were convicted of a nuisance, the enlargement of a mill pond, against the tenement of Robert de Renevill (unidentified) in Yorkshire.[51] The principal defendant, Robert de Manegebi (possibly Maunby), and the third-named, William Clericus (Clerk), were each fined one mark. The amercements of the remaining defendants, William the clerk's son, William Molendinarius (Miller), and Roger de Colecestr (Colchester), were not specified. They were ordered to restore the mill pond to its former size and pay damages of 12d. Incidentally, here again, the damages were very much lower than the amercements. It was evidently a case of a lord, Robert de Manegebi, acting in his own interests. Richard Cook may have been his dependent servant, similar to John, son of Walter, above.[52] Perhaps his circumstances were enough to identify his poverty to the court, which consequently recognized his inability to pay the fine. The last three defendants, and possibly the clerk, look like Robert's tenants if not dependants, although there is no certainty. The status of most of the defendants before the court at Westminster in 1214 is likewise problematic. Twenty-eight men were convicted of disseising Simon

[50] *Curia Regis Rolls*, ed. by Flower, VII, 62: 'Willelmus Piscator pauperimus est' (William Fisher is very poor). William and his wife Cecilia lost to John Aurifaber (Goldsmith) in Burgo (Broughton), Northamptonshire. This case is also an interesting example of the sale of a property originally held in villeinage.

[51] *Curia Regis Rolls*, ed. by Flower, V, 262: 'Perdonatur Ricardo' (Richard is pardoned).

[52] Above, p. 51.

of Barton, Warwickshire, from his tenement there.[53] Over seventeen names the clerk inserted the amount of that man's amercement, but over six he wrote 'nichil' (nothing). (The amercements of the remainder were added at the end of the account.) The word 'nichil' strictly speaking referred to the subject's lack of money and not the amercement itself. In practice the clerks used the same word for the state into which the losing litigant ipso facto fell and the fine which it incurred.

The men here labelled with 'nothing' were excused their fines because they were poor or, perhaps, villeins. The unfree possessed nothing, since they and all their goods were possessions of their lord. Villein or not, the six were an insignificant part of a group which included clearly prosperous individuals. William of Buckingham evidently exercised enough authority to organize a gang to eject the plaintiff. He was amerced 20s. and ordered to pay damages of two marks (26s. 8d.). Two defendants amerced one mark each, Hubert Prepositus and Walter Pwateman, may have been his leading men since their names indicate that they held office. Hubert was a steward and Walter a close serving man. The remaining amercements were each of the standard half-mark. If the six with nothing, and Richard Cook, were dependants following a lord and in his household, they were partially, if not wholly, insulated from the outcome of a case in which they were involved. They were certainly not as directly affected as impoverished principals who faced destitution if they lost. However, there is nothing in the six men's names to indicate either status or occupation.[54] It is possible, then, that they were free men but destitute. Such a large group indicates disseisin by intimidation, if not outright force, and its organizers were likely to attract those in need and with little to lose. A further similar case from Norfolk came before the same court, as did two more from Northamptonshire. They involved twenty-three, seventeen, and sixteen defendants respectively, some of them women.[55] Groups of this size have the appearance of a rabble, and it is notable that they were rare at the turn of the twelfth century but increased during the early decades of the thirteenth. It is possible therefore that the Warwickshire six, and others, were destitute through the civil unrest of John's reign, to which Stenton alludes.[56]

[53] *Curia Regis Rolls*, ed. by Flower, VII, 287.

[54] Nicholas Bagge, William de Hulm, Simon son of Aldith, John de Grena, Robert Largus, Walter Nobilis.

[55] *Curia Regis Rolls*, ed. by Flower, VII, 153–54, 61–62.

[56] *Rolls of the Justices in Eyre*, ed. by Stenton, p. lxiii.

An anomalous case of 1196 which appears to involve poverty features a family of three, two brothers and their mother, who made an unsuccessful attempt to disseise Geva of Burcot (Wood Burcot), Northamptonshire, of her holding there and in Karswell (Cress Spring).[57] The jury at the Northampton assize stated that it was the second-named defendant, Hugh, son of Geoffrey, who was the actual disseisor. He had given the land to his brother John and he himself, the clerk noted, had nothing. Yet it was John, the first-named defendant and not the original disseisor, who was amerced 10s. and ordered to pay the same amount in damages. This may have been a clever but failed attempt by the family to wrong-foot the court, since the first-named defendant was always the principal actor. Perhaps they had thought to win on a technicality, that the case would be dismissed on the grounds that the writ wrongly named John as the disseisor, or that the law entitled John to remain in possession because he himself had not committed the disseisin.[58] Additionally he and Juliana their mother argued their case in some detail, to the point of calling the sheriff to warranty, but all to no avail. The record shows that the family had a sound grasp of the terms of the assize, which they may have tried to exploit, and that in the circumstances the court seems to have applied the spirit, rather than the letter, of the law. No amercement was mentioned regarding Juliana.

My fifth and final category concerns cases in which both parties exploited the assize legitimately for what Meekings terms 'a collusive conveyance'.[59] This was an agreement for the disposal of a specific holding between themselves, which they brought to court under the guise of a dispute. One or other litigant withdrew the action and put himself or herself, as the losing party, in mercy. Withdrawal was deliberate and quite different from default, where one litigant simply failed to appear and the case therefore collapsed. There are too many examples of withdrawal — approximately one hundred scattered through the rolls — for there to be no intent, and it was evidently worth the additional fine for wasting the court's time by not prosecuting these cases. The costs were probably divided between the parties, and there are some blatant examples of one party standing surety for the other.[60] Litigants often appear to be prosper-

[57] *Curia Regis Rolls*, ed. by Flower, I, 29: 'Juratores dicunt quod ita disseisivit eum [*sic*] Hugo et postea tradidit terram illam Johanni [...] et Hugo nichil habet' (The jurors say that Hugh has so disseised her and afterward he handed that land to John [...] and Hugh has nothing).

[58] Bracton, *De legibus*, ed. by Woodbine, III, 77–82, 51–52.

[59] *The 1235 Surrey Eyre*, ed. by Meekings, I, 73, 40.

[60] *The Earliest Lincolnshire Assize Rolls*, ed. by Stenton, *cc.* 413, 1439.

ous, but it is also possible that many suits were between people of humble status. Adjacent cases before the Lincoln eyre of 1206, in which both defendants acknowledged disseisin, may be illustrations of these.[61] In the first case, the plaintiff was pardoned the damages awarded to her. The second was evidently a family affair, since the litigants were brothers and the damages were born by a third sibling. I have found only two such cases which involve litigants whose poverty is certain. The first was recorded in 1212 at Buckingham, when Alice, daughter of Estmer, amerced herself having withdrawn against Alexander de Hamslap (Hanslope), and his wife Edith, over property in Stoni (Stony) Stratford, Buckinghamshire.[62] The record states unequivocally that the fine was pardoned because of her poverty, but she too had pledges for the prosecution who were subsequently fined. It seems unlikely that the pledges would not have known about and been involved in the collusion which was, at the time, a valid procedure. Secondly, in 1213 at Westminster, Muriel, widow of Henry Clericus (Clerk), withdrew her suit against Richard, son of Philip, and amerced herself regarding a tenement in Empingham, Rutland.[63] No other details are given except that she was very poor and therefore, presumably, excused both the fine and the cost of the writ.

These cases demonstrate that the value of an agreement reached in court was well understood by the poor who, with the prosperous, went to considerable lengths to have their private property arrangements formally recorded and witnessed, using the *curia regis* through novel disseisin as a means of achieving this. However, the record for these cases does not indicate whether it was the writing down of the agreement or the witnessing of it by the court that was the more valued at this early stage. Clanchy points out that, in the twelfth century, a record was not a document but a spoken testament which initially needed four knights to ensure that it was correctly conveyed from one point to another.[64] Writing came to be the preferred medium through the example of the higher ranks, percolating down to the peasantry by the end of the thirteenth century. Nevertheless, the way in which these litigants used the assize, regardless of how they viewed the written word, is a significant indicator of the positive attitude toward the court shown by humble people in ordering their

[61] *The Earliest Lincolnshire Assize Rolls*, ed. by Stenton, *cc*. 1433–34.

[62] *Curia Regis Rolls*, ed. by Flower, VI, 382: 'Pardonatur, quia pauperrima est' (It is pardoned, because she is very poor).

[63] *Curia Regis Rolls*, ed. by Flower, VII, 52: 'Ipsa pauperima est' (She is very poor).

[64] Clanchy, *From Memory to Written Record*, pp. 76–77, 263.

affairs. There seems to have been no move by the authorities to prevent this use, which might be another example of legal pragmatism. Whether or not it was originally foreseen that the assize would be used in this way, it is possible that the courts came to recognize this use as a pre-empting and stabilizing factor in the potentially problematic field of property-holding.

The approach taken by humble freeholders towards their adversaries and the courts indicates that, for the most part, they had confidence in the assize.[65] Its immediate popularity shows that they needed and welcomed it. They knew how to become a plaintiff in the royal court, how to conduct themselves, and what to expect. Some showed a limited understanding of its terms, but many used it intelligently. Yet the use of the assize by the poor raises the question of why so many poor freeholders felt able to take a course of action that cannot have endeared them to their superiors, since the majority of defendants were lords under whose jurisdiction most plaintiffs probably continued to live. Most must have felt they had little choice when, deprived of their holding, they faced the loss of both livelihood and social standing. Even so, going to court was still a choice and one unavailable to the poor before the promulgation of novel disseisin in the mid-twelfth century. The records for these cases, however, do not sufficiently explain how humble people came to possess the necessary qualities to undertake such a procedure, which differed considerably from local custom, and to lodge their grievance before the relatively new, royal courts.

Part of the answer may lie in the many demands on the ordinary men and women of that time, which are likely to have widened their perspectives. The poor freeholder as well as the prosperous was involved in the organization of local affairs. Christopher Dyer writes that villagers, as much as lords, were responsible for the decline or growth of a settlement and for the husbandry of its land.[66] Susan Reynolds concludes that village residents of every degree co-operated in the management of their fields and woods because few held large acreages, and all were 'farmers, parishioners, and neighbours', although there was plenty of dissension in other respects.[67] Freeholders great and small were equally implicated in the economic and social aspects of local markets, and also in the concomitant legal requirements of those markets when, as smallholders, they boosted their income through crafts or trade. Musson points out that attendance as required at manor, hundred, county, church, and other courts

[65] *The Earliest Lincolnshire Assize Rolls*, ed. by Stenton, p. xviii.

[66] Dyer, *Everyday Life in Medieval England*, pp. xii, xiv, 11.

[67] Reynolds, K*ingdoms and Communities*, pp. 101–54, 152.

provided the humblest villager with experience of the legal world.[68] In addition, there were the itinerant court of the king and the visiting eyres, which must have extended popular awareness beyond local affairs.

The attitude of the king and his justices towards poor freeholders cannot have been lost on them. They were permitted into the royal courts even when they had no money. Once there, they may have been dealt with sympathetically by justices who could permit flexibility of procedure. Yet the courts were careful to apply the terms of the assize strictly, as the many plaintiffs who were out of time discovered, and there seems to have been an intelligent delivery of justice with mercy. The possibility of support by the courts must have given encouragement to tenants oppressed by their lords. Further, behind courts and justices, and at times with them, stood the king himself, who had always been theoretically available for the dispensation of justice to his subjects. In practice only the wealthy were previously able to avail themselves of this,[69] as Richard Anstey's famous pursuit of Henry II early in his reign illustrates.[70] But novel disseisin enabled the poorest freeholder to gain access to royal justice, indirectly through the *curia regis* if not directly from the throne. That so many brought the action is a strong indication of their trust in it.

[68] Musson, *Medieval Law in Context*, p. 97.

[69] Baker, *An Introduction to English Legal History*, p. 13.

[70] Brand, *The Making of the Common Law*, pp. 1–2.

Works Cited

Primary Sources

Bracton, Henry de, *De legibus et consuetudinibus Angliæ*, ed. by George E. Woodbine, trans. by Samuel E. Thorne, 4 vols (London: Harvard University Press in association with The Selden Society, 1977)

Curia Regis Rolls of the Reigns of Richard I and John, ed. by Cyril Thomas Flower, 7 vols (London: HMSO, 1922–35)

The Earliest Lincolnshire Assize Rolls, AD 1202–1209, ed. by Doris Mary Stenton, Lincoln Record Society, 22 (Lincoln: Lincoln Record Society, 1926)

The Earliest Northamptonshire Assize Rolls, A.D. 1202 and 1203, ed. by Doris Mary Stenton, Northamptonshire Record Society, 5 (London: Northamptonshire Record Society, 1930)

Pleas before the King or his Justices, 1198–1202, ed. by Doris Mary Stenton, Selden Society, 67, 68, 83, 3 vols (London: Selden Society, 1953–67)

'Roll of the Justices in Eyre at Bedford, 1202', ed. by G. Herbert Fowler, in *Publications of the Bedfordshire Historical Record Society*, 1 (Apsley Guise: Bedfordshire Historical Record Society, 1913), pp. 144–247

Rolls of the Justices in Eyre, Being The Rolls of Pleas and Assizes for Lincolnshire 1218–9 and Worcestershire 1221, ed. by Doris Mary Stenton, Selden Society, 53 (London: Selden Society, 1934)

Three Rolls of the King's Court in the Reign of King Richard the First, AD 1194–1195, ed. by Frederic William Maitland, Pipe Roll Society, 14 (London: Pipe Roll Society, 1891)

The 1235 Surrey Eyre, ed. by Cecil Anthony Francis Meekings, Surrey Record Society, 31, 32, 37, 3 vols (Guildford: Surrey Record Society, 1979–2002)

Secondary Studies

Baker, John Hamilton, *An Introduction to English Legal History*, 4th edn (Oxford: Oxford University Press, 2007)

Brand, Paul, *The Making of the Common Law* (London: Hambledon, 1992)

Clanchy, Michael T., *From Memory to Written Record: England, 1066–1307* (Oxford: Blackwell, 1993)

Dyer, Christopher, *Everyday Life in Medieval England* (London: Hambledon, 1994)

Musson, Anthony, *Medieval Law in Context: The Growth of Legal Consciousness from Magna Carta to the Peasants' Revolt* (Manchester: Manchester University Press, 2001)

Reynolds, Susan, *Kingdoms and Communities in Western Europe, 900–1300*, 2nd edn (Oxford: Clarendon Press, 1997)

Sutherland, Donald Wayne, *The Assize of Novel Disseisin* (Oxford: Clarendon Press, 1973)

van Caenegen, Raoul Charles, *The Birth of the English Common Law*, 2nd edn (Cambridge: Cambridge University Press, 1988)

R. Eliezer of Metz's Twelfth-Century Exclusion from Charity of the Jewish *Avaryan B'mezid* ('Deliberate Transgressor')

Alyssa M. Gray

The Jewish legal culture of northern France and Germany ('Ashkenaz') underwent a sea change in the twelfth and thirteenth centuries with the emergence and spread of the critical and dialectical methods of talmudic interpretation practiced by the Tosafists.[1] The Hebrew word *tosafot* means 'additions', and the reference is to scholars' dialectical 'additions' (the scholars themselves eventually becoming known as *tosafot*, or 'Tosafists' in English) to the renowned eleventh-century talmudic commentary of Rabbi Solomon ben Isaac of Troyes ('Rashi', 1040–1105). The Tosafist revolution is contemporaneous with the so-called 'twelfth-century renaissance', and contemporary scholars continue to debate the extent to which Christian scholarship may have been a factor in the flowering of the Tosafist enterprise.[2] Aspects

* My thanks to Professor Judah D. Galinsky for his careful reading of an earlier draft of this essay and his many helpful comments and suggestions. The author alone is responsible for the content.

[1] 'Talmudic' refers in this essay to the Babylonian Talmud (hereinafter referred to as 'Bavli' or 'Talmud'). The Bavli, redacted in Iraq in the seventh to eighth centuries, came to be accepted by medieval Jews as the foundation of Jewish life and practice. Its study was a principal pillar of the intellectual cultures of Jews in Ashkenaz, Muslim al-Andalus, North Africa, Christian Spain, Italy, and Provence.

[2] On this 'renaissance', see generally Haskins, *The Renaissance of the Twelfth Century*. Ivan

Alyssa M. Gray (agray@huc.edu) is Professor of Codes and Responsa Literature and Emily S. and Rabbi Bernard H. Mehlman Chair in Rabbinics, Hebrew Union College-Jewish Institute of Religion.

Approaches to Poverty in Medieval Europe: Complexities, Contradictions, Transformations, c. 1100–1500, ed. by Sharon Farmer, IMR 22 (Turnhout: Brepols, 2016) pp. 67–92
BREPOLS PUBLISHERS 10.1484/M.IMR-EB.5.105460

of that renaissance, notably a focus on individual scholarly inventiveness and achievement, are characteristic as well of Tosafism.[3] Two of the greatest Tosafists — 'great' in terms of incisiveness of intellect and lasting influence — were the northern French R. Jacob ben Meir Tam of Ramerupt (1100–1171) — a grandson of Rashi — and his nephew R. Isaac of Dampierre (d. 1189). Twelfth-century French Tosafists were largely occupied with dialectical analysis of the Babylonian Talmud, and their contributions were preserved in edited collections of written *tosafot* that came to be printed alongside the Talmud text in early modernity. These *tosafot* analyse textual difficulties in talmudic passages or inconsistencies within or between them. Some *tosafot* reconcile talmudic texts with contemporaneous Jewish practices seen as inconsistent with them. French and German Tosafists also produced free-standing legal compilations that could be studied independently of the Talmud. Notable among these is the influential thirteenth-century French work *Sefer mitzvot gadol* by R. Moses of Coucy.[4] German Tosafists of the twelfth and thirteenth centuries produced large legal works containing various genres of legal material, notably talmudic commentary, legal rulings, and responsa (written responses to legal queries).

In writing his *Sefer mitzvot gadol*, R. Moses relied, *inter alia*, on a twelfth-century work entitled *Sefer yere'im* (hereafter SY), the 'Book of Those That Fear [God]'.[5] The latter was composed by R. Eliezer ben Samuel of Metz (*c.* 1115–98), who had studied with R. Jacob Tam.[6] Although a student of the northern French master, R. Eliezer came to be located in the Franco-German border community of Metz and, as we will see below, was influenced by aspects of twelfth- to thirteenth-century German (Jewish) Pietism as well as northern French Tosafism.[7] R. Eliezer wrote SY between 1171 and 1179. In a short

Marcus briefly summarizes contemporary scholarly observations about the creative twelfth century in 'The Dynamics of Jewish Renaissance', pp. 29–31. See now also Kanarfogel, *The Intellectual History*, pp. 84–110.

[3] For more on the relationship between the Tosafist enterprise and the contemporaneous twelfth-century renaissance, see Grossman, *The Early Sages of France*, pp. 21–24 and passim (Hebrew); and Faur, 'The Legal Thinking of Tosafot', pp. 53–55. See now also the very recent reflection on the relationship between Tosafism and contemporaneous Christian scholarship in Kanarfogel, *The Intellectual History*.

[4] On *Sefer mitzvot gadol*, see most recently Galinsky, 'The Significance of Form'.

[5] *Sefer yere'im*, ed. by Schiff.

[6] On R. Eliezer of Metz, see Urbach, *The Tosaphists*, I, 154–64 (Hebrew).

[7] See Kanarfogel, *Intellectual History*, p. 7 n. 16. The German Pietists (in Hebrew, *hasidei Ashkenaz*) were a social and religious group in twelfth- and thirteenth-century Germany, with

preface to the work R. Eliezer claims that his Tosafist contemporaries' intensive involvement with talmudic dialectical analysis occupies them to such an extent that they pay little attention to 'what the Creator commanded; how to uphold his statutes and laws'. R. Eliezer represents that SY will lay out a 'concise path' so that 'the reader might run within it and the seekers of God would find [that which is] correct', resulting in their learning to revere God.[8] Despite R. Eliezer's carefully drawn contrast between his contemporaries' talmudic dialectics and what he represents as SY's concise presentation of God's commandments, there is in fact much dialectical analysis of talmudic passages in SY, as one might expect of a student of R. Jacob Tam.[9] Overall, the work has little utility as a practical legal guide; discrete legal topics are not clearly set out nor all material relevant to one topic collected under one heading. The work may be classified as part of the medieval Jewish 'book of commandments' genre; it is a work intended for study and edification, not practical legal guidance.

In Chapter 156 of SY, R. Eliezer — also known to have been a charity collector/distributor — quietly revolutionized one aspect of rabbinic charity law.[10]

a particular mystical and ascetic outlook. The principal Pietist teachers and guides were R. Samuel *he-Hasid* ('the pious'), his son R. Judah *he-Hasid* (of Speyer and then Regensburg), and the latter's disciple R. Eleazar of Worms. The Pietists' literature was produced primarily in the first half of the thirteenth century; the principal works are *Sefer Hasidim* and the *Rokeah* of R. Eleazar of Worms. On the Pietists, see, e.g., Soloveitchik, 'Three Themes in the *Sefer Hasidim*'; and Marcus, *Piety and Society*. For the Pietists' impact on Tosafism, see, e.g., Kanarfogel, *'Peering through the Lattices'*.

[8] R. Eliezer innovatively divides the work into seven 'pillars', each of which is subdivided into 'hooks'. The seven pillars are: (1) commandments pertaining to prohibited sexual relations; (2) commandments pertaining to foodstuffs; (3) commandments pertaining to items the benefit of which is prohibited; (4) commandments pertaining to monetary prohibitions involving taking money improperly from another or withholding monies that should be given to another; (5) prohibitions that render the violator 'evil' in the eyes of Heaven and other human beings, but which do not involve robbery or monetary benefit; (6) prohibitions regarding speech that render the violator 'evil' in the eyes of Heaven but not other human beings; and (7) prohibitions not regarding speech that render the violator 'evil' in the eyes of Heaven but not to other human beings. In the two-volume Israeli reprint of the 1892 Schiff edition, the first six 'pillars' are discussed in Volume I, and the seventh in Volume II.

[9] As noted by Judah Galinsky, SY consists of three elements: (1) a list of commandments with their biblical and talmudic sources, the list set out as presented in the ninth-century law code *Halakhot Gedolot*; (2) Tosafist dialectical analyses of selected commandments; and (3) practical treatments of certain commandments. For more discussion of the overall structure of *Sefer yere'im*, see Galinsky, 'The Significance of Form', pp. 305–08.

[10] R. Eliezer is identified as having been a charity collector/distributor in a legal ruling

R. Eliezer represents that Deut. 15. 7–8 ('if [...] there is a needy person [...] one of your brothers [...] open your hand') and Lev. 25. 36 ('let him live by your side as your brother') do not obligate the giving of charity to one he calls the *avaryan b'mezid* ('deliberate transgressor').[11] The category *avaryan b'mezid* is a creation of R. Eliezer, as is the *avaryan b'mezid*'s exclusion from charity. This essay's purpose is to explore R. Eliezer's legal innovations, rigorously analyse the talmudic hermeneutic by which he fashioned them, and contextualize the innovations historically.

The analytic journey being long and winding, a short summary at the outset may be helpful. The Bavli nowhere prohibits — nor even discourages — the provision of charity to a Jew who violates Jewish law. Indeed, the Bavli's discussions of charity and Jewish transgressors do not overlap. The legal literature of the post-talmudic Babylonian Geonim also does not provide that Jewish transgressors are to be denied charity because they transgress.[12] In R. Eliezer's own Franco-German milieu, there existed an atmosphere of tolerance toward Jews who transgressed out of a want of self-control (as opposed to rebellion against Judaism), well exemplified by a ruling of the prominent northern French exegete and legalist Rashi. R. Eliezer breaks new ground by excluding from charity the Jew who transgresses to indulge his appetites; moreover, he coins a neologism to describe this transgressor: *avaryan b'mezid*, or 'deliberate transgressor'. This neologism effaces the self-indulgent nature of the transgression, which was an important factor in the earlier Franco-German tolerance of this transgressor. R. Eliezer excludes the *avaryan b'mezid* from the application of a number of other Jewish laws as well, employing an implicit hermeneutical rule according

by R. Isaac of Dampierre, included in R. Isaac b. R. Moses of Vienna's thirteenth-century Ashkenazi legal compilation *Or Zarua*, Mif'al Torat Hahmei Ashkenaz edition.

[11] These translations are excerpted from the Jewish Publication Society (JPS) Bible translation. In these and all other cases, I part company with JPS and render the Hebrew *akh* and its variants literally as 'brother'.

[12] The Geonim ('excellencies') were heads of the Iraqi academies once located in the towns of Sura and Pumbedita, and eventually located in Baghdad. Although there were likely Geonim in the seventh century and possibly a bit earlier, the establishment of the Abbasid caliphate in Baghdad in the mid-eighth century resulted in an expansion of Geonic influence over Jewish communities throughout the Abbasid empire. The Geonim saw themselves as heirs of the talmudic sages, and were instrumental in the process of making the Bavli an authoritative source for the Jewish people. Geonic literature was very important to later medieval Jewish legal developments. The Gaonate as an institution began to lose influence in the tenth and eleventh centuries. For a helpful overview of the Geonic period, its principal figures, and its literature, see Brody, *The Geonim of Babylonia*.

to which biblical expressions denoting kinship or brotherhood are interpreted to exclude the *avaryan b'mezid*, whose transgression of the law is seen as putting him outside the moral universe of the reader of SY. R. Eliezer's creation of the category *avaryan b'mezid* and his exclusion of this transgressor from charity and a host of other Jewish laws may be explained by a confluence of twelfth-century factors: the hardening of anti-Jewish attitudes in Christian northern Europe, the growing threat of Jewish apostasy, contemporaneous canon law developments that also unfavourably viewed giving charity to sinners, and the influence on R. Eliezer of the twelfth- to thirteenth-century German Pietist movement, which also viewed with disfavour the provision of charity to Jewish sinners.

As noted, R. Eliezer's declaration that law-abiding Jews are not obliged to give charity to the *avaryan b'mezid* brings together two large bodies of law and lore that up to the twelfth century had remained distinct: charity for the poor and the identification, classification, and legal status of those Jews who deliberately and habitually do not adhere to rabbinic law, whether in whole or in part.[13] Neither the Bavli nor its predecessor compilations ever indicate that impoverished transgressors are to be denied charity *because* they transgress. In the context of charity, Bavli twice mentions a category of people labelled 'not proper', or 'not appropriate' (*sh'einam[n] mehuganim[n]*), but in neither case (B. Bava Kamma 16b; B. Bava Batra 9b) can it be unequivocally asserted that the 'impropriety' is due to a want of religiously compliant behaviour.[14] Apropos

[13] R. Eliezer of Metz's Chapter 156 has not figured prominently in earlier scholarly treatments of medieval Jewish religious disobedience and its personal status consequences. See the references in Blidstein, 'Who Is Not a Jew?', p. 387 n. 67; Goldin, 'Juifs et juifs convertis au Moyen Age', p. 866 n. 49; Katz, '"Af Al Pi She-hata Yisrael Hu"', p. 266; and Horovitz, '"V'yehiyu Aniyyim B'nei Veitekha"', p. 227 nn. 50, 51. Horovitz is the only one to point out that 'R. Eliezer of Metz was the first who ruled, in *Sefer yere'im*, that under certain conditions "we are not obligated to give charity" to a Jew who transgresses one of the commandments'.

[14] This essay will make frequent reference to passages in the Bavli, and so a note on talmudic citation will be helpful. All references are to the standard printed edition of the Bavli. Contemporary printed editions of the Bavli are based on the nineteenth-century printed edition typeset by the Romm family in Vilna (known as the 'Vilna', or 'Vilna-Romm' edition). The specific printing used in the preparation of this essay is *Babylonian Talmud* (Vilna-Romm edition with commentary). The Bavli is subdivided into thirty-seven tractates. In citing a text from the Bavli, the prefix 'B' is utilized, to distinguish the Babylonian from the Jerusalem Talmud. The tractate name then follows (in the main text, the referenced tractates are 'Bava Kamma' and 'Bava Batra'), and then the page number, with an indication as to whether the reference is to the recto ('a') or verso ('b') side of the page. As the tractate names are often not relevant to the subject-matter of the passage under discussion, this essay will leave these untranslated so as not to unduly complicate the unfolding analysis. Returning to the expression

of religious noncompliance, Bavli interprets Ex. 22. 27 ('You shall not [...] put a curse upon a chieftain among your people') to mean that one must not curse a 'chieftain' who 'performs the acts of your people', that is, one who conforms to the rabbinic way of Torah.[15] Bavli extends this interpretation of Ex. 22. 27 to include people who are not 'chieftains'. People who do not 'perform the acts of "your people"' (and who have not repented) may be struck (B. Yevamot 22b), are not to be honoured by their heirs after death by having property they stole returned to its rightful owners (B. Bava Kamma 94b, B. Bava Metzia 62a), need not be informed of Divine punishment for failing to abide by their word (B. Bava Metzia 48b), and may be cursed (B. Sanhedrin 85a–b, B. Makkot 8b). No talmudic passage interprets Ex. 22. 27 to exclude the one who does not 'perform the acts of your people' from receiving charity.

The most extensive discussions of Jewish transgressors in late antique rabbinic literature involve the terms *mumar* and *meshumad*. *Mumar* refers to those who deliberately do not adhere to rabbinic law, whether in whole or in part. The term implies a habit or tendency to transgress. Late antique rabbinic compilations prior to Bavli tend to prefer the term *meshumad* ('the destroyed one') to *mumar*, although in neither case is there more than a handful of occurrences.[16] The early Babylonian scholar Rav Huna (third century) sees public Sabbath desecration as the very definition of *mumar* (B. Eruvin 69a), but Bavli refers

under discussion in the main text, it also appears in the Talmud on B. Eruvin 100b, B. Rosh Hashanah 22b, B. Yevamot 108a, B. Ketubot 22a, B. Ketubot 54a, B. Nedarim 20a, B. Kiddushin 70a, B. Bava Kamma 16b, B. Bava Kamma 80a, B. Bava Batra 9b. On B. Bava Batra 9b, the sage R. Nahman b. Isaac interprets Prov. 21. 21 to mean that the person who strives to do good and kind deeds will encounter 'proper' (*mehuganim*) people to whom to give charity, for which he will receive (Divine) reward. The obvious implication is that giving charity to 'improper' people will not be rewarded, but what 'proper' and 'improper' mean is not explained. It need not be assumed that *mehuganim* refers to religiously compliant behaviour. The same is true of the use of the term with reference to charity recipients in the biblical prophet Jeremiah's time (B. Bava Kamma 16b = B. Bava Batra 9b).

[15] This exegesis is found at B. Yevamot 22b, B. Bava Kamma 94b, B. Bava Metzia 48b, B. Bava Metzia 62a, B. Bava Batra 4a, B. Sanhedrin 85a, and B. Makkot 8b.

[16] The term *mumar* appears in the standard Vilna-Romm printed edition of the Bavli, whereas the manuscripts of both the Bavli and earlier rabbinic literature tend to prefer the term *meshumad*. The overwhelming deployment of *mumar* in the printed edition of the Talmud appears to be the result of early modern censors' replacement of *meshumad* with a term felt to be less offensive. Medieval Jewish legal compilations also overwhelmingly tend to use the term *meshumad*. For more on this, see Schiffman, *Who Was a Jew?*, pp. 46–49 and 92–93 nn. 34–36. Throughout this essay I will employ whichever term is found in the source under discussion; if no source is under discussion, I will refer to the *mumar*.

to many other types of *mumarim*, notably the '*mumar* to desecrate Sabbaths publicly (and privately)' (e.g., B. Eruvin 69a–b), the '*mumar* to pour libations (to idols)' (B. Eruvin 69a–b), the '*mumar* for idolatry' (e.g., B. Hullin 4b), the '*mumar* for foreskins' (e.g., B. Hullin 5a), the '*mumar* to eat forbidden fat' (e.g., B. Horayot 11a), the '*mumar* as to one thing' (B. Eruvin 69a–b), and even the '*mumar* to the entire Torah' (e.g., B. Eruvin 69b).[17] There is the general indication of a pattern in Bavli that later fourth-century Babylonian scholars make use of the broader categories *mumar l'tei'avon* (*mumar* due to appetite) and *mumar l'hakhis* (*mumar* due to spite); categories based on motive, not on type of transgression.[18] The *mumar* due to appetite sins out of a want of self-control (and thus will eat forbidden meat when permitted meat is unavailable) while the *mumar* due to spite sins out of a spirit of rebelliousness (and will eat forbidden meat even if its permitted alternative is available).[19] R. Eliezer's *avaryan b'mezid* appears from the context of SY Chapter 156 to be essentially identical to the *mumar* (or *meshumad*) *l'tei'avon*. Moreover, the talmudic *mumar* is a habitual transgressor who is seen as retaining a Jewish identity, as exemplified by the not-uncommon term *yisrael mumar* (Israelite *mumar*).[20] Late antique rabbinic literature does not know of a Jew's adopting another religious identity; only in post-talmudic law does *mumar* or *meshumad* come to be used to refer to apostates from Judaism.[21] Significantly, none of the talmudic discussions of

[17] Bavli's principal discussions of the *mumar* are found on B. Eruvin 69a–b, B. Gittin 47a, B. Sanhedrin 27a, B. Avodah Zarah 26b, B. Horayot 11a, and B. Hullin 3a–6a.

[18] Yet on B. Horayot 11a these terms appear to be employed by the early scholars R. Yohanan (third century, land of Israel) and Rabbah b. Bar Hana (third century, Babylonia). A full investigation of this issue — including whether and to what extent the various attributions are reliable — cannot be undertaken in this essay.

[19] There are hints in Bavli of a lenient attitude toward the *mumar* due to appetite. B. Gittin 47a implies that there is an obligation to redeem a '*mumar* due to appetite' from captivity, and B. Avodah Zarah 26b indicates that law-abiding Jews are obligated to return lost objects to the *mumar* due to appetite and preserve his life. Lastly, B. Hullin 3a and 4a provide that a law-abiding Jew may eat the meat of an animal slaughtered by a *mumar* due to appetite, provided that the latter's knife was checked and found to be free of blemishes prior to the slaughter.

[20] See, e.g., B. Eruvin 69a; B. Kiddushin 18a.

[21] See, e.g., the discussion in Katz, "'Af Al Pi She-hata'", pp. 261–69; and in Goldin, "Juifs et Juifs Convertis", especially p. 865 and following. Hillel Newman has also recently observed that talmudic sources lack a systematic treatment of the laws of the *mumar*, noting the interest in this topic in the post-Jerusalem Talmud '*ma'asim*' ('case law') literature of the fifth-sixth centuries, produced in the context of the increasing Christianization of the land of Israel. See Newman, *The Ma'asim of the People of the Land of Israel*, p. 108 (Hebrew).

mumarim — whether due to appetite, spite, or anything else — addresses the giving of charity to these individuals.

The 'Mumar Due to Appetite' in the Legal Discourse of the Babylonian Geonim and Ashkenaz prior to R. Eliezer of Metz

Jacob Katz observes that when confronted with the reality of apostasy to Christianity and Islam, post-talmudic Jewish legal scholars characteristically sought to deal with the phenomenon by giving new meaning to older talmudic terms. As *mumar* or *meshumad* came to be applied to apostates, the terms referred to someone who removed himself completely from his erstwhile community. The talmudic distinction between the '*mumar* due to appetite' and '*mumar* due to spite' ceased to be employed over time except in the context of paraphrases of talmudic material.[22] Katz is correct, yet his gentle hint that the persistence of these terms in the context of paraphrasing talmudic sources is a mere atavism goes too far. We can learn from the interpretation and deployment of these talmudic passages about scholars' attitudes toward transgressors who fell short of apostasy, especially the '*mumar* due to appetite'. What follows is not a complete survey of all pertinent *mumar* source materials, but an overview of important Geonic and Ashkenazi approaches to the *mumar* due to appetite up to the time of R. Eliezer of Metz.

Babylonian Geonic legal literature is devoid of any hint that *mumarim* of whatever sort are to be denied charity on account of their transgressions.[23] As to eleventh- and twelfth-century Ashkenaz (northern France and Germany), Avraham (Rami) Reiner suggests the existence of a lenient tendency toward the *mumar* due to appetite.[24] He demonstrates that there existed in eleventh- and twelfth-century Ashkenaz a reading of a talmudic passage on B. Sanhedrin 27a ('the *mumar* who eats improperly slaughtered meat due to appetite — all agree

[22] See Katz, "'Af Al Pi She-hata", pp. 262–63. See also Goldin, "Juifs Et Juifs Convertis", p. 865 and following. Goldin's contention that the term *meshumad* comes to be used as a catch-all term by the end of the twelfth century for transgressors ranging from transgressors due to appetite to forced converts has some support from the thirteenth-century Jewish polemical treatise *Nizzahon Vetus* and also from Chapter 156 of SY, although the matter can hardly be considered settled.

[23] For an overview of Geonic consideration of the *mumar*, see Blidstein, 'Who Is Not a Jew?'. The major topics at issue were marriage and divorce (including levirate marriage), inheritance, and charging interest.

[24] This may have roots in Bavli; see n. 19, above.

he is invalid [as a witness]') that said the opposite: the *mumar* due to appetite *is* a valid witness because he is not an 'evildoer', and he is not an 'evildoer' because he eats forbidden meat to 'put his soul at ease' (not out of rebellion).[25] This latter, tolerant reading is found in R. Eliezer ben Nathan of Mainz's (1090–1170) legal compilation *Even Haezer* as well as in the thirteenth-century Karlsruhe-Reuchlin Talmud manuscript. Reiner shows that Rashi believed the exclusionary reading to be the correct talmudic text but strongly (and non-intuitively) interpreted it in a way that made the exclusionary reading a vehicle for the rejected text's explicit lenient approach to the *mumar* due to appetite.

This Ashkenazi leniency toward the *mumar* due to appetite is also borne out in Rashi's responsum 175, wherein Rashi rules that the undefined *meshumad* is a 'brother' from whom it is forbidden to take interest and that 'an Israelite who sins is still an Israelite' (B. Sanhedrin 44a). Rashi is referring in responsum 175 to the apostate, and naturally the same rule would apply to the *mumar* due to appetite.[26] Rashi's grandson R. Jacob Tam (R. Eliezer's teacher) tersely disagreed with Rashi as to the apostate, as did R. Tam's nephew R. Isaac of Dampierre.[27]

Tosafot to B. Avodah Zarah 26a (s.v. *ani*) explicitly point out that it is obligatory to save the life as well as the lost property of the *mumar* due to appetite (as per Deut. 22. 3) who is also a 'brother' whom other Jews are commanded to 'enable to live' as per Lev. 25. 36, and of course one may not lend to him at interest.[28] All this is not true of the *mumar* due to spite. Although there is no

[25] Reiner, 'Mumar Okheil Nevelot L'tei'avon — Pasul?'. My thanks to Prof. Judah Galinsky for providing me with a copy of this article.

[26] In responsum 176, he points out that according to 'my masters' it is only forbidden to lend at interest to the *meshumad* due to appetite. See Blidstein, 'Who Is Not a Jew?', p. 385, who casts doubt on the authenticity of this responsum. Blidstein's doubt is reasonable, and I share it. The language of the brief responsum 176 appears to be taken from R. Eliezer's Chapter 156, right after the point at which R. Eliezer discusses Rashi's interpretation of B. Sanhedrin 44a ('an Israelite who sinned'), which Rashi discusses in responsum 175. Moreover, responsum 176 is the only place in which Rashi appears to come close to using a phrase like R. Eliezer's ubiquitous *avaryan b'mezid*. It strains credulity to imagine that had Rashi coined the term, he would only have used it once, in this very short responsum. See *Responsa Rashi Solomon ben Isaac*, ed. by Elfenbein.

[27] For R. Isaac's view, see Urbach, *The Tosaphists*, I, 242–43; Blidstein, 'Who Is Not a Jew?', pp. 385–86. Blidstein also points out (p. 385 n. 60) that there were scholars who agreed with Rashi, most of whom 'were his near contemporaries'. See also Katz, '"Af Al Pi She-hata"', p. 266.

[28] As noted at the beginning of this essay, the dialectical analyses of the Tosafists were preserved in written *tosafot* that were eventually printed together with the talmudic text. The

explicit talmudic or Tosafistic statement on giving charity to the *mumar* due to appetite, it is reasonable to assume that scholars who saw the *mumar* due to appetite as a 'brother' would not have objected to his being given charity.

R. Eliezer's Creation of the Avaryan B'mezid *in SY*

R. Eliezer creates the new category *avaryan b'mezid*, which maps onto the older category '*mumar* due to appetite'. In Chapter 156 he refers to the *avaryan b'mezid* as one who transgresses 'one of all the commandments stated in the Torah and did not repent'. Chapter 156's prohibition against taking interest from both the '*meshumad* due to appetite' — the phrase R. Eliezer employs — and the *avaryan b'mezid* marks these two categories as overlapping. This prohibition distinguishes these transgressors from the undifferentiated *meshumad*, defined by R. Eliezer as one who 'abandons the permitted and eats the forbidden', thus marking him as the '*meshumad* due to spite'. R. Eliezer also refers to the undifferentiated *meshumad* as a *min*, or 'heretic'.

How and why did R. Eliezer create the new category *avaryan b'mezid*? A talmudic passage found on B. Horayot 11a deals with the case of someone 'who eats improperly slaughtered meat due to appetite' but who mistakenly believed on a certain occasion that he was eating permitted meat. Later realizing that he had actually eaten forbidden meat, the person wished to bring an expiatory sacrifice. Bavli disallows this because 'since he eats [improperly-slaughtered meat] due to appetite he would also eat it deliberately [*b'mezid*] and he is a *meshumad*'.[29] Notwithstanding the person's sincere regret in this particular case, he is someone who eats improperly slaughtered meat deliberately, and thus may not offer an expiatory sacrifice. Although certainty is impossible, R. Eliezer may have appropriated B. Horayot 11a's description of the 'appetite' transgressor as someone who eats *b'mezid* (deliberately), bringing it together with B. Shabbat 40a: 'It is permitted to call one who transgressed a religious act prescribed by the Rabbis a 'transgressor' (*avaryana*)'. Indeed, R. Eliezer refers to B. Shabbat 40a's *avaryana* explicitly in Chapter 180 of SY. The link to tractate Horayot is strengthened by R. Eliezer's further description of the *avaryan b'mezid* in Chapter 156 and elsewhere as one who transgresses 'one of all

Tosafist text under discussion here is the *tosafot* passage found in the standard reprinting of the Bavli (based on the Vilna-Romm edition), on the recto side of page 26 of tractate Avodah Zarah ('strange worship', or idolatry), beginning with the word '*ani*, 'I'.

29 This translation is from Paris, Bibliothèque nationale de France, MS Suppl. Heb. 1337.

the commandments stated in the Torah', a phrase which is found prominently, among other places, in M. Horayot 1.1.[30]

If correct, this reconstructed genealogy of *avaryan b'mezid* suggests an advantage the new category has for R. Eliezer over the talmudic '*mumar* due to appetite'. B. Horayot 11a highlights the fact that the *mumar* due to appetite transgresses *deliberately*; driven by appetite, he *intentionally* flouts the law. The label *avaryan b'mezid* minimizes — more, it effaces — the 'appetite' motivation. By highlighting the intentionality of the transgression and eliminating a reference to its roots in unbridled appetite, R. Eliezer paves the way toward a harsher, less understanding approach to the appetite transgressor than existed earlier in Ashkenaz. There is more. The thirteenth-century polemical text *Nizzahon Vetus* accounts for Jewish apostasy by pointing to the apostate's desire 'to eat all that his heart desires', and indulge in wine and whoring, as well as to 'free himself from all the commandments and cling to transgressions'[31] While an anti-Christian polemic — and one composed decades after R. Eliezer — *Nizzahon Vetus* does suggest that there were Franco-German Jews who saw a link between appetite transgression and apostasy.[32] Thus to R. Eliezer, the *avaryan b'mezid* — who sins intentionally, albeit due to appetite — may be understood as teetering at the top of a slippery slope to apostasy.

In SY, R. Eliezer largely — although not entirely — breaks with the older Ashkenazi leniency toward appetite transgressors by expanding the range of legal topics as to which there is exclusion of the *avaryan b'mezid* beyond those discussed in the Bavli and earlier post-talmudic legal literature.[33] R. Eliezer

[30] The reference is to tractate Horayot in the Mishnah (*c.* 200 CE), chap. 1, para. 1 in the standard scholarly printed edition *Shishah Sidre Mishnah*, ed. by Albeck. The Mishnah is the basic legal document of rabbinic Judaism. It is subdivided into six 'Orders', or general categories of law, and subdivided into sixty-three tractates. The Jerusalem (*c.* fifth century) and Babylonian (*c.* seventh to eighth centuries) Talmuds are literatures resulting from centuries of analysis of the Mishnah and contemporaneous second- to third-century rabbinic literatures. Neither Talmud covers the entire Mishnah; as noted earlier, the Bavli has (only) thirty-seven tractates.

[31] *The Jewish-Christian Debate*, ed. by Berger, p. 144 (Hebrew section). The translation is my own.

[32] The people Israel's acceptance and observance of the Torah and its commandments — in contrast to the classical rabbinic portrayal of the Gentile nations' rejection of the Torah — was an important point of emphasis in Jewish anti-Christian polemic as far back as Rashi. See Grossman, *Rashi*, pp. 166–170 (Hebrew); Grossman, *Rashi: Religious Beliefs and Social Views*, p. 70 (Hebrew).

[33] There are two notable exceptions. First, B. Avodah Zarah 26b considers the '*mumar* due to appetite' as a 'brother' whose lost objects must be returned to him as commanded

effectively operates according to an unstated hermeneutical rule that the *avaryan b'mezid* is to be excluded from nearly all biblical terms denoting kinship or neighbourliness. Notably, R. Eliezer newly excludes the *avaryan b'mezid* from a number of commandments, the observance of which would tend to strengthen bonds between parents and children, and between one Jew and another. R. Eliezer's exclusionary hermeneutic results in the near-expulsion of the *avaryan b'mezid* from the universe of moral concern of a reader of SY. In sum, for R. Eliezer's predecessors the *mumar* was a character who needed to be taken into account in the proper application of laws pertaining to interest, family law, and the law of evidence. For R. Eliezer, the *avaryan b'mezid* is to be almost entirely written out of the community's concerns; he is an 'other'. To R. Eliezer, observance of the commandments is a sine qua non for a Jew's inclusion in the community. Indeed, in Chapter 30 of SY, he states that the scriptural phrase 'the congregation of the Lord' (Deut. 23. 2–3) refers to 'all those who keep God's commandments, whether in the [holy] land or outside of it'.

A survey of SY's rulings concerning the *avaryan b'mezid* will illustrate this point. In Chapter 224, R. Eliezer interprets Lev. 19. 18 ('Love your fellow as yourself') to include only 'one like you, who places himself under the yoke of Heaven and loves the commandments like you'. But 'if he is an evildoer, you are not commanded to love him, but it is a commandment to hate him (Prov. 8. 13: 'To fear the Lord is to hate evil'; Ps. 139. 21: 'O Lord, You know I hate those who hate You')'. No talmudic source excludes the transgressor from Lev. 19. 18, although such an exclusion does appear in the sixth-to seventh-century rabbinic work *Avot deRabbi Nathan* (version A, Chapter 16). The twelfth-century French legal/liturgical compilation *Mahzor Vitry* (Chapter 425) also excludes from Lev. 19. 18 the one who does not 'perform the acts of your people' (cf. Ex. 22. 27), which it may have derived from *Avot deRabbi Nathan*. R. Eliezer never refers to *Mahzor Vitry* by name in SY. The presence of this exegesis of Lev. 19. 18 in both twelfth-century French works suggests that it may have had some currency in northern France.

Although a commandment to hate a fellow Jew might seem to violate Lev. 19. 17 ('You shall not hate your brother in your heart'), R. Eliezer counts among the exceptions to that commandment a person 'who is not worthy' (*sh'eno hagun*, Chapter 195). An 'unworthy' person is one who does not demonstrate

by Deut. 22. 3. Second, in Chapter 156 R. Eliezer retains and even provides additional talmudic argumentation in support of his teachers' prohibition against taking interest from the *meshumad* due to appetite (=*avaryan b'mezid*). The latter is thus largely — although not entirely — excluded from the community's universe of moral concern.

'brotherhood' as to the commandments, which R. Eliezer asserts is required by the Talmud on B. Bava Kamma 88a.[34] R. Eliezer also excludes the *avaryan b'mezid* from Lev. 25. 17 ('A man should not wrong his peer') in Chapter 180, where he quotes the talmudic teaching attributed to R. Hanina b. R. Idi (B. Bava Metzia 59a) that Lev. 25. 17 only applies to 'the people that is with you in the Torah and the commandments'. R. Eliezer interprets R. Hanina b. Idi's teaching thusly: 'we have learned that scripture only cautioned against [using] oppressive language toward the fearers of God. But if he is an *avaryan b'mezid* even as to one thing and did not repent, it is permitted to oppress him with words'. R. Eliezer also refers in Chapter 180 to B. Shabbat 40a, which permits calling a transgressor of rabbinic law 'transgressor' (*avaryana*); this is clearly an exception to the interdiction of oppressive speech and, as noted earlier, may partly explain his crafting of the phrase *avaryan b'mezid*. One may also curse (Chapter 189) and strike (Chapter 217) a transgressor. As to the latter case, R. Eliezer comments, 'if he is an *avaryan* even as to one commandment it is permitted to strike him', based on a creative reading of B. Sanhedrin 85b, B. Yevamot 42b, and B. Bava Metzia 73b.

R. Eliezer also excludes transgressing parents from commandments entitling them to respect. In Chapter 174, R. Eliezer makes the point that if one's father is a 'transgressor [*avaryan*] on the words of the Torah — even as to one transgression — and he did not repent, [the son] is not cautioned on his account' (that is, the son is under no obligation not to curse him). R. Eliezer links this exclusion to the rabbinic exegesis of Ex. 22. 27 ('You shall not [...] put a curse upon a chieftain among your people'), although, as he points out himself, Bavli does not derive the prohibition against cursing a parent from Ex. 22. 27. In Chapters 221–22, discussing the honour and reverence due to one's parents, R. Eliezer points out that 'and if his father transgresses deliberately [*oveir* [...] *b'mezid*] one of the commandments stated in the Torah and did not repent, [the son] is exempt from his "reverence" and "honour"' (citing B. Bava Metzia 62a).

R. Eliezer's Exclusion of the Avaryan B'mezid *from Charity in Chapter 156*

With all this as prologue, let us look more closely at R. Eliezer's exclusion of the *avaryan b'mezid* from charity. In Chapter 155, R. Eliezer introduces Lev. 25. 36 and the rabbinic interpretation that it obligates a Jew to 'enable a brother to

[34] An exclusionary exegesis of Lev. 19.17 is also found in Maimonides's (1138–1204) 'Laws of the Murderer and of the Preservation of Life', 13. 14 in his monumental law code *Mishneh Torah*. R. Eliezer's justification of the exclusionary exegesis in SY is unique to him.

live'. Chapter 155 leads smoothly into Chapter 156, 'lending to the needy' (Deut. 15. 7–8). After some discussion of the key scriptural terms 'lend' and 'sufficient for whatever he needs', R. Eliezer writes:

> And if [the needy person] is a deliberate transgressor [*avaryan b'mezid*] of any one of the commandments stated in the Torah and has not repented, [the giver] is required neither to 'let him live by his side' nor to lend to him, as it is written 'And let him live [...] as your brother' (Lev. 25. 36) and as to lending it is written 'one of your brothers' (Deut. 15. 7). And since he has transgressed deliberately he has exited the category of 'brotherhood', for we require 'brotherhood' as to the commandments.

Aspects of the interpretive career of Lev. 25. 36 deserve discussion in light of its importance in R. Eliezer's Chapter 156 and other medieval sources. Lev. 25. 36 reads in full: 'Do not exact from him advance or accrued interest, but fear your God. Let him live by your side as your brother'. The last clause ('Let him live...') is quoted in M. Nedarim 9. 4, where the implication is that a Jew has an obligation to save another Jew's life so that the latter can 'live by your side as [a] brother'.[35] In M. Nedarim 9. 4, this clause is juxtaposed to the mishnaic phrase 'lest he become impoverished and you are unable to support him'.[36] It is not crystal-clear in context that M. Nedarim 9. 4 understands Lev. 25. 36 as a charity verse, although the preceding verse refers explicitly to one's brother's impoverishment. Moreover, even according to the most minimal reading, supporting one's impoverished brother might indeed save his life and enable him to 'live by your side'. Further, Lev. 25. 36 is interpreted on B. Bava Metzia 62a as mandating the return to another Jew of interest he has paid; or, at a higher level of abstraction, as the giving of monies to another Jew, which charity may be also. After Bavli, the Geonic-era legal compilation *She'iltot* (*c.* eighth century) and the twelfth- to thirteenth-century German Pietist compilation *Sefer Hasidim* do indeed understand Lev. 25. 36 as a charity verse.[37] *Sefer Hasidim* is of particular importance for understanding R. Eliezer and SY, as we will later show. Significantly, no late antique rabbinic source interprets Lev. 25. 36 to exclude

[35] The reference is to tractate Nedarim ('vows') in the Mishnah, chap. 9, para. 4.

[36] The reading 'lest' follows the Mishnah manuscripts Budapest, Akademia, Kaufmann A 50 and Parma, Biblioteca Palatina, 3173 (De Rossi 138). 'De Rossi' refers to the Christian Hebraist Giovanni Bernardo De Rossi (1742–1831), whose collection of Hebrew manuscripts included this important Mishnah manuscript.

[37] See the eighth-century legal compilation *She'iltot* by R. Aha meShabha, ed. by Mirsky, §147; *Sefer Hasidim*, ed. by Wistinetzki and Freimann, pp. 221, 474, paras 888, 1950.

transgressors from the category of 'brother' or from charity, and, in the Middle Ages, R. Eliezer is the first scholar to use Lev. 25. 36 to exclude transgressors from charity.

Having introduced the unrepentant *avaryan b'mezid* and his exclusion from Deut. 15. 7 and Lev. 25. 36, R. Eliezer sets out four talmudic passages. The first two (B. Bava Kamma 88a and B. Makkot 23a) are used to establish that 'brotherhood' among Israelites means the brotherhood of shared observance of the commandments, and that only a repentant transgressor can be restored to 'brotherhood'. R. Eliezer's treatment of the third talmudic source (B. Avodah Zarah 26a–b) requires closer attention. In that passage, one scholar teaches that idolaters and 'herders of small cattle' are neither to be raised up from, nor lowered into, pits.[38] From the fact that these herders are not to be rescued, R. Eliezer deduces that 'there is no commandment to "enable them to live"' (Lev. 25. 36). So, if the 'herders of small cattle' are literally not to have their lives saved, they are also not to have their lives saved via charity. Another part of B. Avodah Zarah 26b poses a problem for R. Eliezer. Deut. 22. 3, which requires the return of lost objects to their owners, also refers to 'brotherhood' ('anything that your brother loses'). Bavli points out unequivocally that Deut. 22. 3's 'brother' includes the *meshumad*.[39] This is problematic for if the *meshumad* is 'brother' enough to have his lost objects returned, then why is he not 'brother' enough to be given needed charity? R. Eliezer resolves the problem by interpreting Deut. 22. 3's seemingly redundant general phrase 'anything that your brother loses' with an emphasis on 'loses': the *meshumad* is included within the law of returning lost property, but he is not a 'brother' for purposes of other laws, notably charity. Consequently a law-abiding Jew is commanded to return a *meshumad*'s *own* property to him, but a *meshumad* is not a 'brother' to whom others are commanded to give *their* property (such as in the form of charity).

[38] 'Herders of small cattle' contravene a rabbinic prohibition against raising these animals in the land of Israel; they are presumed to be indifferent about where their animals graze, and are thus presumptively thieves who may allow their small cattle to graze on other people's lands. Thieves are understood to be a type of transgressor due to appetite. In the Mishnah and Tosefta see, e.g., M. Bava Kamma 7.7; M. Demai 2.3; Tosefta ('T') Shevi'it 3.13; and T. Bikkurim 2.16. The Tosefta (meaning 'addition') is a compilation contemporaneous to the Mishnah and largely of a similar style. Although it was once assumed to be a commentary on the Mishnah, scholars now are open to the possibility that parts of the Tosefta (at least) might have been sources for the Mishnah. See, e.g., Hauptman, *Rereading Mishnah*.

[39] This is R. Eliezer's version of B. Avodah Zarah 26b. The Vilna-Romm printed edition reads *mumar*.

That it is the *meshumad* due to appetite who is eligible to have his lost objects returned yet is ineligible for charity is apparent from R. Eliezer's related ruling in Chapter 168, where he emphasizes that lost objects are to be returned to the transgressor due to appetite.[40]

A brief narrative on B. Gittin 46b–47a also poses a challenge to R. Eliezer. According to the story, a sage named R. Ami was approached by a man who had sold himself into servitude as a gladiator and wanted the sage to redeem and rescue him. Other rabbis pointed out to R. Ami that the man was a *meshumad* who had been observed eating forbidden meats, but the sage opined that perhaps the man had eaten them due to appetite (and, implicitly, not due to rebelliousness).[41] The rabbis then pointed out to R. Ami that the man 'abandoned the permitted and ate the forbidden' — and thus was a transgressor due to spite. Upon learning this, R. Ami told the man, 'Go, they will not allow me to redeem you'.

On the face of it, it appears that R. Ami and the other rabbis implicitly agree that had the man been a *meshumad* due to appetite, he would have deserved rescue, and R. Eliezer acknowledges this: 'From this it may be inferred that the one who eats meat that died by itself due to appetite, it is a commandment to redeem him even though he is an evildoer.' Although Lev. 25. 36 is not cited within this talmudic narrative, it is logical to infer that rescuing someone from captivity is 'enabling him to live' (Lev. 25. 36), and, once Lev. 25. 36 is applicable, it should be entirely applicable — thus also requiring that a *meshumad* due to appetite be given charity. This reading of the story (and implicitly, of Lev. 25. 36 as well) is, however, clearly at odds with R. Eliezer's overall point that the *avaryan b'mezid* is excluded from 'brotherhood' and hence from Lev. 25. 36.

[40] Nevertheless, R. Eliezer also points out in the middle of Chapter 156 that the *meshumad*'s (due to appetite) lack of 'brotherhood' is the reason it is also permitted to lend at interest to him, since he is not a 'brother' as per Deut. 15. 7–8 ('one of your brothers [...] open your hand and lend him sufficient for whatever he needs'). This is inconsistent with R. Eliezer's position at the end of Chapter 156 that the permission to lend at interest only applies to the *meshumad* due to spite. At the end of Chapter 156 R. Eliezer accepts his teachers' prohibition against lending at interest to the *meshumad* due to appetite and even offers additional argumentation in support of the prohibition. For more on the views of Rashi, R. Jacob Tam, R. Isaac of Dampierre, and others on the issue of taking interest from and paying interest to the *meshumad*, see, e.g., Katz, 'Af Al Pi She-hata', and Kanarfogel, 'Changing Attitudes toward Apostates', pp. 311–17.

[41] Once again, *meshumad* is R. Eliezer's reading; the Vilna-Romm edition of the Bavli reads *mumar*.

R. Eliezer elides this reading of the story by interpreting it together with B. Avodah Zarah 26a–b. B. Avodah Zarah 26a–b, as noted earlier, says that the herders of small cattle (who are presumptively thieves and thus transgressors due to appetite) and idolaters are neither to be raised up from pits into which they have fallen nor lowered into them. Reading this passage together with a gloss of the talmudic sage Rav Yosef (also found on B. Avodah Zarah 26a), R. Eliezer declares that rescuing idolaters is forbidden. Although the passage equates idolaters and small cattle herders — thus implying that rescuing the latter should also be forbidden — R. Eliezer rejects that interpretation in favour of a forced distinction: rescuing idolaters is forbidden, but rescuing small cattle herders is neither obligatory nor forbidden. R. Eliezer candidly acknowledges the weakness of his reading, which unconvincingly declares 'forbidden' the very same act of rescue of an idolater that is labelled 'neither obligatory nor forbidden' when performed for the small cattle herder. He points out that he prefers this forced reading to a reading that would render forbidden the giving of a gift to the small cattle herder (= *meshumad* due to appetite). R. Eliezer applies this reading of B. Avodah Zarah 26a–b to B. Gittin 46b–47a. He suggests that R. Ami was not obligated to redeem the man, but initially wished to do so anyway: 'It appears to me that R. Ami wished to redeem [the presumptive *meshumad* due to appetite] above and beyond what the law requires.' However, upon learning that the man was in fact a transgressor due to spite, R. Ami then realized that the rescue was actually forbidden. R. Eliezer's reading of B. Gittin 46b–47a maps onto the behaviour he prescribes in Chapter 156 for law-abiding Jews: there is no obligation to 'enable [the unrepentant *mumar*/*meshumad* due to appetite = the *avaryan b'mezid*] to live', although it is not forbidden to do so. Matters are different as to the *mumar* due to spite, whose rescue — including a 'rescue' through charity — is actually forbidden.

R. Eliezer also dismisses an implicit challenge based on Rashi's interpretation of B. Sanhedrin 44a ('a Jew, even though he has sinned, is a Jew'). R. Eliezer limits that principle to the marital context to which Rashi had applied it, in which 'brotherhood' is not an explicit scriptural criterion of inclusion. To R. Eliezer, if a scriptural verse points to kinship, then 'brotherhood as to the commandments' is required and is the hermeneutic key that will exclude the *avaryan b'mezid*.

To summarize the conclusions of Chapter 156: the unrepentant *avaryan b'mezid* need not be given charity (or rescued from harm), as there is no obligation to do so. It is prohibited, however, to lend to him at interest. On the other hand, the one 'who abandons the permitted and eats the forbidden' is neither to be given charity nor rescued from harm, and may be charged interest.

Withholding Charity from the Avaryan B'mezid*: A Result of Textual/Hermeneutical or External Factors?*

In her exploration of legal differences between the Avodah Zarah tractates, Christine Hayes argued that before seeking to explain legal differences through resort to external, historical factors, scholars should exhaust internal — textual and hermeneutical — factors. Moreover, talmudic passages 'that feature a violation of exegetical norms or some other novelty invite cultural historical analysis'.[42] Hayes's insights apply *mutatis mutandis* to this case of R. Eliezer's exclusion from charity of the *avaryan b'mezid* (as well as to his expansion of the exclusion into the other areas surveyed earlier). Of R. Eliezer's various exclusions of the *avaryan b'mezid*, the only one that is directly rooted in the Talmud is the *avaryan b'mezid*'s exclusion from Lev. 25. 17 (B. Bava Metzia 59a) in Chapter 180 (see above). As to the specific case of charity, we have already noted that there is no talmudic or even post-talmudic basis for the *avaryan b'mezid*'s exclusion. Moreover, R. Eliezer's readings of B. Avodah Zarah 26a–b and B. Gittin 46b–47a are not at all compelled by the texts themselves. Avodah Zarah's inclusion of the *mumar* due to appetite as a 'brother' for purposes of returning lost items does not — *contra* R. Eliezer — necessarily imply that giving the *mumar* the property of others (e.g., charity) is not required. The Bavli's straightforward implication on B. Gittin 46b–47a that the *mumar* due to appetite must be rescued from captivity is not — *contra* R. Eliezer once again — represented as a supererogatory obligation. R. Eliezer's strong readings of these passages are curious, and invite inquiry into possibly motivating factors external to the texts. Not only that, but his use of 'brotherhood' in the performance of the commandments as a hermeneutical principle by means of which he excludes the *avaryan b'mezid* from an unprecedented range of intra-Jewish and even familial obligations also suggests the influence of external factors.

R. Eliezer's Text in its Twelfth-Century Context

This essay earlier constructed a genealogy of the term *avaryan b'mezid*, suggesting that its roots lie in M. Horayot 1.1, B. Horayot 11a, and B. Shabbat 40a. R. Eliezer further describes the *avaryan b'mezid* in Chapter 156 (and other places) as one who transgresses 'one of all the commandments stated in the Torah'. This latter phrase is found in late antique rabbinic literature, in one

[42] Hayes, *Between the Babylonian and Palestinian Talmuds*, p. 29 and passim.

case in a martyrdom context: a Jew commanded by a persecutor to violate 'one of the commandments stated in the Torah' should prefer violation to death except in the cases of murder, sexual immorality, and idolatry.[43] Further, Bavli (B. Sanhedrin 74a–b) makes it clear that in a time of widespread persecution (called a time of *shemad*, literally, 'destruction'), an order to violate even the most seemingly insignificant form of Jewish practice must be disobeyed, even if it is not a commandment, and even if death results. Thus, the phrase 'one of all the commandments stated in the Torah' suggests the supreme significance of *each* commandment. While the twelfth century cannot accurately be described *in toto* as 'a time of *shemad*', it was a time of severe deterioration in Christian attitudes toward Jews in northern Europe. Haym Soloveitchik has characterized the period from 1096 to 1146 in northern Europe as one in which Jew-hatred turned 'pathological'.[44] The first stirrings of the blood libel occurred in the twelfth century, and Jews were accused of the murder of Christians six times between 1147 and 1192. Gavin Langmuir has noted the growing tendency in the twelfth century to associate alleged Jewish murders of Christians with Jewish ritual requirements, which deepened Christian fear of the Jews.[45] Moreover, the twelfth-century focus on reason and the conviction that Christianity's claims may be supported by reason led to a view that dissenters — notably Jews — are non-rational and consequently undeserving of tolerance.[46] Jewish apostasy was also a widespread phenomenon during this time, and Pope Alexander III (1159–81) and King Louis VII of France (d. 1180) even forbade the return of Jewish apostates to their erstwhile communities.[47] These dark developments may be correlated with a change in Franco-German Jewry's attitude toward its transgressors. We have already noted Rashi's lenient attitude toward the apostate in the eleventh century and the twelfth-century retreat from that leniency on the part of R. Jacob Tam and R. Isaac of Dampierre. Apropos, it may have seemed to R. Eliezer of Metz that the *avaryan b'mezid* (= *mumar* due to appetite), although not (yet) an apostate, had put

[43] There are two examples in the Jerusalem Talmud (*c.* fifth century). See, e.g., Y. Shevi'it 4.2, 35a; Y. Sanhedrin 3.5, 21b. The 'Y' prefix stands for *yerushalmi* ('Jerusalemite').

[44] Soloveitchik, *Principles and Pressures*, p. 116 (Hebrew). See also his larger discussion on pp. 115–18. See also Chazan, *Medieval Stereotypes and Modern Antisemitism*, pp. 74–94 and passim.

[45] Langmuir, *Toward a Definition of Antisemitism*, pp. 263–81.

[46] Funkenstein, 'Changes in the Patterns of Christian Anti-Jewish Polemics'; Abulafia, *Christians and Jews*, pp. 85–87.

[47] See Goldin, *Uniqueness and Togetherness*, especially pp. 86–88 (Hebrew).

himself on a path to further transgression and was violating Jewish law in a historical context of persecution and apostasy that was similar to the situation limned in the Talmud, in which one must be prepared to die rather than transgress. The changed external reality, along with the growing irrelevance of the old talmudic categories '*mumar* due to appetite' and 'spite', may have motivated both R. Eliezer's creation of the new category *avaryan b'mezid* and his radical exclusion of the latter from the circle of 'brotherhood'.

Although unique in his approach, R. Eliezer of Metz was not the only scholar of his time to propose that Jewish transgressors be denied charity. Ephraim Kanarfogel has observed that R. Eliezer's preface to SY echoes the Pietists' critique of over-involvement in dialectic, which could undermine the fear of God.[48] It is therefore relevant to note that the German Pietist work *Sefer Hasidim* (SH), like SY, includes passages that strongly discourage giving charity to unworthy recipients, including sinners.[49] In Paragraph 840 SH alludes to B. Bava Kamma 16b in noting that it is better to give charity to 'fearers of Heaven' than to 'unworthy' persons (*sh'einam mehuganim*), who are also identified here as 'impudent' or 'licentious' (*peritzim*). Giving to such people is a 'sin' because the giver is thereby 'upholding rebels against the Holy One, blessed be He in the world'.[50] In Paragraph 857 the narrator advises that when faced with the choice of giving to a 'righteous person' or an 'evildoer', the giver must prefer the 'righteous person', and 'the evildoer can go to hell'. Even if the 'evildoer' threatens to sin if he is not given charity, the giver must not give to him, unless he threatens to commit murder.[51] R. Eliezer's exclusion of the *avaryan b'mezid* from charity would appear then to be a pointed expression of the pietistic impulse he shared with the German Pietists and SH, although he parts

[48] Ephraim E. Urbach had pointed out the connection between R. Eliezer and the Pietists some years ago, but, as observed by Ephraim Kanarfogel, he tended to minimize the relationship. See Urbach, *The Tosaphists*, I, 161 and n. 54 (the Pietist R. Eleazar of Worms refers to R. Eliezer as 'my teacher and master'). For a fuller treatment of R. Eliezer's link to the Pietists, see Kanarfogel, *'Peering through the Lattices'*, pp. 69 n. 105, 102 n. 16, and passim.

[49] See the discussion of SH's limits on charity to 'unworthy' recipients in Horovitz, '"V'yehiyu Aniyyim B'nei Veitekha"', pp. 226–28.

[50] *Sefer Hasidim*, ed. by Wistinetzki and Freimann, p. 212. But see also Soloveitchik, 'Three Themes in the *Sefer Hasidim*', pp. 330–35, who understands such negative terms as references to non-Pietists (however otherwise pious).

[51] *Sefer Hasidim*, ed. by Wistinetzki and Freimann, pp. 215–16.

company with them by permitting the giving of charity to the *avaryan b'mezid* as a supererogatory religious act.[52]

R. Eliezer's exclusion of the *avaryan b'mezid* from charity is also interestingly echoed in twelfth-century canon law developments. The mid-twelfth century was a foundational period for the canon law, with the appearance in *c.* 1140 of Gratian's *Decretum*. Gratian quotes and does not resolve a conflict between John Chrysostom, who urged 'indiscriminate charity' for all; Augustine's exclusion from charity of actors, prostitutes, and gladiators; and Ambrose's teaching that 'faithful Christians' should take priority. One commentator, the Decretist Rufinus (writing in *c.* 1157–59), sets out a detailed argument for charitable discrimination. According to Brian Tierney, Rufinus was among those scholars who held 'that there was a class of undeserving poor who were to be denied alms on principle even when ample resources were available'.[53] Tierney notes that Rufinus held that charity was to be refused 'especially' to an idle man capable of work, and that 'especially' implies that Rufinus had other exclusions in mind. Rufinus's successors identified such other exclusions in light of Augustine, who frowned on giving 'to those who followed an evil way of life'.[54] Although Gratian and Rufinus were located in Bologna, Tierney points out that '[a] number of French works of the 1170s also made use of the distinctions and categories proposed by Rufinus', although they did not necessarily accept all of his conclusions.[55]

R. Eliezer's and the Decretists' shared twelfth-century interest in discrimination in charity is striking, as is the overlap between R. Eliezer's Chapters 174 and 221–24 — excluding sinning parents from honour — and the Decretists' contemporaneous discussions about whether one's sinning father is entitled to alms in preference to a virtuous stranger.[56] While it is difficult to imagine a direct conduit by which the *Decretum* and the commentaries and *summae* of the Decretists would have come to R. Eliezer's attention, it is known that there were intensive scholarly and cultural, as well as social and economic contacts between French Jews and the ambient Christian culture at this time.[57] Nor

[52] Cf. Horovitz, '"V'yehiyu Anniyyim B'nei Veitekha"', pp. 227–28.

[53] Tierney, 'The Decretists and the "Deserving Poor"', p. 368.

[54] Tierney, 'The Decretists and the "Deserving Poor"', p. 369.

[55] Tierney, 'The Decretists and the "Deserving Poor"', pp. 365–66.

[56] See Rubin, *Charity and Community*, p. 69; Tierney, *Medieval Poor Law*, p. 57.

[57] For discussions of such contacts, see, e.g., Grossman, *The Early Sages of France*, pp. 24–29 and passim (Hebrew); Urbach, *The Tosaphists*, I, 19–21; Ta-Shma, 'Halakhah and Reality';

were the German Pietists impervious to Christian developments. Yitzhak F. Baer noted many years ago that SH shares ideas held in the ambient Christian environment, even noting that many social ideas found in SH were 'based on talmudic tradition, but recast in a new idiom in the spirit of medieval Christianity'.[58] Baer's observation further illuminates R. Eliezer's charity innovation: while loosely based on Talmudic sources, R. Eliezer's break with the talmudic (and earlier post-talmudic) past in ruling that charity not be given to the *avaryan b'mezid* is similar to contemporaneous canon law's interest in charitable discrimination. Indeed, Jewish and canon law of the time also exhibit a shared interest in charitable gifts and prayers on behalf of the dead.[59]

Conclusion

Despite the growing body of scholarship on medieval Jewish apostasy and the *mumar*, R. Eliezer of Metz's contributions to legal doctrine have been noted, but have remained virtually unexplored. In the twelfth century R. Eliezer creates the category *avaryan b'mezid*, which maps onto the older talmudic category '*mumar* due to appetite'. In a series of novel rulings in his *Sefer yere'im*, he utilizes biblical terms denoting 'brotherhood' or 'kinship' to exclude the *avaryan b'mezid* from the set of those for whom the Jewish community — or even individual families — must demonstrate active concern on the ground that the *avaryan b'mezid*'s transgressions remove him from the category 'brother'.

Marcus, 'The Dynamics of Jewish Renaissance '; and Marcus, 'A Jewish-Christian Symbiosis'. But note Daniel J. Lasker's sober assessment that prior to the thirteenth century few Jews learned about Christianity from literary sources, and those who did were mostly collaborators on translation projects or anti-Christian polemicists. See Lasker, 'Jewish Knowledge of Christianity'. Ephraim Kanarfogel has also recently pointed out that with one possible exception, the Tosafists were unfamiliar with Latin, which thus put scholastic literature out of their reach. Kanarfogel nevertheless points to the contacts between Jewish and Christian Bible scholars and the Christian exegetical techniques the Jewish scholars absorbed through conversation and oral exchange. He hypothesizes that a similar sharing of dialectical technique may have occurred through conversation. He concludes that Christian dialectic acted as an 'enzyme' on Jewish scholarship, catalyzing Jewish dialectical learning. We may hypothesize that a similar sharing through oral exchange may have occurred with regard to ideas about charity. See Kanarfogel, *The Intellectual History*, pp. 84–110.

[58] Baer, 'Ha-megamah Ha-datit Hevratit Shel "Sefer Hasidim"', p. 29; Horovitz, '"V'yehiyu Anniyyim B'nei Veitekha"', pp. 227–28. See also Ivan Marcus's brief catalogue of parallel Jewish and Christian cultural developments in 'The Dynamics of Jewish Renaissance', p. 30.

[59] Falk, 'Jewish Law and Medieval Canon Law'.

Among these rulings is Chapter 156's direction that there is no obligation to give charity to the *avaryan b'mezid*. R. Eliezer's unique construction of the new category *avaryan b'mezid* in place of the talmudic '*mumar* due to appetite' is based on talmudic sources: he draws on sources that emphasize the intentional nature of the *avaryan b'mezid*'s transgression and the fact that the unrepented transgression of even 'one of all the commandments stated in the Torah' places him beyond the communal pale. Heightened hostility toward the Jews, increasing Jewish apostasy, the blurring and growing insignificance of the old talmudic *mumar* categories, German Pietist influences on R. Eliezer, and contemporaneous developments in the canon law of charitable discrimination are all factors contributing to or at least illuminating his construction and wide-ranging application of the new category *avaryan b'mezid* in the twelfth century.

Works Cited

Manuscripts and Archival Sources

Budapest, Akademia, Kaufmann A 50
Paris, Bibliothèque nationale de France, MS Suppl. Heb. 1337
Parma, Biblioteca Palatina, 3173 (De Rossi 138)

Primary Sources

(Rabbi) Aha meShabha, *She'iltot*, ed. by Samuel K. Mirsky (Jerusalem: Ha-makhon L'mehkar u-l'hotza'at sefarim Sura, 1959)

Avot deRabbi Nathan, ed. by Shneur Zalman Schechter (New York: Jewish Theological Seminary, 1967; repr. 1997)

Babylonian Talmud, Vilna-Romm edition with commentaries (Jerusalem: Shulsinger Brothers, 1976)

The Jewish-Christian Debate in the High Middle Ages: A Critical Edition of the 'Nizzahon Vetus' with an Introduction, Translation, and Commentary, ed. by David Berger (Philadelphia: Jewish Publication Society of America, 1979)

Maimonides, *Mishneh Torah* (Jerusalem: Hotzaat Shabse Frankel, 1975)

Rabbenu Simchah of Vitry, *Mahzor Vitry*, ed. by Simon Hurwitz (Nürnberg:, 1923; repr. Israel: [n.pub.], 1978)

R. Eliezer ben Samuel of Metz, *Sefer yere'im*, ed. by Avraham A. Schiff (Vilna, 1892; repr.; Israel, [n.pub.], [n.d.])

R. Isaac b. R. Moses of Vienna, *Or Zarua*, ed. by Mif'al Torat Hahmei Ashkenaz, Laws on Charity, 20, rev. edn (Jerusalem: Makhon Yerushalayim, 2010)

R. Solomon ben Isaac (Rashi), *Responsa Rashi Solomon ben Isaac*, ed. by Israel Elfenbein (repr. New York: [n.pub.], [n.d.])

Sefer Hasidim, ed. by Jehuda Wistinetzki and Jacob Freimann (Frankfurt a. M.: M.A. Wahrmann, 1924)

Shishah Sidre Mishnah: With New Commentary, Introductions, Additions, and Completions, ed. by Chanoch Albeck (Tel-Aviv: Dvir, 1978)

Talmud Yerushalmi According to Ms. Or. 4720 (Scal. 3) of the Leiden University Library with Restorations and Corrections (Jerusalem: Academy of the Hebrew Language, 2001)

The Tosefta: According to Codex Vienna, With Variants from Codex Erfurt, Genizah Mss. and Editio Princeps (Venice 1521), Together With References to Parallel Passages in Talmudic Literature and a Brief Commentary. The Order of Zera'im, ed. by Saul Lieberman (New York: Jewish Theological Seminary, 1955)

Secondary Studies

Abulafia, Anna Sapir, *Christians and Jews in the Twelfth-Century Renaissance* (London: Routledge, 1995)

Baer, Yitzhak F., 'Ha-megamah Ha-datit Hevratit Shel "Sefer Hasidim"', *Zion*, 3 (1937), 1–50

Blidstein, Gerald J., 'Who Is Not a Jew? — The Medieval Discussion', *Israel Law Review*, 11.3 (1976), 369–90

Brody, Robert, *The Geonim of Babylonia and the Shaping of Medieval Jewish Culture* (New Haven: Yale University Press, 1998; new edn, 2013)

Chazan, Robert, *Medieval Stereotypes and Modern Antisemitism* (Berkeley: University of California Press, 1997)

Falk, Ze'ev, 'Jewish Law and Medieval Canon Law', in *Jewish Law in Legal History and the Modern World*, ed. by Bernard S. Jackson (Leiden: Brill, 1980), pp. 78–96

Faur, José, 'The Legal Thinking of Tosafot: An Historical Approach', *Diné Israel VI* (1975), 43–72

Funkenstein, Amos, 'Changes in the Patterns of Christian Anti-Jewish Polemics in the 12th Century', *Zion*, 33 (1968), 125-44 (Hebrew)

Galinsky, Judah D., 'The Significance of Form: R. Moses of Coucy's Reading Audience and His *Sefer ha-Mizvot*', *Association for Jewish Studies Review* 35.2 (2011), 293–321

Goldin, Simha, 'Juifs et juifs convertis au Moyen Age: "es-tu encore mon frère?"', *Annales: Histoire, Sciences Sociales*, 54.4 (1999), 851–74

——, *Uniqueness and Togetherness: The Enigma of the Survival of the Jews in the Middle Ages* (Tel Aviv: Hakibbutz Hameuchad, 1997) (Hebrew)

Grossman, Avraham, *The Early Sages of France: Their Lives, Leadership and Works* (Jerusalem: Magnes, 1995) (Hebrew)

——, *Rashi* (Jerusalem: Merkaz Zalman Shazar, 2006) (Hebrew)

——, *Rashi: Religious Beliefs and Social Views* (Alon Shvut: Tevunot, 2008) (Hebrew)

Haskins, Charles Homer, *The Renaissance of the Twelfth Century* (Cambridge, MA: Harvard University Press, 1927)

Hauptman, Judith, *Rereading Mishnah: A New Approach to Ancient Jewish Texts* (Tübingen: Mohr Siebeck, 2005)

Hayes, Christine Elizabeth, *Between the Babylonian and Palestinian Talmuds: Accounting for Halakhic Difference in Selected Sugyot from Tractate Avodah Zarah* (Oxford: Oxford University Press, 1997)

Horovitz, Elimelekh, '"V'yehiyu Aniyyim B'nei Veitekha": Tzedakah, Aniyyim, U'fiquah Hevrati B'kehillot Yehudei Europa', in *Religion and Economy: Connections and Interactions; Collected Essays*, ed. by Menahem Ben-Sasson (Jerusalem: Zalman Shazar Center for Jewish History, 1995), pp. 209–31

Kanarfogel, Ephraim, 'Changing Attitudes Toward Apostates in Tosafist Literature, Late Twelfth-Early Thirteenth Centuries', in *New Perspectives on Jewish-Christian Relations*, ed. by Elisheva Carlebach and Jacob J. Schachter (Leiden: Brill, 2012), pp. 297–327

——, *The Intellectual History and Rabbinic Culture of Medieval Ashkenaz* (Detroit: Wayne State University Press, 2013)

——, *'Peering through the Lattices': Mystical, Magical, and Pietistic Dimensions in the Tosafist Period* (Detroit: Wayne State University Press, 2000)

Katz, Jacob, '"Af Al Pi She-hata Yisrael Hu"', in idem, *Halakhah and Kabbalah: Studies in the History of Jewish Religion, its Various Faces and Social Relevance* (Jerusalem: Magnes Press, 1986), pp. 255-69 (Hebrew)

Langmuir, Gavin, *Toward a Definition of Antisemitism* (Berkeley and London: University of California Press, 1990)

Lasker, Daniel J., 'Jewish Knowledge of Christianity in the Twelfth and Thirteenth Centuries', in *Studies in Medieval Jewish Intellectual and Social History: Festschrift in Honor of Robert Chazan*, ed. by David Engel and others (SJJTP 15; Leiden: Brill, 2012), pp. 97-109

Marcus, Ivan, 'The Dynamics of Jewish Renaissance and Renewal in the Twelfth Century', in *Jews and Christians in Twelfth-Century Europe*, ed. by Michael A. Signer and John Van Engen (Notre Dame: University of Notre Dame Press, 2001), pp. 27-45

——, 'A Jewish-Christian Symbiosis: The Culture of Early Ashkenaz', in *The Cultures of the Jews*, ed. by David Biale (New York: Schocken, 2002), pp. 449-516

——, *Piety and Society: The Jewish Pietists of Medieval Germany* (Leiden: E.J. Brill, 1997)

Newman, Hillel, *The Ma'asim of the People of the Land of Israel: Halakhah and History in Byzantine Palestine* (Jerusalem: Yad Ben Zvi, 2011) (Hebrew)

Reiner, Avraham (Rami), 'Mumar Okheil Nevelot L'tei'avon — Pasul? Mashehu Al Nusah U-ferusho B'ye-dei Rashi', in *The Scepter Shall Not Depart from Judah: Leadership, Rabbinate and Community in Jewish History. Studies Presented to Professor Simon Schwarzfuchs*, ed. by Joseph R. Hacker and Yaron Harel (Jerusalem: Mossad Bialik, 2011), pp. 219–28

Rubin, Miri, *Charity and Community in Medieval Cambridge* (Cambridge: Cambridge University Press, 1987)

Schiffman, Lawrence H., *Who Was A Jew? Rabbinic and Halakhic Perspectives on the Jewish-Christian Schism* (Hoboken, NJ: Ktav, 1985)

Soloveitchik, Haym, *Principles and Pressures: Jewish Trade in Gentile Wine in the Middle Ages* (Tel Aviv: Am Oved, 2003) (Hebrew)

——, 'Three Themes in the *Sefer Hasidim*', *Association for Jewish Studies Review* 1 (1976), 311–57

Ta-Shma, Israel M., 'Halakhah and Reality: The Tosafist Experience', in idem, *Creativity and Tradition: Studies in Medieval Rabbinic Scholarship, Literature and Thought* (Cambridge, MA: Harvard University Press, 2006), pp. 87-101

Tierney, Brian, 'The Decretists and the "Deserving Poor"', *Comparative Studies in Society and History*, 1:4 (June, 1959), 360-73

——, *Medieval Poor Law: A Sketch of Canonical Theory and Its Application in England* (Berkeley and Los Angeles: University of California Press, 1959)

Urbach, Ephraim E., *The Tosaphists: Their History, Writings and Methods*, 2 vols (Jerusalem: Mossad Bialik, 1986) (Hebrew)

From Saint Francis to Salimbene di Adam: Begging in the Early Franciscan World, *c.* 1210–80

Allison Edgren

Historians have long tended to romanticize early Franciscan attitudes towards the poor. In his survey of medieval poverty, for example, Michel Mollat argues that the mendicants were the first to truly understand the poor, to hold them up to the rich and powerful as examples of virtue and to seek to share in their poverty.[1] Recently, however, scholars have begun to challenge this interpretation, questioning the extent to which the friars could have idealized and championed the poor when attitudes towards poverty actually deteriorated as the thirteenth century progressed.[2] While scholars have proposed a variety of solutions to this apparent conundrum, they have only begun to consider what might be revealed by separating the Franciscans' views on begging from their ideas about poverty more generally.[3] Although poverty and begging are often regarded as paired, almost interchangeable, concepts, there is a fundamental difference: poverty is passive, a state defined by an individual's monetary worth, whereas begging, defined functionally, is both active and social, focused on the pursuit of alms and interactions with

[1] Mollat, *Les pauvres au Moyen Âge*, p. 147.

[2] For an overview of this problem, see Hanska, *'And the Rich Man Also Died'*, pp. 119–21.

[3] A volume published in the same year as the conference at Leeds — Prudlo, *The Origin, Development, and Refinement of Medieval Religious Mendicancies* — considers some of the many tensions between the ideas of religious poverty and mendicancy.

Allison Edgren (aedgren@nd.edu) is a Ph.D. candidate in the Department of History at the University of Notre Dame.

Approaches to Poverty in Medieval Europe: Complexities, Contradictions, Transformations, c. 1100–1500, ed. by Sharon Farmer, IMR 22 (Turnhout: Brepols, 2016) pp. 93–115
BREPOLS PUBLISHERS 10.1484/M.IMR-EB.5.105461

potential donors.[4] This distinction is especially important in the case of the Franciscans, as begging, a bold request for material goods, seems to be paradoxically opposed to their emphasis on the joyful, humble acceptance of poverty.[5] For the Franciscans, this was no mere theoretical problem but an obstacle to their way of life. Dependent on the charity of the faithful, the friars had to idealize and practice a model of begging that not only justified their own mendicancy but also portrayed them as more attractive recipients of alms than any other beggars.

At first, the Franciscans struggled with this critical conflict between begging and voluntary poverty. Many of the early mendicant sources — chronicles, hagiographical materials, and even the writings of Saint Francis — reveal an uneasy suspicion that the mere act of begging indicated a flawed character in the beggar, exposing a lazy and greedy desire for unearned material things. By the 1240s, however, the friars had become more comfortable with their own begging. Franciscan authors began to elucidate an idealized model of mendicancy that emphasized the humiliating nature of begging, a model marked by a desire to maintain, not alleviate, poverty and a preference for spiritual rather than material gain. This model of mendicancy was difficult for secular beggars to follow, as it was both spiritually demanding and explicitly focused on religious ends. Even more detrimental to the cause of the involuntary poor, however, were the friars' deliberate efforts to portray themselves, on the basis of this model of begging, as more attractive recipients of charity than their competitors. Both to support their own mendicancy and to undermine their competition, the Franciscans displaced their suspicions about the evils of begging onto beggars outside of the mendicant orders, accusing them of greed and spiritual weakness. The Franciscan attempt to idealize and practice mendicancy thus actually contributed to the condemnation of the begging of the involuntary poor. Arguing for the superiority of their own, spiritually oriented form of begging, the friars encouraged the laity to be suspicious of the motivations and characters of other beggars, linking non-mendicant begging to suggestions of worldliness and greed.

[4] Voluntary poverty is, of course, more active than involuntary poverty. Nevertheless, the activity of voluntary poverty is self-contained, focusing on an individual's material and spiritual change of state. Begging, on the other hand, is active in relation to others, requiring donors as well as beggars.

[5] Kelly S. Johnson briefly notes this paradox in 'The Irony of Voluntary Begging'.

The Franciscan Order arose in the early thirteenth century, one among a number of new religious groups that practiced evangelical poverty. Many scholars argue that the commercial revolution of the eleventh and twelfth centuries was the major impetus for this plethora of new groups, most of which expressed anxiety over the new valorization of money and wealth.[6] The Franciscan rule shows the order's concern over this new economy clearly, as it forbids the friars to even touch money. Even more illuminating is an anecdote that appears in all of the early hagiographical materials on Saint Francis: finding a coin left on the altar as alms, a friar picked it up and, ignoring its worth, threw it onto the windowsill. When Francis discovered that the friar had touched the coin, even to throw it away, he instructed the brother to take the coin in his mouth and put it on a pile of manure.[7]

In embracing a life of poverty and mendicancy, however, the friars were not only rejecting the new economy but also living in imitation of Christ. In opposition to the views of the cloistered monks, who believed in personal poverty but communal property, the Franciscans argued that Christ and his apostles had owned nothing, and instead lived off of the alms of the faithful. The friars therefore gave up their possessions and forsook their families, living as homeless and penniless wanderers, like 'strangers and pilgrims upon the earth'.[8] More than anything else, the Franciscans emphasized humility, for their overarching goal, which they sought through their poverty, was to mimic the self-emptying of Christ.[9]

Recently, though, scholars have begun to question why the Franciscans' pursuit of poverty did not effect a positive change in the status of the poor. Some historians have continued to champion the mendicant orders, suggesting, for instance, that the friars were less influential than commonly believed, that they practiced self-censorship of their views, or that they simply had many enemies who, in turn, attacked poverty.[10] Others tend to be more critical of the Franciscans. For instance, Daniel Lesnick notes that the mendicants did not idealize poverty per se, but rather the love of poverty. Their ideal was not those who were actually poor, but instead those who behaved as if they were

[6] See, e.g., Little, *Religious Poverty and the Profit Economy*, and Henderson, *Piety and Charity*.

[7] Thomas of Celano, *Vita secunda Sancti Francisci*, II. 35, p. 170; English translation in *The Remembrance*, p. 290.

[8] I Peter 2. 11.

[9] Burr, *The Spiritual Franciscans*, p. 2.

[10] Hanska, '*And the Rich Man Also Died*', pp. 120–21.

poor.[11] Lesnick claims that the mendicants therefore spent little, if any, energy analysing working-class poverty and the living situation of the poor.[12] Kenneth Baxter Wolf has developed this idea still further, pointing out a difference between Franciscan attitudes towards voluntary and involuntary poverty. He argues that Saint Francis never truly succeeded in becoming poor, but instead imitated poverty in a way that was spiritually beneficial and socially powerful — but only for elites who adopted poverty voluntarily. The voluntary poor were holy because they had deliberately renounced their worldly goods, but the poverty of the involuntary poor meant little, as it involved no sacrifice.[13] Thus, in Wolf's conception, as in Lesnick's, the Franciscans did little to elevate views of involuntary poverty or to help the poor themselves.

These iconoclastic reinterpretations have provoked a great deal of controversy, but Lesnick and Wolf were not the first to point out that idealizations of poverty did not always help the poor.[14] In the 1970s and 80s, scholars developed an anthropological interpretation of medieval charity as a 'social contract.' This model presents charity as an exchange in which the rich gave funds to the poor, who, in turn, prayed for the souls of their benefactors; the poor thus received physical relief while the rich accrued spiritual benefit.[15] Underlying this idea was a Christian idealization of poverty which argued that the poor, because of their suffering, were closer to Christ and thus more likely to achieve salvation; nevertheless, this conception of charity was not necessarily good for the poor. As Bronislaw Geremek points out, the poor were the objects, and not the subjects, of this model of charity.[16] Through this contractual understanding, the rich not only sought their own salvation but also justified their wealth. Charity was an exchange that reinforced the social order, as 'the poor were nailed to a cross at the bottom of society'.[17]

[11] Lesnick, *Preaching in Medieval Florence*, pp. 147–48.

[12] Lesnick, *Preaching in Medieval Florence*, p. 146. Anne Scott has a similar perspective; her article in this volume argues that the Franciscans were more interested in portraying the spiritual power of poverty than in ameliorating the condition of the poor.

[13] Wolf, *The Poverty of Riches*, p. 4.

[14] For counterarguments to this revisionist trend, see, e.g., Hanska, '*And the Rich Man Also Died*', and Adam J. Davis's contribution to this volume, 'Hospitals, Charity, and the Culture of Compassion in the Twelfth and Thirteenth Centuries'.

[15] For more on this anthropological interpretation of medieval charity, see Rubin, *Charity and Community*, pp. 1–13.

[16] Geremek, *Poverty*, trans. by Kolakowska, p. 21.

[17] Lis and Soly, *Poverty and Capitalism*, p. 22.

Despite all of these recent attempts at reinterpretation, the friars overwhelmingly continue to be studied in terms of their pursuit of poverty, not their pursuit of alms. But the friars were active beggars, and their mendicancy was not only difficult to reconcile with their evangelical poverty, but also hard to explain in terms of a 'social contract' view of charity. The friars had to idealize their own model of charity, one in which they were the subjects, not the objects, of the exchange. By recognizing the difference between begging and poverty, and studying the former separately, it is possible to see how the friars developed this idealization of mendicancy.

At the most basic level, the Franciscans argued that to beg for alms was to imitate the life of Christ. Thus, the rule of 1223 laid out the duties of the friars:

> Et tanquam peregrini et advenae in hoc saeculo in paupertate et humilitate Domino famulantes vadant pro eleemosyna confidenter, nec oportet eos verecundari, quia Dominus pro nobis se fecit pauperem in hoc mundo. Haec est illa celsitudo altissimae paupertatis, quae vos, carissimos fratres meos, heredes et reges regni caelorum instituit, pauperes rebus fecit, virtutibus sublimavit.
>
> (And as pilgrims and strangers in this world, serving the Lord in poverty and humility, let them go confidently for alms. It is not right that they should feel ashamed, because the Lord made Himself poor in this world for us. This is that height of most exalted poverty which has made you, my most beloved brothers, heirs and kings of the Kingdom of Heaven, made paupers in things, raised up in virtue.)[18]

While the rule of 1223 was given formal approval by Pope Honorius III and was therefore the standard rule of the order, an earlier rule, based on the version presented to Pope Innocent III in 1209 or 1210, was composed at the Chapter of 1221. In this earlier rule, Francis encourages begging as an *imitatio Christi* even more clearly, urging the friars to beg without reservation, as 'Jesus Christus [...] posuit faciem suam ut petram durissimam, nec verecundatus fuit; et fuit pauper et hospes et vixit de eleemosynis' (Jesus Christ [...] set his face like flint and was not ashamed; and he was poor and a stranger and he lived on alms).[19]

[18] Francis of Assisi, *Regula bullata*, VI. 2–4, p. 190; English translation in *The Later Rule*, p. 103. I have made some slight alterations to the English translations quoted in this article.

[19] Francis of Assisi, *Regula non bullata*, IX. 4–5, p. 140; English translation in *The Earlier Rule*, p. 70.

Francis's first rule also gives a more detailed justification for the friars' quest for alms, one which reflects the logic expressed in the 'social contract' view of medieval charity:

> Et eleemosyna est hereditas et iustitia, quae debetur pauperibus, quam nobis acquisivit Dominus noster Jesus Christus. Et fratres, qui eam acquirendo laborant, magnam mercedem habebunt et faciunt lucrari et acquirere tribuentes; quia omnia quae relinquent homines in mundo peribunt, sed de caritate et de eleemosynis, quas fecerunt, habebunt praemium a Domino.
>
> (Alms are an inheritance and a justice which are owed to the poor, which our Lord Jesus Christ acquired for us. The brothers who work at acquiring them will receive a great reward and enable their donors to gain and acquire one; for all that people leave behind in the world will perish, but for the charity and the alms which they gave, they will have a reward from the Lord.)[20]

Once again, the poor beg because it gives the rich the chance to provide for their own spiritual well-being. Francis is clearly on the side of the poor in this dynamic, as he stresses the idea that the poor are owed alms, but the overall picture of charity remains the same. The problem with this interpretation is that, although it explains why people should give alms to the friars, arguing that the friars deserve charity is not the same thing as being able to justify the act that acquires those alms. The traditional social contract view of charity is therefore insufficient to explain Franciscan mendicancy.

Instead, Francis advocates the practice of begging on the basis of its humiliating nature.[21] His argument is predicated entirely on the assumption that medieval society considered begging to be shameful, as he encourages the friars to rejoice in living at the fringes of society, 'inter viles et despectas personas, inter pauperes et debiles et infirmos et leprosos et iuxta viam mendicantes' (among common and contemptible people, among the poor and the weak and the sick and the lepers and the beggars next to the road).[22] Begging was even more humiliating than simple poverty as, active itself, it invited an active response, giving those who were solicited for alms an opportunity to express their contempt of poverty and their poor petitioner. In particular, begging exposed the friar to the spiritually beneficial danger of persecution. Thus, the early rule encourages the Franciscans to thank God 'quando facerent eis

[20] Francis of Assisi, *Regula non bullata*, IX. 8–9, pp. 140–41; *The Earlier Rule*, p. 71.

[21] This justification of begging is present only in the earlier rule.

[22] Francis of Assisi, *Regula non bullata*, IX. 2, p. 140; *The Earlier Rule*, p. 70.

homines verecundiam et nollent eis dare eleemosynam [...] quia de verecundiis recipient magnum honorem ante tribunal Domini nostri Jesu Christi' (when men create shame in them and refuse to give them alms [...] because of this shame they will receive great honour before the tribunal of our Lord Jesus Christ).[23] Through these exchanges, the friars ritually confronted others and confirmed their social inferiority. This could be difficult for a friar to accept: several sources portray Francis himself as being initially reluctant to beg from a large group of people, hindered by his shame.[24] Eventually, however, Francis always overcame his embarrassment, and he frequently encouraged his followers to do the same. Thus Thomas of Celano reports that Francis 'verecundiam mendicandi inimicam saluti dicebat; verecundiam in mendicando [...] sanctam esse confirmans' (used to say that being ashamed of begging was an enemy of salvation, asserting that shame while begging [...] was holy).[25] This sentence, while seemingly paradoxical, summarizes well the Franciscan conception of begging. As the very act of begging humbled the beggar, being ashamed to beg showed a reluctance to humble oneself.

Despite this positive portrayal of begging, even the earliest Franciscan writings show some ambivalence about the practice. While Francis encourages the friars to beg, he also instructs them to work to earn their own support, following the teachings of II Thess. 3. 10, ('Whoever does not wish to work shall not eat') and Ps. 128. 2 ('You shall eat the fruit of your labours; you are blessed and it shall be well for you').[26] The earlier version of his rule repeats twice, both in the section on working and the section on begging, that friars can 'vadant pro eleemosynis sicut alii pauperes' (go for alms like other poor people) only 'cum necesse fuerit' (when it is necessary).[27] Thomas of Celano's *First Life of Saint Francis* (1228/29) further reflects this ambivalence: of the six instances in which Thomas explains how either the needs of Francis were met or the needs of the Franciscans in general ought to be met, in two instances the necessities of life are obtained through begging, in two they are a reward for performed labour, and in two more they appear magically through divine providence.[28]

[23] Francis of Assisi, *Regula non bullata*, IX. 6, p. 140; *The Earlier Rule*, p. 70.

[24] Thomas of Celano, *Vita secunda*, I. 8, p. 138; *The Remembrance*, p. 252.

[25] Thomas of Celano, *Vita secunda*, II. 41, p. 174; *The Remembrance*, p. 295.

[26] Francis of Assisi, *Regula non bullata*, VII. 4–5, pp. 134–36; *The Earlier Rule*, pp. 68–69.

[27] Francis of Assisi, *Regula non bullata*, VII. 8, p. 136; *The Earlier Rule*, p. 69; Francis of Assisi, *Regula non bullata*, IX. 3, p. 140; *The Earlier Rule*, p. 70.

[28] These episodes fall, respectively, in Thomas of Celano, *Vita prima Sancti Francisci*, I. 14

Moreover, both early mendicant and non-mendicant authors carefully considered the ways in which begging was tied to greed. For instance, in the early form of his rule, Francis warns his brothers to take care lest they 'pro nullo turpi lucro terras circueant' (wander throughout the world for filthy gain).[29] While the abuse of begging for profit was a straightforward sign of greed, medieval authors also wrestled with a more subtle question: did the mere act of begging suggest a greed for temporal things? The Franciscans largely combated their anxiety on this subject by emphasizing their refusal to touch money, and indeed, their complete disregard for it. There are thus many stories in which Francis and his followers are offered alms, but refuse them; perhaps the most popular of these is the report of Francis's efforts to convert a Saracen sultan during the Fifth Crusade. Mendicant and non-mendicant authors alike admired the fact that Francis, realizing he could not convert the sultan, spurned the pile of riches the sultan offered him. In Bonaventure's account of the tale, the sultan marvelled that Francis was 'non mundanarum rerum, sed salutis animarum avidus' (greedy not for worldly possessions but the salvation of souls).[30] Efforts to downplay the Franciscans' mendicancy were such that Burchard von Ursberg, who witnessed the beginnings of the order, wrote admiringly in his world chronicle (1229/30) that the friars 'neque pecuniam nec quicquam aliud preter victum accipiebant, etsi quando vestem necessariam quisquam ipsis sponte conferebat; non enim quicquam petebant ab aliquo' (accepted neither money nor anything else besides food, except when someone voluntarily gave them a needed garment; for they would not ask anything from anyone).[31] The fact that a mendicant order could be portrayed positively because it did *not* ask for alms indicates the existence of very real reservations about the friars' begging.

and 16; I. 7 and 15; and I. 14 and 20 (pp. 28 and 33; 15 and 31; and 28 and 42); English translation in *The Life of Saint Francis*, pp. 214 and 220; 195 and 218; and 213 and 229–30. The Franciscans did, of course, consider begging to be an instance of divine providence: God provided for them through the alms of the rich. However, in instances of direct supernatural intervention, the friars do not have to beg from an earthly intermediary. The heaven-sent donor appears magically when needed, bearing food or clothing to provide for the needs of the friars.

[29] Francis of Assisi, *Regula non bullata*, VIII. 12, p. 140; *The Earlier Rule*, p. 70.

[30] Bonaventure, *Legenda maior Sancti Francisci*, IX. 8, p. 601; English translation in *The Major Legend*, p. 603.

[31] Burchard von Ursberg, *Die Chronik des Propstes*, p. 108; an English translation of Burchard's writings on the Franciscans is available in *Francis of Assisi: Early Documents*, I, 593–94 (p. 594).

This ambivalence over begging also appears in the diction of the Franciscan authors. Despite the fact that the Franciscans are now commonly known as one of the 'mendicant' orders, in early texts the friars are far more likely to go for alms, to seek alms, or even to ask for alms (*vadare pro eleemosyna*, *quaerere eleemosynam*, or *petere eleemosynam*) than they are to beg (*mendicare*). In the earliest texts, moreover, the term *mendicare* is usually applied to non-Franciscan beggars. Francis himself, for instance, only ever uses a form of *mendicare* once, to identify to the outcast 'beggars next to the road.'[32] Similarly, in Thomas of Celano's *First Life*, the friars *mendicant* only once; otherwise, the verb refers to secular beggars.[33] This careful word choice had several advantages. First, it shifted attention away from the problematic act of begging and onto the question of charity. While the friars might not have been able to offer a strong justification for their mendicancy, they had the weight of the entire Christian tradition behind them when they argued for the charitable giving of alms. Second, the repeated emphasis on *eleemosyna* underscored the religious quality of the friars' actions, helping to set them apart from other beggars and, hopefully, suspicions about material greed.[34]

In addition to de-emphasizing their mendicancy, Franciscan authors also sought to avoid accusations of greed by writing that a friar was not begging for himself, but for the ill, other members of the poor, or the maintenance of a church. Thus, the *Versified Life of Saint Francis* by Henry of Avranches (*c.* 1232–34) claims that Francis, after he had given away everything of his own, 'audet | ore verecundo propriam confundere frontem | mendicans a divitibus quid donet egenis' (dares | to cover his own face with a shamed expression | begging from the rich what he might give to the needy).[35] As many scholars point out that it is unlikely that the Franciscans actually gained enough from begging to play any real role in poor relief, this trope is particularly striking.[36]

[32] *Corpus des Sources Franciscaines*, v: *Opuscula sancti Francisci, Scripta sanctae Clarae*, ed. by Jean-François Godet and Georges Mailleux, p. 154.

[33] *Corpus des Sources Franciscaines*, I: *Thesaurus Celanensis*, ed. by Georges Mailleux, p. 362.

[34] Augustine Thompson also looks at the different terms used for begging, arguing that *mendicare* was not originally seen as a religious practice, but actually as a degrading activity for clerics. See his 'The Origins of Religious Mendicancy', p. 24.

[35] Henry of Avranches, *Legenda Sancti Francisci versificata*, x. 69–71, p. 471; English translation in *The Versified Life of Saint Francis*, p. 500.

[36] For example, Wolf, *The Poverty of Riches*, pp. 23–25, and Little, 'Religion, the Profit Economy, and Saint Francis', pp. 157–58.

This emphasis on caring for the poor, moreover, points to another weakness in the Franciscan idealization of begging, one which might best be formulated by turning a biblical quotation into a question: is it better to give or to receive? Although the friars advocated mendicancy, they were also instructed to care for the poor and the ill. The hagiographical materials on Saint Francis provide an excellent illustration of this dilemma, as in all of the early documents, the number of stories in which Francis aids the poor greatly outnumbers the ones in which he himself begs. Although hagiographical materials produced in the second half of the thirteenth century contain more stories about Francis's begging, narrowing the gap in numbers, the bias remains the same. A good illustration is Thomas of Celano's *Second Life of Saint Francis* (1246–47). Thomas's second biography of Francis has far more stories about begging than his first, but episodes in which Francis gives to others still outnumber those in which he receives, eleven to eight. Similarly, when distilling Francis's life into short lessons in *The Minor Legend of Saint Francis* (1260–63), Bonaventure removed all references to begging, but not those to charity.[37] Quantitatively, at least, it seems that the Franciscans continued to believe that is better to give than to receive.

The proliferation of stories about Francis's begging is only one indication of a change that took place around the 1240s.[38] At this time, questions about why the Franciscans deserved alms and unease about the connection of begging to greed took on new force as Franciscan authors, responding to internal controversy over adherence to Francis's rule, began considering the topic of begging more frequently and in greater detail. Although the Spiritual Franciscans may not have formed a distinct group within the Franciscan Order until the 1270s, as David Burr argues, many friars before that time were concerned that the order was becoming lax in its observance of poverty.[39] Elias of Cortona, for instance, was deposed as General Minister of the Franciscan Order in 1239 amid general complaints of his corruption and rich living.[40]

[37] Bonaventure, *Legenda minor Sancti Francisci*; English translation in *The Minor Legend*.

[38] More stories in general were added to the hagiography in this period, as Franciscan authors deliberately sought out new stories about their founder, but the change in quantity of stories about begging is nonetheless marked.

[39] Burr, *The Spiritual Franciscans*, pp. 39–40.

[40] Burr, *The Spiritual Franciscans*, p. 15.

Additionally, although the antifraternal movement was not truly launched until the controversy in Paris a decade later, there was some general antimendicant sentiment against which the friars needed to defend themselves. In particular, as the order grew larger, the laity became increasingly reluctant to support the growing number of mendicants. Thus, *The Anonymous of Perugia*, written around 1240/41, first reported people refusing to give Franciscans alms, instead replying, 'Dimisistis res vestras et vultis comedere alienas' (You have renounced your own possessions and now you want to consume those of others).[41] The anonymous author's response to this accusation is weak (he claims that people persecuted and ridiculed the friars because the Franciscan mission was so unusual, which, while likely true, does not actually address the issue), but other authors engage the question of why the mendicants deserved alms more vigorously, seeking to justify their mendicancy both internally and to the laity.

Generally, the Franciscans began to argue that they earned their alms through both physical and spiritual work. Jacques de Vitry, although not a mendicant himself, was an admirer of the movement, and one of the first to elucidate this notion. While a cardinal at the Curia (1228–40), Jacques preached to an assembly of Franciscans, describing the ways in which they could work: by contemplating, preaching, or labouring physically. The friars had long believed that they merited alms because of their imitation of Christ and the apostles, but the role of begging as a method of gathering repayment for this work now became more explicit. Jacques, for example, warned friars who failed to perform any of these activities: 'Illos quidem non dicimus indigentes, qui de manuum labore vivere possent, et mendicant. Hi non paupers, sed raptores judicantur' (We do not call those people poor who are able to live by the work of their hands and yet beg. These people are judged not to be poor, but robbers).[42] Not only would these lazy brothers be condemned in the afterlife, Jacques continued, but they could also rightly have their begging met with demands for their labour.[43] Similarly, Thomas of Celano argues in his *Second Life* that friars who failed in their virtuous emulation of evangelical poverty were no longer due alms.[44] While earlier texts, like Francis's rule, emphasized people's duty to give

[41] *Legenda S. Francisci anonymi Perusini*, chap. 3, ed. by van Ortroy, p. 39; English translation in John of Perugia, *The Beginning or Founding of the Order*, p. 41.

[42] Jacques de Vitry, 'Sermo primus ad Fratres Minores', chap. 2, p. 119; portions of this sermon are translated in *Francis of Assisi: Early Documents*, I, 585–88 (p. 587).

[43] Jacques de Vitry, 'Sermo primus ad Fratres Minores', chap. 2, p. 119.

[44] Thomas of Celano, *Vita secunda*, II. 40, p. 173; *The Remembrance*, p. 294.

alms to the poor, these later writings focused on what the friars had done to earn those alms, and how their spiritual or physical labour permitted them to collect their just recompense through begging.

The Franciscans even began to develop the idea that begging itself was work. In one story, recorded in the *Scripta Leonis* (*c.* 1246–60), Francis casts out a brother who was too ashamed to beg, telling him: 'Vade uiam tuam, frater musca, quoniam uis comedere laborem fratrum tuorum et uis esse otiosus in opere Dei' (Go on your way, brother fly, for you want to consume the labour of your brothers and want to be idle in the work of God).[45] The same text also contends that it is a kind of 'seruilia opera' (servile work) for the friars 'se humiliari et inclinare ad eundum pro helemosinis' (to humble and lower themselves to go for alms).[46] This was a dramatic change. Francis did write in his early rule that the friars 'laborant' to acquire alms, but his repeated demands that the friars perform other kinds of work for their support shows that begging did not, in his mind, fulfil the biblical mandate on labour in and of itself.[47]

A further indication of the rising acceptability of begging is the fact that Franciscan authors writing after the mid-thirteenth century increasingly used the verb *mendicare* to describe their actions, although they continued to prefer various constructions dealing with the seeking of alms. For example, Thomas of Celano's *Second Life* used the verb *mendicare* eight times to refer to the friars and only once for secular beggars, reversing the emphasis of his *First Life*.[48] This linguistic shift is indicative of a larger change in thought. In the earliest stages of the order, the friars were uncomfortable with their mendicancy, and their language therefore focused on their pursuit of alms; but as the friars

[45] *Scripta Leonis*, chap. 2, p. 196; English translation, p. 197. Francis often used the word *musca* (fly) to refer to money or men who did not have what he considered to be a proper disregard for material wealth. See *Scripta Leonis*, p. 23. Brooke's *Scripta Leonis* derives from six fourteenth- and fifteenth-century manuscripts, the earliest and most complete of which is Manuscript 1046 of the Biblioteca comunale Augusta in Perugia, generally dated to 1311. This manuscript has been edited and published under a number of different titles and in a variety of forms, including *Legenda Antiqua*, *I Fiori dei Tre Compagni*, *Legenda Perugina*, and *Compilatio Assisiensis*. Brooke's edition is comprised of the stories from these six manuscripts which she believes, on the basis of meticulous text-critical analysis, to be the original writings of Francis's companions Leo, Rufino, and Angelo. For an updated defence of her method and her attribution of these stories to Francis's companions, see her *The Image of St Francis*, pp. 104–17. I am using Brooke's edition because of her focus on this early material.

[46] *Scripta Leonis*, chap. 2, p. 194; English translation, p. 195.

[47] Francis of Assisi, *Regula non bullata*, IX. 9, p. 140; *The Earlier Rule*, p. 71.

[48] *Corpus des Sources Franciscaines*, I, 362.

worked out a justification for their begging, they shifted the focus back onto the act of begging itself.

Once the friars had carefully thought out the issue of their mendicancy, they were truly able to idealize it, and even to argue that begging was ennobling. This contention appears most often in connection with a story in which Francis visits the cardinal bishop of Ostia, one of the many new stories about begging that appeared in the 1240s. To summarize the story: Francis once visited the bishop, who had invited some of his knightly relations to a meal. Francis, however, who had gone out begging for alms, chose to eat those alms at the feast. Later, the bishop turned to Francis, claiming that Francis had shamed him by going out for alms. Francis replied by praising the ennobling character of begging:

> Nolo uerecundari ire pro helemosinis, ymo uolo habere et tenere secundum Deum pro magna nobilitate et regali dignitate et honore illius summi regis, qui cum sit Dominus omnium, pro nobis fieri uoluit seruus omnium et, cum esset diues et gloriosus in maiestate sua, pauper et despectus uenit in humanitate nostra.
>
> (I do not want to be ashamed to go for alms, on the contrary I want to hold it and keep it before God as a great nobility and a royal dignity and an honour of that greatest king, who, although He is Lord of all, wished for our sake to become the servant of all, and although he might be rich and glorious in his majesty, came to us poor and despised in our humanity.)[49]

Other authors use similar language: Thomas calls it a 'regalem [...] dignitatem et nobilitatem insignem' (royal dignity and an outstanding nobility), while Bonaventure extends the metaphor of royalty, claiming that to abandon alms for a feast would be 'dignitatem regale [...] relinquere pro feudo divitiarum falsarum vobis ad horam concesso' (to relinquish a royal dignity for a fief of false riches granted to you for an hour).[50]

The idea that the friars' mendicancy was simultaneously humiliating and ennobling was the logical conclusion of Franciscan efforts to idealize begging. As described above, the friars believed that begging conveyed spiritual benefits in the next world because it was humbling in this one. As the friars became more comfortable with their own mendicancy, some of that honour began to be reflected in the present world, resulting in a conception of begging as a noble activity.

[49] *Scripta Leonis*, chap. 2, p. 196; English translation p. 197.

[50] Thomas of Celano, *Vita secunda*, II. 43, p. 175; *The Remembrance*, p. 296; Bonaventure, *Legenda maior*, VII. 7, p. 589; *The Major Legend*, p. 582.

But mendicancy was not merely a theoretical question for the Franciscans to resolve. The friars were beggars themselves, and they were thus forced to deal with the practicalities of mendicancy, as well as the ideals.

From the sources, one can construct an image of a begging friar: dressed in a tunic and trousers with a fastening cord and a small cape, a Franciscan's clothing self-consciously displayed his poverty to potential donors, particularly if, as per the rule, it was patched with sackcloth or other bits of cloth.[51] Sometimes the friars begged for alms in public places, like streets and main squares, and other times they went from door to door. Salimbene di Adam's *Chronicle* (1283–88) describes how the friars begged in circuits, bearing a cloth-covered basket for their alms. Each friar would choose a route on which to beg, then leave his basket below and walk up to the houses to seek bread.[52] At each door, Francis instructed the friar to greet the inhabitant: 'May the Lord give you peace.'[53] The petitioner would then request alms, saying, for example, 'Amore Domini Dei facite nobis helemosinas, cuius comparatione nichil est terra uel celum' (Give us alms for the love of the Lord God; in comparison to this earth and heaven are nothing).[54] If the friar was not turned away with insults, he would then bear his bounty back to his basket before continuing on.

But the Franciscans were not the only people seeking alms. First there were the secular (and involuntary) poor, those who were unable to support themselves by working — the crippled, the ill, the elderly, and so forth. In addition, there were a variety of other religious (and pseudo-religious) groups seeking alms. Salimbene complains that after the rise of the mendicants, 'quicumque vult imponit sibi caputium et mendicat et gloriatur se religionem novam fecisse' (whoever wants to may put on a hood and go begging and boast that he has founded a new religious order).[55] Often these pseudo-religious beggars donned the robes of the mendicants, their sandals, their cord, or another

[51] Francis of Assisi, *Regula non bullata*, chap. 2, pp. 124–26; *The Earlier Rule*, pp. 64–65; Wolf, *The Poverty of Riches*, pp. 16–18.

[52] Salimbene di Adam, *Cronica*, p. 46; English translation in *The Chronicle*, p. 20. The English edition does not include the opening section of Salimbene's chronicle, which is based on Sicardo of Cremona's chronicle, although parts are quoted in George G. Coulton's earlier translation, *From St. Francis to Dante*.

[53] Francis of Assisi, *Testamentum*, p. 208, l. 2; English translation in *The Testament*, p. 126; Luke 10. 5; Matt. 10. 12–13.

[54] *Scripta Leonis*, chap. 2, p. 92; English translation, p. 93.

[55] Salimbene di Adam, *Cronica*, p. 22; Coulton, *From Saint Francis to Dante*, p. 275.

piece of their clothing.[56] Conditioned in mendicancy by the friars, Salimbene writes, the people gave generously to these fakers, whose sheer number burdened society.[57] When condemning a new mendicant order, the Order of the Sack, he thus quotes a lady Giulitta de Adelardi, 'In veritate dico vobis, fratres, tot habebamus sacculos et peras ad horrea evacuanda, quia non indigebamus ordine Saccatorum' (In truth, Brothers, I say to you that we had so many sacks and scrips emptying our barns that we had no need of the Order of the Sack).[58] Despite Salimbene's polemical motivation, the sentiment of these words is undoubtedly accurate, and it was with this logic that Gregory X dissolved all new mendicant orders in 1274.

As with any limited resource, the number of beggars led to competition for alms. There is thus an uncomfortable ring of truth to Bonaventure's report that Francis envied and imitated anyone in more dire need than himself, 'tamquam si aemula paupertate concertans' (just as if fighting a rival in poverty).[59] The Franciscans needed to attract alms to themselves and away from other beggars, and, in order to do so, they not only had to distinguish themselves from other beggars, but they also had to teach this difference to the laity. For, as Salimbene claimed:

> Nam tantum relinquunt in testamento rudes seculares, qui non habent scientiam discernendi, uni muliercule in heremitorio commoranti, quantum uni collegio, in quo sunt XXX sacerdotes, qui quasi cotidie pro vivis et mortuis celebrant.[60]
>
> (Rude laymen, who have no knowledge of discernment, leave in their wills as much to one little woman abiding in a hermitage as to a convent in which there are thirty priests, who almost daily celebrate mass for the living and for the dead).

In the end, the Franciscans distinguished themselves by exploiting the same weaknesses that they had discovered in their own idealization of begging: questions of merit and greed.

One method that the friars used to set themselves apart from other beggars was to argue that they had earned the alms they requested while other groups had not. Thus, when attacking the Apostles of Gerard Segarello, Salimbene con-

[56] Salimbene di Adam, *Cronica*, p. 254; *The Chronicle*, p. 248. The *Cum secundum* of Honorius III (1220) limited the wearing of the Franciscan habit to friars alone.

[57] Salimbene di Adam, *Cronica*, p. 254; *The Chronicle*, p. 248.

[58] Salimbene di Adam, *Cronica*, p. 255; *The Chronicle*, p. 249.

[59] Bonaventure, *Legenda maior*, VII. 6, p. 589; *The Major Legend*, p. 581.

[60] Salimbene di Adam, *Cronica*, p. 22; Coulton, *From Saint Francis to Dante*, p. 275.

tended that this group sinned by 'accipiendo helemosinas et non rependendo beneficia' (receiving alms and returning no benefits).[61] Moreover, by accepting these unearned alms, the Apostles 'defraudant illos, quibus de iure helemosine sunt concesse, quia ordinavit Dominus his qui evangelium annuntiant de evangelio vivere' (cheated those to whom alms are conceded by law, because the Lord ordained that they who preach the gospel, should live by the gospel).[62] By 'they who preach the gospel', Salimbene obviously has his own order in mind, for, as noted above, the Franciscans increasingly argued that they had earned their alms through preaching and contemplation. Salimbene's arguments thus both attack the new group and support the begging of his own order.[63]

Moreover, for those seeking a religious reward in exchange for their alms, the Franciscans argued that they, imitating the life of Christ and begging alms in his name, were the most appropriate recipients of charity. Salimbene takes this idea to its extreme when condemning the Pastoureaux:

> Irascebantur ergo Gallici, qui in Francia remanserant, tunc temporis contra Christum, usque adeo ut nomen Christi super omnia nomina benedictum blasphemare presumerent. Nam petentibus illis diebus fratribus Minoribus et Predicatoribus a Gallicis helemosinam pro nomine Christi, stridebant dentibus super illos et illis videntibus, vocato aliquo alio pauper, dabant ei denarios et dicebant: 'Accipe pro nomine Machometti, qui potentior Christo est.'
>
> (At that time, those French who had remained in France became angry with Christ, to such an extent that they dared to blaspheme the name of Christ, blessed above all names. For in those days, when the Friars Minor and Preachers asked the French for alms in the name of Christ, [the French] gnashed their teeth at them and, with them [the friars] watching, called some other poor man, gave him coins and said, 'Take this in the name of Mohammed, who is more powerful than Christ.')[64]

Similarly, Bonaventure writes in *The Major Legend of Saint Francis* (1260–63) that even a Saracen, 'intellecto tandem, quod amore Dei pauperes effecti' (realizing in the end that they [the Franciscans] had become poor out of love of

[61] Salimbene di Adam, *Cronica*, p. 285; *The Chronicle*, p. 284.

[62] Salimbene di Adam, *Cronica*, p. 285; *The Chronicle*, p. 284.

[63] David Foote has recently examined Salimbene's attempts to justify Franciscan mendicancy in detail, arguing that this exchange of pastoral care for alms together with the *imitatio Christi* and the presentation of opportunities for the wealthy to practice chairty, which I discuss above, formed the basis of Salimbene's rationalization of begging. Foote argues for a more positive placement of the involuntary poor in this scheme of mendicacy than I suggest in this essay. See his 'Mendicants and the Italian Communes', pp. 218–27.

[64] Salimbene di Adam, *Cronica*, p. 445; *The Chronicle*, p. 453.

God), was moved to offer the friars support.[65] The message here is not very subtle: if even Muslims gave the Franciscans alms, and if choosing to bestow alms on non-mendicants was the act of a heretic, then good Christians ought to support the friars.

These are, of course, the most extreme examples, and in general the Franciscans found it necessary to actually explain why they merited alms more than other beggars, and not just polemicize. Once again, the major issue in their explanations was greed. The mendicant strategy might best be illustrated with an example that first appeared in *The Anonymous of Perugia*. Two Franciscans visited the city of Florence and begged a woman for shelter for the night. The woman and her husband, both suspicious of the friars, forced them to sleep on the porch without any blankets, so that if they turned out to be thieves, they would be able to steal nothing more than the firewood. The next morning, the woman saw the friars humbly at prayer in the church. A man named Guido was going around, distributing alms to the poor congregated in the churchyard for alms.

> Qui cum accessisset ad fratres et denarium unum cuilibet sicut aliis vellet dare, illi accipere renuerunt. Quibus ille dixit: 'Quare denarios non accipitis sicut ceteri pauperes, cum ita vos videam inopes et egenos?' Respondit ei unus ex eis, Frater Bernardus nomine: 'Verum est utique pauperes sumus, sed paupertas nostra non ita gravis est ut pauperum aliorum, quia per Domini gratiam, et eius consilium adimplendo pauperes facti sumus.'

> (When he approached the brothers and wished to give to each a coin as to the others, they refused to take it. He said to them: 'Why do you not accept coins like the other poor people, when I see you thus, poor and in want?' One of them, Brother Bernard, replied to him: 'Certainly it is true that we are poor, but our poverty is not as burdensome as the poverty of others, for we have become poor by the grace of God and in fulfilment of His counsel.')[66]

Astonished, the woman then approached the two and gladly offered them hospitality, but it was the man who had been distributing coins who took the Franciscans to his home and lodged them for several days. Thus, the friars in this story self-consciously distinguished themselves from the mass of the poor by refusing alms. Ironically, it was their self-proclaimed relative lack of interest in alms that marked them as the worthier recipients of those alms, and they actually received more than any of the other beggars because of their lack of greed.

[65] Bonaventure, *Legenda maior*, IV. 7, p. 574; *The Major Legend*, p. 555.

[66] *Legenda S. Francisci anonymi Perusini*, chap. 5, p. 41; John of Perugia, *The Beginning*, p. 44.

The Franciscan sources thus portray two separate models of begging. In one, the Franciscans beg for spiritual rather than temporal reward. This is why, to return to the story of the Saracen sultan, Francis refused to accept the reward of the sultan he could not convert. He sought to obtain a soul for God, not a mountain of treasure. The other system, the one followed by non-Franciscan beggars, sought material gain. This division is clearly displayed in many Franciscan texts, as secular beggars, seeking money, often appear in contrast to a nearby, benevolent Franciscan.

Conforming to this same mould is the story in which Francis gives a cloak, lent to him by a friend of the order, to an old beggar woman so that she can make a tunic. The old woman took the cloth but found it insufficient and returned to Francis for more. Francis then encouraged his companion, the original owner of the cloak, to give her more fabric.[67] Francis's presence in this story makes several vital points: first, it marks the mendicant as the more worthy recipient of alms by showing that the donor had originally selected Francis as the target of his charity; second, it allows Francis to demonstrate his lack of attachment to material goods and his virtue in giving to another when poor himself; and third, it emphasizes the material needs and desires of the old woman in contrast to those of Francis. Similar are the stories in which Francis gives his cloak to a poor man so that the beggar can exchange it for money, or to a poor peasant, who is angry at the sins committed against him by his temporal lord, on the condition that the peasant forgives his lord.[68]

In each instance, the non-Franciscan beggar receives a material reward, while the friar pursues the spiritual instead. It is important to note that the Franciscans are rarely portrayed in direct competition with other beggars, with both a friar and a secular beggar asking for alms at the same time. Instead, the morally superior Franciscan is either passive or actively giving, facilitating an association of begging with greed. Once again, the relative merits of giving and receiving are invoked to demonstrate Franciscan superiority. Moreover, the connection of the two sides of this divide becomes almost permanent when the Franciscans begin claiming that all the goods they receive as alms are merely 'lent' to them until they find someone in greater need.[69]

On the question of greed, the Franciscans had a further advantage; as the voluntary poor, they could (or at least they claimed they could) get by on fewer

[67] Thomas of Celano, *Vita secunda*, II. 53, p. 182; *The Remembrance*, p. 304.

[68] Thomas of Celano, *Vita secunda*, II. 55 and 56, p. 183; *The Remembrance*, p. 305.

[69] Thomas of Celano, *Vita secunda*, II. 54, p. 182; *The Remembrance*, p. 304.

alms than regular beggars. Since the mendicants chose to be poor, they sought to sustain, not to alleviate, their poverty. Indeed, they claimed that they always took less than was necessary for their survival, so as to leave more for the other poor.[70] Believing that God provided for them through alms, they felt no need to store up goods against future need; in fact, later texts suggested that foresight was actually a form of greed under the 'specie necessitatis' (pretext of necessity).[71] Once again, the friars sought to set themselves apart from other beggars through their comparative lack of greed, encouraging the laity to recognize and reward their spiritual superiority.

As time passed, the character of the non-mendicant beggars portrayed in Franciscan texts degraded further. Take, for instance, the curious case of the brother who is punished by Francis for suspecting a poor man. Until around 1240, the brother was punished for questioning whether the beggar was really a rich man pretending to be poor (a statement which, as Wolf points out, has a certain irony coming from the mouth a member of the voluntary poor).[72] In later texts, like the *Scripta Leonis*, this sentiment suddenly changes, and the brother suggests instead that while the man is poor, 'forsitan in tota prouincia non est uolumptate ditior illo' (perhaps in the whole province there is not anyone more desirous of riches than he is).[73] Francis, of course, still punishes the brother, but the change in sentiment is revealing. In other stories from the same period, the people from whom the Franciscans beg alms increasingly express a worry that their petitioner, an unknown beggar, might be a thief or an idler. The emphasis here is the difference between the relative merits of voluntary and involuntary poverty, a division that has been well studied by scholars. It was not poverty alone that made the poor good but rather their joy in poverty.[74] Those who could not tolerate their poverty with humility were not virtuous; to quote Bonaventure, 'paupertas est caminus [...] consumens illos qui cum impatientia et cupiditate ad acquirenda terrena sunt pauperes' (poverty is a furnace consuming [...] those who are poor, with an unwillingness to endure and a desire to acquire earthly things).[75] Begging, by its very nature, sought a material reward;

[70] *Scripta Leonis*, chap. 111, p. 284; English translation p. 285.

[71] Thomas of Celano, *Vita secunda*, II. 37, p. 171; *The Remembrance*, p. 291.

[72] Wolf, *The Poverty of Riches*, p. 29.

[73] *Scripta Leonis*, chap. 89, p. 240; English translation p. 241.

[74] For a summary of medieval attitudes towards voluntary and involuntary poverty, see Rubin, *Charity and Community*, pp. 54–98.

[75] Bonaventure, 'De S. patre nostro Francisco. Sermo II', pt 2, p. 579; English translation in 'The Morning Sermon on Saint Francis', p. 756.

the question was whether this search for material gain demonstrated a greedy and sinful character. Increasingly, the friars suggested that for non-mendicant beggars this was, indeed, the case.

The early Franciscans did not set out to foster suspicions about begging. In advocating a model of humble, spiritually oriented begging, they were striving to reconcile their practice of mendicancy with their pursuit of evangelical poverty, trying to find a way to adhere to their own deeply held beliefs. However, by presenting their efforts to acquire alms as worthy because of their deliberate choice to follow the example of Christ, their spiritual work at prayer and preaching, and their voluntary poverty, the Franciscans set a high standard of virtue for all beggars. Moreover, because of these efforts at self-justification, when the friars had to compete with other beggars for alms, they had a ready-made method with which to discredit their opponents — attacking the aspects of begging that troubled them in their own practice of mendicancy. Actively encouraging negative attitudes towards their competition, the friars urged the laity to condemn as greedy and sinful those beggars who failed to meet their own stringent spiritual requirements. Despite the Franciscans' original intentions, therefore, their efforts to idealize and practice a model of mendicancy that supported their voluntary poverty actually contributed to the deterioration of attitudes towards the involuntary, begging poor.

Works Cited

Primary Sources

Bonaventure, 'De S. patre nostro Francisco. Sermo II', in *Opera Omnia*, IX (Quaracchi: Typographia Collegii S. Bonaventurae, 1901), pp. 575–82

——, *Legenda maior Sancti Francisci*, in *Analecta Franciscana*, 12 vols (Quaracchi: Typographia Collegii S. Bonaventurae, 1885–1983), X (1926–41), pp. 555–652

——, *Legenda minor Sancti Francisci*, in *Analecta Franciscana*, 12 vols (Quaracchi: Typographia Collegii S. Bonaventurae, 1885–1983), X (1926–41), pp. 653–78

——, *The Major Legend of Saint Francis*, in *Francis of Assisi: Early Documents*, ed. by Regis J. Armstrong, J. A. Wayne Hellmann, and William Short, 3 vols (New York: New York City Press, 1999–2001), II, 525–683

——, *The Minor Legend of Saint Francis*, in *Francis of Assisi: Early Documents*, ed. by Regis J. Armstrong, J. A. Wayne Hellmann, and William Short, 3 vols (New York: New York City Press, 1999–2001), II, 684–717

——, 'The Morning Sermon on Saint Francis: Preached at Paris, October 4, 1267', in *Francis of Assisi: Early Documents*, ed. by Regis J. Armstrong, J. A. Wayne Hellmann, and William Short, 3 vols (New York: New York City Press, 1999–2001), II, 747–58

Buchard von Ursberg, *Die Chronik des Propstes Burchard von Ursberg*, ed. by Oswald Holder-Egger and Bernhard von Simson, Monumenta Germaniae Historica: Scriptores rerum Germanicarum in usum scholarum separatim editi, 16 (Hannover: Hahn, 1916)

Corpus des Sources Franciscaines, ed. by Georges Mailleux, Jean-Francois Godet, and Pierre Beguin, 7 vols (Louvain: Publications du CETEDOC, Universite Catholique de Louvain, 1974–90)

Francis of Assisi: Early Documents, ed. by Regis J. Armstrong, J. A. Wayne Hellmann, and William Short, 3 vols (New York: New York City Press, 1999–2001)

Francis of Assisi, *The Earlier Rule (The Rule without a Papal Seal)*, in *Francis of Assisi: Early Documents*, ed. by Regis J. Armstrong, J. A. Wayne Hellmann, and William Short, 3 vols (New York: New York City Press, 1999–2001), I, 63–86

——, *The Later Rule*, in *Francis of Assisi: Early Documents*, ed. by Regis J. Armstrong, J. A. Wayne Hellmann, and William Short, 3 vols (New York: New York City Press, 1999–2001), I, 99–106

——, 'The Morning Sermon on Saint Francis: Preached at Paris, October 4, 1267', in *Francis of Assisi: Early Documents*, ed. by Regis J. Armstrong, J. A. Wayne Hellmann, and William Short, 3 vols (New York: New York City Press, 1999–2001), II, 747–58

——, *Regula bullata*, in *Écrits*, ed. by Kajetan Esser, trans. by Théophile Desbonnets and others, Sources Chrétiennes, 285 (Paris: Editions du Cerf, 1981), pp. 180–99

——, *Regula non bullata*, in *Écrits*, ed. by Kajetan Esser, trans. by Théophile Desbonnets and others, Sources Chrétiennes, 285 (Paris: Editions du Cerf, 1981), pp. 122–79

——, *The Testament*, in *Francis of Assisi: Early Documents*, ed. by Regis J. Armstrong, J. A. Wayne Hellmann, and William Short, 3 vols (New York: New York City Press, 1999–2001), I, 124–27

——, *Testamentum*, in *Écrits*, ed. by Kajetan Esser, trans. by Théophile Desbonnets and others, Sources Chrétiennes, 285 (Paris: Editions du Cerf, 1981), pp. 124–27

Henry of Avranches, *Legenda Sancti Francisci versificata*, in *Analecta Franciscana*, 12 vols (Quaracchi: Typographia Collegii S. Bonaventurae, 1885–1983), x (1926–41), pp. 405–521

——, *The Versified Life of Saint Francis*, in *Francis of Assisi: Early Documents*, ed. by Regis J. Armstrong, J. A. Wayne Hellmann, and William Short, 3 vols (New York: New York City Press, 1999–2001), i, 421–520

Jacques de Vitry, 'Sermo primus ad Fratres Minores', in 'Jacobi Vitriacensis (1180–1240): Sermones ad Fratres Minores', ed. by Hilarin Felder, *Analecta Ordinis Minorum Capuccinorum*, 19 (1903), pp. 114–22

John of Perugia, *The Beginning or Founding of the Order and the Deeds of those Lesser Brothers who were the First Companions of Blessed Francis in Religion (The Anonymous of Perugia)*, in *Francis of Assisi: Early Documents*, ed. by Regis J. Armstrong, J. A. Wayne Hellmann, and William Short, 3 vols (New York: New York City Press, 1999–2001), ii, 29–58

Legenda S. Francisci anonymi Perusini, in 'La Leggenda latina di S. Francesco secondo l'Anonimo Perugino', ed. by F. van Ortroy, *Miscellanea Francescana*, 9 (1902), 33–48

Salimbene di Adam, *The Chronicle of Salimbene de Adam*, ed. and trans. by Joseph L. Baird, Giuseppe Baglivi, and John R. Kane (Binghamton: Medieval and Renaissance Texts and Studies, 1986)

——, *Cronica fratris Salimbene de Adam: Ordinis minorum*, ed. by Oswaldus Holder-Egger, Monumenta Germaniae Historica: Scriptores, 23 (Hannover: Hahn, 1905–13)

——, *From St. Francis to Dante: A Translation from the Chronicle of the Franciscan Salimbene (1221–1288)*, ed. by George G. Coulton (London: Nutt, 1906)

Scripta Leonis, Rufini et Angeli: Sociorum S. Francisci, ed. and trans. by Rosalind B. Brooke (Oxford: Clarendon Press, 1970)

Thomas of Celano, *The Life of Saint Francis*, in *Francis of Assisi: Early Documents*, ed. by Regis J. Armstrong, J. A. Wayne Hellmann, and William Short, 3 vols (New York: New York City Press, 1999–2001), i, 169–308

——, *The Remembrance of the Desire of a Soul (The Second Life of Saint Francis)*, in *Francis of Assisi: Early Documents*, ed. by Regis J. Armstrong, J. A. Wayne Hellmann, and William Short, 3 vols (New York: New York City Press, 1999–2001), ii, pp. 231–393

——, *Vita prima Sancti Francisci*, in *Analecta Franciscana*, 12 vols (Quaracchi: Typographia Collegii S. Bonaventurae, 1885–1983), x (1926–41), pp. 1–117

——, *Vita secunda Sancti Francisci*, in *Analecta Franciscana*, 12 vols (Quaracchi: Typographia Collegii S. Bonaventurae, 1885–1983), x (1926–41), pp. 127–268

Secondary Studies

Brooke, Rosalind B., *The Image of St Francis: Responses to Sainthood in the Thirteenth Century* (New York: Cambridge University Press, 2006)

Burr, David, *The Spiritual Franciscans: From Protest to Persecution in the Century after Saint Francis* (University Park: Pennsylvania State University Press, 2001)

Foote, David, 'Mendicants and the Italian Communes in Salimbene's *Cronaca*', in *The Origin, Development and Refinement of Medieval Religious Mendicancies*, ed. by Donald S. Prudlo (Leiden: Brill, 2011), pp. 197–238

Geremek, Bronislaw, *Poverty: A History*, trans. By Agnieszka Kolakowska (Oxford: Blackwell, 1994)

Hanska, Jussi, *'And the Rich Man Also Died; and He Was Buried in Hell': The Social Ethos in Mendicant Sermons* (Helsinki: Suomen Historiallinen Seura, 1997)

Henderson, John, *Piety and Charity in Late Medieval Florence* (Oxford: Clarendon Press, 1994)

Johnson, Kelly S., 'The Irony of Voluntary Begging', in *The Fear of Beggars: Stewardship and Poverty in Christian Ethics* (Grand Rapids: Eerdmans, 2007), pp. 51–69

Lesnick, Daniel, *Preaching in Medieval Florence: The Social World of Franciscan and Dominican Spirituality* (Athens: University of Georgia Press, 1989)

Lis, Catharina, and Hugo Soly, *Poverty and Capitalism in Pre-Industrial Europe* (Atlantic Highlands: Humanities Press, 1979)

Little, Lester K., 'Religion, the Profit Economy, and Saint Francis', in *Through the Eye of a Needle: Judeo-Christian Roots of Social Welfare*, ed. by Emily Albu Hanawalt and Carter Lindberg (Kirksville: Thomas Jefferson University Press, 1994), pp. 147–63

——, *Religious Poverty and the Profit Economy in Medieval Europe* (Ithaca: Cornell University Press, 1983)

Mollat, Michel, *Les pauvres au Moyen Âge: étude sociale* (Paris: Hachette, 1978)

Prudlo, Donald S., ed., *The Origin, Development, and Refinement of Medieval Religious Mendicancies* (Leiden: Brill, 2011)

Rubin, Miri, *Charity and Community in Medieval Cambridge*, Cambridge Studies in Medieval Life and Thought, 4th ser., 4 (Cambridge: Cambridge University Press, 1987)

Thompson, Augustine, 'The Origins of Religious Mendicancy in Medieval Europe', in *The Origin, Development, and Refinement of Medieval Religious Mendicancies*, ed. by Donald S. Prudlo (Leiden: Brill, 2011), pp. 3–30

Wolf, Kenneth Baxter, *The Poverty of Riches: St. Francis of Assisi Reconsidered* (Oxford: Oxford University Press, 2003)

Temptation and the Medieval Italian Inquisition

Jill Moore

Introduction

In his *Practica inquisitionis heretice pravitatis*, written around 1323, Bernard Gui, the long-standing Dominican inquisitor of Toulouse, set out criteria for the conduct of the ideal inquisitor. As well as zeal for the salvation of souls, energy, persistence, and physical courage, Gui, as paraphrased by Henry Charles Lea, urged that an inquisitor should avoid the appearance of harshness or cupidity:

> Like a just judge, let him so bear himself in passing sentence of corporal punishment that his face may show compassion [...] and thus will he avoid the appearance of indignation and wrath. [...] In imposing pecuniary penalties, let his face preserve the severity of justice as though he were compelled by necessity and not allured by cupidity. Let truth and mercy [...] shine forth from his countenance, that his decisions may be free from all suspicion of covetousness or cruelty.[1]

These admonitions were required because, as Gui well knew, inquisitors from both the Dominican and Franciscan orders faced peculiar temptations and moral hazards in discharging their duties. The two orders divided responsibility

[1] Lea, *The Inquisition of the Middle Ages*, pp. 119–20. The passage paraphrased by Lea is found in Gui, *Practica inquisitionis heretice pravitatis*, ed. by Douais, pt IV, 232–33. A discussion of dating is in Gui, *Manuel de l'inquisiteur*, ed. and trans. by Mollat, pp. xi–xv.

Jill Moore (jill.moore@waitrose.com) received her PhD from Birkbeck, University of London, and is working on a book on the social history and organization of the medieval Italian inquisition.

Approaches to Poverty in Medieval Europe: Complexities, Contradictions, Transformations, c. 1100–1500, ed. by Sharon Farmer, IMR 22 (Turnhout: Brepols, 2016) pp. 117–144
BREPOLS PUBLISHERS 10.1484/M.IMR-EB.5.105462

for the inquisition in Italy from 1254 onwards, and it is the tensions of their paradoxical position which will be explored in this paper.

The constitution of both orders demanded personal poverty, and throughout the thirteenth and early fourteenth centuries, general and provincial chapters emphasized the need to avoid the possession or handling of money. Even senior office-holders, such as conventual priors, were enjoined not to hold money personally. As friars, inquisitors were required to obey their superiors and were subject to the order's rules in the same way as others.[2]

As inquisitors, on the other hand, they were personally responsible for running a sizeable and self-financing business, with many staff and an often huge cash flow.[3] Income was generated not only by confiscating heretics' property but also through fines imposed for a variety of shortcomings and thought-crimes and by charging for items such as the yellow crosses worn by penitents. Papal and conciliar directives provided a framework of guidance, but inquisitors had wide discretion. Although their appointment and removal was largely delegated to ministers and priors-provincial, superiors in the order were forbidden to intervene in inquisition business.[4]

The free disposition of large sums of money — in effect, a personal expense account — offered obvious temptations. Inquisitors who chose to push the boundaries could achieve a more comfortable lifestyle than their brothers, indulging refined passions for books, illuminations, jewelled chalices, and fine vestments. With money and office came extensive powers of patronage. Rewarding a helpful brother with a new tunic or appointing a judge to a paid advisory panel were actions which on one level simply recognized service or pro-

[2] *Acta capitulorum generalium Ordinis Praedicatorum*, ed. by Reichert (hereafter *Acta capitulorum generalium*), I, 58 (1251 — deposit holders required); p. 76 (1255 — priors not to carry money while travelling); *Acta capitulorum provincialium Provinciae Romanae*, ed. by Kaeppeli and Dondaine (hereafter *Acta [...] Provinciae Romanae*), p. 36 (1269 — strict observance of constitution against carrying money); p. 37 (1270 — priors must not hold convent's money personally). There are many further examples.

[3] Murray, 'The Medieval Inquisition', p. 170, calculates that the accounted revenues of Mino da San Quirico, inquisitor of Florence in 1332–34, were worth over £1.5 million, or some £3.6 million when revalued to 2012 terms.

[4] Alexander IV's bull, *Catholicae fidei negotium*, issued on 1260 December 11 to inquisitors of both orders throughout Italy (a rare event), confirmed their independence from their superiors in matters of inquisition. A copy preserved in Viterbo indicates the involvement of Cardinal Gian Gaetano Orsini, the future inquisitor-general. See *Regesta pontificium Romanorum*, ed. by Potthast, II, no. 17991; Savignoni, 'L'archivio storico del comune di Viterbo', p. 295, doc. 86.

gressed business. But doing so conferred substantial financial benefits and thus bought favour for the inquisitor's own future. More discreditably, inquisitors could manipulate the price when confiscated property was sold, and so benefit family, friends, and political allies. In several well-known scandals exposed by papal enquiries, inquisitors kept receipts off the books or magnified expenses, thus depriving the Church and its secular partners of their proper revenues.[5]

As religious men and the holders of a powerful office, inquisitors also faced moral and spiritual temptations. They were not immune from carnal urges, and the medieval man in the street certainly thought that some inquisitors abused their position in order to satisfy lust.[6] Other errors were more insidious. The zeal and single-mindedness which made an inquisitor effective could look uncommonly like pride and arrogance to the layman. Complaints of inquisitorial high-handedness are frequent, and some inquisitors certainly took things to extremes.[7] Inquisitors were not meant to participate personally in torture,

[5] The profits from heresy confiscations were, in principle, divided equally between the inquisition, the relevant civic authority, and the wider church; see below. But inquisitors could be creative in minimizing the sums going to others. In 1308, the testimony of Fra Ainardo da Ceneda to a papal inquiry listed seventeen types of fraud, peculation, and diversion of funds to inquisitors' relatives in the Veneto. 'Frater Julianus [de Padua] [...],' he said, 'habebat nepotes et neptes plurimos, quos omnes [....] ditavit, cum antea essent pauperes' (Fra Julianus de Padua had many nephews and nieces, all of whom he made rich, though they had previously been poor). D'Alatri, 'Inquisitori veneti', pp. 175–78. Antonio Rigon's introductory essay to *Il 'Liber Contractuum'*, ed. by Bonato, pp. i–xxxvi, also usefully summarizes the different varieties of financial misbehaviour engaged in by the Franciscan inquisitors of the Veneto.

[6] Friedlander, *The Hammer of the Inquisition*, pp. 88–90 (accusations of immorality, sexual perversion, and rape against the inquisitor of Toulouse, *c.* 1300). In Italy, the Florentine inquisitor Mino da San Quirico demanded that a monk convicted of various offences procure his sister for him as the price of remitting a penalty. Still worse, the assignation took place in a nunnery. See Archivio Secreto Vaticano (hereafter ASVat), *Collectoria* 251, fols 85v–86r. Accusations against Guido da Vicenza were made during the 1299 Bologna riot against his condemnation of two Cathars: *Acta S. Officii Bononie ab anno 1291 usque ad annum 1310*, ed. by Paolini and Orioli (hereafter *ASOB*), I, doc. 139. Boniface VIII's letter of 1303 removing the Friars Minor from the office of inquisition in Padua and Vicenza also seems to suggest a sexual component in harassment and blackmail of women and girls there: see Bronzino, 'Documenti riguardanti gli eretici', p. 302.

[7] In 1263, the Franciscan Florasio da Vicenza excommunicated the Doge and Senate of Venice as fautors of heresy, forcing a grovelling withdrawal by Urban IV, who needed the city's support. See da Milano, 'L'Istituzione dell'Inquisizione Monastico-Papale a Venezia', pp. 190–94. The endorsement on the Venetian inquisition's own copy of the bull shows that Florasio was totally insensitive to the situation he had created: Archivio di Stato di Venezia (hereafter ASV), *Corporazioni religiose soppresse*, S. Maria Gloriosa dei Frari, 91/III perg. 28).

though some were accused of doing so.[8] The process of interrogation and the imposition of appropriate penalties could nonetheless desensitize even the otherwise compassionate. Hence, the requirement for a *socius* able to shrive an inquisitor who overstepped the mark.[9]

The close association between heresy and political disagreement was another potential quagmire for inquisitors in the thirteenth and fourteenth centuries. Papal use of the inquisition for political ends is well attested, as, for instance, during Boniface VIII's conflict with the Colonna.[10] But inquisitors also found themselves pressured to use their powers in many other civic and ecclesiastical power struggles. This is an exceptionally murky area, and it is often hard to disentangle where political and theological issues begin and end. Some inquisitors undoubtedly did use their office to shape local politics to their own liking, pursuing personal agendas even to the point of attracting papal censure. Others colluded with civic authorities.[11]

Finally, it must be noted that the financial structure of the *Officium inquisitionis* could itself influence behaviour. In most of Italy, the running costs of the inquisition were defrayed directly from the proceeds of confiscations and penalties, with the surplus shared both with the local civil authority and the wider church. There was thus a powerful incentive to pursue most energetically the suspects who would generate most income, regardless of the seriousness of their offence.

[8] Friedlander, *The Hammer of the Inquisition*, p. 89 (participation in torture).

[9] For the theological justification of inquisition punishments, see Ames, *Righteous Persecution*, especially chap. 5. De la Roncière, 'L'Inquisition a-t-elle été perçue', examines public acceptance of, and acquiescence in, inquisition activity.

[10] Boniface's conflict with the Roman Colonna cardinals originated in his use of church funds to buy land for his own Caetani family in Colonna territory. He declared them heretics for disobedience: they accused him of not being a true pope, because of his succession following Celestine V's abdication. The feud spiralled into intellectual warfare over the nature of papal power, until eventually the Colonna returned to obedience. From a wide bibliography, see Boase, *Boniface VIII*, pp. 159–85; Maier, 'Due documenti'. For the use of the inquisition, see *ASOB*, I, docs 92, 106–09, 111, and Paolini, *L'eresia a Bologna*, pp. 149–55 (inquisition preaching against Colonna when declared heretics and pursuit of their property).

[11] Biscaro, 'Dante a Ravenna', pp. 85–90, gives examples of the use of inquisitorial powers in Bologna and Ferrara to pursue private grudges against the Pepoli and Este, directly contrary to papal wishes. Lomastro Tognato, *L'eresia a Vicenza*, pp. 27–31, 48–56, discusses the relationship between political supporters of the da Romano dynasty and subsequent heresy convictions. Rigon, in *Il 'Liber Contractuum'*, ed. by Bonato, pp. xxiv–xxv and xxviii, illustrates the tangled web of connexions between the inquisitors of the Veneto and local politics around the turn of the fourteenth century.

Questions

Surrounded as they were by the temptations of power and the competing demands of their different roles, how did inquisitors actually respond? Did they succeed in reconciling their vows of poverty and humility as friars with the financial and political responsibilities of inquisitorial office, or was the task inherently impossible to fulfil? How did inquisitors manage the pressure from several sources to generate profits? And finally, given the wide discretion afforded to them, was there consensus about behaviour which crossed the line?

These questions are examined here with respect to inquisitors in central and northern Italy, between around 1270 and around 1330. The time span is dictated primarily by the source material, but also covers three important developments. During this period, the inquisition — founded only in the 1230s — matured into an organization with a fairly stable structure and representation across most of Italy. The church-state conflicts of the Duecento fragmented into increasingly complex power relationships between varied political and ecclesiastical actors, pulling people and organizations in different directions. Finally, the Cathar heresy, the driving motive for the creation of the inquisition, was effectively eliminated in Italy from around 1300. To maintain a functioning organization, the inquisition required new sources of error and revenue.

The greatest Italian writers of the Trecento maintained that inquisitors, in Florence at least, had comprehensively lost the battle with temptation. Boccaccio's *The Inquisitor's Tale* and a popular poem of the 1290s attributed to Dante, *Il Fiore*, present a picture of inquisitors who were oppressive, high-handed, greedy, hypocritical, cruel, and corrupt. This hostile view drove lasting popular stereotypes and helped to shape subsequent opinion among historians. Controversial condemnations, such as the execution of the astrologer Cecco d'Ascoli in 1327, resonated across centuries.[12]

Was Florence simply unlucky that poor inquisitors coincided with great writers of anticlerical sympathies? The skimpy references to the inquisition from other parts of Italy mean we cannot assume the Tuscan experience was replicated elsewhere, nor tar all Florentine inquisitors with the same brush. Since the patchy source material for Italy derives mainly from complaints and

[12] For Boccaccio and *Il Fiore*, see Smarr, 'The Tale of the Inquisitor'; Biscaro, 'Inquisitori ed eretici a Firenze' (1933), pp. 197–99; and Murray, 'The Medieval Inquisition', p. 172. For Cecco d'Ascoli, see Thorndike, *A History of Magic and Experimental Science*, II, 948–68. Tosti, 'Descriptio Codicum Franciscanorum Bibliothecae Riccardianae Florentinae', lists renditions and recopyings of Cecco's sentence in *volgare* as late as the eighteenth century.

papal enquiries into inquisitors who overstepped the mark, zealous, honest — or even typical — inquisitors are underrepresented.

One way of testing how far inquisitors managed to reconcile their competing obligations is to examine their surviving financial accounts.[13] As Scott Fitzgerald remarked, accounts aren't sexy. They can certainly be falsified, and they provide little clue, for example, about an inquisitor's devotional life or motivations. But (with allowance for manipulation) they permit a detailed view of actual daily behaviour and variations in practice, both between successive inquisitors in the same territory and contemporaries in different parts of Italy.[14]

The accounts suggest that inquisitors can be divided into three groups. One group remained true to their vows of poverty and largely managed to reconcile their inquisitorial duties with their status as humble friars. The second succumbed to temptation, and sometimes to outright criminality. The third group, probably the largest, was not actually fraudulent but lost perspective on the appropriate spending and lifestyle for a friar sworn to poverty. The reasons why this happened bear detailed examination, suggesting in some cases exculpatory factors.

Context, Finance, and Historiography

The study of the medieval inquisition in Italy is still a work in progress. In the century following Henry Charles Lea's seminal study of 1887–88, little attention was paid to the inquisition's operation and financing except in the pioneering work of the anticlerical Gerolamo Biscaro in the 1920s and, after 1950, studies by Mariano d'Alatri. It is only very recently that scholars have begun energetically to fill what Grado Merlo once described as a 'black hole' in analysis.[15]

[13] ASVat, *Collectoria* 133 has the accounts of a sequence of Dominican inquisitors in the Lombard province, also digested by Biscaro, 'Inquisitori ed eretici Lombardi', pp. 501–57, though with some misreadings. ASVat, *Collectoria* 159A, 249, 250, 251, 404, and 421A relate mainly to Franciscan inquisitors in Tuscany and the Veneto.

[14] This paper does not address the inquisition in Naples and Sicily, which under the Angevins was organized along French lines and received subsidy from the king. A useful, if older, study is Amabile, *Il Santo Officio della Inquisizione in Napoli*.

[15] See Lea, *A History of the Inquisition of the Middle Ages*; the chapters relating to organization were separately published in 1963 with an essay by Walter Ullmann and have their own value. Citations are to the 1963 edition. For the dearth of twentieth-century studies, see Merlo, 'Predicatori e Inquisitori'. In 'Frati Minori e inquisizione', Merlo calls Italian inquisition studies in the second half of the twentieth century 'un tema lasciato ai margini, ignorato' (a subject left on the sidelines, unconsidered) (p. 10). Gerolamo Biscaro's path-breaking studies

Vigorous academic centres in Bologna and Milan are now putting flesh on the bare bones of our knowledge of the Dominican inquisitors of the huge Lombard province.[16] For the Franciscan inquisition in central Italy, Mariano d'Alatri's important if somewhat dated study and the much older research of Luigi Fumi are now refreshed by Caterina Bruschi's work for Florence and that of several scholars for Orvieto, Umbria, the Marche, and the Patrimony of St Peter. There remains no modern overarching review of Franciscan activity in the Veneto/March of Treviso in the Duecento, and virtually nothing for the region during the Trecento.[17]

A prominent strand of inquisition scholarship has been the study of formal procedure, as expounded in formularies and how-to manuals.[18] The day-to-day organization of the inquisition's work is much less well covered, as is the often tense relationship with bishops and with the civil authorities on whom inquisitors relied heavily. The quality of these interactions, in a changeable political climate, was central to an inquisitor's ability to undertake his work effectively.[19]

were 'Inquisitori ed eretici lombardi'; 'Inquisitori ed eretici a Firenze', describing the activities of four Florentine inquisitors (subsequent references to the parts by year of publication); and 'Eretici ed inquisitori nella Marca Trevisana'. Del Col, *L'Inquisizione in Italia*, offers a useful general summary of work to date. Though focused on France, Given, *Inquisition and Medieval Society*, is also very valuable in illuminating inquisition methods.

[16] Major studies focusing on the Dominicans and the Lombard province include: Paolini, *L'eresia a Bologna*; Benedetti, *Inquisitori lombardi*; Prudlo, *The Martyred Inquisitor*; and, for a somewhat later period, Merlo, *Eretici e inquisitori nella società piemontese*. Paolini has published prolifically on aspects of inquisition procedure and organization; particularly helpful is 'Le finanze dell'Inquisizione'. See also Parmeggiani, 'L'inquisitore Florio da Vicenza'.

[17] For the Franciscans, see d'Alatri, *L'Inquisizione francescana*, is a reprint with additional material (notably the *Liber Inquisitionis* of Orvieto) of his 1950 *tesi di laurea*, though without updating his original conclusions. Bruschi, 'Inquisizione francescana in Toscana', offers a handy update and bibliography (and the volume in which it appears, *Frati minori e inquisizione*, generally is important). For the Veneto/March of Treviso, we have Biscaro, 'Eretici ed inquisitori nella Marca Trevisana'. Other pieces of the Veneto jigsaw are da Milano, 'L'Istituzione dell'Inquisizione Monastico-Papale a Venezia' and 'Gli antecedenti inediti di un noto episodio dell'Inquisizione francescana'; d'Alatri, 'Inquisitori veneti' and 'Due inchieste papali sugli inquisitori veneti'; *Il 'Liber Contractuum'*, ed. by Bonato; Lomastro Tognato, *L'eresia a Vicenza*; and Marangon, *Il pensiero ereticale*. For Umbria and the Romagna, see Fumi, 'Eretici e ribelli nell'Umbria'; Parmeggiani, 'Inquisizione e frati minori'; and Fussenegger, 'De manipulo documentorum ad usum inquisitoris haereticae pravitatis'.

[18] For a full bibliography, see Sackville, *Heresy and Heretics*. Parmeggiani, *I consilia procedurali per l'Inquisizione Medievale*, opens up the previously neglected world of the legal *consilia* through which the inquisition expanded powers.

[19] Inquisitors' relations with local bishops were subject to many changes of direction in the

Under papal and conciliar directives, it fell to the inquisitor to identify and interrogate suspects and to decide on guilt and punishment, taking advice from a panel of *sapientes* and, if he was wise, the local bishop. But there were many tasks which were meant to be carried out by the civil, not ecclesiastical, authorities. In principle, communes supplied prison facilities, carried out executions, provided a notary and also lay officials for the physical capture of the heretic. A key role of the civil authorities (like that which they performed for other criminals and *banniti*) was their valuation and disposal of heretics' confiscated property, involving either its sale or the demolition of houses tainted by 'heretical depravity'.

The costs of all parties were defrayed from the sale of forfeited goods. The exact details mutated over time, but initially the inquisition took a third of the proceeds, the communes another third, and the remainder went (usually via the inquisitors) to the church generally — at first to the bishops, but by the late thirteenth century to the papal collectors. Thus the inquisition effectively collected two-thirds of seizures. In the 1260s and 70s, there is some indication that the system worked as intended. By around 1300, however, as the inquisition became a solidly established organization, to whose presence even reluctant Venice and Genoa acquiesced, the divisions of responsibilities and the financing scheme were becoming blurred or breaking down in a number of ways.[20]

Inquisitors were now increasingly taking over functions which were properly a civic responsibility. The inquisitor, rather than the *podestà*, began to seize and sell heretics' property. In 1299, the Dominican inquisitor of Bologna rented out a heretic's house only two days after his execution, selling it to the tenant two weeks later without the nuisance of an auction. (He later had to obtain retrospective permission for the sale from the bishop, on the spurious grounds of the *podestà*'s delays.)[21] By 1286, the Franciscan inquisitor of Siena was also evi-

later thirteenth century: see Lea, *Inquisition*, pp. 86–87. Regardless of papal pronouncements, there were notable turf wars and personality clashes, for example between Alberto Ricco, bishop of Treviso, and the inquisitors Rufino and Bartolommeo, who he refused to let preach in his diocese. The dispute had to be resolved by the pope personally in 1263. See Treviso, Biblioteca Comunale (hereafter BCT), MS 957, II, fol. 99 (1263, 17 June)); Serena, 'Fra gli eretici trevigiani', p. 171.

[20] See Paolini, 'Le finanze dell'Inquisizione' for the evolution of the division of spoils. Lea, 'Confiscation for Heresy in the Middle Ages', discusses the principles.

[21] Civic records from Treviso in 1269 demonstrate the intended process. Valuers conducted sales on behalf of the *podestà* and transactions were supervised by a group of twelve to fifteen officials 'deputati [...] super officio heretice pravitatis pro Comuni Tarvisii'. A third of the valuation was handed to the inquisitor, and another to the church. See BCT, MS 957, II,

dently handling confiscations, because the city's accounts record receipts from him.[22] Some inquisitors became *rentiers*, instead of selling forfeited property. In Cremona and Brescia, the inquisitor Marchesio da Brescia collected rents from several properties between 1315 and 1318.[23] Whilst the cost of executions and prisons continued to be met ultimately from the commune's notional third share, it was now frequently the inquisitor who organized and initially paid for both these services, billing the civic authorities as appropriate.[24]

This creeping change in responsibilities between civil and religious authorities was accompanied by — or perhaps precipitated by — alterations in the inquisition's financial arrangements. Initially, it seems to have been envisaged that inquisition running costs would be contained within its third share of confiscation proceeds. By the late thirteenth century, standing costs were rising, as inquisitors acquired dedicated buildings, built their own prisons, and expanded their *familia*. The inquisition's costs now ate into the Church's third (hence the interest of the papacy) and encroached on the civic share. The more the inquisition spent, the less was available for other partners.[25]

This was not a business model that encouraged frugality. Inquisitors had no incentive to keep costs down, other than their own sense of propriety and the practical problems encountered if spending outran income. It is easy to see how conflict could arise between their obligations of poverty and the temptations of money in the hand.[26]

docs 62 (fols 125–27) and 63 (fols 127–29). For the 1299 sale in Bologna, see *ASOB*, I, docs 133, 332; II, doc. 805. The seeking of retroactive permission may indicate that disposals by the Bolognese inquisitor were not yet the norm.

[22] For Siena, see Severino, 'Note sull'eresia a Siena', and Mengozzi, 'Documenti Danteschi', p. 126. In Florence, by the early 1320s, both inquisitor and commune seem equally engaged in the disposal process: see ASVat, *Collectoria* 250, fols 71^{r}–72^{v} for a list of payments due to the commune from forfeits collected by the inquisitor.

[23] For properties kept for rent by various inquisitors, see ASVat, *Collectoria* 133, fol. 188^{v} (rental summary for Brescia for years 1315–18); *Collectoria* 249, fols 40^{r}, 41^{v} (Florence, 1319–20); *Collectoria* 250, fols 6^{r}, 8^{v}, 10^{v} (Florence, 1322–24).

[24] For inquisition maintenance of prisons and billing the commune in Florence, see ASVat, *Collectoria* 250, fols 74^{r}–81^{v}. For inquisitors arranging executions, see *Collectoria* 133, fol. 70^{v} (Thomas de Garzano, inquisitor of Genoa, May 1298); fol. 148^{r} (Giovanni dei Pizigotti, Ferrara, July 1313). At a similar period (1293) the commune of Siena was paying the costs of two burnings: Mengozzi, 'Documenti Danteschi', pp. 128–29.

[25] Paolini, 'Le finanze dell'Inquisizione', pp. 478–79, discusses the rise in costs and some egregious cases where the commune's share was squeezed out.

[26] Indeed, Paolini speculates ('Le finanze dell'Inquisizione', p. 477) that the inflation of expenses claims by inquisitors was a device 'per mantenere un certo spazio di autonomia

Obligations as Friars versus the Demands of the Negotium fidei

The constitutions of the Dominican and Franciscan orders were hard enough for ordinary members of the orders to observe. The basic requirement of personal poverty and an austere lifestyle involved a simple vegetarian and fish diet, with meat reserved only for the sick in the convent infirmary. Prescribed clothing was to be simple and humble and made of low-grade cloth. The wearing of leather or furs was forbidden, which would have been quite a hardship in the mountainous regions of Italy in winter. Friars were obliged to walk everywhere, rather than ride or take carriages. They were forbidden to own or carry money or saleable items such as books, to incur debts, or to make or take loans. Any kind of contact with women was to be avoided. They were warned, too, against involvement in secular affairs and politics.[27]

The repeated admonitions issued by Dominican general and provincial chapters throughout the thirteenth century bear witness to the difficulty of maintaining the rules on dress, diet, and money, as well as the importance still attached to them as the order grew. Some poor convents could not provide basic garments for their members. Others were so enriched by donations and bequests that it was necessary to prohibit the wearing of gold crosses or elaborate vestments. Practical problems of observance for individual brothers arose particularly when (like inquisitors) they took on roles outside the order itself.

finanziaria' (to maintain a degree of financial autonomy) in the face of tougher papal accounting demands in the early fourteenth century.

[27] *Acta capitulorum generalium*, I, 11–12 (1239 — simple clothes; no gold, silver, or precious stones in the convent; no riding or using carriages ('nec equitent nec quadrigent'); p. 49 (1250 — no furs or fur blankets); p. 117 (1263 — no sculptures, paintings and decorative pavements in Dominican premises lest they should tarnish poverty ('qui paupertatem nostram deforment'); p. 272 (1272 — reminder not to carry money); pp. 169–70 (1273 — reminder to obey diligently the rules on not riding and not eating meat). *Acta [...] Provinciae Romanae*, pp. 12–13 (1252 — reminder not to ride or carry money; brothers not to eat meat or be given licence to do so even when dining with senior churchmen outside the convent); pp. 17–18 (1254 — punishment for anyone using transport (*vectura*) to come to the chapter: those unable to attend without transport must stay behind); p. 26 (1262 — lending money or contracting debt prohibited); p. 35 (1269 — fur mantles again forbidden except in infirmary); p. 53 (1280 — comprehensive prohibitions on use of money or taking loans without special licence); p. 83 (1288 — further prohibition on riding; no exemptions except for urgent necessity; all concessions to be scrutinized by next chapter); p. 31 (1265 — involvement in civic affairs banned). The Franciscans engaged in similar debates: see Delorme, 'Explanationes constitutionem generalium Narbonensium', p. 523, for tortured debate on the relative sinfulness of riding a horse versus being in a carriage.

Difficulties were sometimes recognized by constitutional concessions, such as that granted by the 1289 provincial chapter at Viterbo to exempt brothers who were papal notaries and officials from the rules about diet and the obligation to eat only within the convent.[28]

With their need to travel widely away from the convent, to pay, feed, and manage an often sizeable staff, to maintain their own premises and to mix with a wide range of civic officials and secular clerics, inquisitors clearly had challenges in observing these rules. However, they were not collectively exempted from their obligations. The rare specific exclusions in surviving Dominican and Franciscan material confirm that all other constitutions were meant to apply to inquisitors in the same way as to others.[29]

A Dominican prohibition in 1267 that no brother should personally capture a heretic is couched generally but is obviously aimed at inquisitors. It is immediately followed by reinforcement of the rules on carrying money, which may or may not be pointed. In 1268, the general chapter accepted that Dominican inquisitors might need to ride where there was danger or rough terrain, but the provision plainly expects compliance where possible. It does not give carte blanche. Forty years later, recognition that he was normally expected to walk is implied in the way the inquisitor of western Piedmont, Francesco da Pocapaglia, justifies his 1308 accounts:

> Ego frater Franciscus predictus habui necesse emere equos sine quibus inquisitio non potest fieri convenienter in partibus Pedemontis propter loca multum distantia et periculosa in quibus habitant heretici et Valdenses.
>
> (I, Brother Francesco, was obliged to buy horses, without which I would not have been able to carry out inquisition effectively in Piedmont, because the places where the heretics and Waldensians live are very distant and dangerous.)[30]

[28] *Acta capitulorum generalium*, I, 170 (1273 — gold or jewelled crosses or vestments not to be worn); *Acta [...] Provinciae Romanae*, p. 13 (1252 — convent of Arezzo to be supplied with tunics by three other houses); p. 91 (1289 — shortages of tunics and undergarments; papal notaries, vice-chancellor, and chamberlain exempted from requirement to eat in the convent).

[29] Lea, *The Inquisition of the Middle Ages*, pp. 94–99, makes much of inquisitors' freedom from obligations to their orders, but accepts their subjection 'as friars'. See also d'Alatri, *Inquisizione francescana*, pp. 21–24.

[30] 'Acta capitulorum Provinciae Lombardiae', ed. by Kaeppeli, p. 146; *Acta capitulorum generalium*, I, 94 (1268 — inquisitors only to ride when in fear, or undertaking difficult routes). For Francesco's justification, see ASVat, *Collectoria* 133, fols 172^{v}-73^{r}; also Benedetti, *Inquisitori lombardi*, p. 192.

Francesco's need to ride is understandable, given the mountainous nature of his territory. Other inquisitors in northern Lombardy faced similar difficulties, and most chose at some point to use horses. It is harder to appreciate why the inquisitor Florio da Verona, in the plains around Venice and Padua, habitually travelled on land by carriage (*carruca*). But since he died in office, we might assume he was elderly and infirm, and perhaps had a personal licence. The Franciscans in Florence adopted the uneasy compromise of having a retainer take the hired horses back once they had reached their destination.[31]

Using horses led inexorably to other breaches of the rules. Stabling and horse feed were costly, and Dominican constitutions tried repeatedly to prevent stabling at their convents. All-weather riding garments such as leather capes were also generally forbidden, though here an exception was perhaps made for inquisitors.[32]

The major area where inquisitors' personal obligations of poverty conflicted with the necessities of their office was in the handling of money. Confiscations and the imposition of penalties did not just involve seizing goods and property. They meant pursuing business debts owed to people convicted of heresy and investing the proceeds with bankers and money changers, thus involving regular contact with individuals from whom their orders normally urged them to keep their distance. Daily bills and wages also had to be paid, and individual inquisitors' idea of appropriate costs and rewards varied wildly. If there was a temporary cash-flow problem, it was also not unknown for inquisitors to lend or borrow money, sometimes at interest.[33]

The physical handling of cash could be minimized by deploying lay members of the *familia* as purse-holders, or by using a convent's procurator as a purchasing agent. (The Florentine inquisitor, Mino da San Quirico, famously 'observed' the Franciscan rule by requiring his blackmail victims to drop payments directly into his purse, so his hands would not be soiled with lucre.)[34]

[31] ASVat *Collectoria* 133, fols 91^{r} and ten other examples to fol. 95^{r} (carriage). Personal licences were sufficiently widespread in the Dominican order to require periodic mass cancellation, see *Acta [...] Provinciae Romanae*, p. 96 (1290).

[32] *Acta [...] Provinciae Romanae*, p. 98 (1291 — confiscation of all riding equipment and capes, except from *inquisitores heretice pravitatis*). This may be a general exemption, or simply an acknowledgement that, since inquisitors' gear was not financed from convent or provincial funds, the chapter could not seize it.

[33] ASVat, *Collectoria* 133, fols 89^{v}, 95^{v}, and 99^{v} (Florio da Verona — dealings with bankers, money-changing); 249, fol. 42^{v} (Pace da Castelfiorentino — loan).

[34] For example, Boccaccio's 'frati minori che denari non osano toccare' (Friars Minor who don't dare touch money). See Biscaro, 'Inquisitori ed eretici a Firenze' (1933), p. 196 for

The insidious corruption of free access to money was a different matter. A particular source of concern to the Franciscan hierarchy was the inquisitor's discretionary power to impose money penalties for a variety of moral and religious crimes. In 1274, the chapter general at Lyons sought to ban Franciscan inquisitors from imposing such fines because of the conflicts with their rule. However, the ban was immediately (and successfully) contested as an infringement of the papal discretion given to inquisitors.[35] As revenue from real heretics declined, inquisitors from both orders made extensive and creative use of this power to punish 'offences' such as eating meat during Lent or failing to attend the inquisitor's preaching and reading of papal letters.[36] Fines formed a significant part of inquisition incomes: in Ferrara and Modena between 1310 and 1315, the Dominican Giovanni dei Pizigotti collected gross revenues of over 1200 gold florins, mainly from fines on Jewish *conversi*. This amount compared favourably with the papacy's tax take from large regions of Italy.[37]

An inquisitor's asceticism was also tested in dealings with local bishops and abbots and less often with visiting papal legates, some of whom were cardinals. Prelates and princes of the Church were not noted for modest living, and it is noticeable how much inquisitors' expenditure shoots up when hosting such visitors.[38] But some inquisitors encountered even more eminent people in the

citation and p. 191 for Mino. Franciscan inquisitors in Tuscany used a large staff to separate themselves from the actual handling of money; Dominican inquisitors in Lombardy seem not to have done so.

[35] For discussion of the dating and business of the chapters at Lyon in 1272 and 1274, see Callebaut, 'Le chapitre général de 1272'. For inquisitors' opposition to the ban on money fines, and the original text of the prohibition, see d'Alatri, *Inquisizione francescana*, pp. 21–22. Oliger, 'Alcuni documenti per la storia dell'inquisizione francescana', doc. 1, edits the *consilium* taken before 1278 by the Franciscan inquisitors of Tuscany on whether they needed to obey the chapter's ruling against monetary penalties.

[36] ASVat, *Collectoria* 249, fol. 43^{r} (fines for failure to hear papal letters read), fol. 43^{v} (fine of more than 19 gold florins for eating meat in Lent).

[37] ASVat, *Collectoria* 133, fols 138^{v}–163^{r} (Pizigotti's accounts). For Pizigotti, see also Paolini, 'Le finanze dell'Inquisizione', p. 479. For comparison, the *decima* (tithe) in the city and diocese of Ferrara for the period 1313–19 raised less than 5000 Bolognese *lire* (ASVat, *Collectoria* 133, fol. 221^{r-v}) or around 2330 gold florins at the exchange rate used by papal auditors.

[38] For example, Thomas de Garzano, a notably frugal Dominican inquisitor in the March of Genoa, whose living expenses are counted in shillings and pence, had to travel with the master of the order from Pavia in July 1301 on a four-day journey. It cost him 2 *lire imperiali* 20 *solidi*, whereas the return journey in August cost only 12 *solidi* (ASVat, *Collectoria* 133, fol 74^{v}).

course of their work. Francesco da Pocapaglia, inquisitor of Piedmont, was summoned by Pope Clement V himself for discussions at the Council of Vienne in 1311, where he spent several months consulting on the worrying resurgence of Catharism led by the Authier brothers.[39] Francesco also met Robert of Anjou, king of Naples, and negotiated with the marquis of Saluzzo and the dauphin of Savoy, all of whom were suzerains of parts of Piedmont and thus his corresponding civil authorities for inquisition business. Extraordinarily, in 1310, Francesco set off on his own initiative to visit the Holy Roman Emperor, Henry VII, who was then in Italy, and spent a week with him seeking support and privileges.[40]

Inquisitors Who Kept their Vows

Despite the odds, some inquisitors managed to strike a reasonable balance between their roles. Notwithstanding visits to popes, kings, and emperors, Francesco da Pocapaglia was both austere-living and dynamic. During his term of office (from before 1307 until 1316), all his accounts record a surplus to be handed to the papal collectors, despite relatively modest *per capita* confiscations from a long list of captured heretics.

Unlike city-based inquisitors, Francesco lived a life of constant movement, shuttling between Turin, Cuneo, Chieri, and Asti as points of access for the high mountain valleys where Cathars and Waldensians lurked. He lodged in Dominican convents where they existed (paying a donation for his keep), or stayed in Franciscan houses (as in Cuneo), or with village priests. In these stamping grounds, Francesco's expenses during 1307–08 were less than 6 *lire* of Asti a month for himself, his associate, and his *famulus*. But even when visit-

[39] From exile in Italy, the Authier brothers led a revival of Catharism in Languedoc from 1299. Guillaume Authier was executed in December 1309 and Pierre in April 1310, but their followers were not wiped out for some years. The nexus between Cathar remnants in Languedoc and in Piedmont was an issue for inquisitors on both sides of the Alps. For the last gasp of the Cathars, see Barber, *The Cathars*, pp. 176–202, and Lambert, *The Cathars*, pp. 230–71. In ASVat, *Collectoria* 133, fol. 180^{v}, Francesco da Pocapaglia notes his expenses for going to the general council in Vienne 'pro factis fidei et maxime contra Guillelmum Auterium hereticatum in Cuneum et fugitivum nostrum, et contra valdenses de terra Dalfini' (for the business of the faith, especially about Guillaume Authier, who was hereticated in Cuneo and a fugitive from our jurisdiction, and about the Waldensians in the Dauphiné). (The Dauphiné straddled the mountain border between present-day France and Piedmont.) Because Guillaume had been made a perfect (hereticated) in Piedmont, Francesco felt a particular responsibility.

[40] ASVat, *Collectoria* 133, fol. 178^{r} (meeting with emperor and with cardinal-legate); fol. 180^{v} (visit to Council of Vienne); fol. 177^{v} (negotiations with King Robert).

ing the emperor in Turin, his costs were still modest: his week there incurred expenses of 2 *lire* 4 *soldi*. To set this in context, one legal opinion from one of King Robert's judges cost 2 *lire* 10 *soldi*.[41]

Francesco was not a man concerned about clothing. Some inquisitors indulged in elaborate vestments to highlight the ritual aspects of their role. Over ten years, Francesco bought a tunic and scapular (five times), a pair of undertunics (four times), two woollen tunics, and a modest amount of unspecified clothing just before a visit to King Robert. Riding gear was a necessity, but limited to a tabard and three capes (one subsequently relined). The used gear is meticulously detailed to hand on to his successor. Far and away his biggest costs were for maintaining the horses, without which his job was impossible. Equine costs were higher than those of his human companions.[42]

Thomas de Garzano, inquisitor in the march of Genoa from 1297 to1305, was similarly austere.[43] Despite a very mountainous territory of small villages and (apart from Genoa) modest towns, he also tried hard to observe the prohibition on riding. At the beginning of his appointment in November 1297, Thomas's first act was to buy shoes (*calciamenta*), followed a few days later by a pair of walking boots (*calige*). Within four months, by February 1298, he had worn out the shoes pursuing heretics, and in December that year invested in another two pairs of boots. In the following six years, there are at least fourteen references to the repair or purchase of boots and shoes, often two pairs at a time. 1303 was a particularly energetic year, when — despite two months' illness — he got through no fewer than five pairs of boots, plus repairs. Though there were times when he had to use horses, Thomas was clearly much happier on foot. Whereas Francesco was able to sell his mounts for a profit at the end of his tenure, Thomas had to confess to losing his in a mountain stream.[44]

Like Francesco, Thomas stuck to the Dominican diet, though there are frequent references to the purchase of wine, and he allowed himself meat when

41 Monthly cost calculated between papal accounting in November 1307 and feast of the Holy Cross (September 1308), for items identified as for food, drink, or expenses of the inquisitor, *socius*, and *famulus*. ASVat *Collectoria* 133, fol. 177^{r} (cost of *consilium*).

42 ASVat *Collectoria* 133, fol. 188^{r} (riding gear passed to successor); fol. 179^{v} (26 *lire* 14 *soldi* on horsefeed in two transactions).

43 Biscaro, 'Inquisitori ed eretici lombardi', gives Thomas's dates as 1292–94 and 1300–1305 (pp. 448). Benedetti, *Inquisitori lombardi*, follows suit. But ASVat Collectoria 133 fol. 70^{r}, though hard to read, clearly gives the start of Thomas's tenure as 1297 and identifies the following year as 1298. The subsequent chronology is clearly signalled.

44 ASVat *Collectoria* 133, fols 70^{r}–102^{v} (fol. 80^{v} — loss of horse). Also Biscaro, 'Inquisitori ed eretici lombardi', pp. 528–32 for a heavily abbreviated selection from Thomas's accounts.

sick.[45] He had his tonsure rebarbered once a year, and a new tunic made for attending the provincial council. Though he was personally frugal, it is less clear whether he observed the proper distinction between inquisition and civil roles, possibly because of the hotchpotch of secular powers in his mountainous province. He arranged executions and sometimes prison facilities, and organized and paid posses to capture heretics in remote locations.[46] Francesco's regular meetings with various civil authorities to hand over to them their share of confiscations also suggest his office undertook seizures and sales, but civil officials do not feature at all in Thomas's accounts. Overall, though, both men appear to have balanced their obligations effectively, with their exhausting travels alone leaving no doubt about their personal dedication to their task.

Inquisitors Who Didn't

In sharp contrast stands Giovanni dei Pizigotti, inquisitor of Ferrara from 1310 to 1315. He took up office on 25 November 1310.[47] By the third week of December that year, he had already thrown three feasts for the entire convents of Ferrara and Bologna. The feast at Bologna, the largest Dominican convent in Italy, cost over 20 *lire* in Bologna money. In less than five years, Giovanni hosted at least thirty feasts, including dinners for both the provincial and general chapters of the order (Lorenzo Paolini estimates the cost at 164 *lire*). Beyond that, he repeatedly used inquisition funds to buy dinner and wine for the prior-provincial, the Master of the Order and their entourages, and to entertain guests in the convent *hospicium*. His regular personal expenditure on food (including sweetmeats) was astonishing for one living in a convent where food was provided. It reached 59 *lire* in one week in February 1311.[48]

Much other spending was on personal clothing, amounting to 332 *lire* on some eighteen occasions. On three occasions in summer 1312 and early 1313,

[45] ASVat *Collectoria* 133, fol 71^{v} (seven instances in June 1299 of purchase of meat or chicken when sick).

[46] ASVat *Collectoria* 133, fols 70^{v} and 78^{r} (payment for exhumation and burning of dead and possibly live heretics, 1299 and 1304); fols 70^{v}, 72^{r}, and 77^{v} (organization of posses to capture fugitives and take heretics, 1298, 1299 and 1304); fols 72^{v}, 73^{v}, 76^{v}, and 79^{v} (payment of prison expenses, 1299, 1300, 1303 and 1305).

[47] ASVat *Collectoria* 133, fol. 138^{v}. Giovanni seems to have surrendered office in mid-August 1315 (ASVat *Collectoria* 133 fol. 154^{r-v}).

[48] See Paolini, 'Le finanze dell'Inquisizione', p. 479, for summaries of Giovanni's expenditure. ASVat, *Collectoria* 133, fol. 140^{v} (food expenditure, February 1311).

Giovanni spent over 47 Bolognese *lire* a time on clothes.[49] Appreciable sums also went to baptismal robes for 'converting' Jews and to clothing for his staff and associates. Ironically, the provincial chapter held at Ferrara during Giovanni's tenure, and which he attended, resoundingly reiterated that Dominican rules on clothing and bedding must be strictly observed by all friars 'cuiuscumque condicionis vel status existat' (of whatever rank or position they be).[50]

Little of Giovanni's expenditure is visibly related to the prosecution of inquisition business (though he did buy his own prison for 120 *lire*).[51] A huge fee of 175 *lire* in 1313 for a *consilium* by senior clerical and lay doctors probably concerns his confiscation of Jewish goods. Despite a large revenue stream of some 1200 florins, mainly from Jewish 'converts', his outgoings were so high that he had to borrow at interest — something specifically forbidden by the rule — in order to keep afloat. He thus ended his tenure 109 florins in the red. Unsurprisingly, his accounts were questioned by the papal auditors, with each item of clothing indignantly side-lined. The only query on Francesco's accounts was a payment to his notary's wife for doing laundry, during a long stay away from convent facilities.[52]

Giovanni dei Pizigotti was enormously extravagant and, on his own evidence, plainly breached his order's rules on the simple life. But he had help in this. Much questionable expenditure went on entertaining his superiors in the order, including past and present masters, or in cash gifts (beyond the cost of his keep) to local convents. He gave alms to brothers who were ill or poor, but much larger payments to those who were neither, such as 25 *lire* for general advice to Corrado da Camerino, the outgoing prior-provincial. Sometimes he was directly instructed by superiors to make payments which had no place in inquisition expenditure, including endowing a perpetual lamp on the shrine of St Dominic and supporting a student in the university. That he records these particular payments as being made 'on the orders of the Master of the Order' suggests he realized he was crossing a line.[53]

[49] By contrast, Francesco's largest single expense was 10 *lire*, probably of Asti: his accounts do not specify the currency used (ASVat, *Collectoria* 133, fol. 175^{v}).

[50] ASVat, *Collectoria* 133, fol. 147^{v} (baptismal clothes); 'Acta capitulorum Provinciae Lombardiae,' ed. by Kaeppeli, p. 170 (provincial chapter).

[51] ASVat, *Collectoria* 133, fol. 149^{r} (purchase of prison, October 1313).

[52] ASVat, *Collectoria* 133, fol. 142^{r} (interest on loan); fol. 148^{v} (175 *lire* for *consilium*); fols 176^{r} and 177^{v} (payments to notary's wife, one sidelined).

[53] ASVat, *Collectoria* 133, fol. 148^{r} (payment to Corrado); fol. 151^{v} (Corrado described as *quondam* prior-provincial); fol. 154^{r} (purchases on the master's orders).

There is an uncomfortable sense in Giovanni's records, not found with Francesco or Thomas, that senior figures at the centre of the Dominican Order viewed inquisition funds as a cash cow and took advantage of a weak-willed inquisitor to plunder them shamelessly, regardless of the proprieties. Was Giovanni himself simply bowled over by his new position, or a venal careerist? His generosity certainly paid off in personal career terms — he became prior of the Bologna convent in 1317.[54]

Giovanni's temptations were good food, clothing, and buying favour. Other inquisitors expressed their extravagances in ways which did not so obviously flout the rule or alert the auditors. Pace da Castelfiorentino, inquisitor of Florence from 1319 to 1322, had low daily expenses because he mainly resided in the Franciscan convent at Santa Croce, and paid a regular monthly fee for maintenance.[55] Though he loved clothes, his special weakness was for artwork and legal tomes. He ordered the inquisition's books to be illuminated by a miniaturist, bought pictures from Taddeo Gaddi, and commissioned a transcription of the Clementine decretals. In 1323, whilst Pace was the inquisitor's vicar and in practice in charge of the shop, the Florence inquisition commissioned the first known copy of Giovanni d'Andrea's commentary on these decretals. To advise on legal issues, Pace maintained a paid panel of judges, who were entertained monthly with wine and food. This get-together disappeared when Pace's successor took office, suggesting it was essentially a social event.[56]

Pace's accounted personal costs were modest, but the overall cost of the inquisition office was not. His large staff of notaries and assistants lived well when out of Florence, and expenditure on innocuous items such as paper, parchment, and office essentials was several orders of magnitude more than elsewhere. The Florentine inquisition was perhaps more bureaucratic than elsewhere in Italy, but the suspicion of fraudulently inflated pricing is strong.[57]

[54] Rome, Archivum Generalis Ordinis Praedicatorum, *serie* 14, Liber GGG, pt II, fol. 403.

[55] Pace was inquisitor in his own right from August 1319 to July 1322 (see ASVat, *Collectoria* 249, fol. 40r and *Collectoria* 250, fol. 5r). He then acted as vicar for several months until his successor, Michele d'Arezzo, was able to arrive in Florence, and continued to be vicar intermittently thereafter until 1334.

[56] Biscaro, 'Inquisitori ed eretici a Firenze' (1929) pp. 347–75 for Pace; p. 359 (Clementine decretals, art spending); (1929) p. 368; and (1933) p. 201 (more Clementine decretals and dating of apparatus).

[57] Biscaro, 'Inquisitori ed eretici a Firenze' (1929), pp. 358–59 (stationery costs).

The Actually Criminal

Pace must have been worried about aspects of his accounts, because he attempted to delay presenting them to the papal collector, Pons Augier, when ordered to do so.[58] But some Italian inquisitors were so tempted by the possibilities of office that they indulged in overt criminality. Best known is the Franciscan Mino da San Quirico, inquisitor first in Siena, then (between 1332 and 1334) in Florence. Mino combined extortion and extravagance on a grand scale with breath-taking effrontery towards papal legates sent to investigate him. He bought a degree of civic acquiescence by using inquisition powers of property seizure from alleged heretics to help the authorities out of a tough spot with enraged creditors after the collapse of the Scaglia bank. His behaviour was, however, so outrageous that the *guardiano* of the Prato convent complained he was bringing the order into disrepute. The minister-provincial (himself later a notably corrupt inquisitor) did nothing, confirming the suspicion that the senior hierarchy of both the Franciscan and Dominican Orders was now actively complicit in financial misbehaviour by inquisitors.[59]

Other egregious examples of inquisition corruption in this period are from the Veneto. A series of papal inquiries, beginning in 1302, reveal prolonged criminality involving half a dozen Franciscan inquisitors and their staff.[60] Property was sold for a fraction of its worth to relatives or officials. Estates left for charity were diverted to personal uses or for money-lending at interest.[61]

[58] ASVat, *Collectoria* 249, fol. 37r. Pons also required Pace to swear 'sancta dei evangelia corporaliter tacta libro iuranti in manibus' (holding the holy Gospels in his hands) that the accounts were complete and that there was no second set of books.

[59] Biscaro, 'Inquisitori ed eretici a Firenze' (1933), pp. 161–207 for Mino generally; pp. 169–72 (Scaglia bank: by arresting the only holder of any Scaglia assets on suspicion of heresy, Mino pre-empted creditors' demands to the commune for satisfaction); pp. 182–88 (Franciscan testimony against Mino); pp. 187–88 (complaint to minister-provincial). Michael of Cesena, when Minister-General, had ordered that Mino be given no further posts, but this order lapsed with the Franciscan schism (p. 184). See also Murray, 'The Medieval Inquisition', passim.

[60] For this episode, see Biscaro, 'Eretici ed inquisitori nella Marca Trevisana'; d'Alatri, 'Inquisitori veneti' and 'Due inchieste'; *Il 'Liber Contractuum'*, ed. by Bonato; Lomastro Tognato, *L'eresia a Vicenza*, and Marangon, *Il pensiero ereticale*.

[61] The property of Aicardino di Litolfo, left to the poor, was sold for 2600 *lire*, despite being worth 4000 *lire* (*Il 'Liber Contractuum'*, ed. by Bonato, doc. 261). The estate of the noblewoman Agnese da Carrara, similarly left to the inquisition for charity, was wholly diverted into commercial loans at interest, mostly to a tavern-keeper: d'Alatri, 'Due inchieste',

In one complex series of transactions, the threat of prosecution for heresy was used to force a secular cleric, the executor of an estate left for the benefit of orphans, poor widows, and other indigents, to nominate a group of notaries close to the inquisition as *pauperes Christi* in order to seize the property.[62] As elsewhere, revenues were used to buy expensive books (some surviving today in the Biblioteca Antoniana) and for patronage to other members of the order.[63] Accounts were falsified and further manipulated to deny the communes their share of confiscations, even where civic authorities had piously dedicated the proceeds to church-building.[64] This financial malpractice finally drove Padua and Vicenza to complain, in a remarkable dossier presented to Boniface VIII. He sentenced the perpetrators to incarceration and removed the Franciscans from office in the two cities. But sadly the lessons do not appear to have been learnt elsewhere.[65]

Conclusion

My initial question was how medieval Italian inquisitors reconciled their calling as poor friars with the riches and temptations of inquisitorial office. Evidence from the Franciscans in Florence and the Veneto shows that some inquisitors did comprehensively betray both the principles of their order and the modest standards expected of medieval office-holders. They lived up to the picture of greed and corruption presented by Boccaccio and Dante. But at the

pp. 235–36, docs 6–8. The sister of the inquisitor Pietrobono Brusemini was sold land acquired by the inquisition: d'Alatri, 'Inquisitori veneti', p. 181 doc. 46; and *Il 'Liber Contractuum'*, ed. by Bonato, doc. 233.

[62] *Il 'Liber Contractuum'*, ed. by Bonato, docs 213–16.

[63] Marangon, *Il pensiero ereticale*, pp. 62–63, discusses the intellectual credentials of the Veneto inquisitors and the survival of their books.

[64] In Vicenza, for example, the commune had dedicated its third share of heresy confiscations towards the building of the church of San Lorenzo (and sometimes to the maintenance of the Franciscan convent as well). By misrepresenting the sums due to the commune, the Veneto inquisitors were in effect defrauding their brothers and their own church-building effort. The fact that they were able to produce large sums of cash to meet the sentences of the papal inquiry indicates that the money had not gone to the building effort in any other way. See d'Alatri, 'Inquisitori veneti', pp. 186–88, docs 54–55; pp. 199–203, docs 75–88; and 'Due inchieste', pp. 240–41 (settlement of sentences).

[65] A further inquiry in 1308 was required, this time involving not only the Franciscans but also several Dominican inquisitors of Lombardy. It was inconclusive. See d'Alatri, 'Due inchieste'.

other end of the spectrum, and less visible to history, were hard-working and zealous inquisitors such as Francesco da Pocapaglia and Thomas de Garzano, who do appear to have achieved a balance between their two roles.

What to make of the sizeable group between these two extremes? We have seen that some Dominican inquisitors, like Giovanni dei Pizigotti, were egged on in wrongful spending by the very superiors who should have held them to account as as friars. Instead, the upper echelons of the orders became substantial beneficiaries of the diversion of inquisition funds. Franciscan chroniclers blamed failures in the hierarchy for at least some of the scandals in the Veneto, and complaints to the Tuscan minister-provincial over Mino da San Quirico led nowhere.[66] Though inquisitors were not subject to their order in their daily work, it is hard not to think that priors and ministers-provincial could have used their power of appointment and removal to improve standards, or have imposed earlier and more vigorous scrutiny of inquisitors' accounts.[67] If inquisitors notoriously broke their vows, some blame at least must attach to the Dominican and Franciscan hierarchies.

There are also other, and more complex, motivations to consider. Medieval piety was not simple. Giovanni dei Pizigotti did fund a perpetual lamp to St Dominic and made other donations, even if the cost paled beside that of his fur mantle. Florio da Verona, Dominican inquisitor of both Padua and Venice (*c.* 1305–08), was a contemporary of the Franciscan inquisitors imprisoned in 1302, and he must have known the reason for their punishment. Nevertheless, he directed much of his inquisition revenue towards building an *ante mortem* funerary chapel for the Dominican pope, Benedict XI, whose chaplain he had been. We find him paying out for the building of marble steps and for stained-glass windows. He negotiated with current and former inquisitors, such as Guido da Vicenza, now bishop of Ferrara, to fund precious items for its altar. Dominican ordinances forbade such fripperies, and from the point of view of

[66] Biscaro, 'Eretici ed inquisitori nella Marca Trevisana', p. 151 n. 1 cites blame given to *praelati ordinis* in the Veneto.

[67] In fact the requirement to present accounts to the provincial chapter developed notably late: from 1272 for the Franciscans (confirmed by 1292) and in 1294 for the Dominicans. See 'Statuta generalia Ordinis', ed. by Bihl, p. 51, for the version incorporated in Franciscan statutes in 1292 at Paris. Callebaut, 'Le chapitre général de 1272', discusses the confusion, and conflation of business, between general chapters at Lyons in 1272 and 1274, where several measures to control inquisitors were attempted. The Dominicans do not seem to have imposed an accounting requirement until the general chapter at Montpellier in 1294: *Acta capitulorum generalium*, I, 273.

other partners expecting their legal share of heresy confiscations, the spending was clearly dubious. But Florio did not profit personally from this use of inquisition funds. He was motivated by piety and solidarity with his fellow Dominican, not by greed.[68]

For some Italian inquisitors, therefore, the real temptation was perhaps not the personal lure of riches and power, but the opportunity to devote the profits of their labour to the glory of the Church and the benefit of their order. Imposing financial penalties on heretics served a double purpose of saving souls and glorifying God. This particular expression of piety was a long way from original mendicant ideals, but nevertheless it stands distinct from the cupidity and covetousness abhorred by Bernard Gui.

It is more difficult to establish whether Italian inquisitors of the period also followed Gui's admonition to exercise compassion in judgement. For an inquisitor, compassion towards the sinful soul could manifest in ways hard for modern (or even medieval lay) sensibility to appreciate. Lanfranco da Bergamo, inquisitor of Pavia (1292–1305), dragged a suddenly repentant heretic *semi combustus* from the flames, an action praised by Grado G. Merlo as epitomizing good inquisitorial practice, even though the man died agonizingly of burns three weeks later.[69] By contrast, Guido da Vicenza in Bologna refused the sacrament to a condemned heretic pleading for it, causing the Bolognese public to riot in horrified protest.[70] As Christine Caldwell Ames has remarked:

> [I]t is patent that despite its rarity in practice, and the formal jurisdiction of the secular arm when it did occur, inquisitors accepted with frank equanimity the execution of recalcitrant and relapsed heretics. And this was not grudging acceptance, in which inquisitors looked with distant disfavor upon the secular shedding of blood as inimical to their own Christian work.[71]

Away from these extreme cases, 'compassion' could be very selective. The inquisitor Manfredo da Parma (Bologna, 1314–18) abated fines in ten out of the sixteen cases with which he dealt 'intuitu pietatis secundum quod per Inquisitores

[68] See Benedetti, *Inquisitori lombardi*, pp. 6–7, for the Dominican programme of building works and inquisitors' donations to them. For Florio's expenditure, see ASVat, *Collectoria* 133, fols 86^{r-v} (steps, window, etc., of papal chapel), fol. 102^{v} (jewelled ornaments).

[69] See Merlo, 'Le origini dell'Inquisizione medievale', pp. 38–39; Biscaro, 'Inquisitori ed eretici lombardi', p. 513 (accounts of Lanfranco da Bergamo).

[70] For this well-known episode, see Paolini, *L'eresia a Bologna*, pp. 63–79, and Thompson, 'Lay versus Clerical Perceptions of Heresy'.

[71] Ames, *Righteous Persecution*, p. 185.

fieri consuevit' (moved by the piety which inquisitors are accustomed to show). But it took a special *consilium* to persuade him to repay to the victim of false witness money which had been wrongly confiscated — and then only partially, and after at least five years' delay.[72] Thomas de Garzano, the inquisitor of Genoa, was undoubtedly compassionate at a personal level — witness his kindly treatment of his young servant, for whose final illness he travelled from Savona to Genoa in midwinter — but he also deployed torture and was responsible for several executions.[73] Some inquisitors demonstrated Christian charity by doling out pittances to former heretics impoverished because the inquisition had seized all their goods. Others, however, let them turn to crime to feed themselves.[74]

Inquisitorial compassion was clearly not the same animal as the sympathy for others which caused St Francis to abandon his worldly goods. For the inquisitor, punishment for heresy was deserved, and even the best inquisitor had no problems with severe or deceptive treatment of a suspect. There was also an uncomfortable connection between 'compassion' in a modern sense and financial temptation. Condemning a suspect to a heavy fine could be more merciful than imprisonment, execution, or even signing with the cross, but there is no denying that it also filled the inquisition's coffers. The extent to which inquisition penances mutated towards fines, between the mid-thirteenth and early fourteenth centuries, deserves more study.

Temptation, for a medieval inquisitor, was a complex issue: on the one side, rigid attitudes to heresy led to riots and the destruction of friars' property; on the other, ill-judged mercy to a suspected heretic might lead eventually to the stake. And the imposition of heavy financial penalties fuelled the expensive lifestyle which pulled many inquisitors away from mendicant ideals of poverty.

[72] ASVat, *Collectoria* 133, fols 130^{r}–31^{r} (remissions) and fol. 133^{v} (reimbursement). The falsely accused victim, Angelo da Arezzo, had been condemned at least as early as 1311 (*Collectoria* 133, fol. 169^{r}, accounts of *Niccolò da Ripa Transone*). The false testimony was known, and his accusers had already paid large sums in fines, by 1312 (*Collectoria* 133, fol. 163^{v}, accounts of Ruggiero da Petriolo). It was not until spring 1316, some four inquisitors later, that Angelo was partially reimbursed for his wrongful beggaring.

[73] ASVat, *Collectoria* 133, fol. 79^{r}.

[74] Manfredo da Parma gave alms to a poor woman, formerly a heretic, on seven occasions, but this was not pure charity, as she acted as a spy to entrap others; ASVat, *Collectoria* 133, fol. 132^{v}. Lanfranco da Bergamo repeatedly assisted the former heretic, Helena, for similar reasons: Biscaro, 'Inquisitori ed eretici lombardi', p. 510. But Guido da Vicenza forced Contessa, the widow of the heretic Bompietro, whose burning led to the 1299 riots, into such poverty that a year later she was prosecuted for theft. See Paolini, *L'eresia a Bologna*, p. 126 n. 160.

Works Cited

Manuscripts and Archival Sources

Rome, Archivio Segreto Vaticano, Camera Apostolica, *Collectoriae*, vols 133, 159A, 249–51, 404, 421A

——, *Instrumenta Miscellanea*

Rome, Archivum Generalis Ordinis Fratrum Praedicatorum, Santa Sabina, *serie* 14, Liber GGG; *serie* 14 3.51–2, 3.53, 3.54

Rome, Biblioteca Casanatense, MS 1730

Treviso, Biblioteca Comunale, MS 957 (Vincenzo Scoti, *Documenti Trivigiani*, 12 vols)

Venice, Archivio di Stato, *Corporazioni religiose soppresse*: S. Maria Gloriosa dei Frari, 91/III (Convento Frati Inquisizione)

Primary Sources

'Acta capituli generalis Mediolani celebrati an. 1285', ed. by André Callebaut, *Archivum Franciscanum Historicum*, 22 (1929), 273–91

Acta capitulorum generalium Ordinis Praedicatorum, ed. by Benedict Maria Reichert, Monumenta Ordinis Fratrum Praedicatorum Historica, 3–4, 2 vols (Rome: In domo generalitia, 1898–99)

'Acta capitulorum Provinciae Lombardiae (1254–1293) et Lombardiae Inferioris (1309–1312)', ed. by Thomas Kaeppeli, *Archivum Fratrum Praedicatorum*, 11 (1941), 138–72

Acta capitulorum provincialium Provinciae Romanae (1243–1344), ed. by Thomas Kaeppeli and Antoine Dondaine, Monumenta Ordinis Fratrum Praedicatorum Historica, 20 (Rome: In domo generalitia, 1941)

Acta S. Officii Bononie ab anno 1291 usque ad annum 1310, ed. by Lorenzo Paolini and Raniero Orioli, Fonti per la Storia d'Italia, 106–07, 2 vols (Rome: Istituto Storico Italiano per il Medio Evo, 1982)

Bullarium Franciscanum Romanorum pontificum, ed. by Giovanni Giacinto Sbaraglia, 3 vols (Assisi: Edizioni Porziuncola, 1983–84)

'Constitutiones Provinciae Provinciae (saec XIII–XIV)', ed. by Ferdinand Delorme, *Archivum Franciscanum Historicum*, 14 (1921), 415–34

'Explanationes constitutionem generalium Narbonensium', ed. by Ferdinand Delorme, *Archivum Franciscanum Historicum*, 18 (1925), 511–52

Gui, Bernard, *Manuel de l'Inquisiteur*, ed. and trans. by Guy Mollat, 2 vols (Paris: Les Belles-Lettres, 1926–27; repr. 2006, as 1 vol.)

——, *Practica inquisitionis heretice pravitatis*, ed. by Célestin Douais (Paris: Picard, 1886)

Il 'Liber Contractuum' dei Frati Minori di Padova e di Vicenza (1263–1302), ed. by Elisabetta Bonato (Rome: Viella, 2002)

Regesta pontificum Romanorum, ed. by August Potthast, 2 vols (Berlin: Rudolf de Decker 1874–75; repr. Graz: Akademische Druck- und Verlagsanstalt, 1957)

'Statuta generalia Ordinis edita in capitulis generalibus celebratis Narbonae an. 1260, Assisii an. 1279 atque Parisiis an. 1292. Editio critica et synoptica', ed. by Michael Bihl, *Archivum Franciscanum Historicum*, 34 (1941), 13–94, 284–358

Secondary sources

Alatri, Mariano d', 'Due inchieste papali sugli inquisitori veneti (1302 e 1308), in *Eretici e Inquisitori in Italia: Studi e Documenti*, 2 vols (Rome: Istituto Storico dei Cappucini, 1986–87), I, 223–42

——, 'Inquisitori veneti del Duecento', in *Eretici e Inquisitori in Italia: Studi e Documenti*, 2 vols (Rome: Istituto Storico dei Cappucini, 1986–87), I, 139–217

——, *L'Inquisizione francescana nell'Italia centrale del Duecento* (Rome: Istituto Storico dei Cappuccini, 1996)

Amabile, Luigi, *Il Santo Officio della Inquisizione in Napoli* (Città di Castello: Lapi, 1892; repr. 1987)

Ames, Christine Caldwell, *Righteous Persecution: Inquisition, Dominicans and Christianity in the Middle Ages* (Philadelphia: University of Pennsylvania Press, 2009)

Barber, Malcolm, *The Cathars: Dualist Heresy in Languedoc in the High Middle Ages* (Harlow: Pearson, 2000)

Barone, Giulia, 'Guido Capello', in *Dizionario Biografico degli Italiani*, 18 (Rome: Istituto della Enciclopedia Italiana, 1975) <http:www.treccani.it/enciclopedia/guido-capello> [accessed 24 August 2015]

Becker, Marvin B., 'Florentine Politics and the Diffusion of Heresy in the Trecento: A Socioeconomic Inquiry', *Speculum*, 34 (1959), 60–75

Benedetti, Marina, 'Le finanze dell'inquisitore', in *L'economia dei conventi dei frati minori e predicatori fino alla metà del Trecento: atti del XXXI convegno internazionale, Assisi, 9–11 ottobre 2003* (Spoleto: Fondazione centro italiano di studi sull'alto medioevo, 2004)

——, 'Frate Lanfranco da Bergamo, gli Inquisitori, l'Ordine e la Curia Romana', in *Praedicatores Inquisitores – I: The Dominicans and the Medieval Inquisition. Acts of the 1st International Seminar on the Dominicans and the Inquisition, Rome 23–25 February 2002*, (Rome: Istituto storico domenicano, 2004), pp. 157–204

——, *Inquisitori lombardi del Duecento* (Rome: Edizioni di Storia e Letteratura, 2008)

Biscaro, Gerolamo, 'Dante a Ravenna', *Bullettino dell'Istituto Storico Italiano*, 41 (1921), 1–143

——, 'Eretici ed inquisitori nella Marca Trevisana', *Archivio Veneto*, 5th ser., 11 (1932), 148–80

——, 'Inquisitori ed eretici a Firenze (1319–1334)', *Studi Medievali*, n.s., 2 (1929), 347–75; n.s., 3 (1930), 266–87; n.s., 6 (1933), 161–207

——, 'Inquisitori ed eretici lombardi (1292–1318)', *Miscellanea di storia italiana*, 3rd ser., 19 (1922), 446–557

Boase, Thomas Sherrer Ross, *Boniface VIII, 1294–1303* (London: Constable, 1933)

Bronzino, Giovanni, 'Documenti riguardanti gli eretici nella Biblioteca Comunale dell'Archiginnasio, pt. II: 1265–1648', *L'Archiginnasio*, 78 (1983), 285–401

Bruschi, Caterina, 'Inquisizione francescana in Toscana fino al pontificato di Giovanni XXII', in *Frati minori e inquisizione: atti del XXXIII Convegno internazionale, Assisi, 6–8 ottobre 2005* (Spoleto: Fondazione centro italiano di studi sull'alto medioevo, 2006), pp. 287–324

Callebaut, André, 'Le chapitre général de 1272 célebré a Lyon', *Archivum Franciscanum Historicum*, 13 (1920), 305–17

Da Milano, Ilarino, 'Gli antecedenti inediti di un noto episodio dell'Inquisizione francescana a Treviso (1262–1263)', *Collectanea Franciscana*, 5 (1935), 611–20

——, 'L'Istituzione dell'Inquisizione Monastico-Papale a Venezia nel secolo XIII', *Collectanea Franciscana*, 5 (1935), 177–212

Davidsohn, Robert, 'Un libro di entrate e spese dell'Inquisitore fiorentino (1322–1329)', *Archivio Storico Italiano*, 5th ser., 27 (1901), 346–55

De la Roncière, Charles, 'L'Inquisition a-t-elle été perçue comme un abus au Moyen Âge?', in *Inquisition et Pouvoir*, ed. by Gabriel Audisio (Aix-en-Provence: Université de Provence, 2004), pp. 11–24

Del Col, Andrea, *L'Inquisizione in Italia dal XII al XXI secolo* (Milan: Mondadori, 2006)

Delorme, Ferdinand, 'Un homonyme de Saint Antoine de Padoue inquisiteur dans la Marche de Trévise vers 1300', *Archivum Franciscanum Historicum*, 8 (1915), 312–16

Frati minori e inquisizione: atti del XXXIII Convegno Internazionale (Assisi, 6–8 ottobre 2005) (Spoleto: Centro Italiano di Studi sull'Alto Medioevo, 2006)

Friedlander, Alan, *The Hammer of the Inquisition: Brother Bernard Délicieux and the Struggle against the Inquisition in Fourteenth-Century France* (Leiden: Brill, 2000)

Fumi, Luigi, 'Eretici e ribelli nell'Umbria', *Bollettino della Deputazione di Storia Patria per l'Umbria*, 3 (1897), 257–85, 429–89; 4 (1898), 221–301, 437–86; 5 (1899), 1–46; 6 (1900), 205–425

Fussenegger, Gerold, 'De manipulo documentorum ad usum inquisitoris haereticae pravitatis in Romandiola saec. XIII', *Archivum Franciscanum Historicum*, 44 (1951), 71–86

Given, James B., *Inquisition and Medieval Society: Power, Discipline and Resistance in Languedoc* (Ithaca: Cornell University Press, 1997)

Lambert, Malcolm, *The Cathars* (Oxford: Blackwell, 1998)

Lea, Henry Charles, 'Confiscation for Heresy in the Middle Ages', *English Historical Review*, 2 (1887), 235–59

——, *A History of the Inquisition of the Middle Ages*, 3 vols (London: Sampson Low, 1888; repr. Cambridge: Cambridge University Press, 2010)

——, *The Inquisition of the Middle Ages: Its Organization and Operation* (London: Eyre & Spottiswoode, 1963)

Little, Andrew George, 'Constitutiones Provinciae Romanae, anni 1316', *Archivum Franciscanum Historicum*, 18 (1925), 356–73

——, 'Definitiones capitulorum generalium Ordinis fratrum minorum, 1260–1282', *Archivum Franciscanum Historicum*, 7 (1914), 676–82

Lomastro Tognato, Francesca, *L'eresia a Vicenza nel Duecento: dati, problemi e fonti* (Vicenza: Istituto per le ricerche di storia sociale e di storia religiosa, 1988)

Maier, Anneliese, 'Due documenti relativi alla lotta dei Cardinali Colonna contro Bonifacio VIII', *Rivista di Storia della Chiesa in Italia*, 3 (1949), 344–64

Marangon, Paulo, *Il pensiero ereticale nella Marca Trevigiana e a Venezia dal 1200 al 1350* (Abano Terme: Francisci, 1984)

Mengozzi, Guido, 'Documenti Danteschi del R. Archivio di Stato di Siena', *Bullettino Senese di Storia Patria*, 28 (1921), 87–182

Mercati, Angelo, 'Frate Francesco Bartoli d'Assisi michelista e la sua ritrazzione', *Archivum Franciscanum Historicum*, 20 (1927), 260–304

Merlo, Grado Giovanni, *Eretici e inquisitori nella società piemontese del Trecento* (Turin: Claudiana, 1977)

——, 'Frati minori e inquisizione' *Frati minori e inquisizione: atti del XXXIII Convegno internazionale, Assisi, 6–8 ottobre 2005* (Spoleto: Fondazione centro italiano di studi sull'alto medioevo, 2006), pp. 5–24

——, 'Le origini dell'Inquisizione medievale', in *L'Inquisizione: atti del simposio internazionale, Città del Vaticano, 29–31 ottobre 1998*, ed. by Agostino Borromeo (Città del Vaticano: Biblioteca Apostolica Vaticana, 2003), pp. 25-39

——, 'Predicatori e Inquisitori. Per l'Avvio di una Riflessione' in *Praedicatores Inquisitores – I: The Dominicans and the Medieval Inquisition. Acts of the 1st International Seminar on the Dominicans and the Inquisition, Rome 23–25 February 2002*, (Rome: Istituto storico domenicano, 2004), pp. 13–31

Murray, Alexander, 'The Medieval Inquisition: An Instrument of Secular Politics?', *Peritia*, 5 (1986), 161–200

Oliger, Livario, 'Alcuni documenti per la storia dell'inquisizione francescana in Toscana e nell'Umbria', *Studi francescani*, 3rd ser., 3, (1931), 181–204

Paolini, Lorenzo, 'Bonigrino da Verona e sua moglie Rosafiore', in *Medioevo ereticale*, ed. by Ovidio Capitani (Bologna: Il Mulino, 1977), pp. 213–28

——, *L'eresia a Bologna fra XIII e XIV seculo, I: L'eresia catara alla fine del Duecento* (Rome: Istituto Storico per il Medio Evo, 1975)

——, 'Le finanze dell'Inquisizione in Italia (XIII–XIV sec.)', in *Gli spazi economici della Chiesa nell'Occidente mediterraneo (sec. XII–metà XIV): atti del sedicesimo Convegno internazionale di studi tenuto a Pistoia nei giorni 16–19 Maggio, 1997* (Pistoia: Centro Italiano di storia e d'arte, 1999), pp. 441–81

Parmeggiani, Riccardo, *I consilia procedurali per l'Inquisizione Medievale (1235–1330)* (Bologna: Bononia University Press, 2011)

——, 'L'inquisitore Florio da Vicenza', in *Praedicatores Inquisitores – I: The Dominicans and the Medieval Inquisition. Acts of the 1st International Seminar on the Dominicans and the Inquisition, Rome 23–25 February 2002*, (Rome: Istituto storico domenicano, 2004), pp. 681–99

——, 'Inquisizione e frati minori in Romagna, Umbria e Marche nel Duecento', in *Frati Minori e Inquisizione: atti del XXXIII Convegno Internazionale (Assisi, 6–8 ottobre 2005)* (Spoleto: Centro Italiano di Studi sull'Alto Medioevo, 2006), pp. 133–50

Piccolomini, Paolo, 'Documenti senesi sull'Inquisizione', *Bullettino Senese di Storia Patria*, 15 (1908), 233–45

Presutti, Giuseppe, 'Altri documenti su l'omonimo fr Antonio da Padova OFM e l'inquisizione in Lombardia', *Archivum Fransciscanum Historicum*, 8 (1915), 662–67

Prudlo, Donald, *The Martyred Inquisitor: The Life and Cult of Peter of Verona († 1252)* (Aldershot: Ashgate, 2008)

Sackville, Lucy, *Heresy and Heretics in the Thirteenth Century: The Textual Representations* (Woodbridge: York Medieval Press, 2011)

Savignoni, P., 'L'archivio storico del comune di Viterbo', *Archivio della Reale Società Romana di Storia Patria*, 18 (1895), 5–20, 269–318

Serena, Augusto, 'Fra gli eretici trevigiani', *Archivio Veneto-Tridentino*, 3 (1923), 169-202

Severino, Gabriella, 'Note sull'eresia a Siena fra i secoli XIII e XIV', in *Studi sul medioevo cristiano offerti a Raffaele Morghen per il 90° anniversario dell'Istituto Storico Italiano (1883–1973)*, Studi storici, 88–92, 2 vols (Rome: Istituto storico italiano per il Medio Evo, 1974), II, 889–905

Smarr, Janet Levarie, 'The Tale of the Inquisitor', in *The Decameron: The First Day in Perspective*, ed. by Elissa B. Weaver (Toronto: University of Toronto Press, 2004), pp. 148–59

Thompson, Augustine, 'Lay versus Clerical Perceptions of Heresy: Protests against the Inquisition in Bologna, 1299', in *Praedicatores Inquisitores – I: The Dominicans and the Medieval Inquisition. Acts of the 1st International Seminar on the Dominicans and the Inquisition, Rome 23–25 February 2002*, (Rome: Istituto storico domenicano, 2004), pp. 701–30

Thorndike, Lynn, *A History of Magic and Experimental Science during the first Thirteen Centuries of our Era*, 2 vols (New York: Columbia University Press, 1923)

Tocco, Felice, *Dante e l'Eresia: quel che non c'è nella 'Divina Commedia'* (Bologna: Zanichelli, 1899)

——, 'Nuovi documenti sui moti ereticali', *Archivio Storico Italiano*, 5th ser., 28 (1901), 97–104

Tosti, Salvator, 'Descriptio Codicum Franciscanorum Bibliothecae Riccardianae Florentinae', *Archivum Franciscanum Historicum*, 8 (1915), 226–78 and 618–57

Rich and Poor in Western Europe, *c.* 1375–1475: The Political Paradox of Material Well-Being

Samuel K. Cohn Jr

The aftermath of Europe's most catastrophic demographic event, the Black Death of 1348, contributed to a rare occurrence in Western Civilization.[1] In the century, *c.* 1375 to *c.* 1475, the rich ceased to get richer and the poor, poorer. Because of the demographic consequences of the Black Death and subsequent waves of plague, the gap between rich and poor narrowed until the 1470s, when population pressure began to mount again, pushing costs of basic commodities up in real terms. These economic-demographic conditions and their consequences cut across strikingly different social, political, and economic regimes, as with Florentine Tuscany, the Low Countries, Languedoc, Normandy, and parts of England — places then experiencing great differences in military activity and destruction.[2] In Normandy, plague, the

* The author dedicates his essay to the memory of John H. A. Munro (1938–2013).

[1] For the general rise in inequality of income and wealth across Europe and the United States from the eighteenth century to the present, see Piketty, *Capital in the Twenty-First Century*, trans. by Goldhammer.

[2] For these trends in artisan and industrial wages (most often taken from skilled and manual labourers in the building industry), see la Roncière, *Prix et salaires à Florence*; Goldthwaite, 'I Prezzi del grano a Firenze'; Pinto, 'I Livelli di vita dei salariati cittadini'; Tognetti, 'Prezzi e salari nella Firenze tardomedievale'; Geremek, *Le salariat dans l'artisanat parisien*, trans. by Posner and Klapisch-Zuber, pp. 134–35; Victor, 'Les salaires des ouvriers du bâtiment' (which summarizes other works on wages and standards of living of other towns in Spain and finds

Samuel K. Cohn, Jr (Samuel.Cohn@Glasgow.ac.uk), Professor of Medieval History, University of Glasgow, is currently working on Disease and Hate. From the Plague of Athens to AIDS.

Approaches to Poverty in Medieval Europe: Complexities, Contradictions, Transformations, c. 1100–1500, ed. by Sharon Farmer, IMR 22 (Turnhout: Brepols, 2016) pp. 145–173
BREPOLS PUBLISHERS 10.1484/M.IMR-EB.5.105463

Hundred Years' War, and brigandage reduced towns and countryside to what Guy Bois has called a medieval 'Hiroshima'.[3] By contrast, no marauding troops invaded the hinterland of Canterbury, destroying villages, wrecking harvests for a generation or more, or reducing its major city to starvation as happened to Rouen in 1418 and 1419.[4] Yet for both regions, population and economy reached their nadir around 1450, with economic growth and the gap between rich and poor rising again by the 1470s.[5] These basic demographic and economic contours also hold, despite radically different perspectives and ideologies of the historians who have mapped them, as different from neo-Malthusian

the downturn in real wages around 1465); Munro, 'Urban Wage Structures'; Munro, 'Builders' Wages'; Munro, 'Wage-Stickiness, Monetary Changes, and Real Incomes'. For England, the literature on wages and prices is enormous, especially for agricultural labourers. See the trends constructed by Brown and Hopkins, 'Seven Centuries of Building Wages'; Brown and Hopkins, 'Seven Centuries of the Prices of Consumables'; and the critique and revision of these trends by Clark, 'Work, Wages and Living Conditions'. Nonetheless, despite Clark's dampening of Brown and Hopkin's peaks of the fifteenth century, his more extensive and nuanced figures show a similar rise in wages during the latter half of the fourteenth century, peaking in the last decades of the fifteenth century, and its peak *c.* 1470 was not surpassed until well into the nineteenth century; see esp. fig. 3, p. 914. For the literature on pre-industrial prices and wages, see Clark, 'Work, Wages and Living Conditions', pp. 889–90 n. 2. For the historiography across Europe, see Soisson, 'Le bâtiment: sources et historiographie', esp. pp. 95–100. Similar to England, the high point in European real wages for masons before the nineteenth century is reached in the quartile, 1450–75 (p. 97) and in Paris around 1468 (Baulant, 'Le salaire des ouvriers du bâtiment', esp. pp. 479 and 481). By contrast, at the high end of society, an earlier historiography has emphasized the colossal fortunes commanded by the large international banking families of the Bardi, Peruzzi, and Accaiuoli before the Black Death in Florence, that their commercial fortunes and the dowries they offered their daughters dwarfed those of the Medici, Strozzi, and other families of the Quattrocento: see Lopez, 'Hard Times and Investment in Culture'. Fortunes such as those of the Serristori family began to rise exponentially during the last decades of the fifteenth century: see Tognetti, 'The Development of the Florentine Silk Industry'. Herlihy and Klapisch-Zuber, *Les Toscans et leurs familles*, have emphasized the great disparity in wealth between Florence and the dependant towns of its territory and the skewed distribution of wealth within the city in 1427. However, with the next Catasto survey in 1457, the distribution of wealth had become much more egalitarian only to widen significantly again with the third survey in 1478: see Cohn, 'Women and Work in the Renaissance'.

[3] Bois, *Crise du féodalisme*; on Bois and his neo-Malhusian critique, see Herlihy, *The Black Death and the Transformation of the West*, ed. by Cohn, pp. 35–38.

[4] For the English siege of Rouen, see Bois, *Crise du féodalisme*, pp. 285–86; and *Mémoires de Pierre de Fenin*, ed. by DuPont, p. 104.

[5] For the demographic trends from the Black Death to the sixteenth century in Normandy, see Bois, *Crise du féodalisme*; for Canterbury, see Hatcher, 'Mortality in the Fifteenth Century'.

Emmanuel Le Roy Ladurie to Marxist Guy Bois.[6] Moreover, where wages have been studied, the same general patterns appear, despite differences in regime and the impositions of new regional or national legislation on wages and prices, as John Munro has shown in comparing England and Flanders. For the former, wage and price laws were enforced more vigorously and over a longer period than for any country in Europe, while for the latter no such regional laws are to be found.[7] Did these changes in the economic standing of subaltern classes then lead inexorably to improvements in their political power and social status?

In one of the liveliest debates in the recent historiography of late medieval and early modern Europe, Robert Brenner argued vigorously that the demographic changes did not necessarily produce increased liberties for the peasantry across Europe. The crux of his argument rested principally with the diverging fates of peasants east and west of the Elbe. Against the fallout of Black Death and successive plagues, forms of compulsory labour declined or disappeared altogether from most of Western Europe, while in Eastern Europe peasants became more tightly bound to their lords. The difference depended on class struggle and power relations, not demography.[8] Yet Brenner and the debate that followed focused exclusively on the fate of peasantries, not on townspeople or on shifts in the power relations between oligarchies and urban workers and artisans — their privileges and freedoms. To question the neo-Malthusian demographic determinacy — the assumption that the radical shift in the supply and demand of labour after the Black Death led necessarily to improvements in material conditions as well as gains in the political power and social status of lower classes — the historian need not cross the Elbe as Brenner did to find fundamental differences. Different trajectories in the well-being and liberties of

[6] See Aston and Philpin, *The Brenner Debate.*

[7] See Cohn, 'After the Black Death'; Munro, 'Urban Wage Structures'; Munro, 'Wage-Stickiness, Monetary Changes, and Real Incomes'; and, most recently, Lis and Soly, 'Labor Laws in Western Europe'; and Lis and Soly, *Worthy Efforts.*

[8] Brenner, 'Agrarian Class Structure', and Aston and Philpin, *The Brenner Debate*; Wunder, 'Peasant Organization and Class Conflict', took Brenner to task for not seeing the great diversity of agricultural systems in places east of the Elbe in the post-plague period. More recently, however, Thomas Robisheaux has emphasized the sharp demarcation in the agrarian structures and personal freedom of peasants between Western and Eastern Germany: 'The Peasantries of Western Germany, 1300–1750'. In addition, Brenner compared the different developments in France and England, but this comparison concerned the thirteenth century, on the one hand, and the sixteenth and seventeenth centuries on the other; Brenner, 'Agrarian Class Structure', p. 42.

peasants, labourers, and artisans occurred within the very borders of individual Western city-states or monarchies themselves.

From statutes, manorial records, and tribunals, such as King's Bench, scholars have studied more intensively changes in the conditions of the English peasantry than for any other European rural labourers from the thirteenth to sixteenth century. More than with most other peasantries in Western Europe,[9] forms of servitude persisted in England into the fourteenth century. Armed with new wage legislation and administrative structures of the Justices of the Peace, English landlords successfully combated the sudden shift in the supply and demand for labour that favoured workers. Similar to landlords east of the Elbe, the English nobility brought about a feudal reaction that turned the clock back as far as personal freedoms went.[10] Harsher forms of servitude restricted peasant mobility and diminished their rights in the generation after the Black Death. In tandem with these legal and political developments, the real wages of rural labourers did not improve until the 1370s or 1380s. The first economic victors of Black Death demographics were the very ones the English chroniclers pitied as the helpless victims of these swift demographic changes and of supposed peasant greed: the nobility.[11] However, around the time of the English Peasants' Revolt of 1381, the economic well-being and the political, juridical, and social status of the peasantry began to shift. England no longer went the way of the East; instead, market mechanisms began to dominate over coercive labour laws with a corresponding change in land tenure from servitude to copyhold. By the 1420s most demesnes had been leased out, and mechanisms for controlling rural labour had declined, as is eloquently testified in the

[9] Pockets of feudal landholdings persisted in the Italian Appenines, in northern Alpine regions such as Friuli, parts of southern Italian, where large estates of the latifundia remained, and in areas of Spain. On the survival of feudal tenures, vassalage, and servile dependency in the Florentine Appenines, see Cohn, *Creating the Florentine State*; for Friuli, Muir, *Mad Blood Stirring*; for the latifondia in Sicily, Bresc, *Un monde méditerranéen*.

[10] Other regions of Western Europe, not mentioned by Brenner or in the debate that followed, also saw aggressive actions by nobilities that quickly and successfully countered the initial post-plague opportunities of peasants to improve their legal status and extend their political rights as in Denmark (but not generally through the rest of Scandinavia); see Orrman, 'The Condition of the Rural Population', pp. 600–05.

[11] For an example of a prominent modern historian scorning the 'extortionate greed' of English peasants following the Black Death, see Putnam, *The Enforcement of the Statutes of Labourers*, pp. 219–20; for modern historians'praise and acceptance of Putnam's conclusions on the peasantry and the English labour legislation, see citations in Cohn, 'After the Black Death', p. 460.

sharp decline in the number of cases landlords could bring before their manorial courts.[12]

Despite an increase in deserted villages and enclosures, the status and economic prospects of rural toilers improved, as seen with increased leisure time, diet, and disposable income for drink at ale houses, investment in animal husbandry, and housing. Although bad times had not vanished, the periodic severe famines of the pre-Black Death period (in 1196, 1234, 1245, 1252–53, 1258, 1260, 1285, 1289, 1294, 1315–22, 1336, 1346) disappeared along with chroniclers' descriptions of the poor driven to eat bark, cats, dogs, even children.[13] The word *fames* rarely appears in late medieval English chronicles, even with England's last famine of the Middle Ages in 1438. Instead of starvation and cannibalism, chroniclers were now shocked that the wretched were reduced to eating bread made of beans and peas.[14] Not only were there fewer mouths to feed, the crown and municipal governments had become more adept at managing subsistence crises, as in 1391 during a period of wheat shortages in London, when the king organized shipments of grain 'from distant foreign parts for the sustenance and aid of His common people',[15] or in 1438, when London's mayor took it on himself to purchase emergency wheat supplies from Danzig.[16] Such measures were matched in the countryside with the growing effectiveness of parish charities and almshouses.[17] As Amartya Sen has shown for catastrophic famines of the twentieth century,[18] and medievalists now are arguing for the Middle

[12] Dyer, 'The Political Life of the Fifteenth-Century English Village', esp. pp. 146–47. Judith Bennett argues that compulsory service, particularly for women, persisted into the early modern period: 'Compulsory Labor Service'. She does not, however, give any evidence on whether such coerced labour increased or declined from the late fourteenth to the sixteenth century.

[13] See Cohn, *Popular Protest*, pp. 22–23. Even before this period, famines appear to have been prevalent. From narrative sources in the West alone Fritz Curshmann found twenty famines between 1090 and 1260 that swept across single regions; cited in Benito i Monclús, 'Famines sans frontiers en Occident', p. 48.

[14] *A Chronicle of London*, ed. by Nicolas and Tyrell, p. 45.

[15] *Calendar of Plea and Memoranda Rolls*, ed. by Thomas, III: *1381–1412*, p. 174, 1391. ii.8. According to *A Chronicle of London*, ed. by Nicolas and Tyrell, p. 79, it was the mayor of London, not the king, who 'sente his men over the see with gold into divers contres and broughte home corn, so that the prys was well amendyd'.

[16] Bolton, *The Alien Communities of London*, p. 33.

[17] Dyer, 'Did the Peasants Really Starve', p. 70; and McIntosh, 'Local Responses to the Poor', pp. 214–17.

[18] Among other places, see Sen, *Poverty and Famines*.

Ages, scarcity and famine were not solely or even at times principally determined by disastrous harvests, but were influenced by politics, markets, and the distribution of foodstuff.[19] A turning-point in English history occurred around 1375, ushering 'in a new era of cheap and plentiful food' — the end of 'hunger-driven mortality'[20] — and its determinants appear here to have been more than Malthusian matters of overpopulation and insufficient production of grain.

Thus, as far as the English countryside goes, there is no paradox: economic improvements for rural labour marched forward alongside increases in personal liberties and juridical power. But what about English towns? The new era of cheap food and an end to famine contributed also here to improving the material conditions of artisans and workers at least until the 1470s. Post-plague growth of the English cloth industry, moreover, fuelled artisans' economic well-being even in towns that continued to decline demographically through the fifteenth century.[21]

Socio-political developments in English towns for artisans and labourers, however, fail to present the same in-tandem march forward seen in the countryside: for towns, advances in personal freedom, equality, power, and the prestige of subaltern classes instead shifted into reverse. Following the

[19] See Bourin, Drendel, and Menant, *Les disettes dans la conjoncture de 1300*, especially the essays by Bourin and Menant, 'Les disettes dans la conjuncture de 1300 en Méditerranée', and Furió, 'Disettes et famines en temps de croissance'.

[20] Dyer, 'Did the Peasants Really Starve', p. 70. Whether the Peasants' Revolt of 1381 was the crucial event that marked the change from 'feudal reaction' to increased freedom and economic prosperity in the English countryside may still be open to debate. However, I would say that historians now see something in the chronological coincidence of broad social and economic changes sweeping across England by the last decades of the fourteenth century, and that few would now support Dobson's conclusion — 'In general the results of the great revolt seem to have been negative where they were not negligible'; *The Peasants' Revolt of 1381*, ed. by Dobson, p. 27.

[21] For large cities such as London, Bristol, Norwich, and Coventry — as well as smaller towns such as Gloucester, Bury St Edmunds, St Albans, and Salisbury — see Britnell, 'Town Life', p. 153. In the fifteenth century many English towns prospered, but others such as Lincoln, Boston, and Yarmouth did not. The debate, however, has focused on overall growth and not on the prosperity or decline in material conditions of workers and artisans, nor have historians investigated in depth the gap between rich and poor in towns over the century. There is little to show that urban artisans and workers suffered disproportionately to the merchant class: that is, until the late fifteenth and sixteenth century, when population was again on the rise and food and fuel were no longer as cheap. On the growth of the English cloth industry in Essex, see Poos, 'The Social Context of Statute of Labourers Enforcement', p. 50; and more generally, Miller and Hatcher, *Medieval England*, p. 127.

Black Death, and especially after the defeats of 1381, franchises won by artisans in lesser guilds of tanners, tawyers, tailors, joiners, lorimers, and cordwainers were swept aside. Best studied have been London's losses, beginning with the oligarchy's abrogation of artisans' 'Great charter of 1317'.[22] In the late fourteenth and fifteenth century, artisans lost their authority to control quality standards of their own production, rights to elect aldermen and mayors, and to serve in minor posts. These losses became deeply apparent with John of Northampton's mayoral defeat and banishment in 1384. But even after the suppression of Northampton's rivals and execution of Nicholas Brembre during the Merciless Parliament of 1386, there was no turning back to pre-plague artisan representation and freedoms. Instead, with royal intervention, the century's end spelled the opposite, a further concentration of political power within the hands of London magnates. From 1387 onwards, the rights of citizenship narrowed: those born to fathers who were freemen no longer were guaranteed citizenship.[23] And in the 1440s London's ruling elites smashed craftsmen's last attempts to have their earlier electoral rights recognized.[24]

For craftsmen and other burgesses of English monastic boroughs, the decline of liberties was even more devastating than in London. After the defeat and severe reprisals for rebels at Bury St Edmunds and St Albans in the summer of 1381, not only were their short-lived charters destroyed, concessions gained earlier in the fourteenth century were rolled back.[25] Until the dissolution of the monasteries, artisans, even merchants, as in St Albans, were not recognized as citizens but were legally defined by their monastic lords as 'villeins'. The burgesses' defeat at Bury St Edmunds was so crushing that later protest even through legitimate channels such as lawsuits and petitions all but disappeared. Major national conflicts such as Cade's Rebellion in 1450 and the Wars

[22] See Williams, *Medieval London*; *French Chronicle of London*, ed. by Riley, pp. 251–52.

[23] Now they were required to prove it formally by registering with the city chamberlain and being sworn in as freemen; Tucker, *Law Courts and Lawyers in the City of London*, p. 23.

[24] Barron, 'Ralph Holland and the London Radicals'; Barron, 'The Political Culture of Medieval London'. Rigby, 'Urban "Oligarchy" in Late Medieval England', p. 69; *The Great Chronicle of London*, ed. by Thomas and Thornley, pp. 175–76; and 'Eighth Book of the *Polychronicon* from Caxton', ed. by Lumby, Appendix 4, p. 567.

[25] These included rights over the possession of hand mills and election of bailiffs. See Trenholme, *The English Monastic Boroughs*; Lobel, *The Borough of Bury St. Edmund's*; Faith, 'The Class Struggle in Fourteenth Century England'; Freeman, *St Albans: A History*, pp. 96–98; Cohn, *Popular Protest*, chap. 10.

of Roses failed to rekindle earlier dreams for political liberties.[26] Even Henry VIII's dissolution of the monasteries from 1536 did not awaken these burgesses' earlier civic ambitions.[27]

Another scenario of post-plague, post-1381 English cities charts success with new charters of incorporation, first to Bristol in 1373, Newcastle-upon-Tyne in 1400, Norwich (1404), Lincoln (1409), Hull (1440), Southampton (1445), Coventry (1451), and many more during the sixteenth century.[28] But as Christian Liddy has recently shown, these were rights that consolidated the power of these cities' ruling elites in national politics and their partnerships with the crown.[29] As a consequence, not only did the balance of power shift towards tighter oligarchic rule, it also enabled elites to impose a greater disproportionate share of the royal tax burden onto the shoulders of the poor. The same did not occur within English villages: there, the tax distribution remained more or less equalitarian through the fifteenth century: richer villagers came to aid their poorer neighbours.[30]

* * *

Let's now turn to another part of Western Europe — northern Italy — where the configuration of power and the character of cities with their larger hinterlands and greater independence differed sharply from England's. Yet, despite these differences, as well as ones in industry, commerce, the character of political regimes, and trends in post-plague wage and price legislation, the movement of peasants' and urban workers' wages in Florentine Tuscany ran along lines similar to England's. In real terms they rose in the 1370s and remained high until the 1470s. After the plague and scarcity of 1374–75, low bread prices, diversification of crops, increased production and productivity of vineyards, olive groves, and animal husbandry improved the conditions of rural and urban workers alike. Moreover, from the late fourteenth to the sixteenth century, shifts in markets and the structure of textile production from low- to high-quality woollens and increased silk production, further benefited Florentine

[26] Lobel, *The Borough of Bury St. Edmund's*, p. 163.

[27] Lobel, *The Borough of Bury St. Edmund's*, p. 167.

[28] Weinbaum, *The Incorporation of Boroughs*, pp. 63–96.

[29] Liddy, *War, Politics and Finance*, p. 228 and elsewhere.

[30] Ormrod, 'Poverty and Privilege', pp. 641–42; and Dyer, 'Taxation and Communities in Late Medieval England'.

artisans: greater skills were demanded and higher wages paid.[31] New artisan demand for fashions such as men's golden belts and fancy sleeves for women underlie artisans' improved conditions and marked increases in purchasing power that can be seen not only in Florence but across cities of central and northern Italy.[32] Similarly, last wills and testaments show artisans entering the art market in significant numbers for the first time, commissioning religious objects and paintings for family pride and eternal remembrance.[33]

Yet, as in English towns, such improved economic conditions did not mark parallel developments for artisans and peasants in the socio-political realm. Instead, urban elites tightened their control, curtailing the earlier powers of artisans as members of large legislative assemblies such as the Councils of the *popolo* and *comune* in Florence or even larger ones as with Bologna's Council of Six Hundred guildsmen and the Council of Two Thousand in Parma. Florence's political history has been best charted. With the defeat of the Ciompi in late August 1378 followed by the fall of the lower guild regime of the *Arti Minori* in January 1382, textile workers and workers in other sectors lost rights of citizenship and representation. With the factional conflict between the Alberti and Albizzi in the 1390s, minor guildsmen suffered further setbacks within the guild republic: new councils staffed by Florence's wealthiest patricians now controlled military and other important decisions. By the early fifteenth century, a new bureaucratic elite trained in law effectively supplanted the old guild structure of amateur government staffed by guildsmen serving short-term offices.[34] With the return and triumph of the Medici in 1434, legal and illegal forms of intimidation, systematic use of exile, and use of hired thugs to execute 'justice' in back alleyways further abrogated guild rights and narrowed Florence's

[31] Goldthwaite, *The Economy of Renaissance Florence*. Similarly, in Bologna, its silk industry blossomed in the fifteenth century, and it experienced a building boom similar to Florence's in the second half of the century; see Robertson, *Tyranny under the Mantle of St Peter*, pp. 51 and 92. Tognetti, 'The Development of the Florentine Silk Industry', finds similar developments for Venice, Genoa, Bologna, and Milan. For Venice, they began earlier during the second half of the fourteenth century; see Molà, *La comunità dei Lucchesi a Venezia*, pp. 24–36.

[32] Stuard, *Gilding the Market*.

[33] Cohn, 'Piété et commande d'oeuvres d'art après la Peste Noire', and *The Cult of Remembrance*, chaps 6 and 7.

[34] Molho, 'The Florentine Oligarchy and the *Balía* of the Late Trecento'; and Molho, 'Politics and the Ruling Class'. Also, see Najemy, 'The Dialogue of Power in Florentine Politics': 'By 1400 the *popolo* had acquiesced in the elite's leadership and emerging dominance; after this point organized challenges from the guild community no longer materialized' (p. 280). Also see Najemy, *A History of Florence*, pp. 182–87.

power base to one focused on Medicean clientelage.[35] With the Pazzi's failed conspiracy of 1478, Lorenzo's ruthless revenge, and the constitutional change with the creation of a Council of Seventy in 1480, republicanism disappeared all but in name.[36]

Italy's other republics followed similar trajectories: by 1390 Lucca's Guinigi family implemented what Cosimo de' Medici was not able to achieve until a half century later — dynastic rule bearing a republican scaffolding with artisan representation only as a formality.[37] Other city-states such as Bologna, where broad artisan representation had been largely lost by Cardinal Albornoz's expansion of the papal states in the 1350s, mark similar late fourteenth- and fifteenth-century pathways. After a successful revolt in 1376 that brought papal power temporarily to an end in Bologna, artisans regained their representation in broad city councils. Their gains, however, were short-lived; in 1393 the city's leading families curtailed the powers of the guild Council of Six Hundred with an emergency Council of the Sixteen, which by the middle of the fifteenth century had become a permanent body and the principal means through which a tightly knit group of twenty to twenty-five families converted the communal guild government into 'the Bentivolesco financial-political oligarchy' (to use Ian Robertson's expression). Under the leadership of the Bentivolgio, these families possessed in effect hereditary control over the state and pilfered its resources as though they were private patrimonies. A generation before Florence's Pazzi conspiracy, this collegiate oligarchy was enjoying the financial and governmental powers that Lorenzo il Magnifico would achieve only after his draconian reforms in 1480.[38]

Of course, north of the Apennines rule by the *popolo* (groups of citizens from the upper echelons of artisans, shopkeepers, and merchants) and republican councils had a brief history. Philip Jones dismissed it as 'an episode between

[35] Martines, 'The Authority of Violence'. For Lorenzo's reliance on thugs, see below and Kent, 'Unheard Voices', esp. p. 400, for his use of *staffieri* in the countryside following the Pazzi conspiracy.

[36] Mallett, 'Premessa Lettere ai volumi V e VI'; Kent, 'Lorenzo…, Amico degli uomin da bene', esp. pp. 53–55; and Brown, 'Lorenzo and Public Opinion'.

[37] Meek, *Lucca, 1369–1400*.

[38] See Ady, *The Bentivoglio of Bologna*; and Robertson, *Tyranny under the Mantle of St Peter*. On Lorenzo de' Medici's financial corruption and powers in the last decades of his rule, see Brown, 'Lorenzo and Public Opinion'. Unlike his previous work on Cesena, in *Tyranny under the Mantle of St Peter*, Robertson pays less attention to the consequences for artisan representation in Bologna after Paul II's tighter control and management over the papal states in the 1460s.

two periods of aristocratic rule'.[39] By 1250 the *popolo* had fallen to signorial dynasties at Milan (the Visconti), Padua (the della Scala), Mantua (the Gonzaga), Ferrara (the Este), Urbino (the Montefeltro), as well as at numerous other smaller city-states, where 'despots' came and went in rapid succession.[40] Yet, the historiography of these political events has followed too closely the class bias of contemporary chroniclers. Historians have considered almost exclusively political and social relations at the top of political life alone, battles between patrician factions and the hegemony of single ruling families. Few have investigated the rights and prerogatives of citizens more broadly in these so-called 'despots', the role of guilds, the existence of broad councils such as that of Parma's Two Thousand that survived through the fourteenth century, even under the rule of a Neapolitan king,[41] and Bologna's Six Hundred that lasted to the end of the fifteenth century under an oligarchy controlled by families loyal to the Bentivolgio and by 1460 under the thumb of the papacy.[42]

Where historians have peered beneath politics at the top into the world of day-to-day decision-making at the neighbourhood level, as Ian Robertson has done for the Malatesta of Cesena from 1378 to 1465, artisans are seen holding neighbourhood elections and serving minor offices as tax collectors, although their cities did not possess broad legislative assemblies.[43] Even beneath the signorial rule of the powerful Visconti dukes of Milan, the institutions of the city's ancient *comune* continued to survive, including its broad-base Council of Nine Hundred, comprised of merchants and the upper echelons of the artisan and guild community. According to Francesco Cognasso, Milan's government was a combination of signorial and communal institutions — a diarchy — and in times of crises, as in 1402–03, 1412, and 1447, the duchess or duke had to negotiate new reforms by assembling the old communal councils.[44] More recently, Paolo Grillo has emphasized the *longa durata* of popular institutions such as the territorial officers of the *vicinie*, the gate districts, the 'elders' of the

[39] Jones, *The Italian City-State*, p. 585; and Scott, *The City-State in Europe*, chap. 3.

[40] For cities such as Perugia, Bologna, Padua, Asti, Pisa, and Bergamo, see Scott, *The City-State in Europe*, chap. 3, where rule of the *popolo* could survive intermittently over longer periods until the fifteenth century.

[41] See Cohn, *Lust for Liberty*, pp. 140 and 290.

[42] Robertson, *Tyranny under the Mantle of St Peter*, esp. pp. 49–63.

[43] Robertson, 'Neighbourhood Government in Malatesta Cesena'.

[44] Cognasso, 'Il Ducato Visconteo da Gian Galeazzo a Filippo Maria', pp. 77, 90–93, 157–59; and Cognasso, 'La repubblica di S. Ambrogio', pp. 396–97, and 399–403.

parishes, and especially that of the *Capitano del Popolo*. These 'republican' institutions limited the powers of the Milanese dukes, supported popular resistance in periods of crisis, and maintained a collective memory of popular powers to at least the mid-fifteenth century.[45] Even into the sixteenth century, market towns in the duchy such as Caravaggio, Agnadello, Pagazzano, Vailate, and others maintained their local power structures of the *vicinitas*, where collectively citizens enjoyed their prerogatives and heads of households (*capifamiglia*) performed crucial tasks such as the distribution of local taxes. In places heads of families continued to assemble periodically under the porticoes of their communal palaces to elect local representatives, who drafted petitions to the central government or could form general assemblies.[46] Under the papal monarchy of late medieval and Renaissance Rome, artisans of the capital still elected their officials of the *rioni* or neighbourhoods, and these were more than honorific positions. Through the first half of the fifteenth century, revolts of the *popolo* led by elected neighbour captains and under neighbourhood banners struggled against the tax policies and dictates of the curia and could banish popes and their entourage of officers and courtiers from the Eternal City.[47] How these rights and responsibilities of a broad base of citizens along with constitutional powers of great assemblies and representation may have changed from the Black Death to the sixteenth century remains uncharted territory.

Nonetheless, as with the republics, the sense is one of decline in artisans' rights in these northern and monarchical city-states, even if there could be moments of popular resurgence, as at Milan in 1403 following the death of Giangaleazzo Visconti.[48] In Cesena, for example, the Malatesta's loss of power to the papacy in 1465 also swept artisans from their rule at the parish level.[49] In the Milanese territory of the Geradadda, Matteo Di Tullio has recently shown that only two communities continued to possess late medieval general assemblies of citizens by the sixteenth century; and in other market towns, the local governing bodies had been transformed into narrow oligarchies of elites. In Caravaggio, for instance, 95 per cent of the families produced less than 3 per cent of their elected representatives (*consiglieri*) by the sixteenth century.[50]

[45] Grillo, 'The Long Life of the *Popolo* of Milan'.

[46] Di Tullio, *La ricchezza della comunità*, chap. 2.

[47] For these revolts, see Cohn, *Lust for Liberty*.

[48] Grillo, 'The Long Life of the *Popolo* of Milan', pp. 227–30.

[49] Robertson, 'Neighbourhood Government in Malatesta Cesena'.

[50] Di Tullio, *La ricchezza della comunità*, p. 70. Unfortunately, Di Tullio does not show

For the Italian countryside the trajectories of material well-being and political power appear more complex and variegated than in England. Black Death economics spurred urban merchants and even artisans to invest in the land. These commercial investments not only benefited the land and its productivity, they also boosted the well-being of rural toilers, as David Herlihy demonstrated more than forty years ago.[51] Before the Black Death, over-cultivation of grain and high taxation from the city had pushed peasants to the brink of starvation. In some areas, however, the post-plague urban investment and material improvement it spawned did not lead to increased freedom for rural labour. Instead, independent peasants who once owned their plots were converted into *mezzadri* (share-croppers), now forced to move from farm to farm on short-term leases that blunted any rights or customs to the land. These new commercial contracts, furthermore, introduced older forms of 'feudal' deference such as the mandatory presentation of gifts to urban lords on certain holidays and anniversaries.[52]

Yet historians often forget that the *mezzadria* system, even in Tuscany, never occupied more than a third of the rural labour force, at least until the sixteenth century or later.[53] Neither urban ownership nor sharecropping penetrated, for instance, into the highlands of Tuscany, where peasants were either independent landowners or feudal dependents of old magnate families (the Guidi, Ubaldini, Pazzi, Battifolle). War and especially Florence's policy of unequal taxation meant that from the Black Death to 1400 these peasants suffered absolutely and relatively to rural labourers in the Lowlands.[54] But with conflict raging between Florence and Milan at the end of the fourteenth century, these mountain peasants revolted and won handsome political and economic con-

how the representation and the political and economic structures of these market towns may have changed from the fourteenth or fifteenth centuries to the sixteenth. However, given the vast destruction of the relevant documentation in the archives of Milan and its territory, such comparisons might now be difficult, if not impossible.

[51] Herlihy, 'Santa Maria Impruneta'; and later in Herlihy and Klapisch-Zuber, *Les Toscans et leurs familles*.

[52] On mezzadria contracts, see Cohn, *Creating the Florentine State*; *Il contratto di mezzadria*, ed. by Muzzi, Nenci, and Daniela, I and III.

[53] Herlihy and Klapisch-Zuber, *Les Toscans et leurs familles*.

[54] By 1400 the city was imposing tax rates on certain mountain communes that were as much as thirty-five times higher than those levied on favoured parishes in the lowlands near the city walls and where Florentine citizens owned much of the land; see Cohn, *Creating the Florentine State*, p. 78.

cessions — up to fifteen years of tax exemptions, licences to carry weapons and rights to pass them on to their heirs, life-time positions as military officers paid by the Florentine *comune*, authority to hire and equip crossbowmen, and in places even political rights to determine who could settle in their communities and what taxes they should pay. More significantly, these peasant revolts succeeded in transforming Florence's fiscal system from a hodge-podge of unequal community rates to a standardized one throughout the Florentine *contado*, based on landed property and other assets.[55]

These peasants' political gains in turn led to further economic advances. Across northern regions of Florence, the real wealth of highland peasants increased more than elsewhere, the city of Florence included. From their darkest days around 1400, the value of mountaineers' holdings soared seven-fold by 1470.[56] As in England, the material conditions and socio-political powers of Florence's independent peasantry took parallel strides forward through the fifteenth century, even if in Florentine Tuscany that rise began a generation later. The same, however, cannot be said for urban workers. Instead, as in England, they prospered materially, while becoming politically more impoverished.

Cities in other regions of Europe followed roughly parallel paths. With Philip van Artevelde's defeat at Rozebeke in 1382, craft representation in municipal governments in Flemish cities declined and especially so at Bruges after its unsuccessful revolts in 1437–38. Craftsmen lost all rights to elect representatives to city councils; the duke of Burgundy and elite merchants, who did his bidding, now controlled these formerly 'representative' bodies.[57]

To be sure, as recent work by Jelle Haemers and Christian Liddy has argued, craftsmen's losses of constitutional powers at Bruges and York during the fifteenth century did not entirely end their influence on city politics. Through formal petitions and non-constitutional mass assemblies in front of town hall, guildsmen at York, for instance, continued to preserve certain rights such as electing their own 'searchers' to enforce standards in their crafts (unlike in London where craftsmen had lost these prerogatives by 1442). Furthermore, although York's craftsmen no longer possessed constitutional rights to elect aldermen and mayors, by illegal mass assembly occasionally they could still

[55] Cohn, *Creating the Florentine State*, pp. 91–92.

[56] Cohn, *Creating the Florentine State*, pp. 91–99.

[57] At Bruges, another rebellion proved successful in 1477; see Haemers, 'A Moody Community?; Haemers, 'Factionalism and State Power'; and Dumolyn and Haemers, 'Patterns of Urban Rebellion'.

oppose the election of those especially despised, as in 1420, 1462, 1464, 1471, and 1473.[58]

Similarly, in Florence, craftsmen, even workers, had not lost all power, despite the steady erosion of their representative powers within Florence's large legislative assemblies after the defeat of the Ciompi in 1378. The nature of that power had, however, changed. Steadily through the fifteenth century, their abilities to bargain and petition for collective privileges — such as rights to bear arms, election of local officials, grants of tax concessions and governmental assistance after war, fire, plague, and other natural disasters — had all but disappeared.[59] In their place, as the Medici archives now attest with thousands of letters that mounted exponentially through the second half of the fifteenth century, individuals, if no longer communities, could beseech Medici lords to grant concessions for tax relief, remissions of criminal sentences, or awards of minor posts in the provinces.[60] Nevertheless, at least one new collectivity of the poor did emerge in Laurentian Florence. Youth gangs known as *potenze* patrolled neighbourhoods. In return for Lorenzo's patronage, they heeded his calls in times of need as after the Pazzi conspiracy when 'the boys of the Millstone Corner, numbering 30 or more' assassinated the Medici's enemies.[61] These informal powers rendered through new patronage networks, however, were a far cry from the previous corporative and constitutional rights workers and artisans had enjoyed from the late thirteenth to the beginning of the fifteenth century. By the end of Cosimo's rule, artisan power had been transmogrified into a new atomized 'Renaissance individualism': now artisans, shopkeepers, and even merchants had become dependent on the Medici's *noblesse oblige*. After the Pazzi conspiracy, their collective and constitutional powers all but disappeared.

[58] Liddy and Haemers, 'Popular Politics in the Late Medieval City'.

[59] On these collective petitions, see Cohn, *Creating the Florentine State*, pt III; by the 1450s these petitions decline sharply within the acts of the *Provvisioni*, and after 1478 fail to appear.

[60] On these archival letters and patronage through letters of supplication and recommendation, see Brucker, *Renaissance Florence*; Kent, 'Ties of Neighbourhood in Quattrocento Florence'; Kent, '"Be Rather Loved Than Feared"'; Kent, 'Unheard Voices'; Kent, *Cosimo de' Medici and the Florentine Renaissance*; and Connell, *La città dei crucci*, chap. 3.

[61] Kent, 'Unheard Voices', p. 391, and Kent, 'Renaissance Patronage', pp. 10–11; Kent, 'Ties of Neighbourhood and Patronage in Quattrocento Florence', p. 95. On Lorenzo's organization and reliance on the *potenze*, also see Trexler, *Public Life in Renaissance Florence*. On the *potenze* during the Grandduchy, see Rosenthal, 'The Spaces of Plebeian Ritual', and work in progress by Francesca Fantappiè.

For Florence and most towns in Italy and England, the demographic pressures of the 1470s led to a worsening of economic conditions and perhaps predictably to further erosion in corporative powers with a growing dependency on the patronage of elites.[62] This pattern, however, was not everywhere the same, as is attested by the history of Bruges and its successful artisan revolution of 1477 against the Habsburg princes and their native oligarchy (but which lasted only a generation).

Armed revolt, moreover, was not the only route by which artisans could revive their former corporatist political power. As in many English and northern Italian towns, artisans in Castilian cities had also lost their corporative privileges and rights of election during the last quarter of the fourteenth century. However, between 1475 and 1511 guildsmen in towns along the northern coast of the Iberian peninsula successfully protested against the powers of an entrenched noble patriciate. As research in progress by Jesús Angel Solórzano Telechea shows, these ends were achieved through oath-taking and assemblies without reverting to armed resistance. Instead, the artisans took their protest to the king of Castile, petitioned for electoral reforms, and accused their noble rulers of abuses of justice, unfair taxation, and usurping from guildsmen former rights to electoral offices. With the Ordinances of Vitoria in 1476, which spread to seventeen other coastal towns, the crown allied with guild communities against the old lineages.[63] This alliance between the crown and 'a middling sort' was not, however, the rule. For the rest of Castile, craftsmen's strategies to regain their lost late-fourteenth-century prerogatives were different. They protested not only against the old urban families but against the king, expelling royal magistrates and proclaiming their towns to be independent city-states. In the second decade of the sixteenth century, they formed a Holy League against the crown but in 1521 were defeated and lost any further opportunities to revive their earlier fourteenth-century guild representation.[64] Nonetheless,

[62] This was the general development despite episodic shifts in these cities' political history as with the temporary ousting of the Medici at Florence, the formation of the Great Council of over three thousand, and an eighteen-year return to patrician rule of the old merchant elite and noble Florentine families; for this political and social narrative, see Brucker, *Renaissance Florence*, chap. 4; and most recently, Najemy, *A History of Florence*, chap. 13.

[63] In some towns, guildsmen were able even to ban the old noble lineages from holding offices. This alliance between the crown and 'the middling sorts' against the nobility, however, rapidly reinstated a new oligarchy in these towns, ones composed of the upper echelons of the guild community, such as at Chincilla in 1484.

[64] Jesús Angel Solórzano Telechea, 'Commons' Requests and Political Changes in the

despite these differences in political histories at the end of our period, the century 1375 to 1475 appears for Flanders and the towns of northern Castile similar to that of England and northern Italy — one of economic gains but of simultaneous political losses for urban artisans and guildsmen.[65]

Thus to find sharp differences in the social and political consequences of the sudden changes in the supply and demand of labour wrought by the fourteenth-century plagues, the historian need not rely only on the different outcomes between countries as far removed as England and Poland. Within the very backyards of city-states and monarchies across Western Europe, such striking contrasts in status and rights against the same demographic consequences can easily be sighted. While peasants generally benefited materially and politically from the post-plague demographic transformation, the same demographics proved a mixed blessing for urban artisans and workers: it brought economic gain but at the cost of political losses. To be sure, further towns elsewhere in Western Europe need to be studied to see whether their trajectories in economic well-being and political freedoms correspond with the paradoxical experiences presented here. Further divergences and wrinkles in these patterns might be found, as in Cologne after a revolt of the Neubürger against the old patrician families in 1396, when some artisans gained limited rights and a say in city government through the first decade of the fifteenth century.[66] More

Towns of Northern Spain in the later Middle Ages', paper presented at a workshop at Durham University: 'Rebels in Medieval and Early Modern Europe (Durham, 28–29 April 2011). See Solórzano Telechea, 'Protestas del común y cambio político'. This is part of a larger project entitled 'Ciudades y villas portuarias en la articulacíon del litoral atlántico en la Edad Media'.

[65] For a similar pattern, also see Geremek, *Le salariat dans l'artisanat parisien*, trans. by Posner and Klapisch-Zuber, esp. chap. 3. As with Lis and Soly, *Poverty and Capitalism*, chap. 2, Geremek emphasizes the negative side of workers' economic and social conditions after the Black Death, the increase in apprenticeship under worse conditions, the loss of artisan independence, the increase of putting-out or *Verlagssystem*, the 'proléterization' of certain groups of artisans in textiles.

[66] Militzer, *Ursachen und Folgen*, pp. 102–09. I wish to thank Dr Job Weststrate of the University of Groningen for bringing this case to my attention. Some late medieval Scandinavian towns may have also diverged from these patterns; however, given the paucity of evidence, especially outside Denmark and the larger towns, it is difficult to know. With the post-plague decline in population, smaller towns dependent on local trade tended to suffer economically more than the larger cities such as Bergen, København, Malmö, Stockholm, and Kalmer, which as regional centres prospered from international trade in late fourteenth and fifteenth centuries. Yet even in these larger, more prosperous towns, where crafts guilds tended to develop as in Danish towns and Stockholm, those elected to town councils were of the merchant class, and

exceptional was the pattern of governmental participation seen in late medieval Lisbon. Because of artisan support in 1383 for the regency of the Master of Avis, the crown granted guildsmen powers to maintain law and order and a voice in municipal affairs by establishing the electoral body of the Twenty-Four. This institution endured until the immediate aftermath of the massacre of 'New Christians' in April, 1506, staged in large part by the lower echelons of Lisbon citizens. To punish these citizens and to extend his regal powers, King Manuel abolished the Council of Twenty-Four and replaced Lisbon's municipal government with his own personal rule.[67]

But given the dominant patterns presented thus far, how do we explain these post-plague social trajectories — differences in the political fates of peasants and urban workers; and for urban workers a second dichotomy — economic gains at the expense of political losses? Why were urban patricians more successful than rural landlords (in places the same individuals) in defending themselves against the political demands of their dependants? How did peasants manage to use their improved market position to extend their liberties, while with similar improvements, urban workers lost their pre-plague customs and rights?

Questions about rich and poor in medieval and early modern Europe have focused either on economics or on the ideology and perception of the poor, while questions of political rights have been compartmentalized either within older contexts of constitutional history or in newer ones of popular protest. In the remaining space, I will speculate on reasons for these late medieval dichotomies. Long ago Fernand Braudel taught us that local causes cannot explain pan-regional trends. But historians perforce must begin with the local and then from local contexts build larger models.[68] For now, I will focus on Florence, where a solution comes from examining the consequences of class struggle. For the city,

by the end of the Middle Ages royal controls largely limited the autonomy of these councils; see Dahlbäck, 'The Towns'. Andersen, *Legal Procedure and Practice in Medieval Denmark*, trans. by Pedersen and Pedersen (pp. 204, 364, 366, 369, 396), suggests that participation and power in town governments by craft guilds in Denmark peaked in the thirteenth century and declined thereafter, especially by the mid-fourteenth century when town councillors became appointed for life and merchant elites consolidated their power assisted by the centralization of the crown. I wish to thank Professor Kurt Villads Jensen for bringing the Scandinavian case to my attention.

[67] See Yerushalmi, *The Lisbon Massacre of 1506*, pp. 28–32; and de Gois, *Chronica do felicissimo rey dom Emanuel da gloriosa memoria*, cap. CIII.

[68] Braudel and Spooner, 'Prices in Europe from 1450 to 1750', p. 437.

the decisive turning-point was the revolt of the Ciompi and its suppression in January 1382, the defeat of the new guilds of workmen and the shoring up of patrician power that increased more or less steadily with the reforms of the Albizzi in 1393, the rise of the Medici in 1434, Lorenzo's princely rule after the Pazzi conspiracy in 1478, and the rise of the grand dukes in the sixteenth century. On the other hand, much less has been uncovered about conflict between Florentine peasants and their lords during the fourteenth and fifteenth centuries, the assumption being that such struggles failed to occur in Republican Florence or in northern and central Italy more generally. But during Florence's war with Milan in 1402, peasants across the northern, eastern, and southern peripheries of the Florentine territorial state revolted against the city's excessive war taxes and encroachments into their customary rights, and unlike Florence's urban labouring classes, these peasants won. From issuing death penalties with new and ghoulish ceremonies for mass executions in 1402, war-torn republican Florence was forced to turn about-face in 1403 and negotiate with their peasant victors across the mountainous zones of Florence's territorial state. To protect their borders from further foreign incursions, to reverse the continuing deterioration of the city's tax base, and to end the haemorrhaging mass emigration beyond Florence's borders, the city cut handsome deals with those who only months before had been condemned to death as rebels. Rebel leaders and their villages were now granted life-long tax exemptions, rights to carry arms, and new positions in Florence's *imperium* to guard the frontiers of the territorial state.[69]

Back in the city, artisans' loss of collective power and representation was not solely the result of constitutional changes in the wake of the Ciompi's defeat. As scholars of fifteenth-century patronage for the arts and politics have shown, certain individuals — loyal subjects — even ones down the social ladder, could succeed within the new structures of favours, letters of recommendation, circles of *amicizia* that extended from the Medici and other well-placed families. This patronage system had a double effect on the guild community: it atomized power by diluting and fragmenting old corporatist ideals and possibilities of collective action (either through constitutional means or by illegal assemblies and violence). Secondly, it widened divisions within the lower classes of minor guildsmen and disenfranchised workers, creating a more clearly defined 'middling sort' in Florentine urban society.[70] Certain ambitious and skilled labour-

[69] Cohn, *Creating the Florentine State*, chap. 9.

[70] Najemy, *A History of Florence*, pp. 182–86, 266.

ers in textiles or other trades could now engineer political and economic advantages for themselves and their families in alliance with and loyalty to patrician patrons rather than in solidarity with less skilled workers, the *popolo minuto*, as had happened in 1378.[71]

This growing division between a 'respectable' middling artisan class and those beneath them, who from the late fourteenth century to the early modern period were increasingly satirized in literary works and artistic representations, finds corroboration in the post-plague history of charity.[72] In Florence and other cities of northern and central Italy, a dramatic change occurred in poor relief during the last quarter of the fourteenth century. From pious bequests made indiscriminately to the 'poor of Christ', testators turned to dowry funds given to select members of the poor, young girls chosen according to their own and their families' *buon costume*.[73] As Wim Blockmans and Jelle Haemers have shown for the Low Countries,[74] and Keith Wrightson, John Walter, Steve Hindle, Andy Wood, and others for England,[75] such a reshaping of class lines within working and artisan classes was not peculiar to Florentine history. Changes in poor relief, the upsurge of guides to good manners, and new attention to elocution and language hammered home new and more distinctive divisions within communities beneath the merchant classes. As Frank Rexroth has shown for London, these divisions — greater rewards for the upper echelons of loyal and productive artisans and labourers, and greater vilification and persecution of new immigrants, the truly poor, and other outcasts — were two sides of the same coin. Moreover, these new social and cultural divisions within the labouring classes did not need to wait until the sixteenth century as it seems early modernists have assumed. Instead, at least in London, they became the conscious objectives of elite politics in the wake of the Peasants' Revolt of

[71] See n. 60 above.

[72] On this satire, see Bec, 'La paysan dans la nouvelle toscane'; Bec, *Cultura e società a Firenze*; Cohn, 'Highlands and Lowlands in Late Medieval Tuscany'; and numerous stories by late fourteenth and early fifteenth century writers such as Sacchetti, *Il Trecentonovelle*, ed. by Lanza; and Sermini, *Le Novelle*, ed. by Vigo.

[73] See Cohn, *The Cult of Remembrance*, chap. 2.

[74] Blockmans, 'The Social and Economic Effects of Plague'; and Haemers, 'Factionalism and State Power', esp. pp. 1021–22.

[75] Wrightson, *English Society*; Hindle, *The State and Social Change*, pp. 115 and 227; Wood, *The 1549 Rebellions*, esp. chap. 5; Walter, *Crowds and Popular Politics*.

1381,[76] that is, about the same time we find these same class divisions hardening in the city of Florence.[77]

The emergence of a 'middling sort' with sharper divisions between rich and poor within the communities of labouring classes has until now been studied within regional boundaries — in England, the Low Countries, and Florence — as though these developments were *sui generis* and not ones then sweeping across wide swaths of Western Europe. The next assignment will be to take Braudel's lessons for comparative history to heart, to understand further what trans-regional variables may have conditioned these broader regional changes in class and culture. One new condition was certainly the plague and its recurrences with new notions on how to understand and combat it. Increasingly, this disease sparked new ideas and policies for policing physical and moral cleanliness, further protecting the respectable from the threat of alien and contagious bodies. However, before embarking on such a grandiose project, I wish to close with two simple pleas: first, the study of poverty concerns more than just economics, ideology, and perceptions: it also involves politics; second, various strands of poverty may not always be woven in simple parallel patterns. As the remarkable century following the Black Death reveals, social groups in society could become enriched economically, while simultaneously becoming impoverished politically.

[76] Rexroth, *Deviance and Power in Late Medieval London*, trans. by Selwyn.

[77] For the continuation of these strategies on the part of elites to divide labouring classes in 1930s and at present, see McKibbin, 'Who Benefits?'.

Works Cited

Primary Sources

Calendar of Plea and Memoranda Rolls Preserved among the Archives of the Corporation of the City of London at the Guildhall, 1323–1482, ed. by Arthur Hermann Thomas, 6 vols (Cambridge: Cambridge University Press, 1926–61)

A Chronicle of London, from 1089 to 1483, written in the Fifteenth Century, ed. by Nicholas Harris Nicolas and Edward Tyrell (London: Longman, 1827)

Il contratto di mezzadria nella Toscana medievale, ed. by Oretta Muzzi, R. Nenci, and M. Daniela, 3 vols (Florence: Olschki, 1987–92)

'Eighth Book of the *Polychronicon* from Caxton', in *Ranulphi Higden monachi Cestrensis*, ed. by Joseph Rawson Lumby, 9 vols, Rolls Series, 41 (London: Longman,1865–86), VIII, 522–87

French Chronicle of London, 1259–1343, in *Chronicles of the Mayors and Sheriffs of London, 1188–1274*, ed. by Henry Thomas Riley (London: Trübner, 1863), pp. 248–67

Gois, Damião de, *Chronica do felicissimo rey dom Emanuel da gloriosa memoria* (Lisbon: Aluarez, 1619)

The Great Chronicle of London, ed. by Arthur Hermann Thomas and Isobel Dorothy Thornley (London, 1938)

Mémoires de Pierre de Fenin, comprenant le récit des événements qui se sont passés en France et en Bourgogne sous les règnes de Charles VI et Charles VII (1407–1427), ed. by Mlle. DuPont, Société de l'histoire de France (Paris: Renouard, 1837)

The Peasants' Revolt of 1381, ed. by Richard Barrie Dobson, 2nd edn (London: Macmillan, 1983)

Sacchetti, Franco, *Il Trecentonovelle*, ed. by Antonio Lanza (Florence: Sansoni, 1984)

Sermini, Gentile, *Le Novelle di Gentile Sermini da Siena*, ed. by F. Vigo (Livorno: Vigo, 1874)

Secondary Works

Ady, Cecilia, *The Bentivoglio of Bologna: A Study in Depotism* (Oxford: Oxford University Press, 1937)

Andersen, Per, *Legal Procedure and Practice in Medieval Denmark*, trans. by Frederik Pedersen and Sarah Pedersen (Leiden: Brill, 2011)

Aston, T. H. , and C. H. E. Philpin, eds, *The Brenner Debate: Agrarian Class Structure and Economic Development in Pre-Industrial Europe* (Cambridge: Cambridge University Press, 1985)

Barron, Caroline M., 'The Political Culture of Medieval London', in *Political Culture in Late Medieval Britain*, ed. by Linda Clark and Christian Carpenter, The Fifteenth Century, 4 (Woodbridge: Boydell, 2004), pp. 111–33

——, 'Ralph Holland and the London Radicals, 1438–1444', in *The English Medieval Town: A Reader in English Urban History, 1200–1540*, ed. by Richard C. Holt and Gervase Rosser (London: Longman, 1990), pp. 160–83

Baulant, Micheline, 'Le salaire des ouvriers du bâtiment à Paris de 1400 à 1726', *Annales: ESC*, 26 (1971), 463–83

Bec, Christian, *Cultura e società a Firenze nell'età della rinascenza* (Rome: Salerno, 1981)

——, 'La paysan dans la nouvelle toscane (1350–1530)', in *Civiltà ed economia agricola in Toscana nei secc. XIII–XV: problemi della vita delle campagne nel tardo medioevo (Pistoia, 21–24 aprile 1977)* (Pistoia: Presso la sede del Centro, 1981), pp. 29–52

Benito i Monclús, Pere, 'Famines sans frontières en Occident avant la "conjoncture de 1300": à propos d'une enquête en cours', in *Les disettes dans la conjoncture de 1300 en Méditerranée occidentale*, ed. by Monique Bourin, John Drendel, and François Menant, Collection de l'École française de Rome, 450 (Rome: École française de Rome, 2011), pp. 37–86

Bennett, Judith, 'Compulsory Labor Service in Late Medieval England', *Past & Present*, 209 (2010), 7–51

Blockmans, Wim, 'The Social and Economic effects of Plague in the Low Countries, 1349–1500', *Revue Belge*, 58 (1980), 833–63

Bois, Guy, *Crise du féodalisme: économie et démographie en Normandie du début du 14e siècle au milieu du 16e siècle* (Paris: Presses de la Fondation Nationale des Sciences Politiques, 1976)

Bolton, James L., *The Alien Communities of London in the Fifteenth Century: The Subsidy Rolls of 1400 & 1483–4* (Stamford: Richard III & Yorkshire History Trust, 1998)

Bourin, Monique, John Drendel, and François Menant, eds, *Les disettes dans la conjoncture de 1300 en Méditerranée occidentale*, Collection de l'École française de Rome, 450 (Rome: École française de Rome, 2011)

Bourin, Monique, and François Menant, 'Les disettes dans la conjoncture de 1300 en Méditerranée', in *Les disettes dans la conjoncture de 1300 en Méditerranée occidentale*, ed. by Monique Bourin, John Drendel, and François Menant, Collection de l'École française de Rome, 450 (Rome: École française de Rome, 2011), pp. 9–33

Braudel, Fernand, and Frank Spooner, 'Prices in Europe from 1450 to 1750', in *The Cambridge Economic History of Europe, VI: The Economy of Expanding Europe in the Sixteenth and Seventeenth Centuries*, ed. by E. E. Rich and C. H. Wilson (Cambridge: Cambridge University Press, 1967), pp. 374–486

Brenner, Robert, 'Agrarian Class Structure and Economic Development in Pre-Industrial Europe', *Past & Present*, 70 (1976), 30–75

Bresc, Henri, *Un monde méditerranéen: economie et société en Sicile, 1300–1450*, 2 vols (Rome: École française de Rome, 1986)

Britnell, R. H., 'Town Life', in *A Social History of England, 1200–1500*, ed. by Rosemary Horrox and W. Mark Ormrod (Cambridge: Cambridge University Press, 2006), pp. 134–78

Brown, Alison, 'Lorenzo and Public Opinion in Florence: The Problem of Opposition', in *Lorenzo il Magnifico e il suo mondo: Convegno internazionale di studi (Firenze 9–13 giugno 1992)*, ed. by Gian Carlo Garfagnini (Florence: Olschki, 1994), pp. 61–85

Brown, H. Phelps, and Sheila Hopkins, 'Seven Centuries of Building Wages', in *Essays in Economic History*, ed. by E. M. Carus-Wilson (London: Arnold 1962), pp. 168–78

——, 'Seven Centuries of the Prices of Consumables, Compared with Builders' Wage Rates', in *Essays in Economic History*, ed. by E. M. Carus-Wilson (London: Arnold 1962), pp. 179–96

Brucker, Gene A., *Renaissance Florence*, 2nd edn (Berkeley: University of California Press, 1983)

Clark, Gregory, 'Work, Wages and Living Conditions: Building Workers in England from the Magna Carta to Tony Blair', in *L'Edilizia prima della Rivoluzione Industriale, secc. XIII–XVIII: atti della 'Trentaseiesima Settimana di Studi', 26–30 aprile 2004*, ed. by S. Cavaciocchi (Florence: Le Monnier, 2005), pp. 889–932

Cognasso, Francesco, 'Il Ducato Visconteo da Gian Galeazzo a Filippo Maria', in *Storia di Milano, VI: Il Ducato e la repubblica ambrosiana (1392–1450)* (Milan: Fondazione Treccani degli Alfieri, 1955), pp. 21–106

——, 'La repubblica di S. Ambrogio', *Storia di Milano, VI: Il Ducato e la repubblica ambrosiana (1392–1450)* (Milan: Fondazione Treccani degli Alfieri, 1955), pp. 387–452

Cohn, Samuel K., Jr, 'After the Black Death: Labour Legislation and Attitudes Towards Labour in Late-Medieval Western Europe', *Economic History Review*, 60 (2007), 457–85

——, *Creating the Florentine State: Peasants and Rebellion, 1348–1434* (Cambridge: Cambridge University Press, 1999).

——, *The Cult of Remembrance and the Black Death: Six Renaissance Cities in Central Italy* (Baltimore: Johns Hopkins University Press, 1992)

——, 'Highlands and Lowlands in Late Medieval Tuscany', in Mìorun Mòr nan Gall, '*The Great Ill-Will of the Lowlander'?: Lowland Perceptions of the Highlands, Medieval and Modern*, ed. by Dauvit Broun and Martin MacGregor (Glasgow: Centre for Scottish and Celtic Studies, 2009), pp. 110–27

——, *Lust for Liberty: The Politics of Social Revolt in Medieval Europe, 1200–1425* (Cambridge, MA: Harvard University Press, 2006).

——, 'Piété et commande d'oeuvres d'art après la Peste Noire', *Annales: Histoire, Science Sociales*, 51, no. 3 (1996), 551–73

——, *Popular Protest in Late Medieval English Towns* (Cambridge: Cambridge University Press, 2013)

——, 'Women and Work in the Renaissance,' in *Gender and Society in Renaissance Italy*, ed. by J. Brown and R. Davis (London: Longmans, 1997), pp. 200–27

Connell, William J., *La città dei crucci: fazioni e clientele in uno stato repubblicano '400* (Florence: Nuova Toscana, 2000)

Dahlbäck, Göran, 'The Towns', in *The Cambridge History of Scandinavia, I: Prehistory to 1520*, ed. by Knut Helle (Cambridge: Cambridge University Press 2003), pp. 611–34

Di Tullio, Matteo, *La ricchezza della comunità: guerra, risorse e cooperazione nella Geradadda del Cinquecento* (Venice: Marsilio, 2011)

Dumolyn, Jan, and Jelle Haemers, 'Patterns of Urban Rebellion in Medieval Flanders', *Journal of Medieval History*, 31 (2005), 369–93

Dyer, Christopher, 'Did the Peasants Really Starve', in *Food and Eating in Medieval Europe*, ed. by Martha Carlin and Joel T. Rosenthal (London: Hambledon, 1998), pp. 53–71

——, 'The Political Life of the Fifteenth-Century English Village', in *Political Culture in Late Medieval Britain*, ed. by Linda Clark and Christian Carpenter, The Fifteenth Century, 4 (Woodbridge: Boydell, 2004), pp. 135–57

——, 'Taxation and Communities in Late Medieval England', in *Progress and Problems in Medieval England: Essays in Honour of Edward Miller*, ed. by R. H. Britnell and John Hatcher (Cambridge: Cambridge University Press, 1995), pp. 168–90

Faith, Rosamond, 'The Class Struggle in Fourteenth Century England', in *People's History and Socialist Theory*, ed. by R. Samuel (London: Routledge & Kegan Paul, 1981), pp. 50–60

Freeman, Mark, *St Albans: A History* (Lancaster: Carnegie 2008)

Furió, Antoni, 'Disettes et famines en temps de croissance: une révision de la "crise de 1300": le royaume de Valence dans la première du XIVe siècle', in *Les disettes dans la conjoncture de 1300 en Méditerranée occidentale*, ed. by Monique Bourin, John Drendel, and François Menant, Collection de l'École française de Rome, 450 (Rome: École française de Rome, 2011), pp. 343–416

Geremek, Bronisław, *Le salariat dans l'artisanat parisien aux XIIIe et XVe siècles: étude sur le marché de la main-d'oeuvre au moyen âge*, trans. by A. Posner and C. Klapisch-Zuber (The Hague: Moutin, 1968)

Goldthwaite, Richard A., *The Economy of Renaissance Florence* (Baltimore: Johns Hopkins University Press, 2009)

——, 'I Prezzi del grano a Firenze dal XIV al XVI secolo', *Quaderni Storici*, 28 (1975), 5–36

Grillo, Paolo, 'The Long Life of the *Popolo* of Milan: Revolts against the Visconti in the Fourteenth and Fifteenth Centuries', in *The Culture of Violence in Renaissance Italy: Proceedings of the International Conference, Georgetown University at Villa Le Balze, 3–4 May, 2010*, ed. by Samuel K. Cohn, Jr and Fabrizio Ricciadelli (Florence: Le Lettere, 2012), pp. 221–36

Haemers, Jelle, 'Factionalism and State Power in the Flemish Revolt (1482–1492)', *Journal of Social History*, 42 (2009), 1009–39

——, 'A Moody Community? Emotion and Ritual in Late Medieval Urban Revolts', in *Emotions in the Heart of the City (14th–16th century)*, ed. by Elodie Lecuppre-Desjardin and Anne-Laure Van Bruaene, Studies in European Urban History (1100–1800) (Turnhout: Brepols, 2005), pp. 63–82

Hatcher, John, 'Mortality in the Fifteenth Century, *Economic History Review*, 39 (1986), 19–38

Herlihy, David, *The Black Death and the Transformation of the West*, ed. by Samuel K. Cohn, Jr (Cambridge, MA: Harvard University Press, 1997)

——, 'Santa Maria Impruneta: A Rural Commune in the late Middle Ages', in *Florentine Studies*, ed. by Nicolai Rubinstein (London: Faber, 1968), pp. 242–76

Herlihy, David, and Christiane Klapisch-Zuber, *Les Toscans et leurs familles: une étude du Catasto florentin de 1427* (Paris: Fondation nationale des sciences politiques, 1978)

Hindle, Steve, *The State and Social Change in Early Modern England, 1550–1640* (Houndmills: MacMillan, 2000)

Jones, Philip J., *The Italian City-State: From Commune to Signoria* (Oxford: Oxford University Press, 1997)

Kent, Dale, *Cosimo de' Medici and the Florentine Renaissance: The Patron's Oeuvre* (New Haven: Yale University Press, 2000)

Kent, Francis William, '"Be Rather Loved Than Feared": Class Relations in Quattrocento Florence', in *Society and Individual in Renaissance Florence*, ed. by William J. Connell (Berkeley: University of California Press, 2002), pp. 13–50

——, 'Lorenzo..., Amico degli uomin da bene: Lorenzo de' Medici and Oligarchy', in *Lorenzo il Magnifico e il suo mondo: Convegno internazionale di studi (Firenze 9–13 giugno 1992)*, ed. by Gian Carlo Garfagnini (Florence: Olschki, 1994), pp. 43–60

——, 'Renaissance Patronage: An Introductory Essay', in *Patronage, Art, and Society in Renaissance Italy*, ed. by Francis William Kent and Patricia Simons (Oxford: Oxford University Press, 1987), pp. 1–21

——, 'Ties of Neighbourhood in Quattrocento Florence', in *Patronage, Art, and Society in Renaissance Italy*, ed. by Francis William Kent and Patricia Simons (Oxford: Oxford University Press, 1987), pp. 79–98

——, 'Unheard Voices from the Medici Family Archive in the Time of Lorenzo de' Medici', *Rituals, Images, and Words: Varieties of Cultural Expression in Late Medieval and Early Modern Europe*, ed. by F. W. Kent and Charles Zika, Late Medieval and Early Modern Studies, 3 (Turnhout: Brepols 2005), pp. 389–404

Liddy, Christian D., *War, Politics and Finance in Late Medieval English Towns: Bristol, York and the Crown, 1350–1400* (Woodbridge: Boydell, 2005)

Liddy, Christian, and Jelle Haemers, 'Popular Politics in the Late Medieval City: York and Bruges', *English Historical Review*, 128 (2013), 771–805

Lis, Catharina, and Hugo Soly, 'Labor Laws in Western Europe, 13th–16th Centuries: Patterns of Political and Socio-economic Rationality', in *Working on Labor: Essays in Honor of Jan Lucassen*, ed. by Marcel van der Linden (Leiden: Brill, 2012), pp. 299–321

——, *Poverty and Capitalism in Pre-industrial Europe*, 2nd edn (Brighton: Harvester, 1982)

——, *Worthy Efforts: Attitudes to Work and Workers in Pre-Industrial Europe* (Leiden: Brill, 2012), pp. 429–40

Lobel, Mary Doreen, *The Borough of Bury St. Edmund's: A Study in the Government and Development of a Monastic Town* (Oxford: Oxford University Press 1935)

Lopez, Robert, 'Hard Times and Investment in Culture', in *The Renaissance: Six Essays*, ed. by W. K. Ferguson and others (New York: Harper & Row, 1953), pp. 29–54

McIntosh, Majorie K., 'Local Responses to the Poor in Late Medieval and Tudor England', *Continuity and Change*, 3 (1988), 209–45

McKibbin, Ross, 'Who Benefits?', *London Review of Books*, 35, no. 8 (25 April 2013), pp. 3–5

Mallett, Michael, 'Premessa Lettere ai volumi V et VI', in *Lorenzo de' Medici, Lettere: V: 1480–81*, ed. by Michael Mallett, (Florence: Giunti Gruppo, 1989), pp. v–xii

Martines, Lauro, 'The Authority of Violence: Notes on Renaissance Florence', in *Emotions in the Heart of the City (14th–16th century)*, ed. by Elodie Lecuppre-Desjardin and Anne-Laure Van Bruaene, Studies in European Urban History (1100–1800) (Turnhout: Brepols, 2005), pp. 31–40

Meek, Christine, *Lucca, 1369–1400: Politics and Society in an Early Renaissance City-State* (Oxford: Oxford University Press, 1978)

Militzer, Klaus, *Ursachen und Folgen der innerstädtischen Auseinandersetzungen in Köln in der zweiten Hälfte des 14. Jahrhunderts* (Cologne: Wamper, 1980)

Miller, Edward, and John Hatcher, *Medieval England: Towns, Commerce and Crafts, 1086–1348* (London: Longman 1995)

Molho, Anthony, 'The Florentine Oligarchy and the *Balía* of the Late Trecento', *Speculum*, 43 (1968), 23–51

——, 'Politics and the Ruling Class in Early Renaissance Florence', *Nuova rivista storica*, 52 (1968), 401–20

Molà, Luca, *La comunità dei Lucchesi a Venezia: immigrazione e industria della seta nel tardo Medioevo*, Memorie, Classe di Scienze morali, Lettere, ed Arte, 53 (Venice: Istituto veneto di Scienze, Lettere ed Arti, 1994)

Muir, Edward, *Mad Blood Stirring: Vendetta and Factions in Friuli during the Renaissance* (Baltimore: Johns Hopkins University Press, 1993)

Munro, John, 'Builders' Wages in Southern England and the Southern Low Countries, 1346–1500: A Comparative Study of Trends in and Trends of Real Incomes', in *L'Edilizia prima della Rivoluzione Industriale, secc.* XIII–XVIII*: atti della 'Trentaseiesima Settimana di Studi', 26–30 aprile 2004*, ed. by S. Cavaciocchi (Florence: Le Monnier, 2005), pp. 1013–76

——, 'Urban Wage Structures in Late-Medieval England and the Low Countries: Work-Time and Seasonal Wages', in *Labour and Leisure in Historical Perspective*, ed. by I. Blanchard (Stuttgart: Steiner, 1994), pp. 65–78

——, 'Wage-Stickiness, Monetary Changes, and Real Incomes in Late-Medieval England and the Low Countries, 1350–1500: Did Money Matter?', *Research in Economic History*, 21 (2003), 185–297

Najemy, John, 'The Dialogue of Power in Florentine Politics', in *City States in Classical Antiquity and Medieval Italy: Athens and Rome, Florence and Venice*, ed. by Anthony Molho and Kurt A. Raaflaub (Ann Arbor: University of Michigan Press, 1991), pp. 269–88

——, *A History of Florence, 1200–1575* (Oxford: Blackwell, 2006)

Ormrod, W. Mark, 'Poverty and Privilege: The Fiscal Burden in England (13th–15th Centuries)', in *La fiscalità nell'economia europea, secc.* XIII–XVIII, ed. by Simonetta Cavaciocchi, Atti delle 'Settimane di Studi', 39, 2 vols (Florence: Firenze University Press, 2008), II, 637–56

Orrman, Eljas,'The Condition of the Rural Population', in *Cambridge History of Scandinavia*, I: *Prehistory to 1520*, ed. by Knut Helle (Cambridge: Cambridge University Press 2003), pp. 581–610

Piketty, Thomas, *Capital in the Twenty-First Century*, trans. by Arthur Goldhammer (Cambridge, MA: Harvard University Press, 2014)

Pinto, Giuliano, 'I Livelli di vita dei salariati cittadini nel periodo successivo al tumulto dei Ciompi', in *Il Tumulto dei Ciompi: un momento di storia fiorentina ed europea* (Florence: Olschki, 1981), pp. 161–98

Poos, L. R., 'The Social Context of Statute of Labourers Enforcement', *Law and History Review*, 27 (1983), 27–52

Putnam, Bertha H., *The Enforcement of the Statutes of Labourers during the First Decade after the Black Death, 1349–1359*, Studies in History, Economics, and Public Law (New York: Columbia University Press, 1908)

Rexroth, Frank, *Deviance and Power in Late Medieval London*, trans. by Pamela Selwyn (Cambridge: Cambridge University Press, 2007)

Rigby, Steven, 'Urban "Oligarchy" in Late Medieval England', in *Towns and Townspeople in the Fifteenth Century*, ed. by John A. F. Thomson (Gloucester: Sutton, 1988), pp. 62–86

Robertson, Ian, 'Cesena: Governo e società dal Sacco dei Bretoni al dominio di Cesare Borgia', in *Storia di Cesena, II: Il medioevo, 2 (secoli XIV–XV)*, ed. by A. Vasina (Rimini: Ghigi, 1985), pp. 5–92

——, 'Neighbourhood Government in Malatesta Cesena', in *Patronage, Art, and Society in Renaissance Italy*, ed. by Francis William Kent and Patricia Simons (Oxford: Oxford University Press, 1987), pp. 99–110

——, *Tyranny under the Mantle of St Peter: Pope Paul II and Bologna*, Late Medieval and Early Modern Studies, 5 (Turnhout: Brepols, 2002)

Robisheaux, Thomas, 'The Peasantries of Western Germany, 1300–1750', in *The Peasantries of Europe from the Fourteenth to the Eighteenth Centuries*, ed. by Tom Scott (London: Longman, 1998), pp. 111–42

la Roncière, Charles de, *Prix et salaires à Florence au XIVe siècle (1280–1380)* (Rome: École française de Rome 1982)

Rosenthal, David, 'The Spaces of Plebeian Ritual and the Boundaries of Transgression', in *Renaissance Florence: A Social History*, ed. by Rodger J. Crum and John T. Paoletti (Cambridge: Cambridge University Press, 2006), pp. 161–81

Scott, Tom, *The City-State in Europe, 1000–1600: Hinterland – Territory – Region* (Oxford: Oxford University Press, 2012)

Sen, Amartya, *Poverty and Famines: An Essay on Entitlement and Deprivation* (Oxford: Clarendon Press, 1982)

Soisson, Jean-Pierre, 'Le bâtiment: sources et historiographie acquis et perspectives de recherches (moyen âge, débuts des temps modernes), in *L'Edilizia prima della Rivoluzione Industriale, secc. XIII–XVIII: atti della 'Trentaseiesima Settimana di Studi', 26–30 aprile 2004*, ed. by S. Cavaciocchi (Florence: Le Monnier, 2005), pp. 49–107

Solórzano Telechea, Jesús Angel, 'Protestas del común y cambio político en las villas portuarias de la España atlántica a finales de la Edad Media', in *La Comunidad Medieval como esfera pública*, ed. by Hipólito Rafael Oliva Herrer and others (Seville: Secretaiado de pulicaciones Universidad de Sevilla, 2014), 45–72

Stuard, Susan M., *Gilding the Market: Luxury and Fashion in Fourteenth-Century Italy* (Philadelphia: University of Pennsylvania Press, 2006)

Tognetti, Sergio, 'The Development of the Florentine Silk Industry: a Positive Response to the Crisis of the Fourteenth Century', *Journal of Medieval History*, 31 (2005), 55–69

——, 'Prezzi e salari nella Firenze tardomedievale: un profilo', *Archivio Storico Italiano*, 153 (1995), 263–333

Trenholme, Norman Maclaren, *The English Monastic Boroughs: A Study in Medieval History* (= *University of Missouri Studies*, 3 (1927))

Trexler, Richard C., *Public Life in Renaissance Florence* (New York: Academic Press, 1980)

Tucker, Penelope, *Law Courts and Lawyers in the City of London, 1300–1550* (Cambridge: Cambridge University Press 2007)

Victor, Sandrine, 'Les salaires des ouvriers du bâtiment à Gérone au XVème siècle', *Anuario de studios medievales*, 26 (1996), 365–90

Walter, John, *Crowds and Popular Politics in Early Modern England* (Manchester: Manchester University Press, 2006)

Weinbaum, Martin, *The Incorporation of Boroughs* (Manchester: Manchester University Press,1937)

Williams, Gwyn A., *Medieval London: From Commune to Capital* (London: Athlone, 1963)

Wood, Andy, *The 1549 Rebellions and the Making of Early Modern England* (Cambridge: Cambridge University Press, 2008)

Wrightson, Keith, *English Society, 1580–1680* (London: Unwin Hyman, 1982)

Wunder, Heide, 'Peasant Organization and Class Conflict in East and West Germany', *Past & Present*, 78 (1978), 47–55.

Yerushalmi, Yosef Hayim, *The Lisbon Massacre of 1506 and the Royal Image in the 'Shebet Yehudah'* (Cincinnati: Hebrew Union College, 1976)

The *Almoina* of Barcelona during the Catalan Civil War (1462–72): Changes and Continuities in the Conception of Catholic Poor Relief in Late Medieval Europe

Pol Serrahima i Balius*

Introduction

This paper tackles the analysis of the activities of a fifteenth-century cathedral almshouse in the Crown of Aragon, the *Almoina* of Barcelona, during a ten-year-long conflict, the Catalan Civil War (1462–72). The main interest of this paper is to test how a charitable organization that traced its institutional, organizational, and ideological roots to the twelfth century fitted into the socio-economic context of fifteenth-century Barcelona, by studying its behaviour in a period of difficulties. I conjecture that, in the conditions of financial collapse, charitable institutions may have evaded what they considered superfluous commitments in order to maintain those they deemed most important. Thus, by studying the *Almoina* of Barcelona during the Catalan Civil War,

* This paper was written with the financial support of an FI grant from the Generalitat de Catalunya and the scientific support of the following research projects: "Escassetats, caresties, fams i mortaldats a Catalunya a la Edat Mitjana: estudi i corpus documental", directed by Antoni Riera Melis at the Institut d'Estudis Catalans, and "Mercados alimenticios en la Edad Media: actores, mecanismos y dinámicas", directed by Pere Benito i Monclús and financed by the Ministry of Economy and Competitiveness (HAR2012–31802).

Pol Serrahima i Balius (polserrahima@historia.udl.cat) has degrees in History and Medieval Culture from the Universitat de Barcelona. He is currently writing a PhD thesis on markets, politics, and food crises in late medieval Barcelona at the Universitat de Lleida.

Approaches to Poverty in Medieval Europe: Complexities, Contradictions, Transformations, c. 1100–1500, ed. by Sharon Farmer, IMR 22 (Turnhout: Brepols, 2016) pp. 175–205
BREPOLS PUBLISHERS 10.1484/M.IMR-EB.5.105464

which totally devastated the Barcelonese and Catalan economy,[1] I will reveal what were considered to be its ultimate priorities, and this ought to bring us to a better understanding of the mentality that guided its actions.

At the time that the *Almoina* was founded, poverty was generally understood as 'an inherent part of the human condition, regardless of time, space, society and culture'.[2] As Dyer puts it, the biblical notion that stated that 'the poor you have with you always' (Matt. 26. 11; Mk 14. 7; Jn 12. 8) was at the core of the basic conception of poverty and ultimately led to the perception that poverty could not be eliminated. Instead, it only had to be relieved through charity, the exercise of which also helped the non-poor in reaching salvation.[3] However, poor relief was only one aspect of charity, which included not only the love of man but also the love of God. Consequently, charity, in the twelfth century at least, was exercised almost exclusively through the funding of ecclesiastical institutions. These institutions, which were not allowed to make any profit, divided charitable revenues among poor relief activities, the celebration of liturgical ceremonies, and the incomes of churchmen. Poor relief was thus ritualized as only one part of the duties of the good Christian.

The high medieval vision of the inevitability of poverty, which we will call 'essentialist', was alive and well in fifteenth-century Barcelona. For instance, in funerals and on the anniversaries of deaths, it was usual to ritually distribute bread among the poor,[4] who 'were treated more as symbols than as real people', as James Brodman expresses it.[5] However, from the mid-twelfth century, the increasing complexity of urban societies and the ever increasing shifts in their economies was paralleled by a greater awareness of the socio-economic dimension of poverty, which is epitomized by the appearance of a new category of poor people, the *pauperes verecundi*, that is, poor people who were ashamed of their poverty because they had once enjoyed wealth.[6] The word *poor* stopped describing an essential category and started defining an accidental characteristic that could be

[1] For a recent account in English of the Catalan Civil War, see: Ryder, *The Wreck of Catalonia*, which summarizes the most significant titles. Among them, the most relevant is: Sobrequés i Vidal and Sobrequés i Callicó, *La Guerra civil catalana*.

[2] Cohen, 'Introduction: Poverty and Charity in Past Times', p. 348.

[3] Dyer, *Standards of Living*, pp. 235–36.

[4] Riu, 'Alguns costums funeraris a l'Edat Mitjana a Catalunya', p. 46.

[5] Brodman, *Charity and Welfare*, p. 2.

[6] Brodman, *Charity and Welfare*, p. 5. For Catalonia, the oldest known reference to the *pauperes verecundi* dates back to 1163 (Archivo de la Corona de Aragón, GP, cupboard 28, scroll 11). Pere Benito i Monclús kindly provided this reference, which I appreciate.

used to designate anyone who had difficulties in satisfying his basic necessities.[7] As a result of that, it was possible to start seeing poor relief not simply as a side of Christian charity but also as a pragmatic means to maintain social stability.

Many institutions resulting from these new ideas were put to work in the fourteenth century, after the Black Death, when a wave of Christian charity was unleashed. In Barcelona, this wave was at first absorbed by the parishes and the Cathedral, but soon it generated new institutional structures. Boards of secular administrators started managing parochial alms, crafts and special interest groups organized themselves into fraternities,[8] and, most importantly, municipal governments started taking poor relief and public assistance into their hands. In Barcelona, in 1401, this last aspect materialized in the foundation of the *Hospital de la Santa Creu*, which merged the six pre-existent hospitals into a single institution, whose board of directors consisted of two members elected by the Chapter of the Cathedral, and two members chosen by the *Consell de Cent*, the town council.[9] Despite the significant role the Chapter would have in the *Hospital*, its establishment should be seen as a step forward for the *Consell de Cent*, which was consolidating its role as the central promoter of public assistance and poor relief policies in the city.

We know well that, until the nineteenth century, in Catholic Europe, poor relief nearly always had a religious component. However, the interference of the secular power may have helped to introduce new conceptions of poverty that fashioned relatively new (or renewed) charitable institutions. These new conceptions took more interest in controlling and, eventually, eradicating poverty than in the spiritual gains that could be obtained from almsgiving, even when references to such gains were of course a means to persuade possible donors. The success of these new forms of poor relief, along with their pragmatic, rather than essentialist, approach to poverty, could explain why, at the time the *Hospital de la Santa Creu* started getting bigger, the growth of the *Almoina* stopped. From 1407, the number of poor that the *Almoina* assisted would remain stagnant, only to start slowly decreasing in the sixteenth century until its disappearance in the nineteenth. In these circumstances, my paper tries to prove three points: the first is that, in the fifteenth century, the *Almoina* still

[7] Moisa, 'Fourteenth-Century Preachers' Views of the Poor', pp. 166–69.

[8] Cabestany i Fort, 'Confraries i gremis a Barcelona', p. 143; Riera i Melis, 'La aparición de las corporaciones'; Bach 'Confraries medievals'.

[9] Conejo da Pena, 'Assistència i hospitalitat'; Arrizabalaga, 'Hospitals, història i medicina', pp. 205–06; Castejón Domènech, *Aproximació a l'estudi de l'Hospital de la Santa Creu de Barcelona*.

followed the principles upon which it had been established, which were based on the perception of an immutable society in which poverty was an essential condition; second, that this conception played a vital role in rendering such an economic and institutional structure almost indestructible; third, that despite its survival well into the nineteenth century, the role of the *Almoina* in addressing the needs of the poor was already secondary in the fifteenth century, as indicated by the decreasing numbers of poor people whom it supported and the shifting charitable loyalties of the townspeople, who preferred making donations to the *Hospital de la Santa Creu*.

To prove these points, in the first place, this paper will offer an overview of the origin, organization, and functions of the *Almoina*, as well as of the sources we are going to analyse. After that, it will present a detailed study of the management of the *Almoina* during the last decade before the war. This will show how the institution worked in normal times. In the third section, it will turn to study the effects of the war on the institution, and from this data, it will try to prove the aforesaid points.

The Almoina *of Barcelona*

Eleven of the Cathedral almshouses of the Crown of Aragon possessed three characteristics that turned them into a very particular kind of institutions, different in some aspects from the average European almshouses. The *Almoina* of Barcelona was one of them, and so it possessed these three: first, it had been established to manage an endowment that had been granted to the Cathedral Chapter and perpetually assumed by it; second, it administered enough funds to accomplish the task originally mandated by the donors; third, unlike most almshouses of the time, which distributed food ritually on holy days, it distributed meals every day of the year.[10] Among these eleven almshouses, the *Almoina* of Barcelona is probably one of the best explained, even though its effective medieval administration has never before been studied.[11]

The deepest roots of the *Almoina* are to be found in the late tenth and early eleventh centuries, when two bishops of Barcelona endowed the Chapter with

[10] Rico Camps, 'Las Almoinas catedralicias', p. 160. The definition is based on that given in Baucells i Reig, 'Limosnas y Pía Almoina', p. 184.

[11] The two main articles on the establishment, development, and organization of the *Almoina* are Baucells i Reig, 'La Pía Almoina', and Baucells i Reig, 'Gènesi de la Pia Almoina'. The only study of the effective administration of the Almoina refers to the seventeenth century, and it is found in Fatjó Gómez, 'La beneficencia eclesiástica'.

some of their possessions. Those had to be used to feed the canons, the pilgrims, and the poor people. According to Josep Baucells, the form of these contributions shows that eleventh-century donors had not yet made any clear distinction between voluntary and involuntary poverty (I doubt that this distinction was ever done in the context of cathedral charity, but I will come to that later).[12] Other donations followed, but before 1160, all of them were aimed to endow meals only on Lent or on other holy days. In 1161, however, a cathedral sacristan established an endowment in land and money so that three poor people, chosen by the Chapter, could be fed a meal 'amodo cunctis diebus omni tempore' (from this day, everyday, forever).[13] Following his example, other individuals started bequeathing possessions to the Chapter mandating a fixed number of meals to be distributed daily. In 1217, the bishop of Barcelona bequeathed goods to establish the benefice of Sant Miquel, and directed its beneficiate to feed as many poor as he could with the land he endowed to the benefice, thus opening a new stream of donations addressed not directly to the Chapter but to the benefices of the Cathedral.[14]

It must be made clear that such endowments incorporated, as did those from the previous centuries, not only the mandate of distributing meals but also that of celebrating anniversaries, maintaining ecclesiastical benefices, or pensioning ecclesiastical dignities. In the will of Berenguer de Palou, for instance, it was clearly stated that the revenues from his donation had to be used to feed as many poor as possible, but only after the amount needed to maintain the benefice he had created had been deducted.[15] Besides, there were conditions regard-

[12] Baucells, 'La Pía Almoina', pp. 81–82; Brodman, *Charity and Welfare*, p. 9.

[13] Arxiu de la Catedral de Barcelona (henceforth ACB), Libri Antiquitatum, IV, fol. 2^{r-v}, 6, cited in Baucells i Reig, 'La Pía Almoina', p. 88, n. 6.

[14] Baucells i Reig, 'Gènesi de la Pia Almoina', pp. 23–25.

[15] In his donation, Berenguer de Palou also instituted an anniversary for himself, one for his uncle, former bishop of Barcelona, and one for his brother (Baucells i Reig, 'La Pía Almoina', p. 95, n. 47). Baucells i Reig explains that originally Berenguer had wished that the lands he had granted to the benefice of Sant Miquel would suffice to feed twelve poor people. Later on, in his will, he had changed the number to 'as many poor as could be decently attended'. Baucells i Reig asserts that he did so 'thinking that there would be more than twelve poor' (Baucells i Reig, 'La Pía Almoina', p. 94). However, assuming that Berenguer also stated very clearly that the needs of the benefice came first, can we be sure about that? On the occasion of insufficient income, did not the document impel the administrator to allocate expenditure to the benefice rather than to the distribution of meals? In fact, Baucells i Reig himself affirms that the poor fed by this foundation were never more than twelve, but he blames luck. Perhaps, the most important function of these donations might have been funding the benefices or the Chapter.

ing the poor that should be fed. In the case of Master Martí, the third founder of the *Almoina*, he indicated that in providing for the poor from his endowments, preference would have to be given to his relatives.[16] The imposition of such conditions was generalized and corresponds with the idea of Christian charity that aims at creating a sacred and immutable structure adapted to a static society, rather than founding a structure that could tackle the effective needs of the Barcelonese poor people according to the socio-economic context.

Donations accumulated for more than a century until the bishop understood that the administration of the possessions that had been donated to support poor people was becoming increasingly difficult, and that it had to be somehow segregated from the rest of the possessions of the Cathedral Chapter in order to rationalize it. Therefore, after a process that culminated in 1275, all the establishments that included mandates to distribute meals, whether they were daily or occasional, were put under the control of the new entity called, simply, the *Almoina* and, later on, *Pia Almoina*.[17] It was decided that meals would be given out in a specific building, and it was settled that two canons would be elected every two years as administrators of these endowments. The administrators would appoint two procurators from the clergy of the Cathedral, which would later be called *majordoms*. Those would be in charge of effectively managing the rents from the properties and make them suffice to face all the expenses that the donors had ordered, plus the salaries of minor officials, such as the distributor of portions, the collectors of rents, or the baker.[18] The *Almoina* would not build up its own capital. If the possessions produced more than what was required, the surplus was transferred to the main fund of the Chapter; and in case they did not suffice to cover expenses, it was the *majordom* that financed the difference until the end of the exercise, at which point the Chapter would reimburse him the amount risked. Every two years, the *majordoms* would have to show their account books to the outgoing and incoming administrators.

At the time this organization was set, the *Almoina* distributed only thirty-nine daily meals. In less than fifty years, in 1317, the number had risen to 178; and ninety years later, in 1407, to 288 and some 320 in the 1420s.[19] Probably this growth can be explained by the aforesaid wave of popular charity that arose

[16] Baucells i Reig, 'La Pía Almoina', p. 90.

[17] The first mention of this name dates back to 1471. See Baucells i Reig, 'La Pía Almoina', p. 74.

[18] Baucells i Reig, 'La Pía Almoina', pp. 104, 115–17.

[19] Baucells i Reig, 'La Pía Almoina', p. 103; Rico Camps, 'Las Almoinas catedralicias', p. 158. In the fourteenth and fifteenth centuries, Barcelona had a population of approximately twenty-five thousand inhabitants: Cabestany i Fort, 'Evolució demogràfica', p. 89.

during the fourteenth century. Even so, it was the success of this reorganization what made the Chapter able to capitalize the flow of almsgiving so effectively. Between 1317 and 1407, probably under the advice of the *majordoms*, the administrators increased and reorganized the estates administered by the *Almoina*. They made its exploitation more efficient by centralizing the possessions in a few specific locations: they sold isolated or less rentable properties and bought new lands, which were chosen so that the *Almoina* could have revenues in kind, in order to make it self-sufficient. In some occasions, the *Almoina* managed to acquire actual seigneuries, such as the castles of Sitges, Vilafranca de Penedès, or Sant Feliu de Llobregat, which produced not only rents from real estate but also seigneurial rights on the usage infrastructures (mills, bakeries, and roads), on the administration of justice, and on the measuring and trade of flour, meat and, other products.[20] In addition to real estate and seigneurial rights, it received other sources of revenue. In 1288, for instance, Berenguer d'Espiells endowed the *Almoina* with the prerogative to receive a quarter of the annual collection of the *lleuda de Mediona* (a royal tax on commercial imports and exports in Barcelona),[21] an establishment that would turn into one of the main assets of the institution.

By 1407, the *Almoina* had taken the shape that would remain almost intact, at least, until the seventeenth century. Under the observation of the two administrators, the *majordoms* controlled a network of salaried officials who brought the authority of the *Almoina* to its different seigneuries outside Barcelona (called 'foreign administrations') and gathered the product from both land exploitation and seigneurial administration, which in this way converged in the same stream of revenue. These officials transferred the revenues generated by the estates to the *majordom* or to a lessee who had previously paid the *Almoina* a negotiated fee. Besides, the *majordom* also received the rents from the estates the *Almoina* managed in Barcelona and its territory. There, the *Almoina* leased the estates perpetually through the system known as *emphyteusis*, which had the advantage of reducing the aggregate of all the rents in the city to a permanent and fixed sum.[22]

[20] The essential study on the first phase of the formation of the patrimony of the *Almoina* is López Pizcueta, *La Pía Almoina de Barcelona*. Some recent studies include: Vela i Aulesa, 'Aspectes de l'economia d'un domini rural barceloní'; Franklin-Lyons, 'Expansión y consolidación del patrimonio de la Pía Almoina de Barcelona'; Benito i Monclús, 'Del castillo al mercado y al silo'.

[21] Ortí Gost, *Renda i fiscalitat*, pp. 472–73.

[22] That system implied that the owner allowed a tenant (*emphyteuta*) to perpetually and hereditarily make use of the asset in exchange for an initial payment, a perpetual annual fee

In addition to the revenues produced by the estates administered by the *Almoina*, there were other sources of income: the revenues produced by the rights the *Almoina* had on the aforesaid taxes, the pensions from *censals morts*,[23] and the rents still administered by the Chapter and some benefices.[24]

By the fifteenth century, these revenues were used to prepare a meal consisting of meat, bread, and wine for the 320 poor on every *normal* day (between 250 and 300 days a year).[25] On holy days the poor were given three *diners* instead. It has been calculated that feeding these poor might have cost 2592 *lliures* a year,[26] a significant amount that, as we will see, broadly corresponds to reality. In addition, the *Almoina* also funded the anniversaries, masses, benefices, and ecclesiastical dignities ordered by the donors, as well as the payment of salaries. Finally, in its role of feudal lord, it had to finance the upkeep of the seigneu-

(which could either be fixed, depend on the land's productivity, or be mixed), and, especially in rural estates, some other specific obligations. The *emphyteuta* could sell or lease his dominion on the estate, but the owner could rightfully receive a share of the sale (*lluïsme*) or even recover the possession (*fadiga*). On the origins of this institution, see Benito i Monclús, *Senyoria de la terra i tinença pagesa*, pp. 615–728.

[23] A *censal mort* was the obligation to pay, for an unlimited period of time, an annual sum for the interest due on a loaned capital, usually guaranteed with property. To avoid condemnation of usury, it was disguised as the sale of the right to annually receive an amount that could reach 10 per cent of the loaned capital, and it could be redeemed for an agreed fee. Ecclesiastical institutions sometimes bought this category of rights, i.e., they acted as lenders. However, they did not usually buy *censals* themselves but were endowed with the right to receive pensions from such *censals* by the individuals who had gathered them when they were alive. Such was the case of the pensions the *Almoina* received. This lending practice became usual on the 1330s. On its origin, see for instance García Marsilla, *Vivir a crédito en la Valencia medieval*, pp. 177–202.

[24] As the *Almoina* was nothing but an administration, the usual procedure when donating was to establish the endowments to the Chapter or to the particular benefices of the Cathedral. Generally, the *Almoina* was then in charge of administering these foundations and ensuring that the benefices or provostries received the pension or the amounts that the donor had instituted.

[25] Baucells i Reig asserts that there were some three hundred normal days or meat days a year ('La Pía Almoina', p. 109). However, according to the account books of 1461–63, for example, there had been only 256 meat days between 1 May 1461 and the 30 April 1462 (ACB, Capítol de la Catedral, Pia Almoina, Majordomia, 1461–63, fols 69^{r}–71^{r}).

[26] Baucells i Reig, 'La Pía Almoina', p. 110. Barcelonese account currency was based on the Carolingian system: 1 *lliura* (pound) = 20 *sous* (shillings) = 240 *diners* (pennies). In 1462, the *lliura* was worth slightly more than the Florentine *fiorino d'oro*: Sobrequés i Callicó. 'Aspectos economicos de la vida en Barcelona', cited in the database *Currency Exchanges (Spufford)* <http://www2.scc.rutgers.edu/memdb/search_form_spuf.php> [accessed 15 July 2015]: electronic database for medieval currency based on Spufford, *Handbook of Medieval Exchange*.

rial possessions, except for the seigneuries that were leased, in which case, the expenses were to be assumed by the lessees. It has been calculated that, in the fifteenth century, the *Almoina* had an annual budget of 4000 to 4500 *lliures*.[27]

To evaluate the effective administration of the *Almoina*, the account books that the *majordoms* had to present every two years to the administrators appear as the perfect source. These books are preserved today in the Arxiu de la Catedral de Barcelona and form a body of documentation that goes all the way from 1283 to 1683. In some periods, there is only one book per biennium, in some others there are two (one per year, or one for revenue and one for expenditure), and in some others there are four (two per year: a main book and another for detailed expenditure). Regardless of that, all books start on 1 May and end on 30 April of the next year, or two years later.[28]

This paper analyses all the remaining books from 1450 to 1473, which add up to a total of ten.[29] These books open up with the chapters dedicated to the revenues. They record in the first place the aforementioned fixed amounts that the Chapter and various benefices paid every year deriving from these properties that were still administered by them. They follow up with the revenues produced by the rights over tax collection, those gathered from the properties in Barcelona and its territory, and those from the properties outside the city and its territory. Finally, they list the income from the payment of interests, from the *lluïsmes* (the *lluïsme* was a transfer tax received by the owner of a property leased on *emphyteusis* whenever the lessee sold the usufruct of such property) and from the extraordinary payments. Despite the fact that the *lluïsmes* were revenue generated by the properties, their payments are segregated because 5 per cent of what was collected from them constituted the pay of the *majordoms*.

[27] A comparison can be drawn with the annual budget of the *Consell de Cent*, which amounted to 43,120 *lliures* in 1412 and 27,075 *lliures* in 1436; Ortí i Gost, 'Les finances municipals de la Barcelona', p. 275.

[28] On these books, see Benito i Monclús, 'L'Almoina de la Seu de Barcelona'.

[29] Two of them encompass a period of one year (1451–52, 1452–53), and the other eight are organized in biennia (1455–57, 1457–59, 1461–63, 1463–65, 1465–67, 1467–69, 1469–71, and 1471–73). There are three books related to the biennium 1455–57; however, two of them are not general administration books, despite the fact that they are catalogued as such. Instead, what they record are the detailed extraordinary income and expenses caused by a particular event that took place in 1457, which will be dealt with below. The signature of these books is: ACB, Capítol de la Catedral, Pia Almoina, *Majordomia*, 1451–52, 1452–53, 1455–57, 1457–59, 1461–63, 1463–65, 1465–67, 1467–69, 1469–71, 1471–73 (henceforth *Majordomia*, followed by the years of the book).

After the section on revenues, the books record the expenses. They start with those related to food, beginning with grain-related expenses (purchases, transportation, milling, etc.), following with wine purchases, and continuing with expenditure on meat and other kinds of food. Still in that section, they go on with the costs of maintaining the refectory and finish with expenses of wine transportation from the properties to the almshouse. Expenditure on maintaining the benefices, pensioning the ecclesiastical dignities, and paying the mandatory ceremonies comes next, followed up by the salaries, the expenses generated by managing the 'foreign administrations', and, in the end, the extraordinary expenses, which are occasionally categorized. Any arrears were placed at the end of the expenditures section. The books usually closed with a summary of the incomes and outcomes of the exercise.

The Almoina *before the War (1451–59)*

The analysis of the administration of the *Almoina* during pre-war years is summarized in Table 7.1. It shows us, in the first place, that the economy of the institution was mainly based on fixed rents deriving from Barcelona and its territory. These were almost totally exploited by the system known as *emphyteusis*, which allowed the landlord to receive a perpetual fixed rent from a specific estate, thus allowing him to anticipate the revenues he could count on. The properties in Barcelona and its territory were classified in three rolls, known as *capbreus*, which were updated every year.[30] Two of them listed the rents produced by the properties in Barcelona. One was the *capbreu de la ciutat* (*capbreu* of the city), which recorded properties that accrued 504 *lliures* per year. The other was named *capbreu del carnisser* (*capbreu* of the butcher), and registered the rents from a set of properties inside the city that, on its aggregate, produced 646 *lliures* per year — the roll received its name from the fact that the rents recorded on it added up to the average annual cost of the meat bought by the *Almoina*, and its incomes were in fact directly consigned to the butcher who supplied it.[31] A third *capbreu*, that of the *territori* (*capbreu* of the territory), recorded the rents of the properties in the territory of Barcelona, which

[30] The *capbreu* was a kind of roll specifically used to record *emphiteutical* tenancies. In these rolls the tenants confessed under oath the duties they had towards their landlord, so that the administrators could keep track of the state of the property.

[31] In *Majordomia*, 1461–63, fol. 3, it is stated that the amount gathered from these rents 'servey a la carn qui·s despèn a la casa de la Almoina' (is used for the meat that is served in the house of the Almoina).

Table 7.1. Revenues and Expenses during Pre-War Period (1451–1459)

	1451–1453				**1455–1457**				**1457–1459**			
REVENUE	**Ll**	**S**	**D**	**%**	**Ll**	**S**	**D**	**%**	**Ll**	**S**	**D**	**%**
Rents from possessions in Barcelona and its territory	2985	5	4	37.3	2797	19	7	31	2786	19	7	34.3
Rents from direct exploitation of 'foreign administrations'	1674	8	3	20.1	1612	0	2	17	1603	4	2	18
Rents from leasing of «foreign administrations»	921	7	6	11.4	822	2	2	8.3	795	19	6	10.3
Receipts from tax collection	1071	9	10	13.4	1088	13	4	12	1058	14	10	13
Receipts from the chapter and the benefices	406	7	6	5.1	405	3	1	4.4	400	16	2	4.9
Interest from *censals morts*	603	16	4	7.3	528	3	1	5.8	495	2	1	6.1
Lluïsmes	250	18	8	3.1	59	18	7	0.7	471	11	2	5.8
Extraordinary revenues	156	13	9	2	2003	5	4	22	620	13	8	7.6
Total revenues	8074	19	8	100	9317	5	4	100	8371	11	2	100

EXPENDITURE	**Ll**	**S**	**D**	**%**	**Ll**	**S**	**D**	**%**	**Ll**	**S**	**D**	**%**
Food-related	4965	13	4	63.3	4997	17	7	51.1	4800	17	5	55
Masses, pensions, etc.	1639	15	9	20.9	1776	4	9	18.1	1769	1	1	20.3
Salaries	576	8	11	7.4	529	3	0	5.4	537	10	0	6.1
Maintenance of the estates and extraordinary expenses	660	18	6	8.4	2486	10	7	25.4	1620	2	10	18.6
Total expenditure	7842	16	6	100	9789	15	11	100	8727	13	4	100
Balance	231	8	2	–	-472	10	7	–	-356	0	2	–

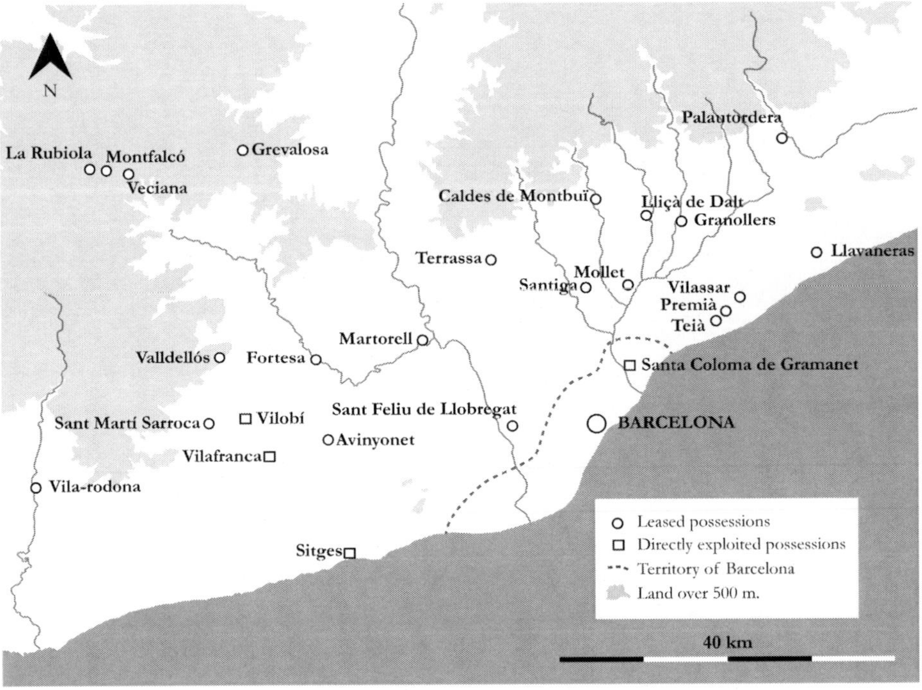

Map 7.1 Location of the Possessions of the Pia Almoina in Catalonia. Map by the author.

produced 223 *lliures* per year. The value of the rents derived from the urban and suburban patrimony was stable and flowed in its entirety during the decade before the war, representing a proportion that oscillated between 31 and 37 per cent of the total income.[32]

The 'foreign administrations' of the *Almoina* supplied about 25 or 30 per cent of its annual budget. They can be ranked in two categories: the ones that were leased and the ones that were not (see Map 7.1). The latter were Sitges, Vilobí, Vilafranca, and Santa Coloma, locations where the officials in charge raised the benefits and transferred them directly to the *majordoms*.[33] One rea-

[32] This figure also includes the leasing of a cellar or warehouse that the *Almoina* owned next to its refectory. This asset was not leased on *emphyteusis* but, instead, at surprisingly divergent prices: in 1451–52 and 1452–53, the *Almoina* received 7 *lliures* a year for its usage; in 1455–57 and 1457–59, on the contrary, it only received 2 *lliures* 10 *sous* for two years of usage.

[33] It is true that the officials of these estates usually leased some of the rents included in them. In Sitges, for example, they leased the butchery year after year and received the annual

son for not leasing these assets was that they were very productive in agricultural terms. Thus, every year it was decided which proportion of the collected cereals and wine was to be turned into money in the local market, and which was to be directly sent to the *Almoina*. In the biennium 1455–57, for example, almost a third of the grain acquired by the *Almoina* came directly from the rents of Sitges, Vilobí, and Vilafranca, while in the next biennium the proportion dropped to less than ten per cent, which means that most of the grain was sold in Sitges.[34] Sitges and Vilafranca provided wine and grain, Vilobí rendered grain, and Santa Coloma specialized in wine. Leaving aside the income in kind, these assets supplied about 20 per cent of the monetary income of the *Almoina*.

In the rest of the estates outside Barcelona, the *Almoina* privileged immediate monetary availability over the possibility of a major profit. Thus, most of the possessions were leased out for periods of one year: the lessee paid an annual fee and acquired the right to collect the aggregate of the revenues of the location, which were exacted by officials of the *Almoina*, and could include rights over bakeries, mills, forges, tolls and fines derived from the exercise of civil jurisdiction. The price of these leases was renegotiated annually, but it remained quite stable over the years.[35] Some possessions outside Barcelona rendered their fruits through other systems: the whole of the revenues of the castle of Avinyonet (Penedès) was perpetually leased on *emphyteusis* to the family of Guillem Vendrell for 50 *sous* a year;[36] the rights over the market of Vilafranca were perpetually endowed to the bishop of Barcelona for 17 *lliures* per year;[37] in Sant Martí Sarroca, the *Almoina* agreed with its subjects to merge all the dues into a single annual payment of 45 *lliures*;[38] and in Valldellòs, Vila-rodona, Raïm, and Veciana, each of the tenants of the manors and plots paid their customary rents

tax paid by the lessees of real estate tenanted in *emphyteusis*. However, these revenues were collected by the official in charge and merged with the rest of the takings.

[34] Serrahima i Balius, 'El pa de la Busca', p. 229.

[35] The rents of Sant Feliu, for example, were leased for 82 *lliures* in 1451–52; 80 *lliures* in 1452–53; 75 *lliures* a year in 1455–57, 1457–59, and 1461–62. *Majordomia*, 1451–52, fol. 4v; 1452–53, fol. 4v; 1455–57, fol. 4r; 1457–59, fols 5v–6r). The rents of Granollers, to put another example, were leased for 22 *lliures* a year all along the same period. *Majordomia*, 1451–52, fol. 9r, 1452–53, fol. 8v; 1455–57, fol. 10v; 1457–59, fol. 15v).

[36] *Majordomia*, 1461–63, fol. 9r.

[37] *Majordomia*, 1461–63, fol. 6r.

[38] *Majordomia*, 1461–63, fol. 6r.

directly to the *Almoina*.[39] The rents from the leased 'foreign administrations' produced about 10 per cent of the biannual monetary income.

The third source of income for the *Almoina* was the set of assets of a fiscal nature: the *lleuda de Mediona*, which was leased every year for 515 *lliures*; two other taxes collected in Barcelona that produced 7 or 8 *lliures* a year;[40] and six *cavalleries*,[41] which had been endowed to the *Almoina* by noblemen and produced *c.* 13 *lliures* per year. Altogether, these holdings yielded some 530 *lliures* a year for the *Almoina*, an amount that could represent up to 14 per cent of the revenues. The interests from the *censals* were next in importance to the fiscal assets:[42] paid by some twenty debtors, they rendered some 250 or 300 *lliures* a year. Following them, the rents received directly by the five previously mentioned benefices[43] and by the Chapter produced a very stable income of some 200 *lliures* a year, which represented about 5 per cent of the biannual income. By contrast, the *lluïsmes* were a very shifting source of income, gathering 0.7 per cent of the budget in 1455–57 and 7.6 in 1457–59.

Finally, extraordinary revenues included any revenue that did not originate from the assets administered by the *Almoina*. Because of their nature, the amounts listed under this category could be very diverse. In the biennium 1451–53, for instance, the *Almoina* only listed *c.* 157 *lliures* under this category (2.3 per cent of the biannual income). In contrast, in 1455–57, *c.* 2003 *lliures* (22 per cent of the income) were listed as extraordinary income.[44] Most of this exaggerated revenue in 1455–57 was received from the general fund of the Chapter in order to finance a sudden and unexpected surge of legal and military expenses produced by a so-called 'questió de Citges amb Cervera' ('question of Sitges with Cervera', a quarrel over the jurisdiction of Sitges), which

[39] *Majordomia*, 1461–63, fol. 17r.

[40] One of them was the so-called *lleuda de n'Aderró*, which was in fact a fraction of the *lleuda del vi* (a royal tax on imports and exports of wine). The other one was a half of the annual takings of the *crides del vi* (an impost on the sales of wine inside the town). Both rents were leased annually.

[41] Originally, the *cavalleria* (Catalan for 'cavalry') was a feudal tax that a castellan received from the castle he held for the king. The size of the tax was proportional to that of the army he had to provide his lord with when needed, also called *cavalleria*; Sabaté, 'Les castlanies i la comissió reial de 1328', pp. 202–04. In the fifteenth century, they may have still been received by the descendents of such castellans.

[42] See n. 23.

[43] See n. 24.

[44] *Majordomia*, 1451–52, fols 21r–24v; *Majordomia*, 1455–57, fols 22r–24v.

neither the assets administered by the *Almoina* nor the private capital of the *majordom* sufficed to face.[45] Consequently, the central administration of the Chapter had to provide the *Almoina* with funds not administered by it, which in fact meant nothing more than transferring funds from one administration to another. This would reinforce the idea that all the assets owned by the Chapter were seen as a whole, whether they were administered by the *Almoina* or by the canons as a whole.

Having discussed the revenues, we must turn to the expenses, whose main source was food acquisition, transformation and distribution. The biggest part of it was due to meat, grain and wine provisioning.[46] When it comes to grain, we do not know the amount of bread that each poor person ate. Nevertheless, it has been calculated that the *Almoina* acquired between 700 and 1000 *quarteres* of grain a year.[47] Wheat was the most common variety, but barley and oats were sometimes used as well. Combining purchases in the Barcelonese cereal market with the aforementioned imports from Sitges, Vilafranca, and Vilobí, the *Almoina* attained the required quantity. When grain was imported from the estates, the *Almoina* did not have to pay for it, but transportation costs were also high. Besides, whatever the origin of the cereal was, once it had been

[45] Unfortunately, following *Majordomia*, 1455–57, fol. 24^{v}, ten pages are missing. Therefore, there is no way to know the exact nature of these extraordinary revenues.

[46] On the diet of the poor of the *Almoina*, see: Echániz, 'La alimentación de los pobres asistidos'; López Pizcueta, 'El "Mal Any Primer"'. The elements that integrate the diet of the fifteenth century are the same as those of the thirteenth century. As regards the amounts distributed, our information is, by now, incomplete.

[47] Serrahima i Balius, 'El pa de la Busca', p. 221. Measurements referred to in this paper are the *quartera* and the *somada*. The *quartera* of Barcelona was a measure of capacity for grains. It was divided into 12 *quartans* and equalled 69.518 liters (Alsina, Feliu, and Marquet, *Pesos, mides i mesures*, p. 210; Ortí i Gost, 'El forment a la Barcelona baixmedieval', p. 394). The *somada* was used to measure liquids. According to some references in the account books of the *Almoina*, it was divided into 12 *quarters*, each of which equalled 3.792 liters (Alsina, Feliu, and Marquet, *Pesos, mides i mesures*, pp. 220–21). Therefore, a *somada* could equal some 45.5 liters. Finally, the *lliura* measured meat. It was divided into 12 *unces* and weighed 400 g (Alsina, Feliu, and Marquet, *Pesos, mides i mesures*, pp. 169–70). With the data from these sources, it is practically impossible to calculate the amounts of bread consumed by the poor people at the Almoina. Even when we have data about the amounts of wheat milled at the end of the biennium, we have no way to calculate exactly how much flour was extracted from it. Besides, we do not know at what rate this flour was transformed to bread and, what is more, if all the bread produced was consumed by the poor. Thus, it is impossible to try to calculate from our data the amounts of bread eaten daily by the poor.

brought to the granaries, it had yet to be sifted, milled,[48] kneaded, and baked before it was served as bread in the refectory. As the prices of grain were less stable than the prices of meat, expenditure on bread was more fluctuating than that on meat: taking into account all the transportation and manufacturing costs, the *Almoina* had spent *c.* 1671 *lliures* in 1451–53, *c.* 1755 *lliures* in 1455–57, and *c.* 1402 *lliures* in 1457–59.[49]

The account books let us know a bit more about meat distribution. Every 'normal day', forty-nine pounds of mutton meat were distributed at the refectory (approximately 208 g of meat per person), which adds up to some 12,400 pounds of meat annually that, costing an average of a bit less than 12 *diners* per pound, should have cost the *Almoina* about 615 *lliures* per year. The 646 *lliures* produced by the rents of the *capbreu del carnisser* sufficed to cover this quantity. Finally, the *Almoina* needed some 550 *somades* of wine each year.[50] As it happened with grain, a good deal of the wine was also produced in the *Almoina*'s vineyards of Santa Coloma, Sitges, and Vilafranca. Even if it was not produced in the land of the *Almoina*, practically all the wine consumed came from nearby. The cost of purchasing and transporting the wine to the house of the *Almoina* had reached *c.* 1577 in 1455–57 or *c.* 1783 *lliures* in 1457–59.[51] Other food-related expenditure included: fish and other less important edibles, the money given to the poor on fast days, the cost of the firewood needed to operate the ovens and heat the refectory, and the cost of washing the tablecloths and maintaining the cellar and the refectory. During the 1450s, food and related items accounted for 51 to 63 per cent of the total expense.

The cost of masses, pensions for the dignities, and maintenance of the benefices represented an amount between 18 and 21 per cent of the budget in the 1450s. The pensions to the beneficiates cost around 990 *lliures* per biennium. The anniversaries that had to be celebrated in the Cathedral amounted to some 400 *lliures* per biennium, and those celebrated out of the Cathedral amounted to some 220 *lliures*.[52] Next in importance was expenditure on the maintenance of the estates of Sitges, Vilafranca, Vilobí, and Santa Coloma de Gramanet,

[48] Only in some rare occasions did the *Almoina* buy flour. See Serrahima i Balius, 'El pa de la Busca', pp. 221–22.

[49] *Majordomia*, 1451–52, fols 30^{v}–31^{v}; *Majordomia*, 1452–53, fols 27^{r}–29^{v}; *Majordomia*, 1455–57, fols 30^{r}–34^{v}; *Majordomia*, 1457–59, fols 42^{r}–45^{r}.

[50] *Majordomia*, 1461–63, fol. 148^{v}.

[51] *Majordomia*, 1455–57, fols 35^{v}–41^{v}; *Majordomia*, 1457–59, fols 51^{r}–60^{r}.

[52] See, for instance, *Majordomia*, 1451–52, fols 32^{v}–42^{v}.

which was permanent and noteworthy: in the 1450s, it ranged between *c.* 160 *lliures* in 1451–53, and an annual average of *c.* 787 *lliures* in 1457–59.[53] The salaries were fixed, and thus the variation from one year to another was very small. Salaries were the least significant line of expense, representing between 5.4 and 8.3 per cent of the annual budget in the 1450s.

In addition to the ordinary expenses, the *Almoina* needed to cover the extraordinary expenses, which, during the 1450s, as was the case with the extraordinary revenues, ranged from *c.* 128 *lliures* in 1452–53 to *c.* 1700 *lliures* in 1455–57.[54] On the last biennium, as mentioned before, a conflict broke out between the *Almoina* and Cervera. In that context, the *Almoina* had to pay for lawyers, messengers, and even finance military actions, actions that were subsidized with funds from the other assets of the Chapter. The study of the other two books of 1455–57 should give us a hint on the entire litigation.[55]

On the whole, the data shows that the annual budget of the *Almoina* ranged from 4000 to 4500 *lliures* a year in the fifteenth century. It also shows that administrators were especially interested in stabilizing the flow of revenues, and that the rents from real estate and seigneurial property, as well as the takings from tax collection, generated 80 per cent of the budget of the *Almoina*. In normal times, around 60 per cent of that revenue was spent on poor relief, but a good part of it, around 20 per cent, was allocated to other aspects of charity — such as anniversary masses and ecclesiastical benefices. The proportion between income and expense was generally balanced. In 1451–53, the *Almoina* spent *c.* 231 *lliures* less than it had collected, which means that the possessions it administered generated an income for the whole Chapter. In contrast, in 1455–57 and in 1457–59 the *Almoina* spent more than it had gathered, thus being a burden for the Chapter. This was especially true in 1457–59, when the Chapter had to spend about 1700 *lliures* in behalf of the *Almoina* in order to cover the expenses derived from a judicial process.

[53] *Majordomia*, 1452–53, fols 55^{v}–58^{v}; *Majordomia*, 1455–57, fols 51^{v}–72^{v}. In Table 7.1, these are put together with the extraordinary expenses, because in some of the account books they were put under the same category.

[54] *Majordomia*, 1452–53, fols 60^{r}–65^{r}; *Majordomia*, 1455–57, fols 73^{r}–110^{r}.

[55] These books are listed as *Majordomia*, 1455–57 (bis) and *Majordomia*, 1455–57 (*terç*).

The Almoina *during the Civil War (The Books of 1461–73)*

The Catalan Civil War (1462–72) was fought between the king of Aragon, John II, and the government of Catalonia, the *Generalitat*, which was backed by the *Consell de Cent* and many other municipalities. It affected the *Almoina* in different ways. On the one hand, it limited its capacity for revenue collection. The main causes for that were the permanent presence of enemy troops in Catalonia, the general decay of the Catalan economy, and the harsh campaign instigated by the *Generalitat* and the *Consell* to increase fiscal pressure on the possessions of the Chapter of the Cathedral, due to their financial needs and their suspicion that the canons could sympathize with the king of Aragon.[56] On the other hand, war provoked a generalized increase of foodstuffs prices. Firstly, because King John II banned his states (including Sicily, Aragon, and Sardinia, which generated a significant part of the grain supplies) from trading with Catalonia, and also managed to eventually blockade traffic with other providers such as France and Provence. Secondly, because, from July 1462, when his troops entered the country and occupied a few key locations in the south, John instigated a ten-year-long campaign of scorched earth that limited the productivity of the territory. This campaign would end in November 1471, when King John launched a siege on Barcelona that would last for almost a year, until October 1472, when he finally rode into town.

Table 7.2 on pp. 194–95 offers a clear picture of the effects of war on the revenues of the *Almoina*. Only the rents from the places nearest to Barcelona, such as Caldes or Granollers (Vallès), Llavaneres (Maresme), or Sant Feliu (Baix Llobregat), were kept more or less safe — they flowed until the siege of Barcelona in 1472. The revenues produced by the rest of the assets were damaged drastically. Those derived from tax collection, for instance, were diminished in the most severe way. Bernat Grau, who had leased the *lleuda de Mediona* for the last years, did not lease it in 1462–63 'per rahó de la Guerra' (because of the war).[57] He did not want to risk his own capital, for he foresaw that the war would cause the decay of trade, as it actually did. Forced to collect the *lleuda* by itself, the *Almoina* only got *c.* 318 *lliures* between May 1462 and April 1463: had Bernat leased the tax at the same price as the year before, he would have lost 38 per cent of his investment. Incomes derived from the

[56] This last aspect has been studied in Torres i Ferrer, 'La Catedral de Barcelona', see particularly pp. 129–31.

[57] *Majordomia*, 1461–63, fol. 2v.

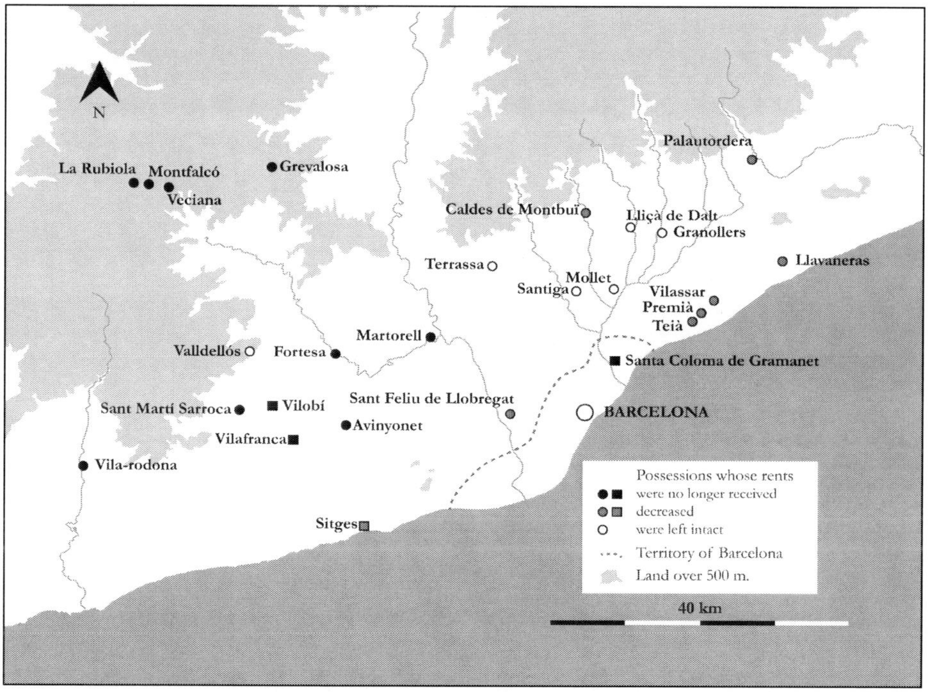

Map 7.2 The Effects of War on the Possessions of the Pia Almoina. Map by the author.

Lleuda would drop unavoidably year after year, for Barcelona would become less and less attractive to traders as war went on. The lowest point was reached between May 1469 and April 1471, when only *c.* 150 *lliures* were collected, 85 per cent less than what had been the usual biannual revenue before the war. Income from other taxes also shrank considerably,[58] but its relevance was minor compared to that of the *lleuda*.

In addition, many of the rents gathered from the estates outside Barcelona were also damaged or destroyed. Those originating from Valencia and Mallorca were immediately cut after the blockade of commercial relations between Catalonia and the rest of the states of the Crown.[59] Rural rents from estates in the more exposed locations diminished or disappeared, because the possessions

[58] The *lleuda de n'Aderró* was not received from 1464 until 1472, the *crides del vi* had lost half of its value, and the *cavalleries* could not be received from 1465 until 1471.

[59] Already the quantities corresponding to 1461 were not paid, for they had to be received by the end of April 1462, a point at which war seemed already unavoidable, possibly because the payment was made once at the end of the biennium (*Majordomia*, 1461–1463, fol. 17^r).

Table 7.2. Revenues and Expenses During the War (1461–1473)

	1461–1463				1463–1465			
REVENUE	**Ll**	**S**	**D**	**%**	**Ll**	**S**	**D**	**%**
Rents from possessions in Barcelona and its territory	2749	19	3	46.9	2743	18	7.5	45.1
Rents from direct exploitation of 'foreign administrations'	451	10	1	7.7	745	3	8	12.
Rents from leasing of 'foreign administrations'	692	15	6	11.8	654	10	0	10.
Receivings from tax collection	867	8	10	14.8	623	2	4	10.
Receivings from the Chapter and the Benefices	404	12	4	6.9	397	7	8.5	6.5
Interests from censals morts	194	10	7	3.3	492	12	5	8.1
Lluïsmes	116	10	3.5	2	146	9	10.5	2.4
Extraordinary Revenues	380	1	2	6.5	280	14	9	4.
Total Revenues	5857	8	0.5	100	6083	19	4.5	10

EXPENDITURE	**Ll**	**S**	**D**	**%**	**Ll**	**S**	**D**	**%**
Food-related Expenditure	3499	6	16.5	51.1	2744	9	0	45.
Expenditure in Masses, Pensions, etc.	1654	5	10	24.2	1330	18	1	23.
Salaries	672	2	0	9.8	550	8	0	9.
Maintenance of the Estates and Extraordinary Expenses	1019	15	19.5	14.9	1019	16	7.5	22.
Total Expenditure	6845	12	6	100	6020	1	5	10
Arrears	138	7	10.5	–	253	15	0	–
Balance [Revenues – (Expenditure + Arrears)]	-1126	12	4	–	-189	17	0.5	–

1465–1467				1467–1469				1469–1471				1471–1473			
Ll	S	D	%	Ll	S	D	%	Ll	S	D	%	Ll	S	D	%
2745	17	1	53.7	2741	6	5	53.6	2741	6	5	59.5	2741	6	5	63.5
535	9	4.5	10.5	301	4	2	5.9	162	18	8	3.5	200	0	0	4.6
605	6	0	11.8	623	10	8	12.2	608	6	8	13.2	253	4	10	5.9
223	13	4	4.4	174	0	4	3.4	154	4	2	3.3	251	1	11	5.8
368	16	6	7.2	369	1	10	7.2	347	16	2	7.5	259	17	4	6
408	0	0	8	430	10	0	8.4	430	3	0	9.3	447	5	3	10.4
113	18	6.5	2.2	7	0	0	0.1	0	0	0	0	0	0	0	0
116	3	2	2.3	468	8	1	9.2	165	14	7	3.6	161	16	1	3.8
117	17	0	100	5115	1	6	100	4610	9	8	100	4314	12	10	100

Ll	S	D	%	Ll	S	D	%	Ll	S	D	%	Ll	S	D	%
677	15	0	30.6	1523	10	8	37.9	1041	10	2	28.1	374	8	2	12.7
294	18	2	23.6	1148	14	7	28.6	1011	0	10	27.3	681	16	3	23.1
571	16	0	10.4	486	4	0	12.1	459	18	7	12.4	362	4	0	12.3
936	18	11.5	35.3	863	12	1	21.5	1193	19	1	32.2	1527	13	1	51.9
482	18	1.5	100	4022	1	4	100	3706	8	8	100	2946	1	8	100
385	13	2	–	550	8	0	–	1269	11	12	–	1783	19	7	–
750	14	3.5	–	543	12	2	–	-365	11	8	–	-415	8	3	–

were destroyed or badly harmed. Fortesa, for example, was sacked in 1463, and taken by the king the next year (see Map 7.2).[60] The *quadra* of Raïm was said to be 'completely uninhabited' since the beginning of the war.[61] The rents from other estates such as Sant Martí Sarroca, Vilobí, or Vilafranca could not be collected a single time after 1464. The reasons were not indicated in the books, but it is almost sure that the occupation of the southern area of Catalonia by the royalist forces had a lot to do with it (in fact, Vilafranca became a royalist stronghold in 1464). The revenues proceeding from Sitges also decreased significantly. The income produced by the *lluïsmes* also maintained a certain stability between 1461 and 1466, but then dropped in 1467–69, when they were reduced to only 7 *lliures* (down from *c.* 114 *lliures* during 1465–67), reflecting a situation of economic decay that did not foster financial transactions.[62]

A difference has to be drawn between the assets that were destroyed or left unproductive, in which case the *Almoina* forgave the payments, and those whose tenants faced difficulties paying their fees. In the latter case, the account books record the payments as effected, and later on warn about the arrears, which slowly increase: from *c.* 138 *lliures* in 1461–63 to *c.* 1783 *lliures* in the books of 1471–73.[63] Most of the debt was accountable to the tenants of the possessions in the city and its territory. By the end of the war, the tenants of possessions listed in the *capbreu del carnisser* owed *c.* 529 *lliures* to the *Almoina*; those leasing estates recorded in the *capbreu del territori* owed *c.* 415 *lliures* (almost three whole annuities); finally, the tenants of possessions of the *capbreu de la ciutat* owed up to *c.* 275 *lliures* (altogether, urban and suburban tenants accounted for 70 per cent of the arrears).[64]

Another good part of the debt was accountable to the defaulting of the interests of the *censals*. In 1461–63, most of the debtors had been freed from their obligations because of the war, but, as compensation, other *censals* that the *Generalitat* and the *Consell de Cent* paid to the Chapter, and that produced some 430 *lliures* a year, were consigned to the *Almoina*. Even so, the *Generalitat* and the *Consell de Cent* could only face their obligations for a while. In the book for 1467–69, they are shown to be in arrears for 550 *lliures*.[65] However,

[60] *Majordomia*, 1461–63, fol. 15ᵛ; *Majordomia*, 1463–65, fol. 15ʳ.

[61] *Majordomia*, 1461–63, fol. 15ʳ.

[62] *Majordomia*, 1467–69, fol. 88ᵛ.

[63] *Majordomia*, 1461–63, fol. 149ʳ⁻ᵛ.

[64] *Majordomia*, 1471–73, fols 55ʳ–80ᵛ.

[65] *Majordomia*, 1467–69, fol. 89ʳ.

this amount was reduced to *c.* 343 *lliures* in the next biennium.[66] Finally, the rents paid by the benefices were also liable for a part of the arrears. Up to *c.* 190 *lliures* were owed by the benefices to the *Almoina*,[67] which meant that the amount of almost a whole biennium had not been paid.

Because of these combined processes, the *Almoina* underwent a significant reduction of its revenues from the very beginning of the war, but especially after 1466. In 1461–63, it gathered only *c.* 5876 *lliures*, in contrast to the *c.* 8377 *lliures* of 1457–59. In 1463–65, the *Almoina* managed to increase its revenues to *c.* 6081 *lliures* by compensating the diminution of the revenues obtained from the *lleuda de Mediona* with the earning of interests from public debt and an increase of the revenues of Sitges.[68] For the next four years, the size of the total revenues was reduced but could be stabilized. However, the progressive loss of its sources of income caused a significant contraction in 1469–71. Finally, between May 1471 and April 1473, the revenues of the *Almoina* amounted to only 4359 some *lliures* (it gathered in two years what would have been considered an average revenue for one year before the war broke out).

The evident reduction of the *Almoina*'s capacity for revenue collection was paired with an increase in the price of foodstuffs. In May 1461, a year before the outbreak of the war, a pound of meat cost 12 *diners*,[69] a price that remained stable until April 1462, when it rose to 13 *diners*.[70] On August 1462, just a month after the start of the conflict, it had already reached 16 *diners*.[71] Less than two years later, on April 1464, it had reached 18 *diners* per pound.[72] The prices of grain were also high during the war. Whereas the highest price per *quartera* the *Almoina* had paid for wheat during the 1450s was 17 *sous* 6 *diners*, during the dearth of 1456–57,[73] on May 1463, it would have to buy significant amounts of barley at 12 *sous* because wheat had reached 20 *sous* per *quartera*.[74] From February 1466 to July 1466, it would not be possible to buy wheat of any kind

66 *Majordomia*, 1471–73, fol. 17^{r-v}.

67 *Majordomia*, 1471–73, fols 2^{v}–3^{r}.

68 Both the *Generalitat* and the *Consell de Cent* sold *censals morts* whose pensions were to be received by the *Almoina*.

69 *Majordomia*, 1461–63, fol. 69^{r}.

70 *Majordomia*, 1461–63, fol. 70^{v}.

71 *Majordomia*, 1461–63, fol. 71^{v}.

72 *Majordomia*, 1463–65, fols 54^{v}–57^{r}.

73 Serrahima i Balius, 'El pa de la Busca', p. 298 (fig. 30).

74 *Majordomia*, 1463–65, fol. 39^{v}.

for a price under 18 *sous*,[75] and in June 1472, during the siege of Barcelona, it purchased *mestall*, a mix of cereals usually sold at prices ranging from 10 to 12 *sous*, at 17 *sous* 4 *diners*.[76] Similarly, wine prices suffered a sustained rise: from the 10 to 15 *sous* per *somada* the *Almoina* paid in 1461,[77] they got up to 20 *sous* per *somada* in October 1466.[78] Besides, it faced as well a significant increase of the expenses derived from the maintenance and defence of its estates, especially in the central years of the war (in 1465–67, *c.* 1937 *lliures* were allocated on aggregate in maintenance and extraordinary expenses).[79]

Faced with this situation, as the Chapter could not supply capital from the main fund, the *Almoina* had to impose budget cuts, which were centred on the purchase of foodstuffs. As early as September 1462, the total daily amount of meat was reduced from forty-nine to forty pounds, and in April 1464, the *Almoina* stopped serving meat at all. Instead, for a year, money was distributed among the poor every day, but from May 1465, this policy was also abandoned. Wine was served for a bit longer. Already in 1465–67, the amount spent was extremely low, which surely indicates a diminution of the amounts served. From that moment on, the *Almoina* stopped buying wine at all and even transporting it from its estates, and only bread was served. Difficulties in buying wheat pushed the *Almoina*, which hardly ever diminished the quality of the bread served, to buy barley, oats, or mixed grains (*mestall*). Besides, in 1467, the officials assigned all the revenues of the *capbreu del carnisser* to the grain sellers, in an attempt to ensure a source of income for grain.[80] Finally, in May 1472, faced with the rising prices, and being unable to import wheat directly from its own estates because of the siege that had been laid on Barcelona, the *Almoina* stopped buying wheat, thus interrupting completely its poor relief services. Some sources seem to imply that such interruption had already taken place in 1470.[81] However, our account books leave no doubt that the *Almoina* still bought significant amounts of grain during 1471 and the first five months of 1472.[82]

75 *Majordomia*, 1465–67, fols 28v–29v.

76 *Majordomia*, 1471–73, fol. 23v.

77 *Majordomia*, 1461–63, fols 53v–57v.

78 *Majordomia*, 1465–67, fols 35r–37r.

79 *Majordomia*, 1465–67, fol. 109r.

80 *Majordomia*, 1467–69, fol. 4r.

81 ACB, Llibre de la Creueta, fols 21–24, cited in Torres i Ferrer, 'La Catedral de Barcelona', p. 127 n. 62.

82 *Majordomia*, 1471–73, fols 22r–23v.

In addition, the *Dietaris de la Generalitat* (the daybooks of the government) recorded, on March 1473, that the *Almoina* reopened after having been closed 'entorn un any passat' (for approximately one year),[83] which should be proof enough to support our dating.

Budget cuts were not limited to foodstuffs expenditure. The account books also show that spending on liturgical obligations, pensions to the ecclesiastical dignities, and maintenance of the benefices also decreased. However, they did so at a much slower pace. In addition, the aggregate expenditure on salaries decreased as well, which could lead us to think that the remuneration of the workers in the *Almoina* was brought down. Nevertheless, even though, in August 1471, the *Almoina* issued a regulation that stated that salaries should be lowered to a half,[84] the reduction is due in fact to the fewer salaries that were paid year after year, because of the progressive loss of the estates outside the city and the general diminution of activities. In 1461–63, more than thirty people received payment from the *Almoina*, while in 1471–73, only eight actually did.[85] Even so, and despite the regulation, the salaries of those who kept on working remained intact or even increased.[86]

To sum up, the loss of revenue collection capacity, together with an increase in foodstuffs prices and in obligations in terms of maintenance of the properties and others, forced the *Almoina* to change its priorities. Unable to capitalize the revenues from its estates, and facing an increasing amount of non-payments from its tenants, the *Almoina* had to reduce expenses. What may surprise us, however, is the way in which this was done: while expenditure on poor relief was reduced by 93 per cent from 1457–59 to 1471–73, that on the maintenance of benefices, the celebration of masses and anniversaries, and the pensioning of ecclesiastical dignities was cut only 41 per cent in the same period. Thus, the *Almoina* was able to confront the payment of salaries and the maintenance of estates and extraordinary expenses. Even so, the cuts could only invert the negative balances of 1467–69. In all the other exercises, the assets administered by the *Almoina* could not suffice to cover the expenses, and the Chapter, which was also facing financial difficulties during the war, had to cover the difference.

83 *Dietaris de la Generalitat*, ed. by Sans Travé, I, 211.

84 Baucells, 'La Pía Almoina', p. 109.

85 *Majordomia*, 1461–63, fol. 105^r–109^r; 1471–73, fol. 40^r–41^v.

86 The *majordom*, for instance, received, in 1471–73, 130 *lliures* instead of the usual 90 (*Majordomia*, 1471–73, fol. 40^r–41^v).

Conclusions

After this analysis, a new perspective on the role and the significance of the *Almoina* emerges. Modern research has usually stressed that poor relief was the main purpose of the *Almoina* and other institutions of its kind.[87] However, my analysis should make us see its motivations under a new light: the main purpose of the *Almoina* was not poor relief but charity, which was not limited to the love of men (poor relief) but also included the love of God, which embraced the financial preservation of the Church or, in this particular instance, that of the Cathedral Chapter and of the benefices of the Cathedral. In the face of financial difficulties, it was the expenditure in food provisioning that decreased the fastest, while expenditure on maintenance of benefices and liturgical celebrations decreased at a much slower pace. This order of preferences was no novelty: it was already present in the aforementioned will of Berenguer de Palou of 1241, and would still be detected in 1655–69, when the *Almoina* deliberately reduced the portions of the poor in order to fund the benefices and the Chapter.[88] My first point would thus be proved.

But perhaps the question is not only whether the guiding principles of the *Almoina* had been fashioned by an essentialist conception of poverty, but also what interests did this conception serve. The Chapter of the Cathedral of Barcelona was a huge economic structure that sustained itself exclusively on the revenues originated by charitable donations. Charitable donations enlarged the economic basis of the Chapter, and generated obligations, such as new altars, benefices or chapels, and poor relief. The job of the *Almoina* was to administer a very delicate part of these possessions that implied the duty of feeding the poor, having in mind that the main goal was the financial stability of the Chapter. The essentialist conception of poverty, then, helped in explaining that poor relief was simply an aspect of charity, without pragmatic motivations, and this, in turn, offered theoretical ground for reducing investment in poor assistance

[87] López Pizcueta, for instance, asserts that the 'only goal' of the *Almoina* was 'to feed the poor of the city': López Pizcueta, 'Estudio de un patrimonio urbano', p. 427.

[88] The part of the budget destined to poor relief did not even reach 20 per cent. The poor people assisted by the *Almoina* had seen how their ration had been diminished without a reason, while the amount intended to maintain benefices and celebrate anniversaries was increased. Besides, the *Almoina* managed to get surpluses from its administration, which were directly transferred to the Chapter. In fact, the situation got to be so outrageous that it caused the intervention of an episcopal visitor, who tried to reorganize the system (Fatjó Gómez, 'La beneficencia eclesiástica', p. 96).

whenever there was risk of not being able to cope with the love of God, which in fact meant the conservation of the Cathedral. To sum up, the essentialist conception of poverty was key to the sustaining the whole economic structure, not only of the *Almoina* but also of the Chapter of the Cathedral of Barcelona, which is even a bit more than what I proposed in my second point.

This brings us to my last point. In 1457 the *Consell the Cent*, interceding for the *Almoina* in front of the king about the 'question of Cervera', had asserted that the organization fed 'more than three hundred poor' and that its task was 'absolutely necessary' for the city.[89] However, this affirmation may have been exaggerated. As significant economic and political actors, the Chapter and the *Almoina* had a major influence in municipal politics in Barcelona, and, in fact, we have serious doubts about the real value the *Consell de Cent* attributed to the *Almoina* as a part of the poor relief system. Apparently, the only help the *Consell de Cent* granted to the *Almoina* during the war was a credit in order to fund the little army that would have to go to protect Sitges.[90]

In addition, the *Almoina* was losing its appeal for the donors. From 1317 to 1417 it had received sixty-eight donations amounting to more than 490 *lliures* in rents and more than 23,000 *lliures* in cash. In contrast, between 1417 and 1537, it only received seven donations amounting up to some 26 *lliures* in rents and *c.* 2684 *lliures* in cash.[91] Consequently, the number of poor it assisted did not grow — in fact, it went down, from 320 in the 1420s, to 279 in 1536, and to 129 in 1655.[92] By contrast, in the same period, the *Hospital de la Santa Creu*, which already owned the assets of the six hospitals the merger of which it was a result, received much help from the authorities, even episcopal ones. In merely six years, between 1403 and 1409, the *Consell de Cent*, the bishop, and the king granted 7250 *lliures* plus an annual credit of 1950 *lliures* to it.[93] Besides, the *Hospital* was the object of a continuous funding from the *Consell de Cent*: still in 1482, the *Hospital* received an annual subvention of 1300 *lliures* (2000 florins of Aragon).[94] As a consequence, and even though the *Hospital* was never

[89] Arxiu Històric de la Ciutat de Barcelona, Consell de Cent, Lletres closes, VI-20, 1456–57, fol. 80v. The assertion that three hundred poor were fed is also exaggerated according to our sources.

[90] *Majordomia*, 1461–63, fol. 109r.

[91] Baucells i Reig, 'La Pía Almoina', appendix 6.

[92] Rico Camps, 'Las Almoinas catedralicias', p. 158.

[93] Conejo da Pena, 'Assistència i hospitalitat', pp. 315–17.

[94] Lindgren, '¿De qué vivían los hospitales?', p. 530. These subventions were complemented

financially autonomous like the *Almoina*, the number of people it attended grew, from 346 a year, already in 1457, to 1890 in 1566, to 2485 in 1583, and to 4727 in 1596.[95] All this may imply that the claims of the Consell in 1457 were a way of protecting the financial interests of the Chapter rather than the needy people of Barcelona, which maybe did not depend on the *Almoina* anymore. However, it also shows that the essentialist conception of poverty had been the base to build an economic structure that would last for centuries regardless of its ultimate uselessness in alleviating the effects of poverty.

with a preferential treatment. On 1464, for instance, it was stated that those trying to sneak grain or flour into the city would lose it and that two-thirds of it would be given to the *Hospital* (Arxiu Històric de la Ciutat de Barcelona, Consell de Cent. Registre d'Ordinacions, IV-9 (1463–71), fol. 51[r–v]).

[95] Conejo da Pena, 'Assistència i hospitalitat', p. 314. These figures only take into account the admissions of sick patients, leaving aside those who lived permanently in the *Hospital*.

Works Cited

Manuscripts and Archival Sources

Aragón, Archivo de la Corona de Aragón, GP, cupboard 28, scroll 11

Barcelona, Arxiu de la Catedral de Barcelona, Capítol de la Catedral, Pia Almoina, *Majordomia*, 10 vols: 1451–52, 1452–53, 1455–57, 1457–59, 1461–63, 1463–65, 1465–67, 1467–69, 1469–71, 1471–73

Barcelona, Arxiu Històric de la Ciutat, Consell de Cent, Lletres closes, VI-20 (1456–57)

——, Registre d'Ordinacions, IV-9 (1463–71)

Primary Sources

Dietaris de la Generalitat, ed. by Josep Maria Sans Travé, 10 vols (Barcelona: Generalitat de Catalunya, 1994–2007)

Secondary Works

Alsina, Claudi, Gaspar Feliu, and Lluís Marquet, *Pesos, mides i mesures dels Països Catalans* (Curial: Barcelona, 1990)

Aramayona Alonso, Guillermo, 'El cuaderno de 1421 de "el bací dels pobres vergonyants" de la parroquia de Santa María del Mar, de Barcelona', in *La pobreza y la asistencia a los pobres en la Cataluña medieval: volumen misceláneo de estudios y documentos*, ed. by Manuel Riu, 2 vols (Barcelona: CSIC, 1981–82), II, 173–89

Arrizabalaga, Jon, 'Hospitals, història i medicina: l'Hospital de la Santa Creu de Barcelona', in *Actes de la VIII Trobada d'Història de la ciència i de la tècnica* (Barcelona: SCHCT, 2006), 203–09

Bach, Antoni, 'Confraries medievals', *Analecta Sacra Tarraconensia*, 67 (1994), 215–32

Baucells i Reig, Josep, 'Gènesi de la Pia Almoina de la Seu de Barcelona: els fundadors', in *La pobreza y la asistencia a los pobres en la Cataluña medieval. Volumen misceláneo de estudios y documentos*, ed. by Manuel Riu, 2 vols (Barcelona: CSIC, 1981–82), I, 17–75

——, 'Limosnas y Pía Almoina: institucionalización de la caridad para los más necesitados en el área catalana', *Memorie Ecclesiae*, 11 (1997), 161–211

——, 'La Pía Almoina de la Seo de Barcelona: origen y desarrollo', in *A pobreza e a assistência aos pobres na península ibérica durante a idade média*, 2 vols (Lisbon: Instituto de Alta Cultura, 1973), I, 73–135

Benito i Monclús, Pere, 'L'Almoina de la Seu de Barcelona: gènesi i formació d'un sistema integral de comptabilitat', in *Comptes de senyor, comptes de pagès. Les comptabilitats en la història rural*, ed. by Enric Saguer Hom, Gabriel Jover Avellà, and Helena Benito Mundet (Girona: Diputació de Girona. Patronat Francesc Eiximenis, 2013), pp. 73–92

——, 'Del castillo al mercado y al silo: la gestión de la renta cerealista de la Almoina de Barcelona en la castellanía de Sitges (1354–1366)', *Historia agraria*, 51 (2010), 13–44

——, *Senyoria de la terra i tinença pagesa al comtat de Barcelona (segles XI–XIII)* (Barcelona: CSIC, 2003)

Brodman, James William, *Charity and Welfare: Hospitals and the Poor in Medieval Catalonia* (Philadelphia: University of Pennsylvania Press, 1998)

Cabestany i Fort, Joan F., 'Confraries i gremis a Barcelona: segles XIII a XVI', *Finestrelles*, 2 (1990), 141–45

——, 'Evolució demogràfica', in *Història de Barcelona*, ed. by Jaume Sobrequés i Callicó, 8 vols (Barcelona: Enciclopèdia Catalana, 1991–97), III, 73–89

Castejón Domènech, Nativitat, *Aproximació a l'estudi de l'Hospital de la Santa Creu de Barcelona. Repertori documental del segle XV* (Barcelona: Fundació Noguera, 2007).

Cohen, Mark, 'Introduction: Poverty and Charity in Past Times', in *Poverty and Charity: Judaism, Christianity, and Islam* (= *Journal of Interdisciplinary History*, 35, no. 3 (2005)), pp. 347–60

Conejo da Pena, Antoni, 'Assistència i hospitalitat a l'edat mitjana. L'arquitectura dels hospitals catalans: del gòtic al primer renaixement', 2 vols (unpublished doctoral thesis, Universitat de Barcelona, 2002)

Dyer, Christopher, *Standards of Living in the Later Middle Ages* (New York: Cambridge University Press, 1989)

Echániz, María, 'La alimentación de los pobres asistidos por la Pía Almoina de la catedral de Barcelona según el libro de cuentas de 1283-1284', in *Alimentació i societat a la Catalunya medieval* (Barcelona: CSIC, 1988), pp. 173–261

Fatjó Gómez, Pedro, 'La beneficencia eclesiástica en la Barcelona del XVII: la Pía Almoina, 1655–1669', *Estudis: Revista de Historia Moderna*, 12 (1985–86), 71–96

Franklin-Lyons, Adam, 'Expansión y consolidación del patrimonio de la Pía Almoina de Barcelona (1340–1370): la incorporación de Sitges, la Mogoda y la torre Baldovina', paper presented at the 'XII Congreso de Historia Agraria' (13–15 March 2008) <http://www.seha.info/congresos/02_08.pdf> [accessed 15 July 2015]

García Marsilla, Juan Vicente, *Vivir a crédito en la Valencia medieval: de le los orígenes del sistema censal al endeudamiento del municipio* (Valencia: Publicacions de la Universitat de Valencia, 2002)

Lindgren, Uta, '¿De qué vivían los hospitales? Los fundamentos económicos de los hospitales de Barcelona de 1375 a 1500', *Anuario de Estudios Medievales*, 17 (1987), 525–32

López Pizcueta, Tomás, 'Estudio de un patrimonio urbano: la Pía Almoina de Barcelona en los siglos XIII–XIV', *Acta historica et archaeological mediaevalia*, 18 (1997), 427–50

——, *La Pía Almoina de Barcelona: estudi d'un patrimoni eclesiàstic català baixmedieval (1161–1350)* (Barcelona: Fundació Noguera, 1998)

——, 'El "Mal Any Primer": alimentación de los pobres asistidos en la Pía Almoina de Barcelona, 1333–1334', in *1r Col·loqui d'Història de l'Alimentació de la Corona d'Aragó: Edat Mitjana*, 2 vols (Lleida: Institut d'Estudis Il·lerdencs, 1995), II, 613–23

Moisa, Maria A., 'Fourteenth-Century Preachers' Views of the Poor: Class or Status Group?', in *Culture, Ideology and Politics: Essays for Eric Hobsbawm*, ed. by Raphael Samuel and Gareth Stedman Jones (London: Routledge & Kegan Paul, 1982), pp. 160–75

Ortí i Gost, Pere, 'Les finances municipals de la Barcelona dels segles XIV i XV: del censal a la Taula de Canvi', *Barcelona Quaderns d'Història*, 13 (2007), 257–82

——, 'El forment a la Barcelona baixmedieval: preus, mesures i fiscalitat', *Anuario de Estudios Medievales*, 22 (1992), 377–423

——, *Renda i fiscalitat en una ciutat medieval: Barcelona, segles XII–XIV* (Barcelona: CSIC, 2001)

Rico Camps, Daniel, 'Las Almoinas catedralicias en de la Corona de Aragón', in *Catedral y ciudad medieval en la Península Ibérica*, ed. by Eduardo Carrero Santamaría and Daniel Rico Camps, (Nausícäa Edición Electrónica, 2005), pp. 157–214

Riera i Melis, Antoni, 'La aparición de las corporaciones de oficio en Cataluña (1200–1350)', in *Cofradías, gremios y solidaridades en la Europa Medieval* (Pamplona: Gobierno de Navarra, Departamento de Educación y Cultura, 1993), pp. 285–318

Riu, Manuel, 'Alguns costums funeraris a l'Edat Mitjana a Catalunya', *Acta Historica et Archaeologica Mediaevalia*, 1 (1982), appendix 1, 29–57

Ryder, Alan, *The Wreck of Catalonia: Civil War in the Fifteenth Century* (New Abbot: Postscript, 2007)

Sabaté, Flocel, 'Les castlanies i la comissió reial de 1328', in *Estudios sobre renta, fiscalidad y finanzas en la Cataluña Bajomedieval*, ed. by Manuel Sánchez (Barcelona: CSIC, 1993), pp. 177–242

Serrahima i Balius, Pol, 'El pa de la Busca. Proveïment i consum de blat a Barcelona entre 1450 i 1462', in *Crisis frumentàries, iniciatives privades i polítiques públiques de proveïment a les ciutats catalanes de la Baixa Edat Mitjana*, ed. by Antoni Riera i Melis (Barcelona: Institut d'Estudis Catalans, 2013), pp. 161–300

Sobrequés i Callicó, Jaume, 'Aspectos economicos de la vida en Barcelona durante la guerra civil catalana de 1462–72', *Cuadernos de historia económica de Cataluña*, 3 (1970), 215–86

Sobrequés i Vidal, Santiago, and Jaume Sobrequés i Callicó, *La Guerra civil catalana del segle XV*, 2 vols (Barcelona: Edicions 62, 1987)

Spufford, Peter, *Handbook of Medieval Exchange*, Royal Historical Society Guides and Handbooks, 13 (London: Royal Historical Society, 1986)

Torres i Ferrer, María Jesús, 'La Catedral de Barcelona y la Guerra Civil Catalana', *Medievalismo*, 7 (1997), 99–138

Vela i Aulesa, Carles, 'Aspectes de l'economia d'un domini rural barceloní: la Torre Baldovina', in *El mas català durant l'Edat Mitjana i la Moderna (segles IX–XVII)*, ed. by Maria Teresa Ferrer Mallol, Josefa Mutgé Vives, and Manuel Riu (Barcelona: CSIC, 2001), pp. 453–78

Rich Master, Poor Master: The Economic Standing of School-teachers in Late Medieval France

Sarah B. Lynch*

During the 1430s, the city of Lyon carried out a major construction project: the rebuilding and repair of the bridges across the rivers Saône and Rhône. Given the magnitude of the work, the municipal council levied special taxes. Most paid in money but some, especially craftsmen and manual workers, paid in labour. Amid the records for days worked, there appears a strange sight: Simon Bravart, schoolmaster, worked twenty days on the bridges.[1] This would suggest that he was poor, lacking the means to pay the tax. Bravart's appearance as one of the workers on the bridges might indicate

* This article forms part of my PhD research on late medieval elementary and grammar schools in France, specifically in Lyon. A much shorter version of this was presented at the International Medieval Congress at Leeds in July 2011. The monetary systems used in this essay require some introduction. In general, the ecclesiastical records use the *solidi viennois* as their currency, while the municipal records use *solidi tournois*. Occasionally, the cathedral records use the *tournois* system, but this is limited to earlier references before 1300. The florin is also used by the cathedral as a currency of account. The conversion rate between these currencies varied through this period, and any conversions will be based on the rates available for that date. For a more complete guide to medieval currencies and equivalencies, see Spufford, *Handbook of Medieval Exchange*.

[1] 'Item mestre Simon Bravart mestre d'escola a fait ouvre par lui… xx jours', Archives municipales de Lyon (henceforth AML), CC 396, piece, no. 63 (*c.* 1437).

Sarah B. Lynch (sarah.b.lynch@outlook.com) recently completed a doctoral dissertation entitled 'Elementary and Grammar Education in Late Medieval France: Lyon, 1285–1530' for the Institute for Medieval Studies, University of Leeds. She currently teaches at SUNY Oswego.

Approaches to Poverty in Medieval Europe: Complexities, Contradictions, Transformations, c. 1100–1500, ed. by Sharon Farmer, IMR 22 (Turnhout: Brepols, 2016) pp. 207–228
BREPOLS PUBLISHERS 10.1484/M.IMR-EB.5.105465

that all teachers in fifteenth-century Lyon were neither highly paid nor highly regarded. This is only one example, however. Rather than being representative of all schoolmasters, Bravart's case points to the changeable and difficult-to-define professional and economic nature of the medieval school teacher. Little has been written concerning the poverty or wealth of teachers, or on whether the occupation was equated with any particular rank in society. While the economic and social status of university-based masters is relatively easy to discover, that of elementary and grammar teachers in both urban and rural contexts is far less clear and has been generally neglected. Elementary and grammar teachers made up a large proportion of educators active in late medieval France and were the masters to whom the greater part of the population would have been exposed. This essay will not only explore the social and economic positions held by these teachers but also how their presence at almost every level of society demonstrates the wide availability of basic schooling. The focus will be on *Lyonnais* teachers in the fourteenth and fifteenth centuries but examples from other parts of France and from other vocations will be used in order to effectively locate specific masters and mistresses on the social spectrum. In addition, the hierarchies within more formal educational institutions, such as the cathedral school at Lyon, will be examined and compared to more independent, less stable schools in the wider city.

While a certain amount of medieval pedagogical literature is used as background for this study, the substantial evidence found in archives in Lyon has been the most useful in helping to construct a realistic picture of medieval educational structures and the position of teachers both within these structures and in society at large. A considerable range of documents has been identified that provide information concerning schools and teachers in medieval Lyon. Amongst the municipal sources, teachers appear in tax records, records of tenancy and ownership, municipal accounts and the proceedings of the municipal council. The majority of these documents are related to financial matters, making them ideal sources of information on the economic status of those who appear in them. The departmental archives are home to the archives of the principal churches of Lyon, including those of the cathedral of Saint Jean, and the chapters of Saint Paul and Saint Nizier. All three of these institutions had schools and teachers attached to them, and they jealously guarded their rights to provide instruction.[2] The cathedral chapter claimed authority over all

[2] The proceedings of the chapters of Saint Paul and Saint Nizier are less detailed and less complete with regards to the schools that were attached to them. It is clear, however, that they each had choir-boys in their care and appointed *vicemagistri* (deputy choir monasteries) in

the schools of the city, though this was gradually eroded over the course of the fifteenth century. Teachers appear frequently in the archives of these churches, especially in the proceedings of the various chapters, but also in wills and obituaries.[3] Thus we have at our disposal a wide selection of documents concerning both financial matters and teachers, in secular and ecclesiastical situations and over a lengthy period of time. Though some of the references are fragmentary, when brought together they create a detailed image of the wealth, poverty, and careers of medieval schoolmasters. This chapter will examine three groups of teachers in late medieval Lyon in three parts. The first part will address the economic and social standing of teachers within the 'closed' community of the cathedral of Saint Jean in Lyon. Those who worked in this school had the most stability but did not have the opportunity for a great deal of financial gain. The second section will look at independent teachers in the wider city of Lyon who would have been considered marginal in terms of their socio-economic position. Simon Bravart, the bridge-building schoolmaster, belonged to this group. The final section will investigate the 'successful' schoolmasters of Lyon, those who thrived financially and who operated in conjunction with the ruling elite of the city.[4]

The teachers who were associated with the church schools of Lyon where involved in multilayered social and professional hierarchies. After all, these were the schools that were the most stable across an extended period of time and did not depend on profit from their pupils in order to continue. They could therefore develop a range of posts and positions that could be occupied by several people at the same time. A teacher's position in these hierarchies could be affected by an individual's economic background, where the wealthy and aristocratic often occupied the most elevated posts within the school. Yet,

order to teach them. Archives departementales du Rhône (henceforth ADR) 13 G 6–13 G 9 (for Saint Paul) and 15 G 12–15 G 14 (for Saint Nizier).

[3] For the purposes of brevity, this article will focus on the school attached to the cathedral of Saint Jean.

[4] The division between city schools and the cathedral school should not be taken as an argument that 'secular' and 'clerical' instruction was different or separated or that different teachers taught in each set of schools. Clerics were often found teaching in independent 'secular' schools, and, in turn, lay teachers may have been employed by churches. For example, George Bechon, whom the city government (and the *scolasticus*) hoped to make rector of the schools of the city in opposition to the chapter, was a cleric: ADR, 10 G 94, fol. 46 (25 June 1460). See also AML, series BB 7, fols 134^{r-v}.

these hierarchies could also serve as a means of career progression, a ladder up which those of modest means but good education could climb. In Lyon, the cathedral school of Saint Jean had the most developed institutional structure, which was comparable with those at Paris, Chartres, and Cambrai. At the top of this hierarchy was the *scolasticus*, who was both a kind of headmaster or governor of the cathedral school itself and the superintendent of all the schools in the city of Lyon.[5] He was a member of the cathedral chapter of Saint Jean and, as such, was one of the *chanoines-comtes* of Lyon. According to a statute from 1285 concerning elementary and grammar instruction (which first defined the role of the *scolasticus* and his relationship with the master of the school at the cathedral and with the schools of Lyon), he controlled the appointments of all teachers across the city.[6] The position of *scolasticus* was probably the least accessible of all the roles in the cathedral school because nobility was a prerequisite.[7] Below him came the *magister chori* (choir-master) and the *vicemagister* (deputy master) of the choir. It was these men who undertook the day-to-day operating duties of the cathedral school, such as providing suitable accommodation, food, and clothing for the boys, as well as doling out punishment. The *magister chori* was always a perpetual chaplain, while the *vicemagister* was often promoted to that position.[8] The *vicemagister* was responsible for the employment of two other masters, the *magister grammaticae* and the *manicantant* (or song master). Below them, a prefect or *bacallarius* could also be appointed as a type of chaperon or prefect for the boys.

The economic state of some of these functionaries is a little more difficult to define than their relative positions in the hierarchy. However, there does appear to have been a corollary between wealth, salary, and rank. The roles of *scolasticus* and *magister chori* were important within the wider organization of the church and attracted those who were already in possession of an income or fortune. The roles themselves could also be lucrative. The earliest datable reference to a *magister puerorum* (who later came to be known as *magister chori*) was around 1170, when one Pierre Roux left one thousand *solidi* and a silver cup with spoon to Saint Jean.[9] Around 1226, Guillaume de Sainte Columbe, described

[5] ADR, 10 G, 1666, piece 1. For a further discussion of the hierarchy of the cathedral school, see Forest, *L'École cathédrale de Lyon*, pp. 99–110.

[6] ADR, 10 G, 1666, piece 1.

[7] Pourrat, *L'Antique école de Leidrade*, p. 28. See also Forest, *L'École cathédrale de Lyon*, p. 28.

[8] Chaplaincies at the cathedral of Saint Jean were endowed with a steady income.

[9] 'Et Petrus Rufus [Pierre Roux], magister puerorum, qui dedit Sancto Stephano pro

as both *magister puerorum* and *magister chori*, left 110 *libras*, 600 *solidi*, and one silver mark in total to the cathedral.[10] These were substantial bequests, and they suggest that those in the higher echelons of the school administration could have maintained and acquired significant sums during their careers. While these large amounts were hardly earned by school administrators, they suggest that taking on the management of the choir school was not beneath wealthy individuals. Of far more interest are the occurrences of *vicemagistri* and grammar masters in the obituaries of Saint Jean, where they both left and received more modest amounts that would have accounted for a greater proportion of their income as teachers. From the thirteenth century on, these figures function as witnesses and executors. The frequency of school officers acting in this capacity suggests that they were somehow linked to the process of making wills within the cathedral community and perhaps emphasizes their respectability within that community. In 1201, *Johannes grammaticus* was listed as one of the witnesses of the will of an eminent canon, Hugues de Talaru.[11] In the fourteenth century, the *vicemagister* appeared frequently as an executor for several bequests to individuals in the cathedral community, especially to choir-boys. Twice in 1348, the *vicemagister* was charged with dividing and distributing legacies among the chaplains, clerics, and choir-boys.[12] The obituary of Saint Jean, therefore, reveals two things about the masters of the choir school there. Firstly, the senior officers of the school were relatively wealthy and could afford to leave sizable legacies to their cathedral. Secondly, the *vicemagistri* in particular were involved in wider financial activities within the institution that indicate their reputation as experienced and dependable administrators and may also have provided them with additional income.

anniversario suo honorifice faciendo mille solidos et cyphum argentum cum cocleari'; *Obituarium lugdunensis ecclesiae*, ed. by Guigue, p. 149.

[10] 'Et Villelmus de Sancta Columba bonae memoriae, magister puerorum, qui dedit lx libras [pro] anniversario suo; operi ecclesiae centum solidos; majori eleemosinae et minori unicumque L solidos; et ad capsam Sancti Stephani unam marcam argenti; et in acquisitionem de Riorter quingentes solidos dedit'; *Obituarium lugdunensis ecclesiae*, ed. by Guigue, p. 170. Sainte Columbe appeared three times in the obituary of Saint Jean as a witness to wills.

[11] *Obituarium lugdunensis ecclesiae*, ed. by Guigue, p. 185. De Talaru was a member of a local noble family with strong ties to the cathedral at Lyon. Three de Talarus — Jean, Amédée, and Hugues — became archbishops of Lyon later in the fourteenth and fifteenth centuries.

[12] The *vice-magister* distributed various bequests from Andre Beguine, perpetual chaplain, and Humbert Baconeri, doctor in decretals: *Obituarium lugdunensis ecclesiae*, ed. by Guigue, pp. 90–91, 101.

There is little information in any of the cathedral documents about the pay and benefits received by the teaching masters at the choir school, namely, the grammar master and the *manicantant*. Up until the middle of the fifteenth century, there is no mention of specific wages being paid to the *vicemagister*, the song master, or the grammar master, even in the proceedings of the chapter. Instead, the *vicemagister* received substantial payments in money and barrels of grain that were intended to cover the costs of running the entire choir school, including the wages of the teachers he employed. For example, in November 1367, the *vicemagister* was given fifty-four barrels of grain and 100 golden florins.[13] This amount would have had to cover all the overhead of the school including the feeding, clothing, and lodging of the choir-boys, their bedding and fuel for heating, any academic supplies, and the employment of a grammar master. In an agreement concerning the choir-boys drawn up in 1394, Jean Chalendati, *magister scolarum* or *vicemagister*, was commanded to 'hold and keep mutually two masters for the instruction of the said choir-boys, namely one in grammar and the other in song to whom the said master Jean will furnish enough provisions according to their status'.[14] For the purpose of running the entire school, teachers' salaries included, he was given 60 florins and 'fifty-four ass-loads of wheat from the grain of the great alms-giving'.[15] There is no indication of what the teachers would have received for their services out of the total budget but the phrase 'enough provisions according to their status' suggests that would-be masters had expectations and that Chalendati had to match or surpass what they might receive elsewhere. Their status accorded to them certain provisions and perhaps a certain salary. This system of payment differed from that at Chartres, where each master was paid a set salary each year. In 1345, a master in the choir school there received an annual salary of between 10 and 12 *livres tournois*.[16] This was in addition to payments for choir performances, which could amount to 6 *deniers* per day. Provisions for the upkeep of the choir-boys were paid separately from their wages.[17] It is only in November

[13] ADR, 10 G 76, fol. 76 (16 November 1367).

[14] 'Videlicet quod dictus magister Johannes habeat secum et teneat duos magistros ad instruendum dictos clericulos, videlicet unum in grammatica et alium in cantus quibus dictus magister Johannes ministrabit victualia satis honorifica secundum eorum statum'; ADR, 10 G 79, fol. 80^{v} (14 November 1394). See also Forest, *L'École cathédrale de Lyon*, pp. 343–44.

[15] ADR, 10 G 79, fol. 80^{v} (14 November 1394).

[16] Clerval, *Les Écoles de Chartres*, p. 361.

[17] In 1345, 10 *livres tournois* was paid to the masters 'pro pensione debita pro alimentis ipsorum puerorum'; Clerval, *Les Écoles de Chartres*, p. 362.

1445 that we find specific wages being offered for the employment of a grammar master at Saint Jean in Lyon. Master Simon was to receive 12 florins in his first year with the expectation of yearly increments thereafter.[18] This was about the equivalent of 360 *sols tournois*. This wage level does not compare well with those in other trades. In fifteenth-century Forez, just west of Lyon, a master mason or master carpenter could earn around 30 to 45 *deniers tournois* daily. If he worked a total of 250 days per year, allowing for Sundays and other holidays, he could easily earn over 750 *sols tournois*. Simon, however, may have lived at the expense of the cathedral chapter within its cloisters, like other masters before and after him. This would have represented a huge saving on food and lodgings in the burgeoning city of Lyon. An annual wage of 12 florins, therefore, may have been more generous than it first appeared.

Master Simon's appointment as grammar master in the choir school of Saint Jean was the only time before the 1530s that a salary for a teacher was agreed upon and recorded in the proceedings of the chapter. Its uniqueness indicates a problem with the employment and retention of grammar masters at the cathedral. Amidst detailed information on the appointment and promotion of song masters, only three named masters of grammar were appointed in 1374, 1383, and 1445.[19] The post of grammar master was founded in 1362 but had to be reestablished at least twice, in 1394 and in 1431.[20] The last one of these resulted in the appointment of Jean DeFosses as song master in 1432, who, it was carefully noted, knew Latin and could write well.[21] In 1439 there was again a complaint made in the cathedral chapter that no grammar master had been appointed, and the canons threatened to withhold funding for the school if this was not resolved.[22] Master Simon was the last grammar master recorded in the proceedings of the chapter. While it is clear that the choir school found it difficult to hire and retain grammar masters, it is not entirely clear why this was the case. One has to wonder, in the light of Master Simon's contract, if the remuneration was considered enough for an educated man. This leads to the inevitable

[18] ADR, 10 G 90, fol. 122^r (3 November 1445).

[19] These were Petrus on 28 June 1374 (ADR, 10 G 76, fol. 162^v), Petrus Girodus on 30 June 1380 (ADR, 10 G 78, fol. 128^r), and Symondus.

[20] ADR, 10 G 76, fol. 15^v (17 November 1362); ADR, 10 G 79, fol. 80^v (14 November 1394); ADR, 10 G 86, fol. 108^r (25 June 1431).

[21] ADR, 10 G 87, fol. 55^r (28 October 1432). DeFosses did not remain in the post of *manicantant* for long. In 1435, Defosses left the cathedral in order to attend a *studium generale*: ADR, 10 G 87, fol. 178^r (16 July 1435).

[22] ADR, 10 G 88, fol. 167^r (1 December 1439).

suggestion that the market for grammar masters was more competitive than for song masters. Better opportunities beyond the cathedral cloister might have made recruitment and retention of qualified teachers difficult. A lack of grammar masters, however, would not have necessarily meant a complete absence of grammar instruction for the pupils at the school. As seen above, Jean DeFosses was appointed as song master but appears to have had grammar-teaching duties as well. In addition, the *vicemagister*, as well as the *manicantant*, may have been able to take over many of the functions of a grammarian.

The careers of song masters within the school serve as a direct contrast to the situation of the grammar masters. They tended to stay on in their positions for lengthy periods of time. Some are noted for serving as *manicantant* for seven or even ten years.[23] Their goal appears not to have been monetary reward but future preferment. The reason for this longevity in post was almost certainly due to the particular training these men had in the distinctive liturgy of the cathedral of Lyon. Many song masters began their careers at Saint Jean as choir-boys and had acquired a knowledge of its workings. For example, Pierre Sorrel, who was *manicantant* from 1414 to 1418, was appointed *vicemagister* in 1428 because he had been both a choir-boy and song master and knew how to conduct the boys well.[24] Furthermore, song masters tended to receive promotions and much sought-after perpetual offices on quitting their teaching roles. This happened at least six times in the fifteenth century, in 1409, 1418, 1423, 1432, 1453, and 1477.[25] In October 1432, Cornelius Conti was granted an endowed position after serving ten years as *manicantant* of the choir school.[26] The expectations of song masters were, therefore, quite different from those of other teachers. Their focus was on obtaining offices within Saint Jean itself, as their training and experience was concentrated on preparing them for functions there. They were, as it were, career men within the cathedral and had no real intention of leaving. They were content with provisions made for

[23] For example, Humbert de Chaffardon was given a benefice after seven years as *manicantant*: ADR, 10 G 92, fol.160^{v} (10 July 1453).

[24] 'Qui fuit clericulus et matutus de infantia in ecclesia'; ADR, 10 G 86, fol. 15^{v} (15 November 1428).

[25] These were, respectively, Pierre Sorel (1418), André Serrat (1423), Corneille Conti (1432), Humbert de Chaffardon (1453), and possibly Pierre de Chaffardon (1477). If it was Pierre de Chaffardon who was promoted to the deaconate in 1477, that would have meant he had served as *manicantant* since 1462, which would have been a total of fifteen years. The proceedings of the chapter do indicate that Pierre had taught song for a particularly long time (*longo tempore*): ADR, 10 G 99, fol. 37^{r} (13 August 1477).

[26] ADR, 10 G 87, fol. 55^{r}.

their reward from the general school budget in expectation of greater rewards later on. Grammar masters, on the other hand, appear to have been more independent and more influenced by the external market for school teachers. Since the only contract between the chapter of Saint Jean and an individual teacher was with a grammar master, one supposes that he was in a strong bargaining position and could find work elsewhere. This mobility contrasts with the way that song masters were, in effect, bound to the cathedral and its school. Then again, the song master's position was more stable and had a more defined career progression. Chartres cathedral also had two masters, one to teach grammar and one to teach song, but had much more success in retaining grammar masters.[27] According to Jules Clerval, there was a struggle for power between them, where the grammar master acted as headmaster for much of the fourteenth and fifteenth centuries but was replaced in this capacity by the song master in 1484.[28] This perhaps reflected the growing provision of grammar education in towns and cities beyond the choir schools which, in turn, began to focus more and more on musical study.[29]

At first glance, the cathedral school of Lyon was separate from what went on beyond the walls of its cloister. Yet, this was not the case, as not only did its *scolasticus* have nominal authority over all the schools of the city, but its pupils — and, ultimately, teachers — were *lyonnais*. The cathedral school formed part of the educational life of the city and its officials and masters played roles in its society. While the power of the *scolasticus* waned in the course of the fifteenth century in the face of the increased pedagogical involvement of the city's council, he was still the senior pedagogical figure in Lyon. Moreover, while the hier-

[27] The cathedral of Chartres had more control over the schools, not only in the town of Chartres but also in the surrounding countryside. It was likely that there were fewer opportunities for alternative employment as a grammar master in and around Chartres: Clerval, *Les Écoles de Chartres*, p. 55.

[28] Clerval, *Les Écoles de Chartres*, pp. 59–65.

[29] It should be noted that choir-boys whose voices had broken were sent outside Lyon's cathedral cloister to the grammar schools of the town. This happened at least thirteen times between 1406 and 1530: ADR, 10 G 81, fol. 68^{r} (24 January 1406); 10 G 90, fol. 122^{r} (3 November 1445); 10 G 96, fol. 184^{v} (5 July 1468); 10 G 99, fol. 103^{v} (7 February 1478); 10 G 102, fol. 297^{v} (5 November 1495); 10 G 104, fol. 114^{v} (27 November 1500); 10 G 108, fol. 45^{v} (12 November 1516); 10 G 109, fol. 38^{v} (25 June 1519); 10 G 110, fol. 60^{r-v} (14 January 1524); 10 G 111, fol. 10^{r} (16 January 1525)l and 10 G 113, fols 26^{r-v} (25 June 1529). Choir-boys who were at the school attached to Saint Nizier were also sent outside to continue their education. For example, on 20 December 1496, several clerks and choir-boys were given permission to leave in order to attend school; ADR, 15 G 14, fol. 23^{v}.

archy of the cathedral school in particular was effectively limited to those who were clerics brought up and educated within the cathedral community, it did provide employment and opportunity. This hierarchy demonstrated that there were a range of posts available for men from sometimes quite different socio-economic backgrounds and that advancement was possible. Teaching in a choir school could be a career with prospects.

There is little evidence to imply that the stability and professional progression available in an institution like the cathedral school at Lyon was available in the city as a whole. Indeed, the example of Simon Bravart given at the beginning of this essay is far more suggestive of haphazard employment and financial volatility. Despite the supposed authority of the *scolasticus*, the teaching profession in Lyon, even more so than in other cities — such as Paris — seemed to be generally unregulated. As such, assigning schoolmasters and schoolmistresses any kind of social or economic definition is difficult, but not impossible. As discussed above, Lyon has a great deal of information pertaining to the financial condition of its citizens, and teachers, just like members of other professions, appear in tax lists, surveys of property, and so on. The picture an examination of these sources presents is exceptionally variegated. Outside the confines of the choir schools, teachers were much more susceptible to 'market forces'. Schoolmasters and mistresses in Lyon can be divided therefore into two groups: those who were poor and did not have any identifiable affiliation with the municipal authorities, and those who were wealthier and had connections with the civic elite.

The first group, to which Simon Bravart certainly belonged, exhibited the fragile nature of the teaching profession in the late medieval city — they were fully dependent on the fees that they received from their pupils (who would have been less affluent), and they received little or no aid from the municipal council. They operated in a city that did not have the same strict organization that existed in other cities. In comparison to Paris, where the cantor of Notre Dame had real authority over the elementary and grammar schools in the city, the *scolasticus* of Saint Jean appears to have intervened rarely in the everyday functions of the schools of Lyon. In Paris, schoolmasters and schoolmistresses had to receive a fresh licence each year in order to hold classes.[30] The proceedings of the chapter of Notre Dame frequently refer to teachers seeking permis-

[30] The list of rules and regulations drawn up by the cantor of Notre Dame in 1378 covered a range of topics such as the attendance of masters and mistresses at the funerals of their colleagues, the number and sex of their pupils, and the type of lessons that could be provided (reading or Latin teaching). *Chartularium universitatis Parisiensis*, ed. by Denifle, III, 51–53.

sion to run schools, to inherit schools from their parents, or even to leave Paris on pilgrimage.[31] This contrasts sharply with Lyon, where there are only brief and irregular occurrences of the chapter of Saint Jean involving itself in any way with the schools of the city over which it supposedly held pedagogical authority.[32] This general lack of attention on the part of the chapter allowed a more open educational market to develop in Lyon. However, it also resulted in less security for teachers and less stability in fees, which in turn led to the socio-economic marginalization of some of their number.

Possibly the most informative sources on the economic condition of teachers in Lyon were the tax records kept by the municipal council. These records included monies paid to both the municipal government and to the king, through the municipal government's administrative framework. They illuminate the disparate economic situations of teachers since taxation was based roughly on income and property. The only variable that cannot be checked in this situation is the possibility of tax exemptions given by the municipal government.[33] These were given out in two circumstances: when a teacher was poor or when a teacher was exercising his or her profession for the good of the city — the latter were usually those who had some connection with the municipal government. Individual references usually differentiated which was which.[34] The earliest reference to a teacher in the municipal archives is tax-related, that of master Reyaud, *mestre de l'escola*, in 1377.[35] He paid 5 *sols* 2 *deniers tournois*.

[31] Guyotjeannin, 'Les Petites écoles'. For example, in 1437, the chapter of Notre Dame allowed Jaqueta, wife of Johannis Varin, to take over the school held by her mother Gileta La Feniere while she was on pilgrimage. Jaqueta either took a school elsewhere or pre-deceased her mother because Gileta's school was given to Perrota Potiere on her death in 1451. Guyotjeannin, 'Les Petites écoles', pp. 122, 125.

[32] This was in 1460 when the chapter, *scolasticus*, and municipal council were in dispute over who could name a schoolmaster; ADR, 10 G 94, fol. 46r (25 June 1460).

[33] Exemptions may have been granted to a favoured master or to the *de facto* master of the city's schools, or they may have been a throwback to the Theodosian Code, where masters of grammar and rhetoric were released from paying civic taxes and tolls: 'The Emperor Constantine Augustus to Volusianus, We ordain that doctors, grammarians and other professors of letters, and the goods which they possess in their cities, shall be exempt from taxation and shall have the honours due to their functions'. Theodosian Code, ed. and trans. in Cole, *Later Roman Education*, p. 29.

[34] For example, Jehan Hanpenille was refunded his taxes in 1477 because he was poor: AML, BB 16, fol. 29v. In contrast, Henri Valluphin's taxes were reduced because he held a school by which the children of the city profited: AML, CC 254, fol. 111r.

[35] 'Mestre Reynaut mestre de l'escola [...] v s. ii d.'; AML, CC 60, fol. 58r (1 April 1377).

To put this amount in perspective, a hectolitre of wheat cost on average 8 *sols parisien* (or around 13 *sols tournois*) in Paris in 1376.[36] Meanwhile, a notary at the royal court earned 6 *sols parisien* (or around 10 *sols tournois*) per day in 1380.[37] In other words, Reynaud's annual tax bill was less than 100 litres of wheat and was half what an (albeit senior) notary earned per day. In terms of his neighbours, who were paying between 2 and 4 *sols tournois*, he was paying the most. While we cannot extrapolate Reynaud's income from these amounts, it is probable that he was wealthier than his immediate neighbours but was not necessarily earning a lot of money. For example, in the next street one *Hugneta la tabureta* (*la tabureta* was either her surname or a reference to her profession as some sort of cabinet or stool maker), was paying 1 florin 4 *sols*, which amounted to 30 *sols tournois*. In general, the tax records suggest that teachers in Lyon were not usually destitute but did not expect to earn as much as a skilled artisan.

The tax records tell of teachers who were much poorer than Reynaud. Occasionally, one of them received tax exemptions from the local government, but one must assume that some never paid taxes due to their indigence and thus never appeared in the rolls. For example, in 1427, Germaine, schoolmistress, was granted immunity from payment as she was unable to pay.[38] In 1426, Master Henri, scribe or *escripvain*, had to pay 5 *sols*.[39] In 1429, when he was listed as a scribe and as a teacher (*l'escripvaint maistre escole*), he had to pay 3 *sols* 6 *deniers*. There are three possible reasons for this reduction in Henri's tax bill. Firstly, he may have received a reduction in 1429 because he had taken on pupils. He was not the usual candidate for such treatment (masters patronized by the municipality were usually masters in arts teaching Latin grammar and literature), but the fact that he was teaching in a school that focused on teaching writing and possibly some elements of arithmetic (that is, the activities of the *escripvain*) would have been seen as useful by the municipal government. Secondly, the reduction in the amount of taxes owed may have been a result of a decrease in Henri's scribal work. He may have been forced to accept pupils, therefore becoming a master of a school, because he needed the extra money.

36 Miskimin, *Money, Prices and Foreign Exchange*, pp. 155–56.

37 'Maistre Pierre Cramette, pour ses gaiges de notaire, de 185 jours en ce terme, qu'il a esté à la Chancellerie et aux Requestes, 6 s. p. par jour. Argent [...] 55 l. 10s. p.'; *Comptes de l'hotel des rois de France*, ed. by Douët-D'Arcq, pp. 21–22.

38 Déniau, *La Commune de Lyon et la guerre bourgnignonne*, p. 148.

39 AML, CC 67, fols 70r and 87r (1415–1434).

Thirdly, the smaller amount due may have been because there was a general reduction in the tax indemnity for the whole community. For example, while some of Henri's neighbours paid the same amount in both 1426 and 1429, others also saw a reduction of their tax burden. Benoit Morel, listed in 1429 as the jailer of Roanne, saw his tax bill go from 20 *sols* in 1426 to 15 *sols* in 1429.[40] It seems that a general reduction was the most likely reason for Henri's reduction, but since Henri was only listed as a teacher in 1429, the other possibilities may have had a hand. Henri's taxes were some of the lowest in his neighbourhood. He was paying about the same amount of tax as weavers. Only Denis, described as a beggar, was paying less.[41] Henri, therefore, was unlikely to have been doing particularly well financially. This trend of poor writing teachers continued in Lyon. In 1477, a Jean Hanpenille was refunded his taxes 'because he had little or no property and was not involved in anything except teaching children how to write'.[42] The tone of this reference suggests that such activity was not highly regarded by the civic authorities. Nevertheless, Hanpenille was still given a valuable tax exemption. Poor and marginal he may have been, but he, just like other lesser teachers, was providing a vital service in the burgeoning city of Lyon.

While the tax records tell us part of the story, the documents relating to ownership and tenancy of property help establish more firmly how teachers lived. They can also help identify teachers who may not have been paying taxes due to straitened financial situations. Schoolmasters appeared frequently, as both owners and tenants, in these records. The property surveys from 1493 are particularly useful as they preserve the living arrangements of four different teachers. At the top of this list was master Pierre Andre, who owned a substantial house and garden near the church of Saint Paul. It was worth 40 *livres* per year.[43] Next on the list was Jean de Lanoe, master of writing, who rented an entire house for 20 *livres* per year.[44] There was Pierre Fidit, schoolmaster, who rented part of a house from a notary just across from the cemetery of Saint Georges, south of the cathedral cloister. He paid 9 *livres* per year.[45] Finally,

[40] AML, CC 67, fols 70ʳ and 87ʳ (1415–1434).

[41] AML, CC 67, fols 70ʳ and 87ʳ (1415–1434).

[42] 'Semblablement ont donne quicte et renus a maistre Jehan Hanpenille escripvain l'impost a quoy il aeste mis et impose es tailles que lieve Jaques Roctry, actuendu et considere qu'il n'a aucuns biens ou bien peu et qu'il ne se meslesois suelement le aprendre les enfans a escripre'; AML, BB 16, fol. 29ᵛ.

[43] AML, CC 4, fol. 75ʳ (1493).

[44] AML, CC 5, fol. 86ʳ (1493).

[45] AML, CC 5, fol. 59ᵛ (1493).

Michel Bertier, a merchant cobbler, rented part of his house to an unnamed mistress of a school for girls for 5 *livres* per year.[46] Keeping in mind that some of these, like Andre, may have used their house as both a residence and a classroom, a quick comparison of these rents tells a great deal about their social and economic status. Andre was active as a schoolmaster for at least three decades. Though he was almost certainly drawing to the end of his career, his ownership of a house and garden indicates that he had done well. While there is no indication that he was linked to the municipal council, he did receive a tax exemption in 1478 for being a schoolmaster rather than for being poor. Jean de Lanoe also appeared to be doing well, as he was able to rent an entire house. However, he was a writing master, which was not considered as respectable as a grammar master. In fact, the title *maistre d'escolle* was carefully crossed out in the document itself and *maistre d'escripture* was inserted above. Despite doing financially well as a teacher of writing, he could not bear the loftier title of master of a school. Pierre Fidit, whose lodgings were far more modest, was at least granted the title *maistre d'yscolle*.[47] This underlines the social hierarchy that existed between different types of teachers, where a master of writing took second place to a master who taught grammar and literature, no matter his income. At the bottom of the list, in terms of value of residence, was the schoolmistress, one of a handful mentioned in the archives of Lyon. Her lodgings were the cheapest, and she shared the house with at least four others, including a pin maker (*espinolier*). It is likely that she would have taught girls exclusively. (In the rules for teachers in Paris written in 1357, men were to teach boys only and women were to teach girls only.[48]) Usually, girls who were sent to school were sent to acquire only the very basics of reading. Since the price of education rose in accordance with the difficulty and prestige of the subjects being offered, an elementary school with a limited number of pupils would not have turned a large profit.[49] These inde-

[46] AML, CC 4, fol. 31^{v}–32^{r} (1493).

[47] In rural Champagne in the fifteenth century, schoolmasters generally rented modest chambers like those of Fidit, rather than houses like those possessed by Andre and De Lanoe: Guilbert, 'Les Écoles rurales', p. 138.

[48] 'Quilibet magister aut magistra stabit in limitibus gratie sue, ita quod non excedet in numero aut sexu puerorum, seu etiam in qualitate librorum' (Every master or mistress will remain within the limits of their grant, so that he should not be excessive in number or sex of children, or even in the type of books); *Chartularium universitatis Parisiensis*, ed. by Denifle, III, 52.

[49] For a discussion of government-mandated prices for different subjects in Renaissance Italy, see Grendler, *Schooling in Renaissance Italy*, p. 17.

pendent masters and mistresses were very much at the mercy of market forces, dependent as they were on fees paid by their pupils.

Not all masters were consigned to the margins of society in late medieval Lyon. In the same archival documents where the poor teachers of girls and writing appear, the well-educated schoolmasters with connections to the civic elites are also found. These teachers formed a distinct class from their less-fortunate counterparts and were the product of the growing trend for urban governments to invest both time and money in the provision of high-quality education. Communal involvement in education was most prominent in the city-states of central and northern Italy from the fourteenth century.[50] Lyon, with its trading and cultural links to Italy and its powerful urban council, which exerted its independence from local ecclesiastical lordship, was the ideal place in France to develop similar institutional arrangements for education. A city with the ambitions of Lyon needed a suitably instructed body of young men who could meet its own administrative needs as well as function on the national and international stages as lawyers, envoys, and merchants. The children who would benefit from the presence of a high-quality schoolmaster were, of course, the sons of the town councilors and others who made up the socio-economic elite of the city. If Lyon wanted to do business in the wider world or be taken seriously in the political arena, it had to accept the importance of education and erudition in these areas of activity.[51] In order to take its place as a centre of commerce and culture, it had to educate its children.

Throughout the fifteenth century, the city of Lyon was active in its acquisition and support of schoolmasters. This activity led directly to increased opportunities and remuneration for those it deemed worthy of its attention. The possibility for financial gain was immediate on accepting an appointment from the city. Indeed, it occasionally preceded the teacher's actual arrival in the city. In 1402, the councilors paid Guillaume Lagier, master of arts, a total of 12 *livres tournois* on two separate occasions to induce him to leave his post as

[50] Black, *Education and Society in Florentine Tuscany*; Gehl, *A Moral Art*; Grendler, *Schooling in Renaissance Italy*.

[51] While some humanists, like Petrarch, were able to devote their lives to thinking and writing, most scholars also pursued active careers in the service of various Italian city states. See Witt, *Hercules at the Crossroads*, for a discussion of an important humanist who was also a civil servant. See also Kristeller, *Renaissance Thought and its Sources*, pp. 93–95 where it is argued that humanism had its roots in the developments in the output of civic administrators.

rector of the schools at Embrun and come to Lyon.[52] Earlier in the same year, the council had sent Jean Gilet to Dijon in order to hire an assistant there.[53] This was poaching, of course. Lagier, for example, already held a post in a sizable town in the east of France. He was well qualified since he was explicitly named as a master of arts. The councilors of Lyon were seeking the best and the most experienced teachers. But for what purpose? The documents state that Lagier was to become rector of the schools of Lyon. The term *rector* usually suggests that he would be the senior teacher or headmaster of a school under the direct authority of the municipal government. (It did not automatically denote an administrator without teaching duties.) However, there is no evidence that such an institution actually existed in Lyon prior to the sixteen century.[54] Instead, these documents represent an attempt by the councilors to establish a school of this type. It is unlikely that they were successful as there is no other reference to Lagier (or to Gilet) in the municipal archives. If teachers did come and set up schools, they did so in a far less formal capacity. The city council still did not have the full authority to set up and control a school. However, the documents also show that the city was both able and willing to pay schoolmasters to come to Lyon. While the councilors felt that they could not openly flout the authority of the cathedral, they were in a financial position to provide for schoolmasters even if they could not be seen to be directly paying their salary.[55]

As a result of the difficult situation in Lyon, with the cathedral still claiming authority over all the schools in the city and the municipal government wishing to become more involved in the provision of education, we must turn to the tax rolls and the receipts of the town in order to discuss the financial situation of teachers. As stated above, some of those masters who received tax exemptions and reductions did so not because they were poor but because they were teachers. The first example of this is Pierre Andre, who was excused from pay-

[52] AML, CC 385 recto 10, fol. 24^{r} (August 1402); AML, CC 385 recto 11, fol. 14^{v} (November 1402).

[53] AML, CC 385, recto 10, fol. 13^{r} (April 1402).

[54] It was not until the late 1520s that the city formally and openly financed a school rather than an individual teacher: AML, CC 776, pieces 27 and 29 (1529); AML, CC 788, pieces 12 and 13 (1530).

[55] Only once did the chapter and the municipal council of Lyon clash over the appointment of a master. In 1460, the chapter rejected George Bechier or Bechon as master of the schools of the city. This was not only against the wishes of the city but also against the advice of the *scolasticus*, who supported Bechon's appointment: ADR, 10 G 94, fol. 46^{r} (25 June 1460).

ing the royal tax in 1478: 'nichil quia est magister scolarum'.[56] This should be read in conjunction with a later appearance of Andre in the municipal records. As noted above, by 1493, Andre was listed as owning a substantial house and garden near the chapter of Saint Paul.[57] This indicates that he was economically successful and that his initial exemption was a mark of the municipal council's approbation. Such special treatment appeared again in 1514 when Henri Valluphin was excused from paying municipal taxes 'for exercising a school which he holds for the profit of the children of the town'.[58] While Valluphin's notable career will be discussed in more detail below, he was not released from his tax burden because he could not pay it but because he was an important master who taught the children of the city's elite, most notably the sons of the municipal councilors. Elsewhere in France, teachers were exempt from paying taxes because they were clerics. For example, in fifteenth-century Champagne, teachers operated as wine merchants as well as educators not only as a means to supplement their income but also to take advantages of the lower taxes imposed on clerics importing goods into towns.[59] This is possible in the cases of Andre and Valluphin but there is no indication that they were clerics. As far as those calculating the taxes were concerned, they merited these exemptions explicitly because of their activity as schoolmasters.

Other teachers did not receive relief from their taxes, even though they were associated with the municipal government. *Maistre Drogo, maistre d'escole* was listed as paying tax in 1426 and 1429, appearing in the same records as master Henri, the poor *escripvain* and teacher.[60] In comparison with Henri, Master Drogo was doing exceptionally well. He was listed simply as *Masitre Drogo* in 1426 and then as *Maistre Drogo, maistre d'escole* in 1429. He paid 20 *sols* in 1426 and 15 *sols* in 1429 in taxes to the king. As such, he was paying at least 10 *sols* more in taxes than his neighbours, most of whom were weavers (*tissant*) or furriers (*pelletier*). For example, Clunier le Boytoux, tailor or *codurier*, paid 5 *sols* in 1429, while Juneta de Myners, *codurier*, paid 2 *sols* 6 *deniers*. Apart from

[56] AML, CC 97, fol. 24^{v} (May 1478).

[57] AML, CC 4, fol. 75^{r} (1493).

[58] AML, CC 245, fol. 111^{r} (1514).

[59] Guilbert, 'Les Écoles rurales', p. 136. Guilbert's article is one of the best considerations of the social position of elementary and grammar teachers in medieval France. In 1259, *Robertus capellanus* was exempt from paying taxes on some of the rooms he held as a school teacher but not on the room he used for the actual school: *Documents relatifs au comté de Champagne et de Bries*, ed. by Longnon, III, 19.

[60] AML, CC 67, fols 73^{r} and 91^{r} (1415–34).

the obvious fact that Drogo lived in the cloth manufacturing district in Lyon, he was the wealthiest resident on his street based on his tax contributions. While his location may suggest that he was teaching the children of cloth workers, his financial success would suggest otherwise. It was far more likely that his classroom was patronized by the sons of more elite citizens who were able to pay more. After all, his taxes were only comparable to those levied on a salaried official, Henri's neighbour, the gaoler of Roanne.[61] The idea of Drogo being connected in some way with the municipal government is strengthened by his attendance at meetings of the municipal council in the early 1420s, where he is simply referred to as *Masitre Drogue*.[62] He was, therefore, in different social and economic sphere from that of Henri. This was not only due to his connections with more privileged citizens but also to his listing as *maistre descole* as opposed to *escripvain* and *maistre descole*. Drogo's financial position would suggest that he was teaching more expensive subjects like Latin grammar and literature as opposed to less 'elite' subjects, such as writing and scribal work.[63] While such skills were vitally important in a commercial city such as Lyon, traditional education in Latin was still considered more 'valuable'. Comparing Henri and Drogo demonstrates the acute economic differences among those in the same profession.

It is clear that some teachers were connected with the municipal government of Lyon. Some were directly hired by the council while others were given gifts of money or materials in order to run their school. For some, like Master Drogo, there is only circumstantial evidence that links them with the city's ruling fathers. One fact is generally clear: these teachers would have been among the wealthiest pedagogues in the city. Despite the supposed authority of the cathedral's *scolasticus*, some teachers were actively courted by the council to move to Lyon. Such teachers could still be presented as being independent while, at the same time, receiving the patronage of the municipality. This support took on various guises, such as the councilors sending their sons and fees to particular schools or paying the rent on the house used by the favoured schoolmaster. As seen above, George Bechon received 5 *livres tournois*, a sub-

[61] 'Benoit Morel, geoulier de Roanne [...] xv sols', AML, CC 67, fol. 70^r.

[62] Drogue or Drogo attended the council meeting twice, on 10 January 1422 and 13 February 1422. He was not a councillor but he may have been a petitioner, perhaps seeking permission to hold a school: *Registres consulaires de la ville de Lyon*, ed. by Guigue, I, 351, 359.

[63] Grendler, *Schooling in Renaissance Italy*, pp. 17–18.

stantial sum, to cover the rent of the house he was using for a school in 1459.[64] In 1481, Master Jean, 'who held the school of Lyon in the part towards the empire' (that is, in the eastern section of the city), was using a large house valued at 200 *livres tournois* as his school house, and its rent was also covered by the municipal government.[65] These buildings probably served the dual purpose of accommodating the classroom or classrooms and the living quarters of the master. Other payments included one of 15 *sols* 6 *deniers* to Henri Valluphin, one of the most respected, educated, and comfortable teachers recorded in the archives, in order to cover 'expenses furnished by him to provide heating for the little children' in his school.[66] This was clearly a subsidy to the unofficial commune-approved grammar teacher of Lyon. These masters were the most successful of their profession, thanks to their connections to the municipal government.

In many ways, Henri Valluphin represents a case study of the successful teacher in Lyon. Though nothing is known about his own education, by the 1490s he was operating a highly regarded school near the church of Saint Nizier across the Saône from the cathedral of Saint Jean. Some historians associate him directly with the school of Saint Nizier, though the chapter proceedings of the church do not mention him.[67] In 1499, the same year that he received the subsidy for providing heat for his pupils, he paid 33 *sols* 4 *deniers* in taxes.[68] This was twice as much as any of his neighbours, one of whom, a mason, paid 12 *sols* 6 *deniers*. It was more than Etienne Villefranche, master of arithmetic, who paid 25 *sols*.[69] In other words, Valluphin was not a poor man. The fact that the municipal councilors were involved with the day-to-day expenses of his school underlines his importance in their eyes. Almost certainly, that was where they sent their own children to school. While Valluphin did not enjoy a tax exemption in 1499, he was given one later, in 1514, when he was due to pay 25 *sols*.[70] The reason given was that he was exempt because 'he held the school for the profit of the

[64] AML, BB 7, fols 134^{r-v}.

[65] AML, BB 352 and CC 486, piece no. 6. (1481).

[66] AML, CC 538, fol. 13^{v} (1499).

[67] Wadsworth, *Lyon, 1473–1503*, p. 43. Wadsworth asserts that Valluphin was a canon of Saint Nizier but there is no evidence for this in the chapter proceedings of that church.

[68] AML, CC 107, fol. 135^{r} (1499).

[69] AML, CC 107, fol. 124^{r} (1499).

[70] AML, CC 254, fol. 111^{r} (1514).

children of the town'.[71] It is abundantly clear that such exemptions were a tool that the municipal council used to provide for its chosen teachers. Moreover, Valluphin was seen by his contemporaries as a scholar. In 1498, Jose Badius Ascensius, humanist author, publisher, and sometime teacher in Valluphin's school in Lyon, dedicated an edition of the works of Juvenal to him.[72] Badius described Valluphin in the preface as 'the best professor of good sciences: the most famous and eloquent grammarian of his city of Lyon and a distinguished friend'.[73] This was no petty scribe who took in pupils on the side, like Master Henri, or even a modestly provided-for but upwardly mobile song master, like Pierre Sorrel. Valluphin was well known, well respected, and well paid.

* * *

The financial evidence surrounding schoolmasters and mistresses, their tax receipts, their property holdings, their share in institutional budgets, all points to the conclusion that they did not occupy a single socio-economic category. They cannot be clustered under neat headings such as 'well-to-do' or 'poor', or even 'middle-income'. Despite the lack of an overall pattern, there were certain sub-trends in the documentary information that support particular arguments. For instance, the frequent aid provided to specific teachers by the municipal government created new financial opportunities and a new social standing for those lucky enough to receive it. Likewise, the hierarchy of the cathedral school gave employment and advancement, especially to those who had grown up and been training in its liturgical and musical tradition. The appearance of teachers

[71] 'Amodere pour ceste foys a caus de l'exercize de scolage quy tient pour le profit des enfans de la ville a [...] xxv sols tournois': AML, CC 254, fol. 111r (1514).

[72] There is some controversy as to whether a noted Renaissance publisher and writer such as Badius was a teacher, especially in a grammar school. While Wadsworth believes he did function as a teacher during his time in Lyon, most historians focus on his publishing activities there. However, Badius himself is clear when he reminisces about his time spent in Valluphin's elementary/grammar school: 'Cum hisce diebus in ludo tuo lugdunensi, virorum praestantissime, Vergiliana bucolica accuratis interpretarer, animadverti divinum illum ac plane incomparabilem artificem in quintae eglogae bucolica phrasi, amicitiae verae (cujus inter nos indissolubile foedus percussimus) omnis explicuisse numeros' (In those days, when I translated Vergilian bucolics with meticulous care in your elementary school in Lyon, O most excellent of men, I clearly observed that the divine and the incomparable skill in the pastoral diction of the fifth eclogue set forth all the categories of true friendship [which we have sealed between us as an unbreakable bond]); *Bibliographie*, ed. by Renouard, II, 535.

[73] 'Henrico Valuphino artium bonarum professori optimo: ac clarissimae Lugdunesis civitatis grammatico disertissimo et amico primario'; *Bibliographie*, ed. by Renouard, II, 535.

in such a broad range of positions, some better paid and better respected than others, demonstrates that they were a common feature at all levels of urban society in the late Middle Ages. In Lyon, this frequency suggests that elementary education, at the very least, was available to a large number of children. Only demand could allow for the creation of a market big enough not only for specialism (grammar, writing) but also for varying numbers of 'rich' and 'poor' masters. Not all may have been financially successful or secure, but in a relatively uncontrolled economy, enough individuals thought it worth their while to pursue careers as teachers. From the lord *scolasticus* in the cathedral to Henri Valluphin contemplating Virgil and back to Simon Bravart on the bridges, there were many opportunities on many different socio-economic levels for the medieval teacher.

Works Cited

Archival Sources

Lyon, Archives municipales de Lyon, series BB, 7
——, series BB 16
——, series BB 352
——, series CC 4–538
Rhône, Archives départementales du Rhône, series 10 G 76–94
——, series 10 G 1666

Primary Sources

Bibliographie des impressions et des oeuvres de Josse Badius Ascensius, imprimeur et humaniste, 1462–1535, ed. by Philippe Renouard, 3 vols (New York: Franklin, 1963)

Chartularium universitatis Parisiensis, ed. by Henri Denifle, 4 vols (Paris: Delalain, 1889–97)

Comptes de l'hotel des rois de France aux XIVe et XVe siècles, ed. by Louis Claude Douët-D'Arcq (Paris: Jules Renouard, 1865)

Documents relatifs au comté de Champagne et de Bries, 1172–1361, ed. by Auguste Longnon, 4 vols (Paris: Imprimerie Nationale, 1914)

Obituarium lugdunensis ecclesiae: nécrologie des personnages illustres et des bienfaiteurs de l'Église métropolitaine de Lyon du IXe au XVe siècle, ed. by Marie Claude Guigue (Lyon: Scherring, 1867)

Registres consulaires de la ville de Lyon de 1416 à 1423, ed. by Marie Claude Guigue, 2 vols (Lyon: Auguste Brun, 1882)

Secondary Works

Black, Robert, *Education and Society in Florentine Tuscany: Teachers, Pupils and Schools, c. 1250–1500* (Leiden: Brill, 2007)

Clerval, Jules Alexandre, *Les Écoles de Chartres au moyen-âge (du ve au xvie siècle)* (Paris: Picard, 1895)

Cole, Percival R., *Later Roman Education in Ausionus, Capella and the Theodosian Code; with translations and commentary* (Charleston: Bibliobazaar, 2009)

Déniau, Jean, *La Commune de Lyon et la guerre bourgnignonne, 1417–1435* (Lyon: Masson, 1934)

Forest, J. M. H., *L'École cathédrale de Lyon: le petit seminaire de Saint-Jean* (Paris: Delhomme & Briguet, 1885)

Gehl, Paul F., *A Moral Art: Grammar, Society and Culture in Trecento Florence* (Ithaca: Cornell University Press, 1993)

Grendler, Paul F., *Schooling in Renaissance Italy: Literacy and Learning, 1300–1600* (Baltimore: Johns Hopkins University Press, 1989)

Guilbert, Sylvette, 'Les Écoles rurales en Champagne au xve siècle: enseignement et promotion sociale', *Annales de l'Est* (1982), 127–47

Guyotjeannin, Oliver, 'Les Petites écoles de Paris dans la première moitié du xve siècle', in *Finances, pouvoirs et mémoire: hommages à Jean Favier*, ed. by Jean Kerhervé and Albert Rigaudière (Brest: Fayard, 1999), pp. 112–26

Kristeller, Paul Oskar, *Renaissance Thought and its Sources* (New York: Columbia University Press, 1979)

Miskimin, Harry A., *Money, Prices, and Foreign Exchange in Fourteenth Century France* (New Haven: Yale University Press, 1963)

Pourrat, Joseph, *L'Antique école de Leidrade: xie centenaire de sa fondation* (Lyon: Emmanuel Vitte, 1899)

Spufford, Peter, *Handbook of Medieval Exchange*, Royal Historical Society Guides and Handbooks, 13 (London: Royal Historical Society, 1986)

Wadsworth, James B., *Lyon, 1473–1503: The Beginnings of Cosmopolitanism* (Cambridge, MA: Medieval Academy of America, 1962)

Witt, Ronald G., *Hercules at the Crossroads: The Life, Works, and Thought of Coluccio Salutati* (Durham, NC: Duke University Press, 1983)

The Poor and their Power: Images of Poor Women in Medieval Literature and Art

Anne M. Scott

The way poverty is represented in medieval literary texts and visual images often shows it to be a powerful social force and one that the non-poor ignore at their peril. While the socio-economic condition of poverty was shunned as the worst fate that could befall a person, it was also widely interpreted both in sacred and secular literature as a state that brings an individual close to God, and, as such, was lauded as a holy state. This enigma of poverty, often portrayed in literature and in art in the figure of a woman, reflects the ambiguity inherent in attitudes to poverty from late antiquity through to the late Middle Ages.[1] The fact that poverty in its many guises is considered a serious topic for literature reflects the force of the condition. Numerically the medieval poor are strong, and,[2] though the poor are ostensibly powerless, the condition of poverty is widely regarded with such horror by the non-poor that it assumes a menacing power of its own.[3] Poverty stalks the rich and powerful, presenting

[1] I have discussed these concepts in some detail in 'The Enigma of "Lady Poverty" — Beautiful Ideal or Loathly Lady?'.

[2] See Scott, *Piers Plowman and the Poor*, p. 70.

[3] One example from Middle English literature of this menacing power is found in Thomas Hoccleve's *Regiment of Princes*, which graphically records the poetic persona's fear of old-age poverty: Hoccleve, *The Regiment of Princes*, ed. by Blyth. See also the terrifying portrayal of *Povreté* discussed in Scott, '*Le Chastel de Labour*'.

Anne M. Scott (anne.scott@uwa.edu.au) is the editor of *Parergon* and honorary research fellow in English and Cultural Studies at The University of Western Australia.

Approaches to Poverty in Medieval Europe: Complexities, Contradictions, Transformations, c. 1100–1500, ed. by Sharon Farmer, IMR 22 (Turnhout: Brepols, 2016) pp. 229–252
BREPOLS PUBLISHERS 10.1484/M.IMR-EB.5.105466

a mirror of what may befall anyone. Yet it is also widely promoted as the sure means to salvation, a theme that pervades medieval drama, poetry, sermon and didactic text in which charity to the poor is expounded as the way in which the non-poor may win heaven by identifying with the poor Christ of the scriptures.[4]

It is within this larger context that I offer this study of three texts and two related images. The first text, the Franciscan treatise *Sacrum commercium Beati Francisci cum Domina Paupertate* (*c.* 1227) narrates how an outcast Lady Poverty leads Francis and his brethren to the top of a high mountain, where she applauds their devotion to poverty and teaches them how to attain perfection through the renunciation of material goods.[5] A visual image connected with this is the fresco of the marriage of Saint Francis to Lady Poverty, sometimes attributed to Giotto, on the ceiling of the lower basilica of St Francis in Assisi (Figure 9.1). In Chaucer's *Wyf of Bath's Tale* (*c.* 1392–95),[6] the lead female figure, a shape-changing hag, trenchantly represents the virtue of poverty as a moral good to an awkwardly embarrassed young knight. In the third text, the Prologue to Book III of Lydgate's *Fall of Princes* (*c.* 1431–38), the aggressive figure of Glad Poverty defeats Dame Fortune.[7] Lydgate's poem, a rendering of Boccaccio's *De casibus illustrium virorum* (*c.* 1360), is based on Laurence de Premierfait's French adaptation of Boccaccio's original work. Miniatures illustrating Poverty overcoming Fortune appear in several manuscripts of this French version,[8] and in this chapter I will allude to that found in a manuscript in the British Library, Royal 20 C IV, fol. 77v (Figure 9.2).

[4] Langland, in *Piers Plowman*, links the good works necessary for salvation directly with charity to the poor: *Piers Plowman*, ed. by Pearsall, C.I.171–80. The medieval plays of the Last Judgement dramatize Matthew 25. 31–46 and show how generous care of the poor and needy will gain a place in paradise for the caregiver. See 'The Webstar's Play', ed. by Hussey, pp. 438–63, ll. 453–644; and 'The Mercers' Play: Doomsday', ed. by Beadle, pp. 442–53, ll. 285–364. Elsewhere in this volume, Adam J. Davis traces the growth of compassion in the twelfth and thirteenth centuries, presenting a nuanced account of the various motivations that prompted contemporaries to undertake works of mercy towards the needy: 'Hospitals, Charity, and the Culture of Compassion in the Twelfth and Thirteenth Centuries'.

[5] All English references are to 'The Sacred Exchange'. The Latin text is reproduced from *Fontes franciscani*, ed. by Menesto and others. This text, written around 1227 in Umbria by an early follower of Francis, influenced Dante's portrayal of Lady Poverty. See Dresser, '"Sacrum Commercium"', pp. 7, 90–92. For further comment on the genesis of this text, see nn. 20–23 below.

[6] All references are to *The Wyf of Bath's Tale*, ed. by Benson. Benson, supported by other Chaucer scholars, dates this tale *c.* 1392–95 (p. xxv).

[7] All references are to John Lydgate, *Lydgate's Fall of Princes*, ed. by Bergen, III.

[8] Miniatures illustrating Poverty overcoming Fortune appear in several manuscripts of

These three selected texts and two related images that figure poverty allegorically as a poor but powerful woman, illustrate the opposite poles of poverty as powerless and powerful. Recognizing the shared heritage and potential cross-influence between significant writers of the European late Middle Ages reinforces the view that poverty, though apparently terrifying, is a state that can lead a person to great moral heights, and I have particularly selected my three texts because Lady Poverty, the Wyf of Bath's hag, and Glad Poverty combine loathliness with poverty and with power. Each of the three female figures is repulsive to most, yet becomes a mentor promoting variously total voluntary poverty in union with Christ (Lady Poverty), true 'gentilesse' at court (Wyf of Bath's hag), and the exercise of Free Will in ordering one's life, with a healthy disregard for the ephemeral gifts of Fortune (Glad Poverty). While only the Wyf of Bath's hag may be properly construed as belonging to the 'loathly lady' tradition of literature,[9] Lady Poverty and Glad Poverty share with her the common characteristics of being marginalized from society, having a repulsive appearance, being without possessions, and having the power to change the lives of those whom they encounter. In discussing Lady Poverty, who elevates Francis, the Wyf of Bath's hag, who redeems a knight, and Lydgate's Glad Poverty, who overcomes Fortune, I will argue that they express the power of the woman, in herself poor, without any of the conventional trappings commonly valued by the world. The kind of poverty represented in the texts under consideration is a strong moral good and contrasts sharply with the material poverty of the socio-economic poor whom society treats as repulsive and often morally reprehensible. Yet it is still poverty, and the power of poverty to be a disturbing force in society is captured in the figure of the loathly lady who represents both the horror and the perverse beauty of poverty.

The Sacrum commercium Beati Francisci cum Domina Paupertate

In addition to the power invested in her, the loathly lady of literature usually possesses wisdom and is a mentor figure, a role portrayed by Lady Poverty in the anonymous Franciscan text, *Sacrum commercium Beati Francisci cum Domina Paupertate*, an allegory composed between 1227 and 1239, which appears

Laurent de Premierfait's French version of Boccaccio, *Des cas des nobles hommes et femmes*. Three examples may be found in British Library manuscripts: BL, MS Royal 20 C IV, fol. 77^{v}; BL, MS Add. 35321, fol. 67^{r}; and BL, MS Add. 11696, fol. 71^{r}. In MS Bodl. 265, fol. 73^{v}, Poverty is represented as a man.

[9] Cognate versions of this tale are discussed by Passmore in 'Through the Counsel of a Lady'.

among the early documents of the Franciscan Order.[10] While this text does not portray Lady Poverty as physically ugly, it is clear from the narrative that she is shunned and outcast by those whose values are centred on the comforts of the material world.[11]

The text of the *Sacrum commercium* portrays Saint Francis's 'marriage' to Lady Poverty as an ideal for a select group of people, empowering them for life in the courts of heaven.[12] Describing the initial encounter of Francis and his brethren with the allegorical Lady Poverty, the text praises the pre-eminence of poverty, 'fundamentum omnium virtutum et custos' (the foundation and guardian of all virtues) (Prologus, l. 2).[13] It tells how Francis and his companions set out to find poverty along the highways and byways, unsuccessfully until they are finally told to seek her upon the heights of a mountain. With his brothers, Francis ascends the mountain and meets Lady Poverty. She tells them her history from Paradise down to their own age, emphasizing how closely she represented God's virtue to humankind while they were naked and without property in Eden, and how far from God and herself human beings strayed once they had to work and embroil themselves in material prosperity to survive in the fallen world. Far from being, as she once had been seen, a beautiful consort to the Almighty, described in the terms Scripture uses for Wisdom, Lady Poverty is shunned and despised by humankind, a loathly lady whose only lover up to now has been Christ.

> Magna ergo dignitas tua et altitudo incomparabilis, cum, relictis omnibus angelorum ordinibus et immensis virtutibus, de quibus magna erat copia in excelsis, venit

[10] The different strands of modern interpretation, and putative dating, have been summarized by Stefano Brufani in the introduction to his 1990 edition, *Sacrum commercium Beati Francisci cum Domina Paupertate*, ed. by Brufani. See also Havely, 'Poverty in Purgatory', for a succinct English language survey of the various theories as to date and authorship.

[11] In *The Romaunt of the Rose* Chaucer describes Poverty as imaged on the outer walls of the garden, a thin bedraggled woman, cowering in weakness and shame: *Romaunt of the Rose*, ed. by Benson, ll. 449–474.

[12] The Franciscan literature shows how far removed from everyday social life is their ideal of Christian voluntary poverty, for although Francis insisted that the early friars live in absolute poverty like the poorest of the poor, by stressing the moral value of their chosen life of poverty, he and his followers have been accused of devaluing the suffering of the socio-economic poor who had no control over whether or not they remained poor. This notion is fully dealt with by Wolf, *The Poverty of Riches*, pp. 1–36.

[13] *Fontes franciscani*, ed. by Menesto and others, p. 1705; 'The Sacred Exchange', Prologue, p. 529.

> te querere in inferioribus partibus terre, iacentem in *luto fecis, in tenebrosis et umbra mortis*. Cunctis viventibus odiosa non modicum exsistebas et omnes te fugiebant et, prout poterant, effugabant. Et, licet aliqui te fugere omnino non possent, non minus ideo eras eis odibilis et exosa. (cap. 5, ll. 9–11)
>
> (How great must be your dignity, then, and how beyond compare your stature! He left behind all the ranks of angels and the immense powers — of which there is a great abundance in heaven — when he came to look for you in the lowest regions of the earth — you who were lying in *the mud of the swamp, in darkness, and in the shadow of death*. All living beings held you in great contempt. All people ran from you and, as far as they could, cast you aside. Even though there were some who couldn't escape from you, you were no less contemptible and despicable to them.)[14]

In this she might be seen as ranking among those poverty figures whose condition reflects the imagery of poverty as the worst of evils.[15] Yet the text of the *Sacrum commercium* describes Francis seeking Poverty in terms that echo the search for the beloved in the Song of Songs: 'cepit sedule velut curiosus explorator circuire *vicos et plateas civitatis*, diligenter *querens quam diligebat anima sua*' (he eagerly began to go about *the streets and piazzas of the city*, as a curious explorer diligently *looking for her whom his soul loved*).[16] But the finding is devoid of any erotic love language; Lady Poverty is a teacher and mentor whose words reflect Scripture and its commentaries, and whose actions are symbolic. Francis invites her to dwell with him and his companions and, after a banquet which consists of half a stale loaf served on a broken platter, they sleep lying naked on the bare earth in a graphic demonstration of the irrelevance of material security.[17] The commitment demanded by Poverty is total and, as the allegory tells it, Francis and his first companions are already practising it before they are rewarded by being united with Lady Poverty.[18] What she confirms for them is the power that poverty brings them, an empowerment that is

[14] *Fontes franciscani*, ed. by Menesto and others, p. 1711; 'The Sacred Exchange', pp. 534–35.

[15] Innocent III's *De miseria condicionis humane* treats poverty as one of the miseries of the human condition, Dei Segni, *De Miseria condicionis humane*, ed. by Lewis, I. 13 and 14, pp. 115–17.

[16] *Fontes franciscani*, ed. by Menesto and others, p. 1706; 'The Sacred Exchange', p. 530.

[17] In medieval spiritual writing, stripping off clothes is not erotic but symbolic of being voluntarily divested of everything material. Francis's gesture of stripping in front of his father and the bishop is part of this medieval understanding of nakedness. See McIlroy, *The English Prose Treatises of Richard Rolle*, pp. 134–35.

[18] Barbara Newman gives a similar interpretation, ranking Lady Poverty among her goddesses, in *God and the Goddesses*, pp. 3–9.

both spiritual and earthly. When Lady Poverty asks to be taken to their cloister or enclosure, Francis walks her to a hill overlooking the valley. Pointing to the whole world as far as they can see, Francis says: 'Hoc est claustrum nostra, domina' (*This, Lady, is our enclosure).*[19] Their apostolate is not to be confined within a monastic enclosure: they are to travel the world preaching the gospel without barriers. Stripped of all earthly goods, Francis becomes a great spiritual leader whose spirit ennobles his followers.

The *Sacrum commercium* belongs to the early writings of the Franciscans — 'an exhortation written to encourage Francis's followers to live in an authentic way the saint's biblical vision of poverty'.[20] It has been viewed as one of the texts that reflects the divisions in the order between the Spiritual Franciscans, who believed that they should hold literally to the evangelical poverty of Christ and his apostles, and those, eventually the mainstream, who accepted that, in order to be able to conduct their work of preaching and teaching, it was necessary to have a certain amount of stability, roofs over their heads, food on the table, and books in their libraries. Francis himself was in sometimes violent conflict within the evolving order, since he held fast to the idea that to follow Christ one must strip oneself of material possessions.[21]

The motivation for this single-minded search for poverty on the historical Francis's part is a personal desire to make poverty his means of uniting with Christ, and demonstrates the power of the medieval concept of poverty to complicate the ideology of both institutional and personal life. For in order to do this he enacts a kind of violence in the process of embracing poverty. His dramatic divesting of his clothing and rejection of his father's mercantile way of life is in itself a violence, and some of the early Franciscan legends echo the violence with which Francis rejects money, throwing out the coins his brethren had collected and tearing down roof tiles in gestures symbolic of avoiding anything that suggests earthly stability.[22] While modern stories about the saint concentrate on his gentle love of nature, the medieval reality is more robust. The early history of the Franciscans demonstrates that Francis's way of life required him

[19] *Fontes franciscani*, ed. by Menesto and others, p. 1730; 'The Sacred Exchange', p. 552.

[20] Armstrong, introduction to 'The Sacred Exchange' p. 523.

[21] A full account of the conflicts and dissensions of the early Franciscan Order is given in the monograph by Lambert, *Franciscan Poverty*.

[22] *Scripta Leonis*, ed. and trans. by Brooke, pp. 106–07.

Figure 9.1 Mystical Marriage of St. Francis and Lady Poverty, Assisi, Lower Church. Photo by Alinari/Bridgeman Images, reproduced with permission.

to be at odds frequently with his brethren, and the dislocation within the order over the meaning of poverty entailed violence in itself.[23]

The visual representation in the lower basilica of Assisi of the relationship of Francis and Lady Poverty links all the themes in allegorical form (Figure 9.1). In the text the word used is *Commercium*, which has been variously interpreted as covenant, alliance, bond, or exchange, and the *Commercium* is made between Lady Poverty and the brethren rather than Francis alone, while the dialogue does not use nuptial imagery. However, the subject of the fresco in the lower basilica of Assisi can be interpreted as a mystical marriage of St Francis and Lady Poverty, a union which is portrayed by Dante, too, in Canto 11 of the *Paradiso*:

> ché per tal donna, giovinetto, in guerra
> del padre corse, a cui, come a la morte,
> la porta del piacer nessun diserra;

[23] Dresser sets the *Sacrum commercium* in the context of early Franciscan conflicts: '"Sacrum Commercium"', pp. 21–32.

e dinanzi a la sua spirital corte
et coram patre le si fece unito;
poscia di dì in dì l'amò più forte.
Paradiso 11, 58–63

(while still a youth he braved his father's wrath,
because he loved a lady to whom all
would bar their door as if to death itself.

Before the bishop's court et coram patre
he took this lady as his lawful wife;
from day to day he loved her more and more.)[24]

The message conveyed by the image stresses the power of poverty, apparently without the impressions of violence. Francis is elevated to the company of the blessed where, standing among the elect, he receives from Christ the hand of his beloved *Domina Paupertas*, in this act becoming an *alter Christus*. Lady Poverty is dressed in the flowing white robes of a mentor figure.[25] Yet though seeming tranquil, this image, too, carries overtones of the violence that accompanies Poverty. The legend of the *Sacrum commercium* is represented in the image by the mountaintop where Francis stands with Christ and his lady, who is still being threatened with stones and sticks by the small earthly people who, legend says, have always rejected her. Her appearance is haggard, old, and ragged[26] — Lady Poverty's robe is patched and torn by the brambles she has encountered[27] — but her stance is magisterial and her demeanour calm and loving.

[24] The translations from Dante are taken from Dante, *The Divine Comedy*, trans. by Musa. The Italian is taken from *Project Gutenberg* <http://www.gutenberg.org/ebooks/1011> [accessed 15 July 2015].

[25] Several writers have commented on Lady Poverty's affinity with Sapientia. See particularly Dresser, '"Sacrum Commercium"', pp. 69–77, and Newman's more recent study in *God and the Goddesses*, pp. 3–9. Her white robe links her symbolically with other mentor figures such as Boethius's Lady Philosophy (Boethius, *The Consolation of Philosophy*, trans. by Watts, bk I, prose 1, pp. 35–37) and Langland's Holy Church (*Piers Plowman*, ed. by Pearsall, C.I.3, p. 56).

[26] Eric Auberbach makes this comment in 'St. Francis of Assisi in Dante's *Commedia*', p. 169.

[27] In a similar way, torn robes grace Boethius's Lady Philosophy, and Alanus de Insulis's Natura: Boethius, *The Consolation of Philosophy*, trans. by Watts; Alanus de Insulis, *The Complaint of Nature*, trans. by Moffat.

There is no doubt that the image in its commanding position is designed to emphasize the great spiritual power that has been given to Francis by his pursuit of poverty, and canonizing it as a mystical marriage gave the image currency in art and literature. Dante, who worked closely with the Franciscans of Santa Croce in Florence,[28] speaks of Poverty as having been the only one to commune with Christ on the cross, saying that, since Christ's death, she has wandered the earth being outcast until she encountered Francis and his companions.

> Questa, privata del primo marito,
> millecent' anni e più dispetta e scura
> fino a costui si stette sanza invito; [...]
>
> né valse esser costante né feroce,
> ì che, dove Maria rimase giuso,
> ella con Cristo pianse in su la croce.
> *Paradiso* 11, 64–66, 70–72
>
> (Bereft of her first spouse, despised, ignored
> she waited eleven hundred years and more,
> living without a lover till he came [...]
>
> alone, though known was her fierce constancy
> that time she climbed the cross to be
> with Christ, while Mary stayed below alone.)

The unmistakeable offensiveness of Poverty to the majority of mankind is always to the fore, whether in visual or textual representation. Dante describes Lady Poverty as shunned, and in the image she is being stoned. She remains a 'loathly lady' who nonetheless has indomitable power which she transmits to those who embrace her.

The Wyf of Bath's Tale

Whereas Lady Poverty belongs to the celestial world, the Wyf of Bath's hag belongs to the world of 'faerye'. In the Celtic and Arthurian traditions, from which the hag in Chaucer's *Wyf of Bath's Tale* springs, the loathly lady is often a shape-changer whose repulsive outside conceals and preserves the power within. Subject to rejection, she chooses the one on whom to place her favour,

[28] Havely, *Dante and the Franciscans*, pp. 8–43.

often demanding from him a physical, sexual embrace.[29] The reward for the male is empowerment, often political,[30] sometimes economic,[31] and, in the case of the *Wyf of Bath's Tale*, marital *maistrye*, but in all the stories, the power of the hag-like woman remains as a constant force, influencing the future of the man.

In Chaucer's *Wyf of Bath's Tale*, the loathly lady from the old world of 'faerye' invokes the 'new world' of Christian doctrine to promote the value of poverty as an ideal of 'gentilesse'. Here Chaucer tells his own version of the story of a knight's encounter with a shape-changing hag who is able to give him the answer to a riddle that will save his life. The knight of Arthur's court, having committed the crime of rape, has been handed over to Queen Guinevere for punishment. She has allowed him one year to find an answer to the question of what women most desire. If he does not find the correct answer, on his return he will die. The hag, who appears to be old, ugly, and poor, tells the knight, correctly, that

> Wommen desyren to have sovereyntee
> As wel over hir housbond as hir love,
> And for to been in maistrie him above;
> *Wyf of Bath's Tale*, ll. 1038–40

(Women want to be in control, both over their husbands and their love, and to be in the position of power.)

What women most desire is to have control. Having thus saved his life, she demands to marry the knight who, though fiercely reluctant, is obliged to honour his promise to do whatever she would demand of him. Being ashamed of having to wed someone who offends against courtly ideals of a suitable bride by being old, ugly, and poor,[32] the knight arranges for the nuptials to be held in

[29] In the story of Niall and the Nine Hostages, a druid charged with finding the true high king takes five brothers to the smith, who makes them weapons and sends them out hunting. Each brother in turn goes looking for water and finds a well guarded by a hideous hag who demands a kiss in return for water. Only Niall gives the full sexual embrace, whereupon the hag is revealed as a beautiful maiden, the Sovereignty of Ireland, who grants Niall not only water but the kingship for many generations: 'Niall Noígiallach', in Duffy, *Medieval Ireland: An Encyclopedia*, pp. 353–54.

[30] Defined by the term *soveraintie*.

[31] The economic influence of the loathly lady can be seen in the poem 'The Weddynge of Sir Gawain and Dame Ragnelle', Dame Ragnelle being an heiress in her own right: see *The Wedding of Sir Gawain and Dame Ragnelle*, ed. by Hahn.

[32] Maurice Keen explains, for instance, that marriage below one's estate would be so detrimental as to debar a knight from taking part in a tournament: see *Chivalry*, p. 211.

private. Once married, the hag gives him the choice of having her old, ugly, and faithful, 'foul and old til that I deye' (l. 1220), or young, beautiful, and sexually potent, in this case taking his chance on her continued fidelity:

> Or elles ye wol han me yong and fair,
> And take your aventure of the repair
> That shal be to your house by cause of me
> *Wyf of Bath's Tale*, ll. 1224–26.

> (Or else you shall have me young and fair, and take your chance on any damage limitation that shall affect your family because of me.)

The knight allows her to make this impossible choice for him, and finds, to his delight, that she sheds her ugly shape and becomes young and beautiful, promising him eternal fidelity.

The complexities of this tale have inspired a strong body of critical response. Among many other interpretations, it is notable as a parody of the knightly quest,[33] an examination of anti-feminism, and a statement of pro-feminism.[34] Since the references to poverty occur in a relatively short section of the tale, it cannot be construed as being a tale 'about poverty'. Nevertheless, at the height of narrative climax, when the knight is about to enter into a marital act of unspeakable loathsomeness, coupling his vital, handsome, young male flesh with the body of a leering, grotesque, old hag, Chaucer allocates 108 lines to a sermon on the merits of poverty offered, crucially, in the context of the hag's proposal to 'amende' the problems of the knight.

This tale fits into a complex discussion of women's authority, culminating in a three part sermon, which Margaret Hallissy plausibly interprets to be the wife assuming the role of teacher — magister.[35] Her 'maistrye' is to assume teaching authority over her husband. Each part of the sermon hinges on a proper understanding of the value of the human being, and makes direct contrasts between the value of possessions and of personal integrity. The knight complains that his bride is old, poor, and of low birth — all stains upon the honour of his name in court.

> Thou art so loothly, and so oold also,
> And therto comen of so lough a kynde,
> That litel wonder is thogh I walwe and wynde.
> *Wyf of Bath's Tale*, ll. 1100–02.

33 Carter, 'Coupling the Beastly Bride and the Hunter Hunted'.

34 Evans and Johnson, *Feminist Readings in Middle English Literature*.

35 Hallissy, *Clean Maids, True Wives, Steadfast Widows*, p. 177.

(You are so ugly and so old as well, And what's more, you are so low-born, it's small wonder that I toss and turn.)

The hag's first rejoinder is that 'gentilesse' — the quality that makes someone 'gentle' or noble — comes from Christ, and cannot be passed on by birth.

> Crist wol, we clayme of him our gentillesse,
> Nat of our eldres for hir old richesse.
> For thogh they yeve us al hir heritage,
> For which we clayme to been of heigh parage,
> Yet may they nat biquethe, for no-thing,
> To noon of us hir vertuous living,
> That made hem gentil men y-called be;
> *Wyf of Bath's Tale*, ll. 1117–23

(It is Christ's will that we derive our gentility from him, not from our ancestors because of their old money. For even though they might give us their whole heritage as a reason for us to claim noble lineage, even so, they cannot, in any way, bequeath to any of us their virtuous manner of life, which is what caused them to be called 'gentlemen'.)

The knight's second complaint is that she is poor. In answer to this she points out that Christ himself chose to live in poverty, and that poverty, therefore cannot be held in scorn. Furthermore, a rich man who covets something is poor, and a low-born man who is content with his rags is rich.

> Glad povert is an honest thing, certeyn;
> This wol Senek and othere clerkes seyn.
> Who-so that halt him payd of his poverte,
> I holde him riche, al hadde he nat a sherte.
> He that coveyteth is a povre wight,
> For he wolde han that is nat in his might.
> But he that noght hath, ne coveyteth have,
> Is riche, al-though ye holde him but a knave.
> *Wyf of Bath's Tale*, ll. 1183–90

(Cheerful poverty is a praiseworthy thing, certainly; Seneca and other scholars will say so. The person who is content with his state of poverty, I consider him rich, even if he hasn't a shirt to his back. He who covets something is a poor fellow, because he wants to have that which is not within his power. But the person who has nothing and longs for nothing is rich, even though you might consider him just a low-born type.)

As to her third problem, age, her solution resolves this once the knight has agreed to let her make the decisions.

Much of the authority on which she bases her discussion, the gospel, and sayings of Seneca, Cicero, Boethius, Juvenal, and Vincent of Beauvais, is commonplace material but unusual in the context of loathly lady tales. She is poor, hideous, and undesirable, but overtly praises the power of poverty, which is translated into virtue, in this making a trenchant rehabilitation of the poor in the eyes of the most powerful non-poor — King Arthur's court. The knight reluctantly accepts the repulsiveness of her poverty and her physical ugliness which affront fourteenth-century notions of 'gentilesse'.[36] He unites himself with the poor old woman, becoming one flesh with her whole undesirability, and is instantly rewarded by finding that she is ravishingly young and beautiful.

The conclusion to Chaucer's version of the well-known fairy tale underlines the poet's compassion for human beings and his acute consciousness of the ethical conflicts thrown up between overarching humane and Christian ideals and the way contemporary society ordains life and lifestyle. For although the story ends with the knight 'bathed in bliss', the reader is left with the strong impression that this knight is ethically far beneath the lady who is the cause of his ultimate bliss. Chaucer does not dwell on the physical details of her loathsomeness,[37] yet being old — and in the forest,[38] outside the civilizing and protecting walls of house and home — she is ipso facto poor, and is certainly regarded so by her knight, who takes exception to her appearance, age, and low estate.

One of the strongest values of Arthur's court is the keeping of one's word. Set against this is the value attached to one's reputation. A knight aspired to gain a wealthy and beautiful bride — this was one way the younger sons of families secured their fortunes. Shame is an integral part of court ethics, and shame dominates the knight's thinking.[39] His insistence on having a private marriage not only highlights his sense of shame in this alliance, but could be construed

[36] Gervase Mathew discusses the cultivation of sensibility at the court of Richard II, which developed expectations of beauty, loyalty, and chivalry in the marriage of a knight to his lady: *The Court of Richard II*, pp. 114–37.

[37] This is in contrast with some of the 'loathly lady' tales, such as *Dame Ragnell*, which glories in the grotesque appearance of the hag.

[38] Hallissy, *Clean Maids, True Wives, Steadfast Widows*, p. 89, points out that a social and moral difference exists between the woman who is enclosed within walls and one who roams the countryside. In the home, woman's chastity is safe; abroad, she is perceived to be 'loose' and penetrable.

[39] This concept is illustrated in the contemporary poem *Sir Gawain and the Grene Knight*, and carries through to Malory's *Morte d'Arthur*. See Trigg, '"Shamed be…"', pp. 77–80.

as an impediment allowing for its future invalidation.[40] He can claim that he gave his word under duress and in ignorance, two impediments to marriage, when in peril of his life he made a promise not knowing what the hag would demand. His 'trouthe' is compromised by these considerations, for it would appear that he is ready to take on the appearance of having married the lady according to this promise, but, perhaps, not to continue in the marriage.

There is often a problem in reading allegorical work because the allegory conflicts with underlying assumptions of the story.[41] While it is true that the allegorical interpretation declares that goodness of the heart (that of the hag) is ultimately shown forth in beauty of the body (the ravishingly transformed lady), nevertheless, the yardstick is definitely worldly beauty as defined by the culture of Arthur's court. Happiness is measured by the knight's possession of a beautiful, sexually potent wife. There is no question of his living in poverty, or with an ugly consort. She is as beautiful 'as any lady, emperice, or queene' (l. 1246). Beauty equates with earthly prosperity.[42] If we press the interpretation of the story to its logical conclusion, it is the hag who adopts the material prosperity of the court rather than the knight who is reconciled to her poverty. Read in this way, Chaucer's final judgement seems to be that poverty is not an acceptable vocation for those who count. The poor old hag becomes a beautiful lady capable of giving the knight all his heart desires and fitting in with the court; the knight has not accepted her poor way of life — he does not choose either way. In the end the hag's poverty seems to become insignificant because it is obliterated. In courtly terms, poverty and happiness cannot be conceived of as going hand in hand, so poverty is sidelined.

Recognizing the tension between allegory and reality in this instance helps the modern reader to appreciate the dichotomy Chaucer expresses between a devotional and intellectual acceptance of the fundamental equality of human beings and the very different ethic dictated by the norms of court life. Yet one cannot ignore or forget that the inherent power is in the lady who had to be embraced as poor, old, and ugly before she could be revealed in the full beauty of her nature, restoring the knight to his standing within the court. Ultimately,

[40] McSheffrey, *Marriage, Sex, and Civic Culture*, pp. 21–25.

[41] Kathleen Hewett-Smith discusses this issue in the context of *Piers Plowman*, where she finds that the social context of the poem militates against the author's desire to make a specific teaching about poverty: 'Allegory on the Half-Acre'. In Chaucer's tale a similar problem occurs.

[42] George Orwell observes how the grinding hardships of poverty rob women of physical beauty: *The Road to Wigan Pier*, p. 20.

in the context of the *Wyf of Bath's Tale*, the 'loathly lady', while propounding the virtues of poverty, belongs to a world of faerie where legendary wealth untold and unimaginable sexual fulfilment are available for those who conform to certain conditions laid down by the fairy mistress.[43] Susan Crane suggests that the lady's 'curtain lecture' does not favour lowborn poverty over gentle wealth, but questions the validity of divisions between these categories.[44] And indeed the knight does, ultimately, profit morally from his alliance with this lowborn yet powerful wife, for, by allowing the hag to decide what appearance she is to take and whether or not she will be a loyal wife, the knight gives up control over his status and destiny, and thus becomes poor in spirit. His acceptance of this loathly lady's poor state, within the context of Arthur's Christian court, brings its own reward of courtly wealth and fame, in a bold gesture that reflects the treasure in heaven promised by Christian scripture for the poor in spirit — 'for theirs is the kingdom of heaven'.

Lydgate's Fall of Princes

My final representation, in Lydgate's Prologue to Book III of the *Fall of Princes*, has similar characteristics to the previous two: an ugly, poor, repulsive woman named Glad Poverty turns out to be immensely powerful. Lydgate's poem, written over a lengthy period, *c.* 1431–38, is a rendering of Boccaccio's *De casibus illustrium virorum* (*c.* 1360), hugely expanded from the original, and commissioned by Humphrey, duke of Gloucester, to be an influential work in the Mirror for Princes genre. Following his source, Boccaccio, Lydgate describes how Andalus, the teacher, expounds to his pupils an *exemplum* on the clash between two women; one, Dame Fortune, apparently powerful, the other, Glad Poverty, actually so. This is vividly illustrated in a manuscript miniature by the Master of the *Cité des dames*, of Poverty overwhelming Fortune (Figure 9.2).

The paradox of the encounter is immediately evident. Fortune, often portrayed as blind, has been, from late antiquity, the impartial controller of destinies, turning the wheel upon which human beings rise to prosperity only to fall as the wheel turns. Poverty as an allegorical figure is usually despised, often allied to vice, and powerless to escape her condition.[45] By contrast, Boccaccio's

[43] The conditions vary from tale to tale, but often involve a promise of secrecy about the identity of the fairy benefactress.

[44] Crane, *Gender and Romance in Chaucer's 'Canterbury Tales'*, p. 156.

[45] In the *Romaunt of the Rose*, Poverty is placed in close proximity to the vices of Avarice

Figure 9.2
'Poverty Overwhelms Fortune', Miniature by the Master of the Cité des dames, Paris *c.* 1420, BL Royal 20 C IV fol.77v. Reproduced with permission.

tale recounts how Dame Fortune, wealthy and powerful, is overturned in hand-to-hand combat by the thin, ragged, and noisome figure of Poverty, a theme imaginatively depicted in several manuscript illuminations and retold by Laurent de Premierfait, followed by John Lydgate. Instead of dealing out good or bad fortune, the allegorical figure is herself held to account for leading people astray, and is herself brought low by the very figure whom most people fear: Poverty.[46]

In the manuscript miniature by the Master of the *Cité des Dames*, of Poverty overcoming Fortune, we witness a powerful allegory, clear-cut and striking (Figure 9.2). Fortune, pinned to the ground, wears the crown and ermine of royalty, as well as her signature blindfold. Poverty, ugly, in rags, athletic, and skilled in wrestling, uses her knees to hold down the opponent, grasping her by the throat. Other parts of the allegorical story are depicted — in the background, Poverty ties Misadventure to a stake. The bystanders who look on

and Sloth: *Romaunt of the Rose*, ed. by Benson, ll. 449–74. In *La voie de povreté*, Poverty is said to be the mother of all misfortune: Bruyant, 'La voie de Povreté et de Richesse'.

46 An analogous portrayal of Poverty as the reverse image of fortune is found in the *Roman de la Rose*, when Fortune's dwelling is described as harsh and forbidding.

in engrossed horror replace the audience of Andalus in the text. They do not interfere to help Fortune, and this reflects the horror of poverty which attacks the fortunate and has to be endured alone.[47] Here, Fortune is vanquished in an extraordinary overturning of stereotypes: she and Misadventure, who normally inflict disaster, are now subjected to the same treatment: powerless Poverty has become powerful.

The text of Lydgate further complicates the encounter. In the visual image we see only the final moments of defeat; the text relates the encounter which has all the belligerence and derision of a parlay between equal combatants — unusual in this context when the customary stance of the poor is to be downtrodden and meek. Fortune taunts Glad Poverty with her hideous appearance:

> 'Mi scornful lauhtre pleynli was for the
> Whan I the sauh so megre, pale and leene,
> Nakid and cold, in gret aduersite,
> Scabbid, scuruy, scallid and oncleene
> On bak and body, as it is weel seene [...].
>
> Hauyng nothing to wrappyn in thyn hed
> Sauff a brod hat, rent out off nattis olde,
> Ful often hungry for defaute off bred,
> Slepyng on straw[e] in the frostis colde.
> And wher thou comest, as men may weel beholde,
> for feer off the, children them withdrawe,
> And many a dogge hath on thi staff ignawe.
>
> To alle estatis thou are most odious,
> Men with the will ha[ue] no daliaunce,
> Thi felashipe is so contrarious,
> Wher thou abidest ther may be no plesaunce.
> Folk hate so dedli thi froward aqueyntaunce,
> That fynali, I dar conclude off the,
> Wher-euer thou comest thi felaship men fle!'
>
> *Fall of Princes*, III. 239–59.

('My scornful laughter clearly was for you, when I saw you so scrawny, pale and thin, naked and cold, in great hardship, scabby with scurvy, and suppurating boils all over your back and your body, quite plain to see [...]. With nothing to wrap

[47] Hoccleve is another English poet who deals with the loneliness and loss of identity that comes to an individual whom poverty strikes; Hoccleve, *The Regiment of Princes*, ed. by Blyth, ll. 827–973.

around your head but for a broad hat, cobbled together from old straw mats; too often hungry for want of bread, sleeping on straw in the cold of frost. And wherever you come, as it can plainly be seen, for fear of you the children run away and many a dog has gnawed on your staff. You are most hateful to people in all walks of life; men have no wish to make love to you, your companionship runs so counter to what people want, where you live there can be no delight. People hate your quarrelsome acquaintance so mortally that ultimately, I conclude as far as you are concerned, wherever you come, people will flee your company.')

Here once more the ugly appearance of Poverty is held up as repulsive. The detail is fairly conventional — in other texts, such as *Pierce Ploughman's Crede*, or *Piers Plowman* itself, similar accounts generate pathos and elicit pity from the reader. Here, the graphic details emphasize the hatefulness of poverty to those for whom material prosperity is a priority.[48]

In response, Glad Poverty stands up to Fortune as an equal: she can do so because she has of her own accord withdrawn from the company of Fortune, and become liberated from relying on her favours.

'Fortune', quod she, 'touchyng this debat,
Which off malice thou doost ageyn me take,
Be weel certeyn, touchyng my poore estat,
I off fre will thi fauour ha[ue] forsake.
And thouh folk seyn thou maist men riche make,
Yit I ha[ue] leuere be poore with gladnesse,
Than with trouble possede gret richesse.'
Fall of Princes, III. 267–73

('Fortune', she said, regarding this debate, which, out of malice you set up against me, you need to know, concerning my poor status, that of my own free will I have given up your favour. And though people say that you can make one rich, yet I would rather be poor with gladness, than possess great wealth with troubles.)

The debate soon moves from words to challenge, and surprisingly, it is Glad Poverty who initiates it. Predictably, Fortune taunts Glad Poverty, stressing her ragged appearance and lack of substance and armour, denigrating her as a worthless opponent since the poor have no ransom to pay, nor are they worth dragging through the streets as a victor's prize. Contemptuously invulnerable to these taunts, Poverty responds that she will vanquish Fortune who, enraged,

[48] *Piers Plowman*, ed. by Pearsall, C.IX.71–97; *Pierce the Ploughmans Crede*, ed. by Skeat, ll. 418–42.

attacks without warning, not recognizing how out of condition she is for a wrestling match. Short of wind, well padded, and stoutly armoured where Poverty is sharp, bony, and clad in rags, Fortune is no match for Poverty who rapidly has the victory.

This complex representation shows two kinds of poverty — that pilloried in Innocent III's *De miseria condicionis humane*, derived from sapiential literature: the unavoidable and hated stroke that can afflict the fortunate at any time, imaged so clearly here, and the voluntarily accepted poverty of those who have renounced Fortune. 'Melius est mori quam indigere' (better be dead than a beggar), says Innocent, quoting Ecclesiasticus.[49] The power of such poverty to overwhelm is depicted in the secular image — the vanquishing of Fortune who, having been powerful herself, has, at one stroke, lost all the power that her material possessions give. The entrée to society and the company of the 'fortunate' is denied to the poor. Poverty, by her aggressive stroke, deprives Fortune of everything that gave her identity. But Lydgate's text makes considerable play of the virtues of Glad Poverty, who is free from the concerns of material possessions. The description of Poverty is repellent, and it is quite clear that although she may have chosen poverty — she says on several occasions that she deliberately set herself free of Fortune — she nevertheless offends those who are not poor. Glad Poverty offends because she does not look miserable, and she does not subscribe to the materialism of Fortune. But she also offends because she demonstrates what happens to those whom Fortune abandons.

Here is no romantic following of poverty, no Christian idealism is invoked. The benefits of poverty are stressed as being the absence of care, and the philosophy behind the sentiments is derived from Juvenal, with his carefree singing tramp,[50] Boethius deriving consolation from Philosophy, and Seneca, whose aphorisms pepper medieval texts. There is no suggestion that Glad Poverty is in line for a heavenly reward, but there certainly is a strong sense in which Poverty has emotional power in the temporal world.

Glad Poverty, as the mouthpiece for the teacher, Andalus, and indirectly for Lydgate, wants everyone to realize that not fortune but free will controls human destiny. This has to be read in the overall context of Lydgate's *Fall of Princes*, which is a handbook for rulers. The message is that both ruler and pop-

[49] Innocent III (Dei Segni, *De Miseria condicionis humane*, ed. by Lewis), I. 13, p. 115; quoting Ecclesiasticus 40.

[50] 'Cantabit vacuus coram latrone viator', Juvenal, *Satire* 10. 22, in *The Satires of Juvenal*, trans. by Kelk, p. 230.

ulace must take responsibility for their actions.[51] Order, represented by Poverty who acts with free choice, is opposed to the folly of those who hold the random Fortune as a goddess.

> Such wilful wrechis that hemsilfe betake
> To putte ther fredam in hir subieccioun,
> Off God aboue the power thei forsake,
> And hem submitte, ageyn[e]s al resoun,
> Vnder Fortunis transmutacioun,
> ther liberte ful falsli for to thrall,
> Namli whan thei a goddesse list hir calle.
> *Fall of Princes*, III. 652–58.

(Such wilful wretches that undertake of their own accord to put their liberty into subjection, abandon the power of God above, and submit themselves, flying in the face of reason, to the changeability of Fortune, subjecting their liberty to captivity for the wrong reason. That is to say, when they call her a goddess.)

Conclusion

Not only do these works all spring from a common heritage of scripture, philosophy, and shared images, but the writers, too, were acquainted with and influenced by each other's work. Chaucer based many of his works on Boccaccio's texts: the *De casibus,* in particular, is reflected in the Monk's Tale. Lydgate revered Chaucer, whose work influenced his own. Chaucer is likely to have known the work of Dante, and Dante is said to have been influenced by the *Sacrum commercium*. Moreover, as both Dante and Boccaccio travelled in central Italy, they may well have seen the Assisi fresco. These important writers raise questions about poverty, a socio-economic condition that impinges on everyone's life and needs to be dealt with rather than being ignored. Recognizing the shared heritage and potential cross-influence between significant writers of the European late Middle Ages reinforces the view that poverty, though apparently terrifying, is a state that can lead a person to great moral heights.

Ultimately everyone is in a position where material possessions may be removed in a flash, and then only those whose happiness is detached from material prosperity can pursue their lives in order to achieve the blessed peace

[51] Anna Baldwin, in speaking of *Piers Plowman*, wrote that the ideal proposed is not for everyone to become rich and comfortable, but for everyone to become poor and just: Baldwin, 'Patient Politics in *Piers Plowman*', p. 100.

of mind promised, not as a reward for, but as a consequence of being poor. Chaucer's hag, the Franciscan Lady Poverty, and Lydgate's Glad Poverty belong to the tradition of loathly ladies, outwardly repulsive but possessing remarkable powers, who are able to bring untold knowledge, wealth, or power to those willing to embrace them. They are also mentor figures, evocative of the *senex puella* of antiquity and the long tradition of the *magistra* represented by such influential literary figures as Boethius's *Philosophy* and Alanus de Insulis's *Natura*.[52] Contemplation of them opens the way to understanding the complexity of attitudes towards the poor and towards their treatment in the European Middle Ages. Just as the loathly lady is treated with a mixture of respect and revulsion, so is poverty. Just as the loathly lady has power over the people who come into her path, so does poverty. And just as the *magistra* has knowledge to impart to an often reluctant learner, so involuntary poverty, a hateful condition, can be turned to good by those who understand its power to elevate the human spirit. The result of the encounter can be devastating when material success is all that is valued by the protagonist. However, when poverty is regarded as a sign of a noble spirit, as it has been since Roman times, then different conclusions must be drawn. Study of these ladies leads one to the initial conclusion that redressing the problems of the socio-economic poor is not the concern of the courtly, gentry, or Franciscan audience for whom the works are written. The 'treasure' that these loathly ladies promise is not material wealth but a new way of regarding that poverty which, whether voluntary or involuntary, must be contemplated as potentially the lot of everyone.

[52] Curtius, *European Literature and the Latin Middle Ages*, pp. 101–05.

Works Cited

Manuscripts

London, British Library, MS Royal 20 C IV
——, MS Additional 35321
——, MS Additional 11696

Primary Sources

Alanus de Insulis, *The Complaint of Nature*, trans. by Douglas M. Moffat, Yale Studies in English, 36 (New Haven: Yale University Press, 1908) <http://www.fordham.edu/halsall/basis/alain-deplanctu.asp> [accessed 15 July 2015]

Boethius, *The Consolation of Philosophy*, trans. by V. E. Watts (Harmondsworth: Penguin Books, 1969)

Bruyant, Jean, 'La voie de Povreté et de Richesse', in *Le mesnagier de Paris*, ed. by Georgina E. Brereton and Janet M. Ferrier, Lettres gothiques (Paris: Librairie Générale Française, 1994), pp. 814–37

Dante, *The Divine Comedy*, trans. by Mark Musa, Penguin Classics, 3 vols (Harmondsworth: Penguin, 1986)

——, *Il Paradiso*, available online via *Project Gutenberg* <http://www.gutenberg.org/ebooks/1011> [accessed 15 July 2015]

Dei Segni, L. *De Miseria condicionis humane*, ed. by R. E. Lewis (Athens, GA.: University of Georgia Press, 1978)

Fontes franciscani, ed. by Enrico Menesto and others (Assisi: Porziuncola, 1995)

Hoccleve, Thomas, *The Regiment of Princes*, ed. by Charles R. Blyth (Kalamazoo: Medieval Institute Publications, 1999) <http://www.lib.rochester.edu/camelot/teams/hoccint.htm> [accessed 29 August 2012]

Juvenal, *The Satires of Juvenal: A Verse Translation*, trans. by Christopher Kelk (Lewiston: Mellen, 2010)

Langland, William, *Piers Plowman: A New Annotated Edition of the C-Text*, ed. by Derek Pearsall, 3rd edn (Exeter: University of Exeter Press, 2008)

Lydgate, John, *Lydgate's Fall of Princes*, ed. by Henry Bergen, EETS, o.s., 123, 3 vols (London: Oxford University Press, 1924)

'The Mercers' Play: Doomsday', in *The York Plays*, ed. by Richard Beadle (London: Arnold, 1982), pp. 442–53

Pierce the Ploughmans Crede, ed. by W. Skeat, EETS, o.s. 30 (London: Kegan Paul, Trench, Trubner, 1867)

Romaunt of the Rose, in *The Riverside Chaucer*, ed. by Larry Benson, 3rd edn (Boston: Houghton Mifflin, 1987), pp. 686–767

'The Sacred Exchange between Saint Francis and Lady Poverty', in *Francis of Assisi: Early Documents*, ed. by Regis J. Armstrong, J. A. Wayne Hellmann, and William Short, 3 vols (New York: New York City Press, 1999–2001), I, 529–54

Sacrum commercium Beati Francisci cum Domina Paupertate, ed. by Stefano Brufani (Assisi: Porziuncola, 1990)

Scripta Leonis, Rufini et Angeli: Sociorum S. Francisci, ed. and trans. by Rosalind B. Brooke (Oxford: Clarendon Press, 1970)

'The Webstar's Play', in *The Chester Mystery Plays: Sixteen Plays from the Chester Craft Cycle*, ed. by Maurice Hussey (London: Heinemann, 1957), pp. 438–63

The Wedding of Sir Gawain and Dame Ragnelle, in *Sir Gawain: Eleven Romances and Tales*, ed. by Thomas Hahn (Kalamazoo: Medieval Institute Publications, 1995) <http://www.lib.rochester.edu/camelot/teams/ragnfrm.htm> [accessed 15 July 2015]

The Wyf of Bath's Tale, in *The Riverside Chaucer*, ed. by Larry Benson, 3rd edn (Boston: Houghton Mifflin, 1987), pp. 116–22

Secondary Studies

Auberbach, Eric, 'St. Francis of Assisi in Dante's Commedia', *Italica*, 22 (1945), 166–79

Baldwin, Anna, 'Patient Politics in *Piers Plowman*', *Yearbook of Langland Studies*, 15 (2002), 99–108

Carter, Susan, 'Coupling the Beastly Bride and the Hunter Hunted: What Lies Behind Chaucer's *Wife of Bath's Tale*?' *The Chaucer Review* 37.4 (2003), 329–45

Crane, Susan, *Gender and Romance in Chaucer's 'Canterbury Tales'* (Princeton: Princeton University Press, 1994)

Curtius, Robert, *European Literature and the Latin Middle Ages* (London: Routledge & Kegan Paul, 1953)

Dresser, Robert M. '"Sacrum Commercium": An Early Franciscan Tract as Theological Literature' (unpublished doctoral dissertation, Fordham University, 1990)

Duffy, Sean, ed., *Medieval Ireland: An Encyclopedia* (New York: Routledge, 2005)

Evans, Ruth, and Lesley Johnson, *Feminist Readings in Middle English Literature: The Wife of Bath and All Her Sect* (London: Routledge, 1994)

Hallissy, Margaret, *Clean Maids, True Wives, Steadfast Widows: Chaucer's Women and Medieval Codes of Conduct*, Contributions in Women's Studies, 130 (Westport, Conn.: Greenwood Press, 1993)

Havely, Nicholas, *Dante and the Franciscans: Poverty and the Papacy in the Commedia* (Cambridge: Cambridge University Press, 2004)

——, 'Poverty in Purgatory: From "Commercium" to "Commedia"', *Dante Studies, with the Annual Report of the Dante Society*, 114 (1996), 229–43

Hewett-Smith, Kathleen, 'Allegory on the Half-Acre: The Demands of History', *Yearbook of Langland Studies*, 10 (1996), 1–22

Keen, Maurice, *Chivalry* (New Haven: Yale University Press, 1984)

Lambert, M. D., *Franciscan Poverty* (London: S.P.C.K., 1961)

Mathew, Gervase, *The Court of Richard II* (London: Murray, 1968)

McIlroy, Claire, *The English Prose Treatises of Richard Rolle*, Studies in Medieval Mysticism, 4 (Cambridge: Brewer, 2004)

McSheffrey, Shannon, *Marriage, Sex, and Civic Culture in Late Medieval London* (Philadelphia: University of Pennsylvania Press, 2006)

Newman, Barbara, *God and the Goddesses: Vision, Poetry, and Belief in the Middle Ages*, (Philadelphia: University of Pennsylvania Press, 2003)

Orwell, George, *The Road to Wigan Pier* (London: Secker & Warburg, 1959)

Passmore, S. Elizabeth, 'Through the Counsel of a Lady: The Irish and English Loathly Lady Tales and the "Mirror for Princes" Genre', in *The English 'Loathly Lady' Tales: Boundaries, Traditions, Motifs*, ed. by S. Elizabeth Passmore and Susan Carter, Studies in Medieval Culture, 48 (Kalamazoo: Medieval Institute Publications, 2007), pp. 3–41

Scott, Anne M. '*Le Chastel de Labour, La Voie de Povreté ou de Richesse* and a Luxury Book, Widener 1, Free Library of Philadelphia', in *Experiences of Poverty in Late Medieval and Early Modern England and France*, ed. by Anne M. Scott (Farnham: Ashgate, 2012), pp. 253–78

——, 'The Enigma of "Lady Poverty" — Beautiful Ideal or Loathly Lady?', in *Interpreting Francis and Clare of Assisi: From the Middle Ages to the Present*, ed. by Constant J. Mews and Claire Renkin (Melbourne: Broughton, 2010), pp. 54–74

——, *Piers Plowman and the Poor* (Dublin: Four Courts Press, 2004)

Trigg, Stephanie: '"Shamed be…": Historicizing Shame in Medieval and Early Modern Courtly Ritual', *Exemplaria*, 19 (2007), 67–89

Wolf, Kenneth Baxter, *The Poverty of Riches: St. Francis of Assisi Reconsidered*, Oxford Studies in Historical Theology (Oxford: Oxford University Press, 2003)

INTERNATIONAL MEDIEVAL RESEARCH

All volumes in this series are evaluated by an Editorial Board, strictly on academic grounds, based on reports prepared by referees who have been commissioned by virtue of their specialism in the appropriate field. The Board ensures that the screening is done independently and without conflicts of interest. The definitive texts supplied by authors are also subject to review by the Board before being approved for publication. Further, the volumes are copyedited to conform to the publisher's stylebook and to the best international academic standards in the field.

Titles in Series

Across the Mediterranean Frontiers: Trade, Politics, and Religion, 650–1450, ed. by Dionisius A. Agius and Ian Richard Netton (1997)

Dictionaries of Medieval Germanic Languages: A Survey of Current Lexicographical Projects, ed. by K. Van Dalen-Oskam, K. Depuydt, W. J. J. Pijnenburg, and T. H. Schoonheim (1997)

From Clermont to Jerusalem: The Crusades and Crusader Societies 1095–1500, ed. by Alan V. Murray (1998)

The Community, the Family and the Saint: Patterns of Power in Early Medieval Europe, ed. by Joyce Hill and Mary Swan (1998)

The Vocation of Service to God and Neighbour: Essays on the Interests, Involvements and Problems of Religious Communities and their Members in Medieval Society, ed. by Joan Greatrex (1998)

Negotiating Secular and Ecclesiastical Power: Western Europe in the Central Middle Ages, ed. by Arnoud-Jan A. Bijsterveld, Henk Teunis, and Andrew Wareham (1999)

Christianizing Peoples and Converting Individuals, ed. by Guyda Armstrong and Ian N. Wood (2000)

Decorations for the Holy Dead: Visual Embellishments on Tombs and Shrines of Saints, ed. by Stephen Lamia and Elizabeth Valdez del Álamo (2002)

Time and Eternity: The Medieval Discourse, ed. by Gerhard Jaritz and Gerson Moreno-Riaño (2003)

The White Mantle of Churches: Architecture, Liturgy, and Art around the Millennium, ed. by Nigel Hiscock (2003)

Love, Marriage, and Family Ties in the Later Middle Ages, ed. by Isabel Davis, Miriam Müller, and Sarah Rees Jones (2003)

The Medieval Household in Christian Europe, c. 850–c. 1550: Managing Power, Wealth, and the Body, ed. by Cordelia Beattie, Anna Maslakovic, and Sarah Rees Jones (2003)

Exile in the Middle Ages: Selected Proceedings from the International Medieval Congress, University of Leeds, 8–11 July 2002, ed. by Laura Napran and Elisabeth van Houts (2004)

Representations of Power in Medieval Germany, 800–1500, ed. by Björn Weiler and Simon MacLean (2006)

Aspects of Power and Authority in the Middle Ages, ed. by Brenda Bolton and Christine Meek (2008)

Behaving like Fools: Voice, Gesture, and Laughter in Texts, Manuscripts, and Early Books, ed. by Lucy Perry and Alexander Schwarz (2011)

Languages of Love and Hate: Conflict, Communication, and Identity in the Medieval Mediterranean, ed. by Sarah Lambert and Helen Nicholson (2012)

Medieval Life Cycles: Continuity and Change, ed. by Isabelle Cochelin and Karen Smyth (2013)

Problems and Possibilities of Early Medieval Charters, ed. by Jonathan A. Jarrett and Alan Scott McKinley (2013)

The Tree: Symbol, Allegory, and Mnemonic Device in Medieval Art and Thought, ed. by Pippa Salonius and Andrea Worm (2014)

Travels and Mobilities in the Middle Ages: From the Atlantic to the Black Sea, ed. by Marianne O'Doherty and Felicitas Schmieder (2015)